# CHINA

## GETTING RICH FIRST

# CHINA

## GETTING RICH FIRST

★

### A MODERN SOCIAL HISTORY

## DUNCAN HEWITT

PEGASUS BOOKS
NEW YORK

CHINA: GETTING RICH FIRST

Pegasus Books LLC
45 Wall Street, Suite 1021
New York, NY 10005

Library of Congress Cataloging-in-Publication Data is available.

ISBN: 978-1-933648-47-7

10 9 8 7 6 5 4 3 2 1

Printed in the United States of America
Distributed by W. W. Norton & Company, Inc.

# Contents

# List of illustrations

Military training for Shanghai university students (Li Jiangsong, ImagineChina, 2004)

Customers choosing a masseuse at a Shenzhen massage parlour (Mark Leong, 2005)

Migrant workers at Shanghai station (Qilai Shen, 2004)

Children of migrant workers at an unlicensed school in the Shanghai suburbs (ImagineChina, 2000)

A farmer in Henan province lies dying of AIDS (Qilai Shen, 2001)

A funeral procession of rural Catholics in the hills of Yunnan province (Qilai Shen, 2003)

Making an offering at a Taoist temple in Guangzhou (Qilai Shen, 2004)

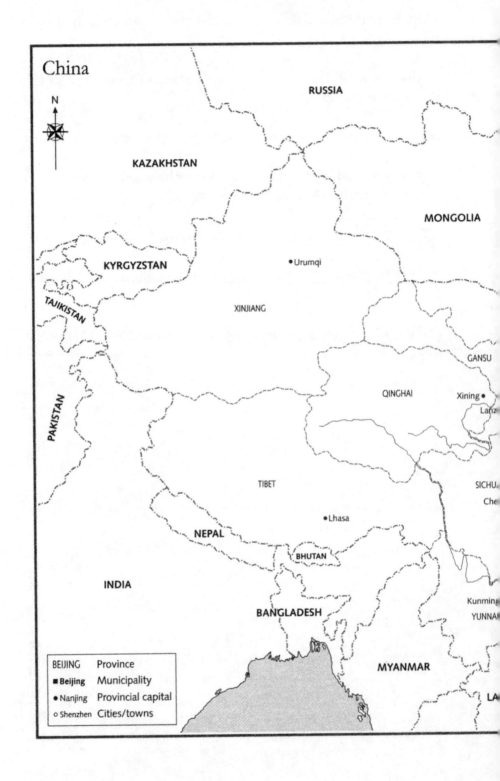

China

N

RUSSIA

KAZAKHSTAN

MONGOLIA

KYRGYZSTAN

•Urumqi

TAJIKISTAN

XINJIANG

GANSU

QINGHAI

Xining •

PAKISTAN

Lanz

SICHU

Che

TIBET

•Lhasa

NEPAL

BHUTAN

INDIA

Kunming

YUNNA

BANGLADESH

MYANMAR

LA

| BEIJING | Province |
| ■ Beijing | Municipality |
| • Nanjing | Provincial capital |
| ○ Shenzhen | Cities/towns |

RUSSIA

HEILONGJIANG

● Harbin

JILIN

● Changchun

INNER
MONGOLIA

● Shenyang

LIAONING

N. KOREA

JAPAN

Hohhot ●

Beijing ■

● Dalian

Tianjin ■

Gulf of Bohai

S. KOREA

HEBEI

Shijiazhuang

SHANXI

inchuan

Yellow River

● Taiyuan

● Jinan

○ Pingyao

SHANDONG

● Qingdao

Yellow
Sea

Zhengzhou

JIANGSU

● Xi'an

HENAN

ANHUI

Nanjing

SHAANXI

Hefei

Zhouzhuang

● Suzhou

● Shanghai

HUBEI

○ Wuhu

● Feixi

Hangzhou

Wuhan

Yangtze River

● Ningbo

ZHEJIANG

■ Chongqing

Nanchang

Wenzhou

JIANGXI

Changsha

HUNAN

FUJIAN

UIZHOU

Fuzhou

● Guiyang

Xiamen

TAIWAN

GUANGDONG

Shantou

GUANGXI

Guangzhou Dongguan

Shunde ○

○ Shenzhen

● Nanning

Zhuhai

HONG KONG

Haikou

HAINAN

Sanya

0          500 km

0          300 miles

For Haichen and all my family, old and new

# Introduction

Sometimes I sit in the café of the Shanghai IKEA – the largest in Asia, or at least it was until they opened an even bigger one in Beijing – and gaze out at the cars, taxis and trucks speeding past on the three levels of elevated highway, and the overhead light railway snaking between them, before disappearing past the 80,000 seat sports stadium into the shadow of the ranks of tower blocks behind. And I can't help wondering, how did this all happen so fast? Can this city of four thousand high-rises and two million cars really be the same slow-paced town of tree-lined streets, dawdling cyclists and low, European-style houses which I first visited as a student just two decades ago, when the hotel across the highway from IKEA was not just another nondescript concrete block, overlooked on all sides by newer, shinier buildings, but the newly built pride of the city, a palace which seemed to have been transported to this semi-rural suburb as if from another world?

To live in China in the early years of the twenty-first century is to be surrounded by change, on a scale and at a pace arguably unprecedented in human history. It's evident not just in the physical landscape, but even in the most mundane details of daily life. Sometimes, in the midst of an everyday scene, I suddenly find myself shocked by the realisation that almost everything around me would have been completely unimaginable in the China of twenty years ago. I was travelling on the Shanghai underground one afternoon, trying not to slide along the shiny plastic seat while gazing aimlessly at the highlights of the latest English football matches on the plasma TV screen on the carriage wall, when my attention was distracted by the loud conversations of my fellow passengers. A young woman carrying a large bag was talking on her mobile phone, checking the address where she was due to deliver some goods; opposite her, a man was yelling into his phone: 'The customer demands it, we have to provide it or we'll lose the contract!' There was nothing particularly unusual about any of this: wherever you go in China these days people are rushing around, frantically conducting business; and mobile phone signals and TV screens are now ubiquitous in the cities, available everywhere from trains to elevators. But I suddenly found my mind wandering to the first time I arrived in Shanghai, in January 1987 . . .

In those days there was no underground network, in fact the city's infrastructure had barely changed since 1949, when the communist revolution brought Shanghai's reign as the most modern metropolis in Asia to an abrupt halt. The only public transport for the journey from the old north station into the city centre was a creaking trolley bus, or a lung-choking ride through the narrow chaotic streets on the back of a motorbike taxi, the only kind available at the time. Plans to build a subway network were not even on the drawing board; the only television sets in the city were the primitive ones sold in state-run department stores for the equivalent of several years' wages for an urban worker. A telephone was an unattainable luxury for most, requiring good political connections, vast expense and many years on a waiting list to acquire – and even then a call to the next town might take several hours to be connected by the operator. The words on the lips of my fellow underground passengers would have been similarly implausible: in the 1980s, doing business was still rare, and frowned on by many as somewhat disreputable. Words such as 'client' and 'contract' were barely part of the Chinese language and any 'customers' who did exist certainly wouldn't have dared to make too many demands, in a society where the state ran the economy, and ideas such as consumer rights and the concept of 'service' were almost unheard of. Making a purchase in those days meant a visit to a government-run department store staffed by sullen assistants whose main aim in life seemed to be to sell as few items as conceivably possible.

China in 1986–7 was a society still struggling to drag itself out of the isolation and backwardness which had enveloped it since the Cultural Revolution, by then officially a decade in the past, but still casting a long shadow. Launched in 1966, this political movement had been designed to restore the authority of Mao Zedong, who had led the communists to victory in China's civil war, but now saw his absolute power challenged by others who wanted a less doctrinaire approach to the economy, after years of disastrous famine in the late 1950s and early 1960s. Mao sanctioned the denunciation of many of his closest colleagues as revisionists and reactionaries, unleashing several years of nationwide political terror, particularly after he encouraged China's young people to throw away their school books and join in the struggle. In the chaotic years from 1966 to 1968, millions heeded his word and joined the ranks of these teenage 'Red Guards'. Pupils denounced teachers, children accused their parents of being closet capitalists, and anyone with any connections to the pre-revolutionary 'old society' was at risk of being subjected to public humiliation, beating or imprisonment – and in many cases death. Houses were ransacked; foreign books, western musical instruments, even clothes from the pre-revolutionary era were destroyed as symbols of reactionary tendencies. Some of China's most cosmopolitan cultural figures were persecuted to death, or driven to suicide, as were some of Chairman Mao's oldest colleagues.

Many schools remained closed throughout the late 1960s, and millions of young people from the cities were 'sent down' to the countryside, in theory to learn about rural life and help the peasants on the collective farms. Universities were shut, reopening in 1973 in the guise of revolutionary centres of proletarian culture – with class background one of the most important criteria for admission. The Cultural Revolution finally officially ended in 1976, after the death of Chairman Mao and the arrest of his wife, Jiang Qing, and her three henchmen – known as the 'Gang of Four'. Most of the young people who had been sent down to the countryside began gradually to return to the towns and cities, but, having missed much of their education, many could only find menial jobs in the state enterprises which dominated every area of China's economy, from restaurants to heavy industry, clothing to candy.

The first signs of significant change came in late 1978, when Deng Xiaoping, one of the veteran communist leaders denounced by Mao in the 1960s for his suspect tendencies, returned to power. He soon pronounced an era of 'reform and opening up', which included a gradual loosening of some of the government's controls over the economy – particularly in the countryside, where farmers who had been forced into collective agriculture were once again allocated plots of land for their own use. In the early 1980s, many farmers began, for the first time, to sell some of their surplus produce on the new 'free markets' which were now appearing in Chinese towns. By the middle of the decade, some of their urban counterparts also began doing a little buying and selling – since the government did not have enough jobs to absorb all those who had returned from the countryside or been demobilised from the military. But the state still controlled the lives of most of China's urban citizens down to the minutest detail, allocating everything from housing to education opportunities, assigning people jobs, and telling them when they could get married. And despite the appearance of the new 'individual units', as the small street traders were euphemistically called, the nation's official goal was still the 'construction of socialism'.

Thus it seemed perfectly reasonable that when I first visited Beijing's Tiananmen Square, on Chinese National Day in 1986, the vast space was bedecked not only with attractive socialist flower arrangements, but also with giant portraits of Marx, Engels, Lenin and Stalin. In the central city of Xian, where I was studying that year, even the foreign students had to use grain coupons – issued to each family by the state, which controlled the price of staple foods – to buy bread from the only bakery in town. One of our teachers, a venerable gentleman always dressed in a neatly pressed blue Mao suit with matching cap, took us to a local shop to practise our vocabulary, and insisted that we must begin every sentence with the phrase, 'Excuse me, comrade shop assistant,' if we were to have any chance of making a successful purchase.

Yet beneath the surface, much was beginning to shift in Chinese society. It was in fact in the 1980s that the country began to make its first faltering contacts with the outside world, and a great thirst for all things foreign was quickly unleashed – not just for consumer products, though the few imported goods which were available became great status symbols, but for ideas and culture of all kinds too. The second half of the decade in particular saw something of an intellectual ferment, though often a rather chaotic and haphazard one, as people clamoured for anything which seemed new. Ageing foreign films such as *Roman Holiday*, finally authorised for showing in China, packed out cinemas around the country. Serious intellectuals discussed the cultural significance of everything from Jean-Paul Sartre to George Michael and Wham!. Students, bored with their compulsory Marxism–Leninism classes, flocked to dancing evenings in the university canteen, a somewhat unusual combination of waltzing, recently acceptable again after years of being banned as lewd and bourgeois (though men and women still rarely dared dance together, which meant the dance floor was filled with twirling same-sex couples), and break-dancing, which had entered China with the showing of a rare modern film.

Still, many people, not least conservatives in China's leadership, had serious reservations about the impact of foreign ideas. In late 1986, university students in several of China's biggest cities held protest marches; these were motivated mainly by anger at poor living conditions and bad university management, but wider criticisms of official corruption were also expressed. The authorities, seeing the protests as an alarming symbol of the erosion of socialist values, responded by launching a nationwide drive for ideological correctness known as 'The Campaign against Bourgeois Liberalisation'. It resulted in the demotion of the relatively liberal Communist Party Secretary General, Hu Yaobang, and the expulsion from the party of leading intellectuals who had begun to call for greater freedom of speech.

Nevertheless, it was clear that there was a growing desire among ordinary people to reduce the influence of the state over their lives, and a widespread thirst for new opportunities. One of the few students who still dared to talk to us that year boldly announced one day that 'actually I quite like bourgeois liberalisation'; a young teacher mooted seemingly fantastical notions of setting up a Chinese green movement. Many young people were particularly frustrated at the way they were simply assigned jobs on graduation. The inability of the authorities to control such ideas – and such dissatisfaction – was emphasised two years later, with the mass student protests in Tiananmen Square and around the country, following the death of the deposed leader Hu Yaobang.

The brutal crushing by the military of these protests in June 1989 was designed to send a message that the Communist Party's authority could not be questioned; it was backed up in the next few years by a series of patriotic education campaigns aimed at young people. And notions of political reform – floated briefly in the 1980s by Hu Yaobang and his successor Zhao Ziyang (himself deposed in 1989 for showing too much sympathy to the student protestors) – were most definitely no longer on the agenda.

Yet the changes in Chinese society did not grind to a halt; if anything they only grew faster. When I first lived in China change was sufficiently slow – and limited in scope – that one could more or less see it taking place: in Xian in 1987, the first imported canned drinks suddenly appeared in the shops one day, for example, and fashionable clothes were so rare that when a new red bomber jacket arrived on the market that spring, it was immediately obvious, since within days dozens of people around the city were wearing it. But in the decade and a half since the early 1990s, much in Chinese society has been transformed so thoroughly as to be completely unrecognisable.

These days, teenage high school students with dyed hair, dressed in the latest fashions from Japan and South Korea or the US, hold hands and kiss in the street. The word for comrade – *tongzhi* – is rarely used by ordinary people any more, except by members of China's homosexual community (whose existence was not even acknowledged in the 1980s) as punning slang for a gay or lesbian. Being 'petty bourgeois' is now enthusiastically recommended in the pages of China's new lifestyle magazines, as a mark of sophistication; an acquaintance who hung some old oil paintings of Marx and Engels on the wall of a new art gallery in a major city was told by local officials to remove them for the gallery's opening ceremony, since they did not fit in with the modern international image which the city's leaders, who were to be in attendance, wished to project.

None of this means that politics no longer matters, or that the Communist Party is not determined to retain its grip on power – but there is no doubt that for many ordinary people life has been turned on its head over the past fifteen years. Much of this transformation is the result of vast upheavals in the country's economic system. In the early 1980s, as China sought to put the chaos of the Cultural Revolution behind it, Deng Xiaoping announced that the nation would have to let 'some of the people and some regions of the country get rich first'. The aim, he emphasised, was to give a new impetus to economic development, which would eventually allow everyone to become better off, and help China become a powerful nation once again.

It took some time for the results of this change of emphasis to become visible. In the 1980s some state-run companies did begin to produce more commercially viable products, and a few areas of southern China were designated as 'special economic zones', with permission to attract investment from nearby Hong Kong and abroad. But the chances of China becoming a major economic power seemed remote. Just before our group of students from Edinburgh University set off to study in Xian in 1986, two of my fellow students met a couple of men in a pub in the Scottish capital, and mentioned that they were about to move to the People's Republic. 'Ah yes, China,' said one of the men, obviously keen to impress, 'that's where they make all the cars, isn't it?' This became a widely repeated joke, since it seemed ridiculous that anyone could confuse Japan, an industrial giant and mass car exporter, with a semi-crippled communist economy which didn't seem to produce much more than Mao suits and cheap plastic junk.

Less than twenty years later, when two Chinese car companies, Shanghai Automotive and Nanjing Automotive, were competing with each other to buy up the remains of MG Rover, and were hailed by many as potential saviours of the near-bankrupt UK car industry, the joke no longer seemed quite so funny. China's car industry has in fact been a late developer compared to many other areas of its economy – but in general a country which accounted for a minuscule percentage of the world's economic output in the 1980s has, in the intervening years, become the manufacturing base for a massive proportion of the world's consumer goods and industrial products. It has also shown ambitions to be more than just a source of cheap labour – not just in the purchase of the MG brand name, but in, for example, the acquisition of IBM's personal computer division by the Chinese firm Lenovo in 2005.

These developments are part of the extraordinary economic boom which began in the early 1990s, after Deng Xiaoping took a trip to southern China and called on the nation to move ahead faster with economic reforms. This put an end to debates among the country's leadership, in the aftermath of the crushing of the Tiananmen protests, as to whether such reforms should be reversed or slowed down. And it led to dramatic changes, not only in the economy, but in society as well, as the government pressed ahead with reforms both of state industry and, later, of its traditional socialist welfare system too.

For many people, this meant far more freedom – to move around the country, and to choose their own jobs – and as the economy developed in new directions, and private enterprise became increasingly tolerated, many found opportunities to earn far more money too. The retreat of the government from the economy also went hand in hand with an opening up of society, spurred by the desire of a new generation, and of people with more money and broader horizons, for new ways of life. As a result, China over the past fifteen years has been a society in a constant state of flux, diversifying and evolving before one's eyes. Almost every week you hear about, or read about in the fast-changing media, a new idea, a new concept, a new fashion, something for which there was no word in Chinese before, yet which has now suddenly become part of the vernacular. Few areas of life have remained untouched: from the rise of the teenager to the growth of home ownership, from soaring divorce rates and greater sexual openness to an increased awareness of consumer rights and the rush to embrace new technology. It's as though China has undergone many of the changes and upheavals seen in western societies in the half-century after the Second World War compressed into just ten or fifteen years – and with a dose of the industrial revolution thrown in for good measure.

And the rush to modernise everyday life has been matched by the headlong transformation of China's physical environment, as cities, towns and even villages have reinvented themselves at breathtaking speed. China over the past fifteen years has become a nation where houses, streets, entire neighbourhoods can disappear almost overnight, to make way for the office towers, apartment blocks, shopping centres and highways of the new urban dream. It's made it possible for those who have succeeded in 'getting rich first' to enjoy vastly changed lifestyles: China's newly wealthy now include some of the world's most extravagant consumers of luxuries, from whisky to designer clothes, Range Rovers to real estate. The urban middle class is growing fast too, swiftly buying into the dream of an apartment, a car and holidays abroad. China may remain officially a communist country, but it can be hard to ignore the sense of aspiration and sometimes of a self-seeking rush for wealth. It's an idea which was emphasised by the advertisement I once saw in a Guangzhou newspaper, in which a real-estate developer proudly promoted its latest exclusive residential development by simply emblazoning Deng Xiaoping's slogan 'Let some of the people get rich first' across the page . . .

Yet if the economic reforms of the past two decades have enabled some people to do very well, they have also left Chinese society deeply divided, with an ever-growing wealth gap between the new urban elite on the one hand, and the millions of laid-off workers from bankrupt state factories and the hundred million or more migrants from rural areas now doing menial jobs in new industries on the other – to say nothing of China's farmers, whose incomes have grown far more slowly than city-dwellers since the 1990s. The nation's rapid urbanisation has also left a legacy of dissatisfaction, among residents driven out of the city centres to make way for new construction, and among those concerned about China's heritage, who have watched as large quantities of historical buildings and traditional districts are demolished in the rush towards modernity.

For an outsider, there's a certain privilege in observing a process which is undoubtedly history in the making. But it can be exhausting too. In 2002–3, I decided I wanted to take a break from working as a journalist in China, and spend some more time in Europe. I soon discovered that the pace of the nation's opening to the outside world meant that having a break from China was no longer so easy. The flight to London was filled with Shanghainese teenagers setting off for summer courses in England; on the streets of English tourist towns, it was suddenly common to hear Mandarin being spoken, and to find young mainlanders working in menial jobs. An English football team, Everton, was now sponsored by a Chinese electronics company. In a bathroom shop in the south of England, the manager explained somewhat apologetically that almost all his products were now made in China. In a family-run umbrella business in Belgium, meanwhile, the owner talked sadly of how the company was about to close its hundred-year-old workshop and start selling the far cheaper products being imported from China. There were Chinese tour groups on the streets of Brussels, and Chinese vendors selling trinkets on the streets in Geneva. And after a long cable-car journey up a Swiss mountain, the staff in the mist-shrouded restaurant at the top turned out to be from Changchun in China's north-east, and Guangdong in the south.

It's perhaps inevitable that Chinese people will follow the nation's goods and companies in becoming increasingly visible around the world, indeed it's a trend which is surely only in its infancy – it's only over the past few years, for example, that it has become easy for ordinary Chinese citizens to acquire a passport, and only a tiny proportion have so far had the chance to travel abroad. And the country's increasing international influence has contributed to a growing global fascination with China and its developments. Yet many Chinese people still bemoan the fact that when they do go abroad, they meet with many misunderstandings about the nature of their country and its society, with some people assuming that they're still stuck in the days of either the Qing dynasty or the Cultural Revolution – or, increasingly, that their country is just one big, threatening economic miracle. And so when I got back to China, to the dynamic and ever-changing city of Shanghai which is my wife's home town, and where I too have now put down some roots, I decided to try to write this book, which looks at how China's society, and the lives of its people, have developed over the past couple of decades. It's a subject which is of course constantly evolving, but I hope that by focusing to a large extent on the stories of individual people who have lived through these changes, I will be able to bring out at least some of the complexities, contradictions and challenges of this nation in motion.

# 1

# Cities in motion

It was a frosty winter's afternoon on the eve of the new millennium, and the Beijing weather seemed to be doing its best to live up to the classical precepts of the city's ancient designers, which decreed that the Chinese capital should be a city of grey. A blanket of smog, ripe with the pungent aroma of coal dust and rice vinegar, hung over the low roofs and grey brick walls of the city's old courtyard houses. Out on the pavement, urban life was all too evident: trolley buses shrieked, bicycle bells rang, babies wailed, the roar of the traffic was shrill and menacing.

But once old Mr Zhao closed the massive pockmarked wooden gates of No. 8, Behind the Art Museum Street, the hubbub faded to a mere hum. Inside, sheltered by the high walls of the courtyard, a watering can lay on the ground; two kittens were scrambling under a gnarled walnut tree, which had shed its leaves for the winter. Mr Zhao bent down to whistle to them. 'These two small cats came running here,' he said, in the precise English and gentle tones of a bygone age. 'My wife fed them; now this is their home.' As he opened the door and ushered me into the single-storey house, the sense of a sanctuary from the world outside grew even stronger. In the warm sitting room, with its heavy carved wood furniture, almost no sound from the street could be heard. Only the chiming of an ageing carriage clock interrupted the silence. 'You see how quiet it is?' said Mr Zhao, with evident pride. 'These walls are so thick – there are no such thick walls now.'

Everything about the house seemed to speak of China's past – from its antique furniture to its two venerable inhabitants. Mr Zhao, at eighty-two, was still sprightly and sharp, but his English retained the flavour of a generation educated in the old missionary-established universities of pre-revolutionary times. His wife, who was bustling around in the kitchen making tea and answering the phone, was still known to some by her long-ago English name Doris, while Mr Zhao himself retained the name Tim, which he had acquired more than half a century earlier. In those days, during the period of the former Nationalist government, he had been a civil aviation pilot flying in and out of China. In 1949, when the revolution brought the communists to power, Mr Zhao, like so many patriotic Chinese intellectuals, decided to give his support to the new government, and flew his plane back from Hong Kong to Beijing. Soon after, his father, a prominent academic, had bought the house, and it had been home to the family ever since.

The building itself had a far longer history, however. From the brick walls topped by a sloping roof of curved grey tiles, to the living room and bedrooms arranged around the small inner courtyard, it was a typical example of traditional Beijing architecture. For over seven hundred years, since the Mongol Yuan dynasty first made the city China's capital, Beijing had been dominated by great swathes of such single-storey houses, connected by narrow lanes, known as *hutongs*, which radiated out in a symmetrical pattern from the imperial palace – the 'Forbidden City' – at the heart of the capital. The grandest of these houses, the homes of princes and aristocrats, had dozens of rooms set around many inner courtyards. Others, like Mr Zhao's, had six or eight rooms, with a front and a rear courtyard. 'This was not a home for the princes, they had better ones,' he said with a smile. 'This house was probably used by junior officials, courtiers, doctors serving these lords or princes.' Yet there was still much to be proud of. He pointed upwards, to the corners of the eaves jutting out over the courtyard. Closer inspection revealed delicate patterns carved onto the face of the tiles. 'These are elephants' eyes,' said Mr Zhao, giving them their traditional name. 'And this one,' he added enthusiastically, 'is called a cat teasing a butterfly; those over there are peony flowers.' Such tiles, he said, helped to date the house – it was only in the mid-seventeenth century, when the Ming dynasty was replaced by the Qing dynasty, that such decoration had been in use.

The intervening centuries had certainly left their traces. Some of the bricks were crumbling a little; a few blades of grass poked out between the tiles. The Zhao family had carried out major renovations when they first moved in, replacing traditional paper windows with glass panes, installing a modern bathroom, and putting in radiators, or, as Mr Zhao put it, 'steam heating'. For a while they had lived here in some style. Then, during the Cultural Revolution of the 1960s, Red Guards had forced Mr Zhao's brother out of the house. The building was subdivided, and another five families moved into the rooms around the front courtyard. The old 'flower pendant gate', the decorative divide between the front and rear of the building, was demolished to create more space. But the house had remained home to Mr Zhao and his wife, and, until her death a few years earlier, his sister too. And despite all it had been through, its character, and the artistry of its creators, was still evident.

Now, though, the home which had sheltered the couple through the upheavals of half a century seemed suddenly fragile. Mr Zhao recalled the moment, a few months earlier, when he first realised this. 'We came home one day, and saw the Chinese word *Chai*, which means demolish, painted on the wall of the house,' he said. 'It was a great shock for us,' he went on, with a slight shiver at the memory. 'Just imagine, we two old people over eighty. That night my wife's blood pressure went up to 185. We didn't know what we could do – or how this could have happened . . .'

The answer, as it turned out, was all too simple. Their home, which had survived the changing of dynasties, two revolutions, foreign occupation, and the violence of the Cultural Revolution, was now under threat from an apparently more implacable opponent – urban development. A couple of hundred yards away, an old street was being widened to create a six-lane highway, and the company in charge was taking the opportunity to carry out new construction alongside the new road. The plans called for the demolition of a whole community of old lanes along one side of Behind the Art

3

Museum Street – the Zhaos' home included. Some of his neighbours, the ones who had been squeezed into the old houses during the Cultural Revolution, had not been too unhappy about leaving, said Mr Zhao. They had grumbled that the new flats offered to them by the government were far away in a distant new suburb, but at least they would no longer have to share bathrooms, or use public toilets out in the lane, as some had done in the past. 'We must admit that some of these people got better living conditions after moving,' he acknowledged. 'And the houses weren't their property, so they didn't mind so much.'

He led me to the rear window of the house and told me to take a look outside. Most of the surrounding buildings had already gone, leaving just a field of rubble stretching out towards the new road; among the debris, a few builders' tents flapped forlornly in the wind. The Zhaos' home was now almost alone, marooned among the wreckage. No wonder many of the couple's friends had urged them to accept their fate and move away. Even Mr Zhao himself admitted that they didn't really feel so safe here now. But still he was not prepared to leave. On the one hand there was a sense of personal injustice; he was convinced that the developers were seizing more land than was necessary – or permitted by local regulations – to build the new road. 'They were only allowed to demolish seventy metres from the road – we're a hundred and fifty metres away,' he insisted.

But perhaps even more important was his outrage at what he saw as the casual destruction of a part of Beijing's heritage. 'It's not just our house,' he said, 'there were others around here which were even better – real old palaces!' By this stage, he was prepared to move out, he said, but only if the building itself would be protected. 'If someone would keep it I would happily give it to them,' he exclaimed, 'but I won't give it to the developer – why should I?!' Mr Zhao's determination was heightened by his memories of a previous savaging of Beijing's history, in the 1950s, when Chairman Mao, inspired by dreams of building a new socialist order, ordered the demolition of Beijing's centuries-old city wall and gates to make way for a ring road. 'We made a big mistake in knocking down the city wall,' Mr Zhao said softly. 'Now we regret it – but it's too late. And now we're going to make a second big mistake, tearing down all the lanes and the courtyards.' He sighed. 'So there will be another regret.'

Coming from a prominent intellectual family, Mr Zhao was well connected, and he had done all he could to enlist the help of historians and architecture professors from the nearby universities, even journalists from the official press. 'Everyone said it would be so sad to knock down these courtyards,' he went on. 'All learned Chinese would like Beijing to maintain its ancient fashion, it's something the nation can be proud of. My house is almost four hundred years old, older than the United States,' he added, his eyes shining. 'Why should people destroy something four hundred years old, for no reason at all?' Of course a city needed to progress, he agreed – but surely there was enough space out in the suburbs for new construction. 'In Paris they didn't tear down the old city,' he said, 'they built the tall buildings around it. In Rome it's the same. Why only in China do they want to tear down everything ancient in the centre of the city?'

So determined was he to save his home that he had succeeded in persuading the local court to hear his case against the construction company. But he wasn't optimistic about the outcome. 'These people all have their connections, they're very powerful,' he said, with a sigh. As he showed me back out into the little courtyard, Mr Zhao paused for a moment under the old walnut tree in the gathering gloom, and acknowledged that he would have little choice but to accept his fate if the court ruled against him. 'If you move me to a tall building what can I do, besides adapting myself to it?' he said, with a sad smile. He bid me a courteous farewell. As he closed the heavy door behind me, the roar of the street again filled my ears. On the grey wall of the house, a sheet of white paper had been roughly pasted – it was the latest eviction order, demanding that the residents of No. 8 Behind the Art Museum Street vacate their home within two weeks.

In fact, the Zhaos' fight continued for almost a year. Eventually, though, to no one's surprise, the court ruled against them. Their

5

house was deemed to be early Qing dynasty (late seventeenth century) rather than late Ming (early seventeenth century), and thus not worthy of protection – though the court did offer them unusually high compensation. By this time the construction company, frustrated at the delay, had already built its buildings a little further away from the house. But no sooner had the old couple finally left for their new apartment in the suburbs than the demolition team moved in, along with a heavy police presence designed to prevent any image of the destruction from being captured on film.

A few years later I went back to look for traces of the Zhaos' former home. So completely had the area changed, it was hard to be sure where it had stood – but it was probably on a small corner of what was now the car park of a large tiled building with tinted windows, which seemed to be an activity centre for retired government employees. When I visited, the car park was almost empty.

Since the 1990s, such stories have become all too familiar in Beijing and other Chinese cities, as the country rushes to embrace 'modernisation', and burgeoning economic development has only added momentum to the process of reconstruction. It's as though China's cities have been hurling themselves towards the future, with little time to think of the consequences – or indeed of the past.

And yet, on my first visit to Beijing, as a student in 1986, it would have been hard to imagine any of this. As the train approached the capital, the strident announcer on the loudspeaker in the carriage launched into a poetic description of the city's thousand years of history; when we drew into the station, a singer trilled operatically, 'Beijing, ah Beijing,' his voice apparently quavering with emotion at the thought of arriving in the great heart of the nation.

And the city did not disappoint. For a vast capital, Beijing had a leisurely charm, typified by the old courtyard houses, and the *hutongs* meandering between them. The word *hutong* is thought to be of Mongolian derivation, dating back to the Yuan dynasty – and the names of the lanes were rich in the history of the city. Those closest to the old imperial palace were named after the gates which led to it, or after the homes of famous noblemen. In the districts where the ordinary people had lived, the street names were reminders of the traders who traditionally worked there: 'Mutton *hutong*', 'Coal Dust *hutong*', 'Goldfish *hutong*'. The grandeur of most of the old houses had faded; many were now home to multiple families, their once-elegant courtyards filled with the trappings of household chores – clothes drying on lines, vegetables hanging from nails on the walls, little piles of black coal briquettes used for cooking stacked up on the ground. The public toilets out in the lanes, which announced their presence from afar, particularly on a breezy day, were a reminder of how basic the facilities were in many of the houses. Yet these neighbourhoods seemed to be the essence of Beijing; old people sat chatting to their neighbours on tiny bamboo chairs, children played hopscotch or twirled hula hoops, shoppers returned from the market with chickens and cabbages piled on the back of their bicycles. Much of the city's life was lived in these areas, as it had been for hundreds of years.

A few skyscrapers, some still under construction, could be seen on the distant skyline, but from our hotel near the Drum Tower – which, at several storeys high, was by far the tallest building in the neighbourhood – it was possible to cycle right across the city and barely leave the old *hutongs*. Occasionally you had to cross a wider street, but most of the traffic consisted of other cyclists or locals out for a leisurely stroll. The ring road constructed on Chairman Mao's orders in the 1960s was virtually empty; most of Beijing's citizens still pedalled their bicycles along the separate cycle lanes on either side.

Beijing was by no means an ideal city. Its low-density buildings meant it sprawled far in all directions, and its slow pace gave it the atmosphere more of a giant village than a modern capital; contemporary amenities were few and far between. But its evident sense of its own history, and the direct connection with its past represented by its towers and temples, courtyards and lanes, gave it a unique, timeless quality, one which many visitors found strangely haunting. It was still possible to see why Lin Yutang, the western-educated scholar who was one of the first to attempt to explain

7

China to the outside world in the 1920s and 1930s, described Beijing as simply 'one of the most beautiful cities of the world'.[1]

I was not in Beijing in 1988 and 1989, the years of social and political convulsion, but by 1990–91, when I returned for several short visits, time seemed suddenly to have caught up with the old city. Political tension following the Tiananmen crackdown could still be felt in the air, but on the ground Beijing had started to change. Massive construction was under way, much of it connected to the hosting of the 1990 Asian Games, which was designed to pave the way for a bid to host the 2000 Olympics. There was a sense of a coordinated effort to keep the people looking forward rather than back – everywhere hopeful slogans proclaimed 'A more open Beijing awaits the 2000 Olympics' – and also of the increasingly powerful interests of construction firms and real-estate developers. Under the auspices of the city's Communist Party boss, Chen Xitong, vast monolithic buildings were being thrown up along Chang'an Jie (the 'Avenue of Eternal Peace'), the city's main east–west boulevard. Because of traditional rules limiting the height of buildings around the Forbidden City, most of these were eight or ten storeys, as broad as they were tall. They had something of the air of the last huge edifices built by the former Romanian dictator Nicolae Ceauşescu in Bucharest in the 1980s – with the addition of sloping Chinese-style roofs. Rumoured to have been added to the design on the personal orders of Chen Xitong, such roofs were widely known to the locals as 'Xitong hats'.

Most of the old areas of courtyard houses were at this time still largely unscathed. But by the next time I visited the city, in 1995, things were different. In Beijing's main shopping street, Wangfujing (the 'Well of the Prince's Palace'), small shops, and blocks of old courtyard houses behind them, had already disappeared, replaced by hoardings proclaiming the imminent arrival of new shopping centres invested by Hong Kong property developers. In other neighbourhoods too there were vast holes in the ground, the beginning of a wave of speculative construction of apartments and shopping malls, aimed both at foreigners and at a Chinese middle class which, as yet, barely existed. Many of the contracts had been

8

awarded when the city was under the control of Chen Xitong, who by now was under house arrest (and was later to be sentenced to life imprisonment) on charges of corruption; these were widely assumed to be linked to the awarding of real-estate contracts. But his fall from power seemed to do little to slow Beijing's changes. The old archways, which had marked the entrance to many of the city's traditional residential neighbourhoods, could now frequently be seen standing isolated, everything around them already demolished.

And when I returned to live in the city as a journalist in 1997, a drive across Beijing could take on a nightmarish quality, as on one memorable late-night taxi ride, when the faint yellow glow of the street lamps lit up a seemingly endless scene of destruction: for many miles, the half-demolished skeletons of courtyard houses lined the road on both sides, like the remnants of some particularly brutal battle. This, I later discovered, was the beginning of the construction of the new traffic artery, known as 'Peace Avenue', which would eventually claim old Mr Zhao's home too.

Such new roads were also a reminder of China's growing love affair with the car; already Beijing's once-empty ring road was now becoming jammed, as the first newly wealthy families went out cruising in their little Japanese-designed hatchbacks. And the city's leaders had now made the decision to transform Beijing into a modern business centre, unleashing another wave of construction, of office buildings and shopping complexes. No matter that some of the new malls quickly went bankrupt, or that even modern buildings (including the world's largest McDonald's) were now also being demolished to make way for bigger construction projects; foreign investors remained excited about China, and were increasingly making their mark on the city. I was invited for dinner at the home of a writer, one of the generation of idealistic intellectuals who had emerged in the late 1970s. How would I recognise his house, I asked. 'No problem,' he said, 'it's the building between the McDonald's and the Kentucky Fried Chicken.'

Sometimes it could seem as though those in charge of Beijing's urban planning were taking cities like Los Angeles as their role models. More and more people were being forced out into the suburbs – either by demolition of their homes or by rising property prices – and with the city's public transport network struggling to keep up, owning a car became increasingly important for many residents. By the early years of the twenty-first century Beijing had five ring roads, yet traffic jams had become a way of life. Growing pollution from roads and building sites meant that the Western Hills, once an inspiring sight on the horizon, were now rarely to be seen from the city centre. Meanwhile a series of attempts by the authorities to 'clean up' the city's appearance led to the demolition of many of the small restaurants, shops and bars which had sprung up during the 1980s and 1990s, and the removal of many of the city's bustling street markets. City-centre pavements now often seemed strangely empty, and residents found themselves with little choice but to head for the newly opened shopping centres and supermarkets.

A joke did the rounds that Beijing was the only place in the world where you had to phone a restaurant before going out for dinner, not to reserve a table, but to check that the building hadn't been demolished. This struck me as a little exaggerated, until one evening when, after driving up and down the same street several times in an increasingly desperate search for a friend's favourite restaurant, we realised that it had indeed been swallowed up by a large building site. We retreated to a large and evidently very popular restaurant on the other side of the road, which was so well established that it even published its own newspaper. The food was good, and a few weeks later my friend decided to go there again; when he arrived he found only a corrugated-iron fence, a large hole in the ground, and signs announcing the city's next construction project.

For Beijing's residents it could be a disorienting experience, though so constant has been the transformation of China's cities that some urban dwellers have come to accept such upheavals as an inevitable part of 'progress'. Seen through the eyes of those who have been away from the city for a while, though, the shock of the process becomes apparent. The poet Yang Lian, who grew up in Beijing but moved abroad in the late 1980s, began returning to the city a decade later. On a walk around central Beijing one day, his long hair shook in disbelief as he surveyed what he saw. 'The skyline has changed absolutely,' he said. He had just travelled across town, and had spotted an old temple in the shadow of a clump of modern buildings. 'It was the Tianning Temple tower,' said Yang Lian. 'Twenty years ago I used to work near there; I remember that tower used to seem so high to me that I used to feel I really had to stretch my neck to see the top. But now,' he went on, 'it's not even half as tall as those modern buildings – it looks like a very old man walking between two young boys.'

The readjustment of scale became even starker when we made our way into an alley behind the new shopping malls of Wangfujing. The old courtyard house where Yang Lian had spent a year as a small child in the 1950s was still there. It had been a fine building, with many courtyards; his great-grandfather, who had owned a theatre around the corner, had bought it from a famous classical painter. 'This was one of the best areas of the city,' said Yang Lian. In those days, he added, the whole area had been made up of such houses, each with trees in its courtyard. 'Beijing was known as the city of trees,' he recalled. 'There were big fruit trees – dates and jujubes – it was very exciting for the children, we always used to climb on the roofs to pick the fruit. And in the summer,' he went on, 'when the crickets were singing in the trees, the children would take a long thin piece of bamboo and put glue on the end to catch them; that was a great game,' he grinned. Other courtyards had been famous for their grapes or their goldfish, he said. 'And in the hottest days of summer, at six or seven o'clock, after sunset when the first gust of wind came, people would take small wooden chairs and sit under the trees, holding big fans, and everyone would get together – it was a really comfortable feeling.'

Now his old family home was used as a government office, and we could only catch a faint glimpse of the front courtyard through a gap in the locked gates. One could only imagine the dramas which had taken place here – not least that of Yang Lian's grandmother,

11

who had been confined to a tiny storeroom at the rear of the house during the Cultural Revolution, and had remained there for three years until she died. Now, with the opposite side of the lane demolished, the house seemed somehow diminished, the tall modern buildings around it appearing to mock the idea that something so puny could have any historical significance. Yang Lian gazed up at the glass towers – or 'pollution of the sky', as he called them. 'In the old days, when you stood in this kind of street you didn't feel that these houses were very low,' he said. 'In fact I always thought they were beautiful. They had thick walls and small windows, so they had a very peaceful feeling – and they were very warm in winter,' he went on. 'And because the rooms faced inwards into the courtyard, you felt protected – not like in these big glass buildings which are open to the outside.' There was a certain logic to the traditional design too, given the sandstorms which swept into the city from the deserts of Mongolia in spring and early summer, and which now battered directly on the plate glass windows of the tower blocks of the new Beijing. Yang Lian frowned. It was inevitable, he said, that the old way of life would change, but the process had been so extreme. 'A city has its own age,' he said, 'it's like a person, it should grow up naturally. Of course it needs to develop,' he went on, 'but it shouldn't be a case of: "I can change your head and your legs and cut you in half and connect you with another body"; the basic person should still be the same one!'

Yet by this time, at the dawn of the new century, the character *chai* could be seen everywhere, on old walls around the city. To an outsider, this willingness to bulldoze the heritage of the nation's capital seemed more than a little baffling, in a country which never ceased to emphasise its pride in its thousands of years of history. And when I went to visit Yao Ying, then the deputy head of Beijing's Municipal Planning Commission, in a quiet office compound on the western side of the city, there was certainly a sense of contemplation about what had been happening. 'Beijing is an important place, we know that, and everyone is very concerned about it,' he said. 'Its planning was very special: the unity of the four sides, the imperial buildings with yellow or green tiles, ordinary people's

12

homes with grey roofs. So it's a very great treasure of cultural heritage.' As he spoke about the city's past, he began to wax quite lyrical. 'Modesty aside,' he went on, 'we can probably say that as a big ancient capital with a long tradition, there was one Beijing and one Paris – and maybe we can say that Beijing was more beautiful than Paris!'

Mr Yao acknowledged that mistakes had been made over the past decade or more. 'When the reforms began, everyone wanted to charge forward at random and throw out everything old,' he said. 'Some historic things were knocked down, some were damaged, some were badly preserved. So there are many regrets. In the 1980s most people didn't know much about architecture or the significance of old styles, or the relation between old things and modernisation,' he added. But now, he suggested, things were starting to change. 'The more modern a country becomes, the more it sees a value in old things,' he continued. 'It's sad, but maybe in a way it's inevitable. Sometimes I think it's only after some losses that you realise the value of things.' Mr Yao noted that the city had just announced a number of small conservation areas, and would try to direct new construction away from the old heart of the city. There were, he admitted, still what he called 'contradictions' between supporters of modernisation and those concerned about Beijing's heritage, but at least, he said, 'there are very few people now who think we shouldn't protect things at all.'

At the same time he insisted that the process of urban renewal could not be stopped altogether. Beijing's old neighbourhoods were harder to adapt for modern life than those of many European cities, he said. 'Our buildings are different from Paris, where the streets are wide and the buildings tall. Here the old lanes were built for rickshaws, and there's hardly enough space for the cars to get through.' The centuries-old brick houses were difficult to maintain too, he added. 'It's hard to improve the living conditions of the people there,' he said, 'which are often very bad, with no running water.' Was it fair, he asked, to expect residents to use toilets out in the lane, even in Beijing's freezing winters?

In fact, many had argued that it was not impossible to reconfigure the old houses for modern life – the poet Yang Lian for example was adamant that it was a question of commitment. 'Yes, these traditional buildings are not so convenient in some ways,' he said, 'but you can put in modern plumbing and heating, maybe use double glazing. I've been in Italy, in France – they've done it. You don't need to be so clever to keep an old town.' But Mr Yao emphasised that preserving old buildings was a luxury for a country which was still relatively poor. 'There's still a lot we have to do in China – and the cost is very high,' he said.

There's no doubt that some of Beijing's residents were quite happy to put the old way of life in the crowded, dusty courtyards behind them, and move to modern apartments – though many did later come to resent the lack of transport and other amenities in the new areas. The shift to these areas brought with it some strange dislocations. In one of Beijing's new suburbs, I visited Mr Lin, who had just moved from his old house in what had once been a village nearby to a tenth-floor apartment. The government had requisitioned their land and given the villagers these flats as compensation. With a toothy grin, the retired farmer proudly showed off his new home, complete with bar in the sitting room. He was happy to be here, he said, and he wasn't lonely because all his neighbours from the old village had moved into the same building too. Still, some of the residents seemed to be finding it hard to let go of their old way of life: on the concrete floor of the corridor in front of the elevator, grain had been spread out to dry, as was often seen on farm forecourts in the Chinese countryside.

For many residents of the old areas, moving to a new home meant not just leaving behind the building where they had lived for decades, but the break-up of friendships and communities, and often the scattering of an entire way of life. For older people in particular, it could be hard to accept. In Houhai, one of Beijing's last old neighbourhoods, set around the lakes to the north of the imperial palace, many of the surviving courtyard houses are ramshackle and much converted, with extra buildings added to accommodate the extra residents who have moved in over the years. Yet a stroll around the area reveals a determination on the part of

14

many of the locals to hold onto their long-established traditions. Neighbours still exchange gossip in the narrow lanes, or take the air by the lake in the evening; tradesmen still pull their handcarts over the little bridges across the canal, advertising their presence with the ringing of a bell. Here, on a winter's afternoon, an elderly man named Mr Yu insisted on inviting me into his home, three rooms of an old courtyard house originally built for a famous general a hundred years earlier, at the end of the Qing dynasty. 'This place is pretty scruffy now, no one cares about looking after it,' he said, as we dodged around the rickety huts which had been built in the courtyard. But he beamed with pride as he showed me his living room, with a high ceiling and a floor of ancient tiles decorated with red and white flowers.

'The structure of these old houses is much better than new ones,' he said, pointing to the thick doorway. 'In the big earthquake of 1976, this place didn't move at all. And you see how high this room is – in new apartments you only have to stretch out your hand to touch the ceiling,' he went on. 'So the air in these houses is much better.' Like many older Beijing citizens, Mr Yu believed in the importance of *di qi* – the air or energy from the ground, which is traditionally thought to be good for the health. His wife was watching television in the corner of the room and laughed as she heard him becoming so philosophical. 'Don't exaggerate,' she said, 'who wants to live in these old places?' She gestured towards the modern apartment in the soap opera on her TV screen. 'How can a place like this compare to these new buildings?' she asked dismissively. But it turned out even she had no wish to leave this old neighbourhood. 'I love walking on the banks of the lake, with the water and the trees, or just having a chat outside,' she said.

The government had its plans, and its ideas of what a 'large international city' (a phrase beloved of Chinese officials) ought to look like, however. And for all the talk of conservation zones, there were few signs of a slowing of the destruction of Beijing's heritage in the early years of the new century. A vast new National Theatre was built, right behind Tiananmen Square, the giant glass dome

15

causing not only puzzlement among many local residents, but the demolition of a whole neighbourhood of old courtyards. Added impetus for change came with the success of Beijing's second attempt to win the right to stage the Olympics, this time in 2008. It was notable that an important part of Beijing's Olympic bid programme was a pledge to create a more modern city. Certainly the International Olympic Committee's decision in 2001 to award the games to Beijing delighted people with interests in the property market, like the middle-aged man I met on a flight to Beijing on the eve of the announcement. He spoke with the brash swagger typical of those with influential connections in China, telling me how he lived in the same compound as various senior officials – and of how much money his real-estate company stood to make from a Beijing Olympics. And within days of the confirmation of the city's selection, a new wave of demolitions began, to build the first of the new transport hubs, widened roads and modern housing which the authorities insisted would make Beijing an 'Olympic city'.

Areas demolished in the intervening years have included old lanes of great cultural significance, like the former homes of famous intellectuals, aristocrats and politicians in Red Flag *hutong*, a couple of blocks from the poet Yang Lian's old family home. Even Brick Pagoda *hutong*, said to be the only surviving lane named in official documents dating back to the Yuan dynasty in the thirteenth century, has been half destroyed, according to one prominent academic.[2] Some estimates put the number of *hutongs* knocked down since the 1990s at between a third and a half of the total.[3] The city did announce a series of plans aimed at restoring a few prestigious old buildings in an attempt to create a heritage showpiece in time for the 2008 Olympics; it has even rebuilt one of Beijing's old gates, taken down in the 1950s, and restored a few relics of the old city wall – though this too has provoked controversy, with the displacement of hundreds of people from their homes to make way for the project. Much money has been lavished on the city's twenty-five designated conservation areas – yet even here there has sometimes been little compunction about tearing down original courtyards, and replacing them with brand new, improved 'traditional' houses, with garages and added floors for the comfort of their wealthy owners. The 'renovation' of the city's traditional entertainment and trading area of Dazhalan, south of the old imperial city, meanwhile, involved the demolition of unique buildings from the nineteenth and early twentieth centuries and the removal of many residents, as part of a plan which included restoring parks and canals which had not existed since the Ming dynasty several hundred years earlier. Ramshackle and crumbling some of these buildings certainly were, but it was still a curious experience to take a stroll through the area, as I did in 2005, and discover red banners strung across the street proclaiming: 'Demolish in accordance with the law in order to promote the preservation of the city's appearance.'

Exactly why official attitudes to Beijing's heritage have been so cavalier is a question which has puzzled many – particularly given China's traditional reverence for its past. The preservation of a few prominent buildings and areas cannot conceal the fact that much of the city's fabric has been pulled apart. Some see this simply as a legacy of the destruction of traditional values during the early decades of communism, the Cultural Revolution in particular. The writer Gu Xiaoyang, who published a moving lament for his demolished *hutong* neighbourhood, has noted that the education he received during his upbringing in the Cultural Revolution years contained 'two lessons at least: violence and a contempt for culture'.[4] Officially, of course, the authorities long ago consigned the Cultural Revolution to history; still, many of those who grew up during that period have come into positions of power and influence in recent decades. Could it be that their education at that time (or indeed the loss of education experienced by many) has left them particularly unaware of issues of culture and heritage?

Other intellectuals, however, believe that the destruction is a relic of traditional attitudes which meant that a new ruler taking over a city – or a new dynasty assuming control of the nation – often sought to erase the traces of what went before, as a symbol of their power. This, one Beijing academic explained to me at some length, was exactly why Mao Zedong demolished the old city wall. Still, the willingness to knock down old buildings and replace them with new 'old-style' constructions can seem particularly mystifying. Some see this as reflecting a traditional communist faith in the power of 'scientific' socialism and man's ability to impose his will on his environment. 'The idea is that I can destroy everything,' says the poet Yang Lian. 'And not only that, but if I can destroy everything, then why can't I rebuild everything too? I made old Beijing disappear; now, if I want to, I can make it re-emerge.' Others are even more cynical. 'I don't even want to talk about this,' says one Beijing intellectual with a sad sigh. 'It's too boring, too ridiculous. In the 1980s I wrote lots of essays about architecture, criticising construction and urbanisation,' he adds 'and then I discovered these criticisms were meaningless – it's all about profit.' Demolishing old buildings and putting up new ones, he insists, gives many people the chance to make money – for some, it's an opportunity to borrow money from the banks, while others can get kickbacks or make huge profits from land deals. Some projects, he claims, have gone ahead when there was no real interest in actually building anything new. 'It's nothing to do with culture or modernisation,' he says. 'It's a web of advantage.'

Some ordinary people too have expressed dissatisfaction with the process of urban development – often more because of its impact on their livelihood than because of any particular concern about heritage. But organising any type of public protest, as some have done, can be a risky strategy. In 2004, two brothers who campaigned against the demolition of their restaurant in Beijing, as part of the reconstruction process for the Olympics, were jailed for several years.[5] The centralised nature of the political system, and the powerful interests of many of those involved in urban reconstruction, has also restricted public debate, and made it hard for any organised conservation movement to emerge. Concerned academics have expressed criticism, some directly to the government through their status as advisers to China's legislature, and others via the media, which has in recent years become increasingly critical of the obsession with modernisation in China's cities. (One prominent newspaper scathingly mocked plans, later shelved, to build one of

18

the world's highest skyscrapers – in a field outside Beijing.)[6] And a few courageous Beijing residents have tried to respond to the loss of their city's heritage – one such group set up a website dedicated to old Beijing, and organised dozens of volunteers to take photographs of vanishing neighbourhoods of the city.[7]

Others have expressed their discomfort at the changes through more extreme means. The Beijing artist Zhang Dali took to spray-painting an outline of his head on the grey walls of half-demolished old buildings, and then photographing the result. Often the head would enclose an old window or doorway, soon to disappear. His art offered a human response to a situation in which individuals have little say.[8] Many people, however, have simply accepted the reality, or contented themselves with expressing their feelings via Beijing's famously mordant sense of humour: the country's English name, 'China', noted one local, sounds almost exactly the same as the Mandarin phrase *chai ne* – meaning 'let's demolish'. 'So if we don't demolish things, how can we call ourselves China?!' he asked.

Perhaps as a passive response to the pace of change, there has also been a growing interest in the history of Beijing and other Chinese cities, symbolised by the popularity of historical TV dramas set in mock-ups of the old capital, and the Old Beijing themed restaurants where staff dressed in traditional gowns transport you from the street to the door in hand-pulled rickshaws (banned from the city's streets after the communist revolution). Bookshops have filled up with volumes of old photographs of the city's history and its traditional way of life; there's a certain irony in watching the crowds of young people poring enthusiastically over such books in the shops, while outside the physical remnants of the past are being razed by the square mile.

There's no question that Beijing's new architectural showpieces can be dramatic – few could fail to be impressed by the Olympic stadium, or by Norman Foster's new terminal for Beijing airport, or the remarkable twisted glass headquarters for China Central Television, designed by the Dutch architect Rem Koolhaas. But such buildings are also symbols of a complete transformation of the traditional scale of the city. Beijing has always been spread over a

19

huge area – but in its old neighbourhoods the sense of perspective remains remarkably intimate; in the narrow lanes, you are never more than a few feet from a building or a person; inside a courtyard house, the high walls seem to keep the outside world at a distance. But when you emerge from one of the surviving old areas onto a main street, the vastness of the modern city, with its wide open spaces, massive roads and huge buildings, can be quite shocking. These days it seems that every corner of the city is loudly proclaiming its desire to become a new 'Central Business District', everywhere huge billboards promote new housing developments with glamorous names and promises of a better way of life, accessible via the city's many ring roads and new expressways. Little wonder that some feel that the planners have effectively erased much of old Beijing and replaced it with an almost entirely different city bearing the same name.

The upheavals in Beijing have been echoed, to a greater or lesser degree, in cities all over China. In some, the replacement of the traditional by the modern is almost complete. In Taiyuan, the ancient capital of Shanxi province in the north, I was shown a book of photographs of the city during its heyday in the late nineteenth and early twentieth centuries, when its role as the centre of China's first banking industry made it one of the country's wealthiest and most modern cities. The pictures showed bustling streets of two- and three-storey buildings, imposing banks, grand hospitals and universities, many in western neoclassical style. Where, I wondered, should I go to find some remnants of the old city – since all I had seen so far was nondescript urban sprawl. There was an awkward pause. 'Actually I don't think there's anything left,' said one of my hosts apologetically. He asked his colleagues, but they all looked blank, as though the question had never occurred to them. There were a few old temples, and some churches, they said, but they couldn't think of any complete streets at all. Eventually I went to explore for myself. Finally, behind the wide dusty roads lined with new shopping centres and half-built concrete blocks, I found what seemed to be the last old street of small buildings with intricately decorated frontages; nearby another similar area had just

20

been demolished, and a single old temple stood alone, marooned on a kind of traffic island.

This approach, of preserving a few prominent buildings, but rarely entire neighbourhoods and communities, seems to be a common one in China. In the north-eastern port of Dalian, the circle of grand old civic buildings in the city centre, built by the Japanese during their brief control of the area a century ago, had been given a shiny new coat of paint when I visited – but just a short distance away, old neighbourhoods of fine European-style houses from the earlier Russian occupation were in the process of being demolished. In Wenzhou, an economic boom town on the south-east coast, one old street of the Portuguese-influenced shop-houses once common in southern China, some with colonnades over the pavement, still survived, but little more. And in Kunming, the capital of Yunnan province in the far south-west, the old red-painted wood-fronted houses which gave the city so much of its character in the early 1990s had all but disappeared when I returned little more than a decade later.

Some trace this process back directly to what has happened in Beijing. In central China, I met Mr Li, an architect and designer, who spent most of his weekends leading a group of like-minded individuals on trips to small towns, often in remote rural areas, to photograph their traditional architecture and document the local way of life. He was convinced that Beijing's development had had a powerful influence on cities and towns around the country. 'Beijing leads the way in China,' he said, 'and they have destroyed the old beautiful Beijing as though they were clearing space in a forest to make room to build houses. And so every provincial capital in China will take Beijing as its model, and do the same thing; and then the county towns will copy this, and the small towns will copy them.' Even in the far-flung towns and villages he visited, this was becoming increasingly obvious, he said. 'There are places I've been to a few times,' he explained, 'and the first time I get there it's really nice, then the next time it's already gone, damaged, lost.' He paused for a moment. 'And after years of looking around, I feel that you actually can't stop this force, that people in an old town will themselves pick up their own hammer to smash it down – it seems to be a natural process which no one can halt.' Perhaps it was understandable, he said, given the nation's orientation towards progress. 'We have a slogan in China's reforms,' he said, 'that "development is an unshakeable logic", and so in the small towns and villages, if their area is poor and backward, their hope is to become like the towns they see on their TV sets.'

Even some of China's most famous and beautiful towns have not been immune to the process. One of the first destinations on many tourists' itineraries in China is the old city of Suzhou. Along with the nearby town of Hangzhou, it has long been hailed by ancient Chinese poets as the epitome of dignity and refinement. 'Above there is heaven, on earth there are Hangzhou and Suzhou,' as the old Chinese saying puts it. Suzhou lies just fifty miles from Shanghai, beside the Grand Canal built in the Ming dynasty to facilitate north–south trade. Until the middle of the nineteenth century it was in fact a far more important city than Shanghai, famed for its fine silk, the elegance of its language, the beauty of its women, and the highly trained scholar-officials who emerged from its Confucian academies. It was these men of wealth and taste who gave the city its most famous legacy, the ornately laid-out private gardens of miniature lakes and painstakingly arranged rockeries, with tiny stone humpback bridges leading to little pavilions for taking the air, and covered walkways providing access to whitewashed, airy rooms set around small inner courtyards. The names of the gardens convey the sense of harmony to which their creators aspired: the Blue Wave Pavilion, the Garden of Cultivation, the Garden of Retreat and Reflection, the Garden for Lingering In. One of the most famous gardens, the Shizilin or Lion Forest, was built by an ancestor of I. M. Pei, the renowned Chinese-American architect who redesigned the Louvre in Paris and added its famous glass pyramid. I. M. Pei, who spent time here himself when he was a child, has said that it was in the gardens of Suzhou that he learned 'the complementarity of man and nature'.[9]

The city itself was similarly revered, for its whitewashed court-yard houses, with delicately carved lattice windows, set along narrow stone-paved lanes. Many of these houses backed onto small canals busy with boat traffic of all kinds. Marco Polo waxed lyrical about the city in his *Travels*, and for generations Suzhou has enjoyed the epithet of the 'Venice of the East'. This was, more or less, the city I saw when I first visited in the 1980s. From the railway station, it was still possible to plunge almost immediately into a maze of old lanes, and emerge a few minutes later onto a paved path beside a canal criss-crossed with small stone bridges. It was a place with an unusually graceful atmosphere. And it's an image on which Suzhou continues to trade: in any guidebook or tour itinerary you will find it described in similar terms. Which is why, one spring day a few years ago, I found myself on a train returning to the city, with a visitor from Britain who wanted to see this oriental Venice of which he had read so much.

We decided to take a leisurely stroll from the station into the town. One seemingly endless walk down a fume-ridden, traffic-clogged road later – and still slightly muddied from clambering over mounds of earth from the latest construction works blocking the pavements – we finally caught sight of our first ancient building, the famous North Temple Pagoda. We climbed to the top for a bird's-eye view of the town – and were confronted with a largely uninterrupted vista of modern blocks, stretching out to the city's new industrial parks in the distance. Back at ground level, we took a taxi to one of the famous gardens – a half-hour slog through traffic jams on a four-lane road lined with concrete buildings. I think it was at this point that my visitor turned to me and asked: 'Are you sure we've come to the right town?' The gardens, listed by UNESCO as a World Heritage Site, were still relatively unscathed, once we found them, but most of the old neighbourhoods nearby had vanished. Around the Lion Forest Garden, old houses were being bulldozed to make way for new developments; across the road from its front gate, a modern leisure area had already opened; it had a strangely lifeless atmosphere, its newly built shops and restaurants virtually empty.

Suzhou, like many cities in China, embarked on the path of modernisation in the late 1980s and early 1990s, when its leaders decided that even a relatively small town renowned for cultural excellence needed to become an economic powerhouse. It opened two industrial zones in its suburbs, and set about creating a grand city centre, removing many of the old, slow-paced canal-side districts in the process. In a nod to traditional style, most of Suzhou's new buildings are only three to five storeys high, with white walls and vaguely traditional style roofs, intended to echo the classic 'South of the Yangtze' style of architecture. But their box-like dimensions and metal-framed tinted-glass windows do little to impress visitors. And genuine old areas are becoming harder to find; one canal which has been proudly 'preserved' now runs down the middle of a six-lane highway.

In search of traces of the old Suzhou, I went with my wife to visit her great-uncle, who at more than ninety years of age still lived in part of the rambling old canal-side house which had been in his family for generations. The large new road nearby meant it was initially hard to recognise the place, but we eventually found ourselves in the narrow lane which ran between houses so close together that the points of their roofs almost touched. We made our way down a dark hallway filled with clutter and old bicycles, and across several small inner courtyards. As we reached the rear courtyard, a beaming old man with wispy white hair, dressed in a traditional padded jacket, came bounding towards us, grinning broadly to reveal his two remaining front teeth. He led us into a room with a paved stone floor and carved lattice windows, and sat us on old wooden stools. After pouring tea, he produced examples of the classical Chinese calligraphy which he still practised, and for which he was still winning prizes. Then, excitedly, he grabbed his brush and ink stone, and proceeded to write, with an impressively steady hand, a classical poem in our honour. Sitting there watching him work, it was as though we had returned to an earlier age. Once the calligraphy was finished, we walked out to the little terrace at the back of the house. The family had often talked of how, during the oppressive heat of the Suzhou summer, melon boats would pass by on the canal behind the house, selling their thirst-quenching wares to grateful residents. But now, as we stood and gazed out across the water, we heard only the roar of traffic. The far bank was still lined with willow trees, but behind them lay a four-lane road, busy with cars, and beyond it a large shopping centre. A few curious pedestrians stared back at us from the bus stop just opposite great-uncle's back door.

There are other famous 'water-towns' in the region south of the Yangtze River which have survived relatively intact. But most of them are far smaller than Suzhou, and if their local leaders have realised their heritage value, they often seek to maximise it by encouraging tourism. The small town of Zhouzhuang, not far from Suzhou, for example, has preserved most of its old buildings, but is generally agreed to have become something of a theme park, the admission ticket needed to enter the town not deterring the throngs of tourists who push past each other on its narrow bridges and tiny streets. The town's popularity has also attracted a large influx of people from other parts of China, who have moved there to try to make money from the tourists, thus changing its traditional character even further. And as the number of Chinese people with money and time to travel – and their own cars in which to do so – increases, and the number of well-preserved old places continues to diminish, the risk of any such surviving towns being overrun by tourists only grows. In the ancient northern town of Pingyao, for example, also listed by UNESCO as a World Heritage Site for its complete city wall and collection of fine houses, the authorities are reported to have begun moving local residents out of the old centre in order to make more space for visitors.[10]

Perhaps it is simply an inevitable process. Certainly there are some in China who have decided that in the face of such rapid development, extreme measures are necessary to preserve the country's traditional architecture. Out in the countryside of southern Jiangsu province, a couple of hours' drive from Shanghai, I visit a compound of imposing old buildings with Jeffrey Wong, a man whose love of traditional architecture is immediately apparent. As we enter the first of the buildings, he runs his hand along an old wooden beam and begins to coo with pleasure. 'I love this,' he sighs. 'Look at this carving, isn't it beautiful? It's so detailed – they

25

hollowed it out from a single piece of wood. That's such a difficult thing to do!' He points to the tiny carved figures. 'And you see these? The whole thing tells a story – isn't that amazing?!' We are standing in a high-ceilinged room, its broad roof beams held up by pillars as thick as entire tree trunks. Jeffrey gazes around reverentially. 'Do you realise that this entire structure was built without any nails? All they had to hold it together were these,' he says, pointing to a small bamboo wedge which has been hammered into the joint of pillar and beam.

We head out of the rear of the building, across a brick-paved courtyard, and up a few stone steps between two tall fir trees. Now we are in an even grander room, with a large curved staircase at the back leading to the upper floor. 'This building is at least 170 years old,' says Jeffrey, pointing out the memorial stone in the wall which commemorates the names of those, long-since dead, who once paid for its upkeep. With three courtyards linking its four main rooms, it's an imposing sight, all the more so because of the stone lions which guard the main entrance. 'This place was built as a clubhouse for the local guild of traders in cow-hide and leather,' says Jeffrey. 'You would arrive in a sedan chair here, and then you would be taken into the reception area.' He glances at the whitewashed outer walls and the charcoal-coloured roof tiles, their carvings of leaves and flowers edged in white, and gives a little sigh of satisfaction. 'It's a perfect example of the South of the Yangtze school of architecture,' he says.

We leave the clubhouse and walk along a little stone path to another old house, its dark roof tiles sweeping upwards in steps, decorated with carvings of animals. Fish are swimming in a small pond in the front yard; an old millstone stands nearby. 'This house was built three hundred years ago,' says Jeffrey, pointing to the characters carved into the millstone: 'Good fortune for all eternity.' Further down the path, we come upon a small grove of bamboo, where a few goats are munching on the grass. In the distance the roof of an old temple can be seen among the trees. As we draw closer, it's clear that the temple building is the focus of much activity. On the roof, several men are hammering away energetically; down below, others are pushing wheelbarrows laden with old roof tiles, which they stack on the ground, the curved tiles piling up in a cascading pattern. Major renovations are clearly under way. We slip past the workers into the darkened main hall of the temple and gaze up at the roof beams, painted deep crimson and decorated with Buddhist symbols. 'Nice, ah?' says Jeffrey softly. 'This is the original paintwork. I'm not going to restore it or repaint it – why should I? This is history!'

Out here in this rural corner of Jiangsu province, a couple of hours away from Shanghai, these old buildings seem in total harmony with their surroundings, a vision of a traditional China becoming rarer and rarer these days. There's just one catch. None of the buildings was actually here a year earlier. They may be typical of the local architecture, but each has been transported here by Jeffrey Wong and his workers from other towns and villages in the region. For five years now, he has been buying buildings like these from the surrounding area, dismantling them brick by brick, and then shipping them to his warehouse, to await eventual reassembly on plots of land like this one, which he has acquired for the purpose. His aim is to protect unique old buildings from the twin perils of neglect and modernisation.

It is an unusual approach to conservation, but then Jeffrey Wong is hardly the typical conservationist. Raised in Hong Kong, but now a Canadian citizen, he made his money in textiles and real-estate investment, before retiring to Shanghai in the late 1990s. He owns a stake in a bar in the city, and in the evenings can often be found there, chatting and laughing with friends over the pulsing music. With his Hawaiian shirts, suntanned features and hair still jet black in his early sixties, he has something of the air of a veteran Hong Kong movie star – and indeed, judging from the frequent calls on his mobile phone, many of his friends are from such circles. But soon after his move to the mainland, Jeffrey stumbled on his new passion. 'I was travelling around the country,' he says, 'and I saw that a lot of the old architecture was not well protected, so I said, what a shame, maybe I should buy one!' What started as something of a joke soon became a reality when he found an old house in Suzhou, just as the city's reconstruction was gathering pace. 'It was a beautiful house,' he recalls, 'and when I saw it I fell in love with it, so I said, can I buy it? And they said OK!'

And once he started, he found it hard to stop. Now he has an ever-growing collection of buildings, more than a hundred in all – of every kind. 'I've got big ones, smaller ones, houses, mansions, farmhouses, pavilions, teahouses, pagodas, towers, temples,' he says. Many are still in the warehouse waiting to be reassembled. 'This is my hobby,' he says. 'I choose which building to rebuild and where to put it, depending on my mood.' He glances at an empty space opposite the temple. 'Over there I'm going to build a pavilion,' he says. 'And I think I need something behind that fence – I'll probably build a brothel,' he adds with a chuckle. 'It's an old whorehouse I collected, with very fine decoration. Of course no girls come with it, hah hah hah!'

The temple where we are standing was, it turns out, built more than two hundred years ago in what's now downtown Shanghai, as a place for fishermen to make offerings and say their prayers before setting out to sea. After the Cultural Revolution, when it was turned into a factory, it eventually reopened, but the temple elders have now decided to replace the original buildings with something grander and more modern. 'If we hadn't found out about it they would have just demolished it and sold off the wood for recycling,' says Mr Wang, Jeffrey's foreman, emerging from behind a pile of bricks. And so they bought the entire structure from the demolition workers and transported it out to the suburbs. It's not the first temple they have saved. 'I have four now,' says Jeffrey, with a grin.

And he has found other buildings of unusual historical significance too – even an entire street. In the small town of Haining, south of Shanghai, Jeffrey read in the local papers about a controversy over plans to demolish the family home of Xu Zhimo, a famous romantic poet of the 1920s and 1930s. Xu, who lived in Britain, and was a friend of the Indian poet Rabindranath Tagore, scandalised Chinese society by advocating marriage for love rather than duty, conducting a high-profile affair, divorcing and remarrying before meeting a suitably dramatic – and modern – end

28

in a plane crash at the age of just thirty-four.[11] He is still admired by many – not least for a famous poem immortalising the English city of Cambridge, where he studied. 'When I heard his home was going to be demolished, I rushed over there to have a look at it,' says Jeffrey. He found a big old house, dating back to the early sixteenth century, when it was built by one of Xu's wealthy ancestors. 'It was in a terrible state, divided up between lots of families,' he explains, 'and the authorities said they weren't going to preserve it. So I said, what a shame, I'm going to take it anyway, whatever the condition.' And while his workers were busy dismantling the house piece by piece, his eye was caught by the entire main street of the town, which was also under threat of demolition. 'That town had, God knows, a thousand years of history,' says Jeffrey, 'and it was the last street of the old town. They said, do you want it? And I said, of course.' The houses, several hundred years old, were in poor condition too, but he dismantled all the façades along the hundred-metre-long street. Now, he says, the whole area has been replaced by a swathe of 'Spanish-style' villas.

Even Jeffrey's attempts to find a new home for his buildings have been affected by the march of progress. No sooner had he erected ten of his houses outside a small village on the edge of Shanghai, than the local government re-zoned the land and started building new villa compounds all around. Jeffrey left three or four houses where they stood, but took all the others down again, and eventually found two new patches of land near a famous old canal town in neighbouring Jiangsu province. Even here, a new main road has recently appeared nearby. But he's doing his best to make sure the local government designates it as a protected cultural area; he's still trying to decide whether to open the buildings up to the public once he finishes, or whether just to bring his friends here, but it has become an increasingly consuming obsession. Jeffrey thinks he may have spent between ten and twenty million dollars so far, though he's not too sure, and he plans to put all his savings into the project before he dies. Not everyone can see why he's doing it, he says – even the workers who renovate the buildings are a little baffled. 'They respect that I'm preserving traditional Chinese culture,' he

29

grins, 'but they still can't really understand what this crazy man is doing spending so much money on these old houses.' At this, he dissolves into a fit of giggles. 'Even my wife doesn't like all this old stuff!' But in his eyes, these buildings are relics of both architectural history – and human history too. 'I love these old buildings,' he says. 'I look at them and I dream of what was there before. I look at the marks on a pillar, and I wonder who made them; in every room there are stories – family conflicts, love stories. In one house you can write a book of a thousand pages.'

Given the fact that he pays for the buildings, I ask whether there's a risk of creating a market for local officials to drive residents from their homes in order to sell him their houses – and whether it isn't sad to move them from their original sites – mightn't this just become another 'old China' theme park? Well, says Jeffrey, he only buys buildings if they are due to be redeveloped – or if the owners want to sell them; he never buys things which will be preserved anyway. And it's all architecture from this one region of China – his aim is to recreate the atmosphere of an old town or village, he emphasises, not build a museum of different architecture. 'That would be ugly', says Jeffrey with a frown. In his opinion, the pace of development in China means that his approach is often the only way to save something of the past. He has met a lot of local leaders in small towns, he says, and few are concerned about conservation. Part of the problem is the legacy of the Cultural Revolution, he agrees, but he believes that it's the opening-up of the post-1980s era which has had the greatest impact. 'Now these mayors make a trip to Europe or south-east Asia, or Hong Kong, and they come back and look at all these old things and they hate them,' he says. 'They tell me, "Jeffrey, don't you think we should get rid of this, it represents the backwardness of our country. Why don't we have Spanish villas, we can have a flush toilet, hot water . . . ?"'

The town where he's based now has had a relatively enlightened leader, he says, but even here there's pressure. Jeffrey points to an old bridge and a few small houses lining the canal. 'If they have visitors from Beijing, and they walk through here and they see this,' he says, 'they'll say, what's wrong with this town, why is it so poor?!' His response, he smiles, is to encourage Chinese officials to visit countries like Italy. 'Look at the Colosseum, how it's been preserved – and what about the Leaning Tower of Pisa, do the Italian government feel ashamed because it's leaning and they don't have money to build a new one?' he asks. 'No, they spend all their money trying to keep it that way.' In recent years, he believes, more people have begun to show an interest in such issues – but he fears it may be too late. 'Maybe in ten years' time lots of people will start to appreciate the importance of these things, but then it will all be in the past – there'll be nothing left if you don't do something about it now.' He has tried, he says, to persuade rich locals to spend some of their money on preserving old architecture. 'There are so many rich guys spending money on beauty contests or whatever to promote their business,' he insists, 'why don't they spend the money to save a house? Then they can say this was saved by me and my company.' But so far, he admits, 'not many listen to me'. Does he ever become depressed at the situation? I ask. Jeffrey thinks for a moment. 'I did at one point,' he smiles, 'but now I'm just happy I can save something . . .'

Others are not so lucky. In a nation with such a complex recent history, the disappearance of the physical remnants of China's past can sometimes make it even harder for those seeking to come to terms with events gone by. The poet Yang Lian has written of how, in an attempt to put some painful memories behind him, he made a trip back to the village outside Beijing to which he was banished for several years during the Cultural Revolution. But by the time he got there it was already too late. The entire village had gone, and a clump of new high-rise buildings was now rising from the dry soil. Of the 'old alleys' and 'crooked gatehouses', which 'concealed so many stories', he wrote, not a trace remained. The place, which held so much meaning for him, had 'vanished so completely that there was not even a name left on the map'.[12]

31

# 2

# Shanghai between old and new

Nowhere has the collision between China's past and its future been more spectacular than in Shanghai, a city with a legendary history which was the crucible of China's modernisation in the first half of the twentieth century, and has returned to the role with a vengeance since the 1990s. To arrive in Shanghai in the early twenty-first century is to be plunged, with a jaw-dropping intensity, into a vision of China's modernisation. For many, the experience begins at the Pudong airport, a huge modernist hangar of steel and glass, designed by a French architect, rising from the mudflats beside the East China Sea. Here the world's fastest passenger train, floating a few centimetres above its track on a magnetic force field, transports travellers to the edge of downtown Shanghai at speeds of some three hundred miles an hour. Alternatively, you can take the new expressway, past the modern residential compounds now devouring the farmland, and up onto one of the vast suspension bridges spanning the Huangpu River. If you're lucky, you might just catch a glimpse of the old colonial waterfront, the Bund, its buildings filling up with luxury boutiques, fine-dining restaurants and contemporary art galleries. But the Bund itself is now dwarfed by the far taller buildings of the new financial district on the opposite bank of the river, where the eighty-eight-storey Jinmao Tower, home to one of the world's highest hotels, vies for attention with the city's TV tower. This massive structure, with its tubular legs and bulbous observation platforms, looms over the city like a giant spaceship from some 1950s futurist cartoon. And across the river, behind the Bund, a sea of skyscrapers – from office blocks and commercial plazas to the residential high-rises which are now home to millions of Shanghai's residents – stretches out, through what remains of the old city, to the new suburbs, and on, towards the banks of the great Yangtze River itself.

The vision is all the more startling when you consider that, even at the turn of the 1990s, when urban renewal was already well under way in much of China, Shanghai was still a city living more on the legend of its past than the promise of a glorious future. During the first decade of the reform era, in the 1980s, it was to the south, to Guangdong province – and particularly the provincial capital Guangzhou – that all China looked. Guangdong's proximity to Hong Kong had made it the obvious place to set up China's first experimental 'Special Economic Zones' aimed at drawing in foreign investment and creating new jobs, and the region was given special dispensation to pioneer many aspects of economic reform. By the second half of the 1980s, Guangzhou (known in former times as Canton) had built China's first highways and flyovers, its smartest hotels, its earliest supermarkets. The city's residents were close enough to the border to pick up Hong Kong radio and television too – and pop music and movies, fads and fashions soon began flowing in from across the frontier. Guangzhou was also one of the first places to accept the development of small-scale private enterprise, and young people from across China began to flock to the city in search of work. Even those who couldn't get there themselves adopted Guangzhou fashions and hairstyles – with the result that by the late 1980s, the most fashionable young men around the country were proudly sporting identical Guangzhou-style 'mushroom' perms.

Shanghai, meanwhile, was not given the same freedom to develop. Its industries, many dating from the pre-revolutionary era, still generated a sizeable part of China's income, but most of this went straight to the central government, leaving relatively little for the city itself. In many ways, Shanghai was a prisoner of its own unique history, still distrusted by the authorities for its decadent, capitalist past.

Shanghai had indeed always been a phenomenon, a city which did not so much grow up gradually as erupt, in the second half of the nineteenth century, after the first Opium War, when the British forced the opening of what was then a medium-size port on the Huangpu River, just south of the mouth of the Yangtze, to foreign trade. To facilitate this trade, the foreigners built their own settlements on the muddy flats beside the Huangpu, to the north of the old Chinese walled town. One of these enclaves was controlled by the French, another, the 'international settlement', consisted of land appropriated by the British and Americans. Within just a few decades, these had become the fastest growing areas in all China. For Chinese citizens from the surrounding provinces, the foreign zones, which had their own police and defence forces, offered sanctuary from the civil wars and rampaging rebel armies which so often convulsed the nation in the later years of the Qing dynasty. For adventurous young men from Europe or America, the International Settlement (never an official colony, but run by a committee of resident western businessmen) offered the chance to make a career, and sometimes a fortune, in trade, finance, or even property speculation. Soon the products of China's first modern factories began to flow out of the city, while opium, imported by the British from India, flooded in. Shanghai swiftly became one of the largest trading ports in Asia.

Such rapid expansion put growing pressure on space in the city, and land became increasingly expensive. And so Shanghai began to build some of Asia's first high-density urban housing, for the workers in the new industries and the burgeoning urban middle class. The result was a unique fusion: small houses built in continuous rows, like nineteenth-century British terraces, with a tiny, compressed version of a traditional Chinese courtyard at the front, shielded from the outside world by high brick walls and massive wooden gates. The granite frames around the gates gave these buildings their name – *shikumen*, or 'stone-framed gate' houses. Above the front gate of each house was a distinctive design, a bird perhaps, or a flower, carved in stone or later moulded in cement. In the first decades of the twentieth century, hundreds of thousands of such houses were built, many on narrow, residential lanes set back from the city's main streets. And each of these lanes – or *longtang* as

34

they were known – had its own name, invariably including some of the many Chinese characters denoting peace, good fortune or prosperity.

And for all the conflicts and unrest which continued to sweep much of China in the years following the overthrow of the Qing dynasty in 1911, Shanghai did prosper. Wealthy industrialists and foreign tycoons built themselves grand western-style villas in the suburbs; hotels to rival the world's finest opened in the city centre; and the imposing banks, clubs and office buildings of the Bund, the half-mile-long waterfront of the International Settlement, became one of the most potent symbols of foreign influence in the Far East. By the 1930s, Shanghai had become a fashionable stop for well-heeled travellers on world tours. Chaplin, Einstein, Auden and Isherwood all visited. Noel Coward wrote his play *Private Lives* while laid up with flu in the Cathay Hotel on the Bund; Wallis Simpson was said to have spent some wild months in the Palace Hotel across the road, in the days before she became the Duchess of Windsor.[1] The city had a sizeable community of longer-term foreign residents too. The ballerina Margot Fonteyn spent a couple of years in Shanghai as a child, while her father was working in the city; another pupil of one of the city's many foreign missionary schools was the writer J. G. Ballard, who spent much of his childhood in an English-style house on Amherst Avenue in one of Shanghai's leafy suburbs. His novel, *Empire of the Sun*, describes the experiences of Shanghai's foreign residents after the Japanese took over the city in 1941 – and it's perhaps revealing that when this was turned into a film in the 1980s, scenes featuring the main character's Shanghai home were actually shot in the English Home Counties, in Surrey, where the buildings were deemed so similar to those of Shanghai suburbia that, with the addition of a few tastefully positioned palm trees, no one would notice anything amiss.[2]

The unique status of Shanghai's foreign settlements – neither full colonies nor fully Chinese-controlled, and therefore accessible without a visa – also made them a haven for refugees. Jews fleeing pogroms in eastern Europe were soon followed by White Russians escaping from the Soviet Revolution. Many settled in the city, opening shops and restaurants. By the late 1930s, they were joined by some 30,000 Jewish refugees from Germany and Austria, who had escaped from Europe by boat, or even overland via the Soviet Union. After the Japanese takeover of the foreign concessions, most of the Jews were eventually forced to move to a designated area of the city – effectively a ghetto. But almost all survived the war – and though most departed soon after, their influence lived on in places such as the famous Shanghai Conservatory of Music, where some of the first teachers were Jewish musicians from Germany and Russia.[3]

Chinese people from all over the country flocked to the city too. Many were peasants seeking work in the city's factories. But the relative security offered by the foreign enclaves during the unstable years of the 1920s and 1930s, their supposed immunity from Chinese justice, and the chance of greater contact with foreign ideas and a more modern way of life, also attracted the talented, the politically radical and the simply ambitious. Sun Yat-sen, the inspiration for China's first revolution in 1911, took up residence in Shanghai when his political fortunes waned, welcoming visitors including Bertrand Russell and George Bernard Shaw. The radical writer Lu Xun, the conscience of China during the early decades of the century, also sought sanctuary in the city from the increasingly dangerous political squabbles elsewhere in the country, remaining in Shanghai until his untimely death in 1936.

Thus Shanghai became a laboratory of China's modernisation, and a centre for the nation's first, faltering interactions with the outside world. It was home to many of the country's earliest modern newspapers – in both Chinese and English – and to its first publishing houses and film studios. (One of the many starlets of the Shanghai movie scene – though by no means one of the most successful – was a young actress named Lan Ping, later better known as Jiang Qing, the third wife of Chairman Mao and leader of the Gang of Four during the Cultural Revolution. Indeed, many believe that her violent persecution of intellectuals in the Cultural Revolution stemmed in part from bitterness and personal feuds dating back to her days in the Shanghai film industry.) Shanghai had China's first stock market, its most advanced banks and factories, and some of its top universities and most modern architecture practices. It was a city of dance halls and jazz bands, massive movie palaces and a gossipy tabloid press. But the legendary 'anything-goes' attitude of this 'Paris of the East' also brought the city a less desirable fame: for its drastic extremes of wealth and poverty, the exploitation of workers in its factories and sweatshops, the myriad brothels, pitiful beggars and the slums of the destitute.

It was therefore perhaps not surprising that it was here too, in reaction to foreign control and the rise of indigenous capitalism, that the Chinese Communist Party was founded, at a secret meeting in a newly built terraced house in Shanghai's French concession in 1921. Nor was it any wonder that, as far as the communists were concerned, Shanghai became a symbol of many of the worst excesses of China's 'old society' – excesses which they set out to eradicate when they eventually came to power twenty-eight years later.

In the early years after the revolution of 1949, Shanghai's bars, clubs and brothels were closed down; its factories were gradually taken into state control, though most remained open, since the new government realised it still needed the city's industry and economic know-how. Many of Shanghai's wealthiest residents – and not a few of the middle classes too – had fled, to Hong Kong or Taiwan or North America, and their former homes were taken over by the state. Some of these buildings became the offices of government departments, while others were divided up to house the families of officials and workers, as well as the hundreds of thousands of military men and refugees from other parts of China who had arrived in the city at the time of the civil war of the late 1940s.

It meant that many of the new proletarians found themselves living in some rather unlikely surroundings: art nouveau apartments for example, or Spanish-inspired town houses, mock-Tudor villas, even neoclassical mansions. In the 1920s and 1930s, after all, Shanghai had been one of the fastest growing cities in the world, luring international architects and designers and adopting many of the latest fashions. Wealthy Chinese merchants had commissioned

37

houses influenced by the homes of the city's foreign residents, though often with a few touches of their own; Chinese architects, meanwhile, went to study abroad – one group, including the young I. M. Pei, went to the US, many of them attending the University of Pennsylvania. Some of these students returned, influenced by the ideas of western modernists, and carried on working right up to the eve of the communist revolution. Thus Shanghai became a unique hybrid: as well as high-density terraced housing, it had luxury red-brick apartment buildings like those of 1930s north London; English-style corner cinemas and fire stations; churches of all types, from Methodist to Russian Orthodox; and an impressive array of art deco and modernist architecture: the grand hotels and office blocks of the business district may not have been as tall as those of New York or Chicago, nor as ornate as those of Miami Beach, but they were certainly unique in Asia. I. M. Pei has said that he was first inspired to study architecture as a teenager in Shanghai in the 1930s, when he used to spend his afternoons playing billiards in a downtown club, from where he was able to watch the construction of the famous Park Hotel, then the tallest building in Asia. 'In Shanghai,' he later recalled, 'I saw the future.'[4]

But after the communist revolution, and the flight of money from the city which accompanied it, new construction slowed dramatically. A few showpiece buildings were erected with Soviet assistance, and some basic housing for workers was built in the industrial suburbs, but the city's central areas were little affected. And despite all the political movements of the 1950s and 1960s – even the Cultural Revolution itself, when Shanghai was the centre of worker radicalism in China – most of the old buildings survived, though many were stripped of their finer fittings. Ironically, in fact, it was in large part these political movements, and China's resulting isolation from the rest of the world, which insulated Shanghai from the pressures for urban development that swept through cities worldwide during the 1960s and 1970s. Foreigners coming to China after the Cultural Revolution were startled to find the physical structure of old Shanghai almost completely preserved. Tess Johnston, an American writer and architecture lover who later made

Shanghai her home, remembers arriving in the city in 1981. 'I'd taken courses on Shanghai's history and knew something about what to expect,' she says, 'but I never thought I would find a complete European city on the shores of the East China Sea. I assumed it would have all been torn down, but I found Shanghai intact – and it was an incredible amalgam of styles: you'd find a wonderful French villa right next to an art deco bungalow; there were arts and crafts houses, art nouveau – for an architecture buff it was like dying and going to heaven!'

For many of the city's residents, though, the experience was somewhat less divine. Millions were living crammed into the city's old neighbourhoods. Houses originally designed for a single family – and perhaps a servant or two – were now often home to five or six families, each inhabiting one or two rooms, and sharing kitchen and bathrooms. The subdivision of Shanghai's houses had begun back in the 1930s, when many people fled into the foreign concessions to escape the march of the Japanese armies across eastern China. The revolution, and the Cultural Revolution too, brought further waves of inhabitants to be squeezed into the old neighbourhoods. Such close proximity bred strong bonds and friendships, but many tensions too – particularly since the decades of political movements often turned neighbour against neighbour. Even today, in the shared houses which remain, there's often an obvious sense of heightened territoriality among people living virtually on top of each other in these tiny spaces: it's not uncommon to find four or five separate stoves in the same kitchen, two or three cold-water taps on the same sink, or several light bulbs on the same landing – each one used, and jealously guarded, by a different family.

Lack of funds, and the often uncertain ownership status of the old buildings, also meant they were generally badly maintained, their paint yellowed and peeling, their kitchen walls blackened with the grease and grime of decades. Facilities such as gas central heating, hot-water boilers, even plumbing, which had been state-of-the-art when the houses were built, had often long since been removed, or had broken down and never been repaired. In the oldest residential neighbourhoods in the inner city, many houses had never had plumbing at all, and residents were still using large wooden buckets for their 'night soil'.

Shanghai's citizens still did their best to live with a little of the style which the city was famous for, dressing as smartly as finance or the political climate allowed, and continuing to indulge in habits, such as eating cream cakes and drinking coffee, which would have been regarded with some suspicion in many parts of the country. Yet in fact many of them actually lived in some of the most cramped and decrepit conditions of any city in China. Even at the dawn of the 1990s, Shanghai was effectively a city still struggling to cope with a half-century-old refugee problem. It retained a reputation for producing China's best-quality consumer goods, from the worsted suits of its old textile mills, to 'Forever' bicycles and 'Shanghai' brand cars, but its industry was rapidly being overtaken by new factories in the Special Economic Zones of the south, and the city's infrastructure was creaking, little changed from the pre-war era. The lack of progress was widely put down to the fact that China's leadership at the time still included a number of veteran revolutionaries who remained deeply suspicious of Shanghai, believing its residents to be far too interested in foreign ideas to be given too much freedom, and that the city, given half a chance, might quickly revert to its former capitalist ways.

Shanghai in the late 1980s, when I first visited, was therefore a city with a decaying grandeur, still unique, but not apparently going anywhere in a hurry. Yet by the middle of the 1990s, when I next returned, it had already embarked on the extraordinary transformation which was to propel it back into the world's consciousness. The giant TV tower now soared over the city, on what had been largely undeveloped land across the river from the old colonial waterfront, and alongside it stood the first few office towers of the new financial district. A city famous for its overstretched transport system suddenly had a shiny new subway line, built in record-quick time; elevated roads now led into the city centre from the old airport, and new shopping centres were beginning to appear on the main streets.

This rapid development had much to do with ageing leader Deng

Xiaoping's insistence, in early 1992, that economic reform should move faster and more boldly, if China were to emerge from its post-Tiananmen doldrums. Finally Shanghai began to enjoy some of the preferential treatment previously granted to the Special Economic Zones of the south; the policy change gave the green light for massive new investment in the city – and a new generation of national political leaders, many of whom had previously worked in Shanghai, were happy to oblige. Once again it was designated as China's financial centre – within the space of a few years in the mid–late 1990s it built a new stock exchange, city government offices, grand theatre, museum and library, as well as a network of new roads, bridges and tunnels. Money poured into the city from around the world. And perhaps because of that fabled sense of superiority which had caused many in China to look on Shanghai and its people with a mixture of envy and suspicion since the 1920s, it seemed determined to regain its status as one of the world's great cities.

Indeed, so obsessed was Shanghai with the idea of change that it built a shrine to it. The Urban Planning Exhibition Centre sits right beside the municipal government offices in People's Square, on the site of the old British race course. It's a central planner's dream, a monument to everything connected with Shanghai's recon-struction, on a scale which can leave visitors open-mouthed. In the high entrance hall, a massive gold sculpture rotates gently on a plinth – a tableau of the grandest buildings of the city's past and future, the colonial edifices of the Bund nestling beneath soaring high-rises, some of them not actually built yet. The enormity of the city's transformation is highlighted nearby, where one whole wall is filled with a huge bronze frieze. It features craggy-looking con-struction workers in the heroic poses of socialist realism, and alongside them ordinary citizens packing their belongings into the backs of removal vans. Its title is *One million residents moving house,* a tribute to the Shanghai citizens who left their old homes in the city centre during the 1990s to make way for new construction and redevelopment. Yes, all one million of them – though the frieze may be due for an update, since as many as another three-quarters of a million people were expected to move in the first decade of the new century, during which another twenty million square metres of the old city were due to be demolished.[5]

The exhibition rooms upstairs fill in the details of Shanghai's ambitions. There's the underground and light rail network, due to expand to around a dozen lines in just a few years, with the final plan for more than twenty; the deep-water port, intended to rival Hong Kong and Singapore as the largest in the world, which was created by flattening two islands some twenty miles out to sea, joining them together and linking them to the mainland via the world's longest offshore bridge. There's the regeneration of the old shipyards and factories along the Huangpu River, to form the garden site for the 2010 World Expo, to say nothing of the magnetic rail line, the new airport terminals, the Formula One racetrack in the suburbs, the massive petrochemical base – and the eleven new satellite towns, each with a different European country as its theme, from the Bavarian-inspired town square of Anting to the Dickensian cottages and half-timbered houses of 'Thames Town', the British-themed area in suburban Songjiang district.

But the true, awe-inspiring centrepiece of the exhibition is to be found on the third floor, most of which is taken up by a vast scale-model of the city. Entitled *Shanghai 2020*, it claims to show the city as it will look in that year, down to every street and major building. It's in different shades, coloured for existing structures, and white or transparent for those yet to be built – a reminder that the city's upheavals are far from complete. The model attracts large crowds, some to stare in awe, some to work out where they should invest in property, others simply hoping to find out whether their own homes will still exist in a few years' time; in a city which puts so much emphasis on planning, it can be remarkably hard for ordinary people to get advance news about what's going to happen to their neighbourhood – and the model is sometimes the only source of information. Whether it's reliable, however, is another matter: change is so constant in Shanghai that even the 2020 model itself has to be revised on a regular basis. For the young guide from the Shanghai government who showed me around this was a source of pride. 'Shanghai is developing day after day,' she said, as we gazed

42

across the giant model. 'People here are very excited. In Shanghai we say that every year you will see a small change, and every three years a great change,' she continued, adding with apparent satisfaction, 'even Shanghai residents can't recognise their old homes after several years.'

And sometimes the pace can be far faster. As in Beijing, Shanghai is a city where old streets can disappear and new buildings appear on the skyline in what seems like a matter of weeks – and the city's software, its shops and restaurants, can transform just as rapidly. After one brief trip abroad, I came back to find that my local hairdresser's had become a bar, the French restaurant was now serving Japanese food, and the optician's I'd visited just before going away had turned into a furniture store. Such stories are an everyday occurrence in Shanghai – though few can top the (possibly apocryphal) tale of a friend who claimed to have walked down a street one morning and passed a large patch of bare earth beside the road, only to come back later the same day and find a public garden, complete with trees, flowers and grass.

There's no doubt that the years of constant change, and the ever more modern environment, have left their mark on the thinking of many of Shanghai's citizens, the younger generation in particular. I began to realise this when I moved to Shanghai from Beijing in 2000 and started looking for a place to live. A clean-cut young estate agent, his mobile phone earpiece permanently lodged in his ear, showed me a folder filled with pictures of modern tower blocks. Did he have anything older? I wondered, thinking of some of the stylish apartment buildings from the 1920s and 1930s. 'No problem,' he said, 'we'll look at some tomorrow.' The next morning we set off to visit the places he'd selected. 'Here we are,' he said with satisfaction, as we drew up at our first stop. We climbed out of the car. In front of us stood a pair of distinctly modern tower blocks, each more than twenty storeys high, tiled in that curious green and pink colour scheme so beloved of Hong Kong property developers. I tactfully pointed out that I had been hoping to see something a little older. 'Well,' insisted the estate agent, 'these are old – they were built in 1995!'

43

Still, while many Shanghai residents have enthusiastically accepted the authorities' obsession with the new, there are others who have found the city's transformation more traumatic. In the early–mid 1990s, when the municipal authorities began moving the first of the million or more citizens out of their old homes, many were only too happy to cooperate. The government was promising a greener, cleaner city, with more parks, and bigger, more modern homes for those who moved. Some of the first to go were the residents of areas which were little more than shanty towns, huts thrown up after the bombing of Shanghai during fighting with the Japanese in the 1930s. And those who lived in some of the city's oldest streets, their tiny two-storey houses made mainly of wood, were also often keen to move out. 'We were so happy,' said Mrs Yan, a Shanghai housewife in her fifties, remembering how she felt when her family left their cramped single room in an old neighbourhood for a flat in a newly built concrete block. 'Suddenly we had our own bathroom – and our daughter even had a bedroom to herself.'

But as the process continued, concerns began to surface. While some old areas of town were being knocked down to make way for the city's new roads, underground lines and other public facilities, other demolitions seemed to be driven more by commercial interests. The government, which needed money to fund its grand plans, was keen to attract real-estate developers to the city; the developers, many from Hong Kong or Taiwan, were, not surprisingly, eager to get their hands on the best areas of town and build high-density, high-rise office towers, shopping centres and residential blocks, as they had done in their own cities. In the great wave of demolitions of the mid–late 1990s, it became clear that some of the more upmarket areas of the former foreign settlements were being affected too, and that people living in relative comfort in better-equipped old lane houses were sometimes being moved before those in the poorest areas, who were supposed to be the main beneficiaries of the city's reconstruction. Even among those who were willing to move if they could get a new home with better facilities not too far from the city centre, there were growing complaints that what they actually got were flats in cheaply built housing blocks, in new suburbs with little infrastructure, up to two hours by bus from the downtown areas where they had lived.[6] (There was also an initial resistance to moving across the river from the older parts of the city to the Pudong new district, as hundreds of thousands of people had to do. In the late 1990s it was still common to hear disgruntled residents muttering the old Shanghai saying, 'Better a bed in Puxi [the old centre of the city] than a house in Pudong.')

There was little that most of the relocated residents could do about the situation, however, since very few of them actually owned their homes. A minority of the old, pre-revolutionary middle class did get their old homes returned to them by the authorities in the 1990s, but most Shanghai citizens were living in accommodation which had simply been allocated to them by the government in the years after the revolution. In theory those who moved were at least entitled to choose between a new flat offered by the property developer, or cash compensation which they could use to buy a home on the commercial market. But the process was far from straightforward: in practice the amount of compensation varied from area to area, and the companies in charge of the relocation carried out separate negotiations with each family. And since these companies were usually private firms hired by the developers, it was to their own advantage if they could persuade residents to accept as little money as possible. What's more, the official compensation standard, which initially took into account the number of people in each family, was later revised, and based largely on the market value of their existing home – in other words, those who had lived in low-quality, tiny accommodation would get less compensation.[7] The government did set a new official target of giving each resident a minimum of eight square metres, but it was not necessarily the spacious new life which many residents of the cramped old downtown districts had been hoping for.

Rumours that a particular area was soon to be demolished might fly around for months or years. Residents, though, would usually hear nothing definite until the last moment, when they would be given just one or two months to pack up their lives and move out of their homes. The lack of information was made clear to me one day when I was wandering through an old neighbourhood where the bulldozers had already started work, and an old lady sitting on a bamboo stool outside her front door beckoned me over and asked whether I was the property developer in charge of demolishing her home, and whether I could tell her which part of the city she would have to move to.

For most people, there was little choice but to go along with the process and make the best of it. But as the relocations gathered pace in the second half of the 1990s and into the new decade, signs of resistance began to emerge. It became increasingly common to pass a half-demolished block and find that there were still lights on in the windows of the remaining buildings, or washing still hanging out to dry. These were the homes of those who had refused to accept meekly the terms offered to them by the relocation firms, and were holding out for what they saw as fairer treatment. Such defiance did not go down well, however. There were repeated stories of strong-arm tactics being used by the relocation firms. 'They turned off all the water and electricity in the lane while we were still negotiating our compensation,' one irate man complained. 'In the height of summer, too – you can imagine how disgusting it was to live here!'

Others told more frightening tales, of people who refused to move being beaten up or threatened. In an old neighbourhood beside what was once Avenue Road, one of the main streets of the former International Settlement, I met two women picking their way among heaps of rubble to reach the last few houses which were still standing in the middle of a demolition zone. They too were defying the pressure to move out because they were unhappy with the level of compensation. 'My friend has 140 square metres here,' said one of the women, pointing to an old *shikumen* house, the carved wooden decoration on its upper windows just visible above the high wall of its courtyard. 'Do you think she needs to move?' Her friend, a middle-aged teacher, said she had been offered a smaller place out in the suburbs, far from her workplace and her son's school. 'I'd be happy to move across the road to one of those,' she said, pointing at a new luxury block which had recently been built opposite. 'Why don't they just let us stay here?' Their greatest anger was reserved for the people carrying out the relocation process and the demolition work. The first woman pointed to a nearby house which was partly propped up by a big wooden joist; jagged edges jutting from one of its walls made it clear that the rest of the structure had already been demolished. 'There's an old lady still living there,' she said, 'but they've already knocked half the place down.' 'Yes,' said her friend angrily, 'some of the workers are like hooligans, they've just got out of jail – they try to scare you so that you'll move out.'

Such stories were not always easy to verify, particularly since the relocation companies rarely spoke to the media. I myself had only one direct encounter with these organisations, which was more surreal than frightening. I once called on a family whose home was due for demolition; the owner opened the door and whispered quickly that they were in the middle of a meeting with the relocation company. Hearing a shrill voice talking insistently inside, I said I'd come back later. But before I could move, a woman in her thirties, evidently the owner of the voice, appeared behind him and demanded to know what I was doing there. I explained that I was a friend who was just passing by and would return another time. But as I set off down the lane I realised she was following me. She caught up with me and began firing off questions. Who was I, where was I from, why was I visiting this family? By this time we had reached the entrance to the lane, and passers-by on the pavement outside were beginning to stare at us. The relocation lady turned to an old couple out for an evening stroll who were watching the scene with interest. 'This foreigner is very interested in the relocation of our residents!' she announced loudly. Finally, having established that I was from Britain, she barked: 'Do you or do you not accept that our two countries have a friendly relationship?' I said I certainly hoped so and jumped into the nearest taxi. I've still never quite worked out whether this last question was a gesture of friendship or a threat, but I was relieved that I did not have to negotiate my own future living conditions with her.

Slowly the authorities began to accept that there had been

47

problems with the relocation process – particularly after one case in early 2005 where an elderly couple, who had refused to move out of their home, died in a fire started intentionally by workers from a relocation company. The deputy head of the company and one of the workers received suspended death sentences; another worker was jailed for life. State media reported that other residents of the same area had previously been attacked and injured by staff of the relocation and demolition companies.[8] Chastened officials began to call for a more careful approach, and the press became more open about some of the problems. 'Certain relocation companies have used evil and vicious methods,' said one newspaper article, which I found pasted on the outside wall of an old house near the Bund by its residents, in silent protest at their relocation to make way for a new luxury development.

And some residents defied the pressures to mount their own defence. In one area, which became something of a cause célèbre, local residents who claimed that some people had never received any relocation funds after leaving their homes staged public protests outside official buildings, including the homes of local government leaders, and hired a lawyer to bring a case against the developer. Their tactics eventually attracted the attention of the central government. The real-estate developer, Zhou Zhengyi, who grew up in Shanghai's rural suburbs and had grown rich through real-estate deals in the 1990s, eventually listing his company on the Hong Kong stock exchange, was arrested on charges of false financial reporting and stock manipulation.[9] More serious allegations, of corruption in the acquisition of the land involved, were rejected by the court; Mr Zhou was eventually jailed in 2003 for three years. The lawyer who tried to defend the residents, meanwhile, was himself arrested, accused of passing state secrets to a foreign organisation – and jailed for the same length of time.[10] His harsh treatment was seen as a warning to other residents not to make their grievances public (though in 2006, after the sacking of Shanghai's Communist Party Secretary on corruption charges, Zhou Zhengyi was rearrested, and later jailed for 16 years – though again on financial charges not directly related to the real estate case).

Nevertheless, the bad publicity which resulted from the case, along with the central government's high-profile campaign, announced in 2005, to create a 'harmonious society', did seem to lead to some attempts to reduce the bitterness surrounding Shanghai's relocations. There were still complaints from residents – but property developers now also began to grumble that moving people out of their homes was becoming more and more complicated. One developer bemoaned the fact that an entire project was being delayed by a single family who were refusing to move; the authorities, he said, were too concerned about negative publicity to put pressure on them. As a result, he added, such residents had been emboldened and were now making increasingly high demands for compensation. To such developers, it was all highly unreasonable: as the head of one Hong Kong real-estate company put it, most of the people being moved did not actually own the buildings or the land where they lived, and therefore deserved to be treated as nothing more than 'squatters'.[11]

There was no doubt that some residents did their best to get what they could out of the system; some re-registered family members who had long since moved away as still living in their homes, in order to get more compensation. One old man I met, who lived on a plot of land earmarked for the Hong Kong developer, complained he was only being offered a million yuan (some £75,000). This was, at the time, enough to buy a three-bedroom flat in a reasonably convenient suburb; but, he insisted, 'the people in the next block got twice as much, so that's what I want too'.

It was not hard, however, to understand why people whose whole lives were being turned upside down would try to extract whatever they could from the process. And for all that the authorities promised that they were improving the facilities in the new suburbs, there was still something rather strange about watching a 'socialist' system moving ordinary working people out of the city centre, where they had lived for most of their lives, in order to replace them with luxury housing, offices and leisure complexes for the benefit of big business, foreigners and China's new rich. The decision to disperse many of Shanghai's densely packed downtown communities was, however, a conscious one, which would benefit the city as a whole, according to Mao Jialiang, the director of the city's planning bureau. 'As Shanghai's economy has developed, the population has grown fast too,' he explained in 2006. 'So we're trying to thin out the population of the city centre, reduce building density, and increase public space and green areas. We hope that many people will move out to the new satellite cities in the suburbs.'[12] And there is no doubt that, with its economic success once again attracting people from all over China, Shanghai has become more crowded than ever in recent years. In 2006 its long-term resident population was just short of eighteen million, an increase of more than one and a half million people in the space of just four years.[13]

The continuing stresses in the relocation process, though, were highlighted by the big red banners suspended across the streets in the old neighbourhoods being prepared for relocation. These encouraged residents to vacate their homes as speedily as possible, promising greater benefits for those who moved first, and seeking to inspire them with dreams of a brighter future. 'Move today for a better tomorrow' was a popular slogan; another vowed to 'reconstruct the old areas, beautify Shanghai, and bring wealth to our children, grandchildren and future generations'. But some banners gave a hint of the problems involved: many of them offered thanks to 'the residents who have actively supported and co-operated with the removal process', which seemed to suggest that not all residents had been quite so forthcoming. Banners proclaiming 'Make absolutely sure that the honest people don't lose out', meanwhile, were designed to reassure citizens about the fairness of the process, but were also a reminder that not everyone was quite so convinced. And other slogans took a less soothing tone, warning citizens that they had a responsibility to cooperate. 'Everyone is equal in the face of reform,' said one; 'Supporting national construction is every citizen's glorious duty!' insisted another. Individuals, it was suggested, must make sacrifices: 'Everyone should make their own contribution to the reconstruction of the neighbourhood,' announced one banner, while others urged

50

residents to 'think about the bigger picture and recognise the broader situation'; or even to 'move your little home [*xiao jia*] to benefit the "big home" [*da jia* – a phrase normally used to mean 'everyone']'.

Yet for many in Shanghai, it could be hard to accept the idea of moving out of the old neighbourhoods – particularly for older people who had lived in the heart of the city all their lives, and were fiercely proud of being China's most modern urban citizens. 'They want to send us so far away, to somewhere by the banks of the Yangtze River,' lamented Mr Wang, a charming man of more than eighty, in his old-fashioned English. A vague gesture of his hand made it clear that he felt this was a place beyond the limits of known civilisation. One of his neighbours put it more bluntly. 'They're going to turn us all into peasants,' she grumbled. In a city where one of the biggest insults in the local dialect is to describe someone as a *xiangwuning* – a country bumpkin or peasant – it must have been a depressing thought.

For many such people, the demolition of the old neighbourhoods and the break-up of these long-established communities also meant a loss of something of the fabric of the city. That was certainly how it felt to the family of Mr Wei, a middle-aged businessman, who lived in a *shikumen*-style house in the old French concession, very close to one of Shanghai's busiest shopping streets. According to family legend, the house had been bought by Mr Wei's grandfather in 1922, when it was newly built, for what was then the princely sum of five bars of gold. After the revolution, the family had given up part of the house to a local official, and now had three rooms, some forty square metres in total. A few years ago, Mr Wei and his wife and daughter had moved out, to a new flat in another part of town. His mother, though, refused to leave the house where she had lived since she married into the family half a century earlier. 'The first time I came here was on my wedding day,' she explained with pride. 'I was carried here in a sedan chair. When I arrived, the whole lane had been laid out with tables for our marriage banquet.' Her own former home was just fifteen minutes' walk from here, she said, but at the time it had felt like she was moving far away – a reminder of just how closely many older Shanghai people were traditionally tied to their local neighbourhood.

Now, though, the area was due to be demolished, to make way for office buildings and an upmarket shopping district. Mrs Wei had been offered a flat across the river in Pudong, almost an hour away by bus, but she wasn't tempted. 'I've never been to Pudong, never been to the suburbs,' she insisted. 'I've always been here, in this area.' Her house was not the best, she acknowledged, but they had put in a new kitchen a few years earlier, and she was happy here. 'It's best to live in your own home,' she said, 'and the neighbours are very good.' Her son nodded: despite the more modern facilities of his new flat, he missed the sense of community. 'Here the doors are always kept open, people can just drop in any time, children can come and go,' he said. 'In the new apartments it's very different – once the door's shut no one comes in.' And to recreate the atmosphere of these old communities in a new area was not easy, he said. 'It's a tradition,' he explained, 'the result of decades living so close together. It's not something that just develops in three to five years.' At this moment, as if to prove his point, one of their former neighbours appeared at the door. He had moved away, but he still came back to see his friends almost every day. Hearing the topic of conversation, he began telling a story about a family who had moved to a new flat and had died as the result of a gas leak. 'No one found them for two days,' he said. 'Over here that could never have happened – the neighbours would have asked where they were today, they would have knocked on the door to check.'

Surely living in such constant proximity with others must be hard, I suggested. No, said their friend, it was never too much, and the best thing was that people helped each other. Mr Wei was starting to look nostalgic. 'Now we're about to move I often dream about things which happened when I was young,' he sighed. His teenage daughter, who with her trendy clothes and Japanese-style make-up looked like a typical product of Shanghai's new generation, glanced up from the textbooks she was reading in the corner of the room. She'd had mixed feelings about the house when she was young, she said: it could get crowded, and the ground floor was quite dark since they had covered up a leaking skylight. But after living elsewhere she still preferred this area. 'I'll miss this place,' she said. 'All my classmates were here, now they've all moved out and I can't find them.' She took me out into the lane for a last look. 'Now foreigners come to Shanghai and they don't see it as an old city,' she said. 'They think it's modern, more and more like America. But to me it doesn't feel like Shanghai any more – not like my Shanghai anyway'.

There's no doubt that Shanghai's singular urban culture has been altered by the disappearance of so many old neighbourhoods. Some see this as being for the good, believing it's time for the old ways to change. But the old traditions are also a part of what makes the city unique: the washing creatively suspended from upper windows on bamboo poles (something the Shanghai government once tried, rather unsuccessfully, to ban); the women of the crowded inner-city districts with their hair piled up in spectacular bouffants, apparently held together with glue; the vendors and rag-and-bone men who wander the lanes calling out their wares or their services; the nightwatchmen who still patrol through each lane in the early evening, ringing a hand bell to remind residents to shut their windows and doors before they go to bed; the locals strolling the backstreets – and sometimes the main streets – dressed in pyjamas – which they consider to be ideal daytime house wear, and so, by extension, quite reasonable to wear when popping out to the shops or running a quick errand.

The demolitions have also erased much of the tangible evidence of Shanghai's spectacular history: the art deco houses removed to enlarge a park and build a petrol station; the old lanes with their decorous entrances, the dates of their construction – mostly from the 1920s to the early 1930s – proudly carved on the walls above them, and their unique names (I once watched a demolition worker setting about the 'Lane of Everlasting Calm' with a sledgehammer); the functional buildings of the late 1940s which some see as the missing link to a long-lost, alternative vision of Chinese modernity; even the old grey bricks from demolished houses which I once saw a man loading onto the back of a truck. 'I export them to Japan,' he explained, 'they love these old bricks there, but they don't have any more of their own, so they buy these ones.' Indeed, Shanghai's short but intense history means that the layers of its past are often buried in tightly packed strata, one on top of the other. In one street, the removal of modern shop signs prior to demolition unearthed not only the hand-painted Chinese names of old shops from the early communist days – the 'New Glow Barbers', the 'Number Five Grain Store' – but older signs too, painted in English, clearly dating from the 1940s or before. One of these advertised 'coal briquettes', which according to a 1946 map of the city was exactly what the shop used to sell. Occasionally, traces of different vanished eras can still be found on a single building: on one grand old block behind the Bund, the faded signs announcing its pre-1949 status as the headquarters of 'Imperial Chemical Industries China' – in other words the local branch of ICI – remain visible alongside peeling Cultural Revolution slogans proclaiming 'Long live Chairman Mao'.

Yet such traces are becoming rarer all the time. For lovers of the city's architectural heritage, watching the disappearance of favourite parts of old Shanghai can be a depressing experience. Tess Johnston, the American writer who was so surprised to find the city almost intact when she moved here in 1981, has, since the early 1990s, spent much of her time documenting Shanghai's old neighbourhoods with her colleague, the photographer Er Dongqiang. 'Sometimes we almost get physically ill when we see some particular treasure going under the wrecker's ball,' she says. For Er Dongqiang, born and bred in the city, the loss is particularly tragic. 'We've thrown out great quantities of human cultural information and heritage,' he has written. 'It's as though the city's muscles have been split, the pulse of its architecture cut off.'[14] One grand old house which met its end was the family home of the grandfather of I. M. Pei – a red-brick mansion dating from around 1900, with sweeping staircases and grand balconies, French stained glass and parquet floors. Descendants of the family, who still lived in the house, were initially assured that it was a historic building and would be protected. The following year, in 2001, they were told it was to be demolished to make way for a new park. Even a plea from

I. M. Pei himself, who had designed a number of prestigious buildings for the Chinese authorities, could not save it. 'I suppose that means this house is just worth a few trees,' Bei Nianzheng, one of the last of the family to live there, said sadly.

I once suggested to Shen Zhengchao of the Shanghai Construction Commission that the willingness to demolish so many old buildings might reflect continuing suspicion of their links with the 'bad old days' of foreign domination in Shanghai. He laughed at the idea. 'No,' he assured me, 'that shadow has faded, and anyway a nation must face up to its history to do well. Shanghai people have a lot of feelings for these old buildings,' he continued, 'they really combine the best architecture from around the world.' And the demolition of large parts of Shanghai's original walled city district, which pre-dates the foreign presence, also suggests that there is no particular political motive to the destruction.

Certainly the city has shown itself capable of protecting old areas when it wants to. Most of the buildings on the Bund, and a number of famous old shops and hotels, were listed for preservation in the 1990s, along with a handful of the most prestigious old lanes. One famous former cinema (now the Shanghai Concert Hall) was even lifted up on a hydraulic cushion, rolled seventy yards and rotated in order to improve its acoustics, which had suffered when the city's overhead expressway was built right outside the front door. The homes of several famous revolutionaries have been treated with similar respect: one was wheeled a few hundred yards and relocated to spare it from the demolition of the surrounding neighbourhood; and two separate houses where Chairman Mao once lived were also preserved, while everything around them was knocked down. And perhaps most famously, the site of the Communist Party's first meeting in 1921 – a small *shikumen* terraced house in the old French Concession – became the catalyst for one of the city's best-known renovations of an old neighbourhood.

The house, which was turned into a museum after the revolution, stood in the midst of a typical Shanghai neighbourhood of small residential backstreets. In the 1990s, the area, close to one of the city's main business and shopping districts, was earmarked for

55

redevelopment, and the land acquired by a Hong Kong property developer. The authorities insisted that the Communist Party museum, and a few buildings around it, should be protected. But Ben Wood, the American architect hired by the developer, was determined to preserve far more of the original area, and eventually persuaded his employers to keep almost the entire city block in which the museum was situated, to create a pedestrianised leisure zone. He was inspired by both the architecture and the atmosphere of the old lanes. 'The character of these buildings is just amazing,' he said, when he showed me around during the reconstruction work. 'You might think you were in the area around Spitalfields in London, with these tiny lanes – or some of the older parts of Paris, with all these decorative French-style carvings.' Many people had told him that these houses were 'just slums', he said, but he was determined to prove them wrong. 'I knew that on any given day in Shanghai they were tearing down a couple of hundred of these houses,' Ben Wood explained, 'and I wanted to demonstrate to people that you could take the existing fabric of a city and make it commercially viable for the twenty-first century.'

The area, renamed Xintiandi (literally: new heaven and earth), quickly became hugely popular, the chic restaurants and boutiques which now occupied the renovated buildings doing a roaring trade, the terraces outside its cafés filled with tourists and local yuppies until late into the night. The concept swiftly caught on – soon other cities around China were seeking help from Ben Wood and the developer, the Shui On Group, to revive old neighbourhoods of their own cities. Not everyone was convinced. Some conservationists complained that many of the buildings preserved just a façade, that the soul of the area had been lost when its two thousand original residents were relocated, and that the new amenities were too expensive for ordinary people to enjoy. Others saw it as merely a token gesture by the authorities towards historical conservation, while large areas of similar buildings continued to be demolished all around.[15]

Still, there were some hints, by the middle of this decade, that the authorities were at least starting to think a little more about

56

preserving some of the city's remaining heritage. Professor Wu Jiang, dean of the school of architecture at Shanghai's Tongji University and a long-standing advocate of greater conservation, was appointed deputy head of the city's Planning Bureau, and played an important part in the drawing up of new lists of protected buildings and the establishment of new conservation areas. In 2005 the planning department also began to put stone plaques on the walls of protected structures, giving a short explanation of their background. It was hardly a radical step, but it was still the first time the Shanghai government had publicly acknowledged the pre-communist history of many of these buildings. Professor Wu also made efforts to protect some of Shanghai's unique old industrial architecture – another new idea for the authorities. It wasn't always easy, he acknowledged. One state-run company was furious to find that one of its old factory buildings had been listed as a historical site – since it had been intending to demolish it and put up a new office block which it could rent out. But Professor Wu believed that attitudes were beginning to change. We were talking on an observation platform looking out over an old factory, which was to become part of the site for the 2010 World Expo in Shanghai; it was one of a number of striking old industrial buildings which Wu Jiang and his colleagues had tried to preserve as part of the Expo development. 'In the past people didn't always listen or understand what we were talking about,' he said, gazing at the glass and iron roof of a former steelworks, 'but I think that now that the city's economy is more developed, conservation is becoming the demand of the majority of the people.'

The increasingly high value of old houses on Shanghai's property market, many of them snapped up and renovated by foreign investors, may also have played a part in protecting a few more fragments of the city's history from redevelopment. And in recent years there's no doubt that the local media has become more outspoken in its calls for the preservation of the city's heritage. But it's clearly too late to save some areas, or to bring back the old ways of life for many of the city's inhabitants. Where old neighbourhoods have survived, it seems inevitable that more and more will be turned into fashionable restaurants and wine bars, or homes for wealthy overseas buyers. And outside Professor Wu's new conservation zones, the city's grand plans for redevelopment continue. The sacking of Shanghai's Communist Party Secretary on corruption charges connected to the use of money from the city's pension fund in 2006 did lead to closer scrutiny of some real-estate deals, since some of the cash had ended up in several developers' construction projects. But there was little sign that real-estate companies would suddenly lose interest in this most popular of cities. To drive out of the centre of Shanghai towards the suburbs these days is to be confronted with an extraordinary landscape of cranes, construction sites and half-built or freshly completed town houses and high-rises, stretching for a solid hour in any direction. Indeed, there are some who believe that Shanghai's obsession with progress will make it one of the world's most modern cities, defining the early twenty-first century in the way New York or Chicago defined the urban environment of much of the last century.

For the moment, though, Shanghai remains a city caught between two worlds – where the hyper-modern exists cheek by jowl with the old, the quaint, even the rustic. It can sometimes seem as though an old village or a small European town has been picked up and scattered at random among the skyscrapers of a modern central business district, or that two entirely separate cities coexist on the same spot: the high-rise splendour of the new, futuristic metropolis, and alongside it the remnants of the old Shanghai, the refugee city, with its lanes with their completely different pace of life still surviving behind the glossy façades of the main streets – and it's entirely up to the viewer which of these two worlds they choose to see. Part of the city's charm lies in the unexpected glimpses which result: an old wrought-iron balcony filled with flowerpots on a busy downtown street; elderly residents, apparently oblivious to the startling transformation of the neighbourhoods around them, continuing to play cards, stroll around in their vests and parade their pet birds in cages among the concrete plazas and ornamental gardens which form the entrances to the city's new office blocks.

Whether such sights will survive for long is less certain.

Shanghai's fascination with change goes back a long way – even in the 1920s and 1930s the city was continuously demolishing buildings, including those on the waterfront, and replacing them with newer and bigger ones – and it's a state of mind which seems to be in Shanghai's blood. What does seem clear is that in a city which has led China's rush towards the future over the past decade and a half, few people's lives will remain quite the same in the years to come.

# 3

# Aspiration nation

On a crisp winter morning in 1999, I approached the entrance of a large, hangar-like building beside Beijing's Third Ring Road. I had never been here before, but the atmosphere was strangely, perhaps reassuringly, familiar. Friendly staff ushered me upstairs to the office area and showed me in to a small room. Inside, the youthful manager jumped up from his chair and gave me a friendly handshake, introducing himself as Mr Gustavsson. With his sandy-yellow hair and even yellower shirt, he seemed a picture of energy and enthusiasm. But when he sat back in his chair and began to describe the experience of the past few weeks, there was a hint of exhaustion in his voice. 'I have worked for this company for fifteen years,' he said, in his lilting English, 'and I have never seen anything like it.' He seemed to pale a little at the recollection. 'The Saturday before last we had 35,000 people in the store,' he continued, 'it looked like a tornado had gone through the place!' Now, he said, he was starting to get used to the situation. 'But in the beginning it was frightening, all those people, it was . . .' He paused for a moment, as though searching for the right words to describe his feelings, then seemed to abandon the attempt. 'It was . . . wooh!' he sighed, with a shrug of his shoulders. As a former professional footballer in his native Sweden, it seemed safe to assume that Mr Gustavsson had seen some crowds in his time. But apparently nothing in his past career had quite prepared him for the frenzy of recent days. Mr Gustavsson was, it perhaps goes without saying, the newly appointed manager of the Chinese capital's first branch of IKEA.

It was just over a month since the store had opened, and the response had been, to say the least, enthusiastic. 'We had to cancel three advertisements because there were too many people,' said Mr Gustavsson. Even the district Communist Party secretary had dropped in to cast an eye over the soft furnishings. And the masses too had been making the most of the amenities. 'It's amazing,' Mr Gustavsson went on. 'On Saturdays there are people sitting in all the sofas and the easy chairs; they have their own tea, their biscuits, their newspaper, and . . . yeah, they're having a picnic!' He gave an ironic chuckle. 'And one thing I have never seen before – we had a guy sleeping in a bed for an hour, and when he woke up he explained that he just wanted to test the bed.' He shrugged again. 'And OK, why not?!'

The public reaction was perhaps hardly surprising. It was not that China's citizens had had no interest in furnishing their homes before; back in the 1980s, as people began putting the austere days of the Cultural Revolution behind them, there was a sudden fascination with attaining the new basics of life – a television set, stereo, fridge and washing machine. These, along with a full set of furniture, were known collectively as the 'forty-eight legs', and quickly became prerequisites for any man who wanted to find a bride.[1] But in those days the products of the Chinese furnishing industry were somewhat hit-and-miss. When I lived in China in the 1980s, one of the most coveted items was a two-seater sofa, upholstered in luminous green velour, with a central armrest which folded down to reveal an inlaid picture of a panda chewing on a sprig of bamboo. Such sofas could often be seen perched precariously on the back of bicycles, being manoeuvred through the traffic by courageous delivery men. Gradually, as foreign films and TV series made their influence felt in the late 1980s and early 1990s, more people began trying to mimic 'western style'. China's new generation of budding private entrepreneurs, the laoban or 'boss class', could now be found relaxing on massive leather sofas or seated at vast wooden desks. The emphasis was very much on the showy and imposing: rococo was in, gold ornamentation was all the rage, and, for those with money to spare, imported furniture from Italy and Spain was particularly popular. And because the big international lifestyle stores had not yet arrived in China, some unlikely players were able to carve out a niche in the market. In the years before the opening of IKEA, Beijing consumers consoled themselves with such delights as the 'Romanian Furniture City' – a huge emporium in the basement of a rather empty shopping centre, filled with immense beds, tables and chairs made of ornately carved heavy wood.

Now, with more people moving from old buildings into new homes, the arrival of Sweden's finest seemed to have tapped into a general desire for a cleaner, more modern style. Introducing the people of Beijing to the joys of pale wood, self-assembly bookcases and space-saving sofa beds was not necessarily a simple business, however. A stroll around the newly opened store's kitchenware department, for example, revealed several shoppers holding up assorted utensils for closer inspection, with expressions ranging from puzzlement to downright suspicion on their faces. 'What's this in aid of?' asked one man irritably, brandishing a plastic salad fork. 'Don't we have chopsticks for that?' he demanded, perhaps not unreasonably, after being told of its function.

Nevertheless, the tiny, carefully arranged display rooms, designed to convince even the residents of cramped public-housing flats that a minimalist Scandinavian lifestyle could be theirs, seemed to be winning some people over. 'This shop can change many things about the thinking of the Chinese people,' said a middle-aged man I met there one Sunday. 'We never had the idea that a home could be like this, with so many colours, such a clean style.' And indeed there seemed to be many young people in the store, leading aged relatives around by the hand and pointing out to them the function of various appliances. As one young professional put it, such places provided an opportunity to show her parents' generation that the way they lived was due for an overhaul. 'These older people have been through difficult times,' she said, 'and so they've never had the luxury of being interested in design or style. Take my parents, for example – all they care about is something simple that works. And after all the hard times,' she added, 'they tend to keep everything. My mother doesn't like to throw anything away, so the house is full of boxes – and she doesn't know how to

62

use space efficiently either.' Subtle lighting was a similarly alien concept. 'They just want bright lights, to see better and save electricity,' she explained, 'so their homes always feel like a meeting room or an office.' But perhaps now things were starting to change, she said. 'One of my friends brought her mother to IKEA for the afternoon,' she recalled, 'and after a few hours her mum said, "I really think I should throw out a lot of the stuff we have at home."' The young generation too could learn something, she believed. 'Lots of young people want something different, different colours,' she explained, 'but they don't know how to do it – if you go to their homes it often looks a mess, all mixed up. So here they can get some ideas.'

Mr Gustavsson had also begun to realise that his store was playing a slightly unexpected role. 'I think people see us not so much as a shop, perhaps more as an exhibition of modern European lifestyle,' he said thoughtfully, as he surveyed the crowds in the sofa department. There were still some potential cultural misunderstandings to be overcome. One young Beijing couple proudly installed a new folding sofa bed in their spare room, only to find that the husband's parents were less than impressed when they came to stay. 'You don't want us to stay long, then?' asked his mother with a hurt look, when she set eyes on this rather temporary-looking piece of furniture. Still, others happily embraced the new style. Not long after the Beijing store opened, I went to visit a friend at his parents' home in a typical old government-built apartment block. As usual I made my way through the darkened entrance hall, trying not to trip over the ramshackle array of dust-coated bicycles, most of which seemed not to have been moved for years, and climbed the bare concrete staircase to their small flat. But when my friend opened the door I was surprised to find his elderly parents reclining on a cream-coloured sofa in front of a new pine table. 'It was time for a change,' said his father, with a satisfied smile.

The growing interest in new types of living environment around the turn of the century came as many people were moving into new homes, not only because of relocations caused by urban reconstruction, but also as a result of radical reforms in China's housing policy which gathered pace in the second half of the 1990s. Until the middle of that decade, the vast majority of housing in Chinese cities still belonged to the state. Despite all the country's economic reforms since the 1980s, most urban residents still lived in homes which had been allocated to them by their 'work unit' – the state-run enterprise, government department or public institution for which they worked. Housing had been a fundamental part of the Communist Party's 'new deal' after the 1949 revolution: not only were existing old houses divided up to accommodate more people, but in the early years of the new state, and again in the years after the Cultural Revolution, large quantities of functional housing blocks for workers were built in towns around the country. The flats were generally cramped, but tenants paid little more than a token rent. This housing was usually for life; as the authors of a recent book called *Housing has changed China* wrote, the biggest threat that the leaders of a work unit could use in those days was 'we'll take away your flat', or 'we won't allocate you a flat'.[2] Retired workers kept their homes, so if state-run work units wanted to employ more staff, they often had to construct new buildings to house them.

By the 1990s, the government had come to see the provision of such accommodation (and of other forms of welfare too) as both a burden on its own finances, and a major drag on the profitability of state-run enterprises. This, it believed, was seriously hampering the ability of Chinese businesses to compete internationally. From the early 1990s onwards, experiments took place in a number of cities with so-called 'housing accumulation funds', a type of social insurance pioneered in Singapore, which allowed workers with steady jobs to pay a percentage of their salary into a personal housing account. This amount was then matched by their work unit or employer, and employees could draw on these funds to take out loans for buying or renovating their own homes.[3] Finally, in 1998, the leadership made the momentous (and for many Chinese people shocking) decision to phase out the provision of 'welfare housing'. It announced that from 1st July that year (coincidentally the seventy-seventh anniversary of the founding of the Chinese

64

Communist Party), the provision of new low-rent 'welfare' housing, would come to an end. The rents paid by those living in existing public housing would also rise significantly (though they remained low by most standards). Newly built homes would from now on only be available for purchase – and citizens would be encouraged to take out mortgages to do so.[4] The government's aim, besides reducing its welfare burden, was to stimulate the commercial housing market, encourage new construction and create large numbers of jobs in building and other related industries.

Suddenly slogans began appearing on advertising hoardings around China's big cities, promoting the first mortgages offered by the country's commercial banks. There were a few measures to soften the transition. The housing accumulation funds, now available in most cities, were one aspect – in Shanghai for example, some quarter of a million families had made use of these to buy homes by the year 2000 (though there were soon complaints that the amounts available – a maximum of a hundred thousand yuan, or around £7,000, per family in 2003 – were not enough to keep pace with fast-rising house prices).[5] And many work units also now sold off their housing stock to their staff, at prices heavily discounted from market rates. The idea of buying their own home was one which many older people, accustomed to paying almost nothing, found hard to come to terms with. But those who did buy at the subsidised levels were soon to be grateful, as China's rapidly evolving property market brought soaring house prices to most cities by the early years of the new century. Staff in some wealthier work units also benefited from a flurry of new building by their employers in the last years of the old welfare-housing policy. A manager at a state-run company in Shanghai once described to me how she had acquired a newly built apartment of a hundred square metres, in a popular part of the city, for just a few thousand pounds in the late 1990s. 'It's pretty hard to believe now,' she said, eyes wide. 'It must be worth more than twenty times that today.'

In one sense, it was something of a giant giveaway of state assets, a little reminiscent of the Thatcher government's sell-off of council housing in Britain in the 1980s – though the Chinese authorities might perhaps argue that it was actually true socialism in action. What followed, however, was certainly closer to the Thatcherite model, as the market economy began to take hold of the housing sector. It took a while for many people to realise the full significance of this, but once they did, the cost of housing quickly shot to the top of everyone's list of anxieties; many people began hoarding their savings as a result, frustrating the government's desire to stimulate consumer spending during the Asian economic downturn of the late 1990s. Eventually, some employers, mainly wealthier state enterprises and new foreign businesses, began to offer housing subsidies of their own – either by contributing to mortgage payments, or by providing low-interest loans themselves. It was seen as a good way to attract, and keep, good staff.

The new system undoubtedly did achieve its aim of stimulating the construction industry and the property market. In a nation where, at the start of the 1990s, very few urban residents owned their homes, buying a place of one's own now swiftly became a national obsession. For the wealthy it was often just a good investment. But many ordinary citizens also seemed determined to scrimp and save in order to make a downpayment on a mortgage. Between 1998 and 2005, the total value of mortgages taken out by individual Chinese citizens was estimated to have increased thirty-five-fold to 1.8 trillion yuan (some £130 billion).[6] Some were able to use their accounts in the housing accumulation fund to help pay the cost. But interest rates were rising too, and soon around a third of mortgage-holders were spending more than half their salaries on their mortgage, according to one survey. State media began describing such people as 'housing slaves', and experts began to raise questions about why so many people insisted on buying when it would have been much easier, and cheaper, for them to rent.[7] But there was a sense that in a society where old certainties were shifting rapidly, a home of one's own was now increasingly seen as an important guarantee of stability. And there was no doubt that for those who had a little more money to spend, the commercial housing market was now offering possibilities which would have been unimaginable just a few years before . . .

Cai Liang was leafing through a brochure, with a serious expression on his face. 'It's a tricky choice,' he said. 'Which one do you recommend?' We glanced at the tastefully stylised artist's impressions. 'I'm not sure about that turret,' he said, 'but this balcony's not so bad.' He flipped the pages. On the front cover was an image of a large house standing in a luxuriant garden with a large lawn; above it was printed, in bold type, 'Oriental Hollywood'. It was, needless to say, the catalogue for a new luxury residential development in the suburbs of Shanghai, where Mr Cai was thinking of buying a villa. It was a big moment for him. Thus far in his life, he had spent a childhood in a shared old house in a Shanghai lane, half a decade of the Cultural Revolution in a village in the countryside, and a few years sharing two rooms with his in-laws back in Shanghai, before moving with his wife to a small apartment in a noisy downtown neighbourhood. Now, though, his luck had changed. After years of faithfully investing in the Shanghai stock market, for very little return, share values had suddenly gone through the roof. Now everyone wanted to buy his shares. Mr Cai had seen his opportunity, and sold up quickly.

So now, with money in his pocket, he was making his choice. Or trying to: he was finding the decision difficult, perhaps because there were so many options. Would he prefer the half-timbered 'British mansion'; the 'Spanish villa', with its whitewashed walls and red roof; or perhaps the 'French chateau', with its grey stone gables and matching turret? The customer simply bought a plot of land in the new development, selected their favourite type of house from the brochure, and the builders would get to work.

In the end Mr Cai plumped for an Italian villa. He asked the developer to change the original plan, and leave out one of the rooms upstairs; this made his hexagonal living room about six metres high, giving him plenty of space to hang a large chandelier from the ceiling. The floor and the pillars were covered in marble that he'd picked up from a quarry in the neighbouring province, and the large 'Italian rustic-style' marble fireplace completed the effect. Mr Cai and the family could sit beside it in their armchairs and gaze across the room at their forty-inch flat-screen television; or listen to some of his favourite classical music on his imported speakers. If he felt in the mood, he could even go into the study and pick out a tune on the piano himself. Upstairs, the four bedrooms were spacious and light, one set aside for his mother-in-law to stay in at the weekend, if she wanted to get away from the crowded city centre.

'It's such a nice environment, isn't it?' said Mr Cai, as we stood on the balcony one spring afternoon, looking out over the garden. The plants weren't quite as flourishing as those in the brochure, but it was certainly nice and green, and made an ideal place for them to raise a few chickens (not strictly permitted by the estate's management regulations, but nonetheless popular among the new residents). Beyond the garden was a small stream, criss-crossed by miniature wooden bridges, and further away other houses in various European styles. Mr Cai pointed to one building. 'That guy's garden is double-size,' he said, clearly impressed. 'He went abroad to study and then came back to China to work; he bought two plots of land, but he only built one house on them.' Another neighbour was the talk of the district: he was thought to be an official from another province, because he only appeared at weekends, and the ceilings of his house were rumoured to be covered in gold-leaf.

Life in this oriental Hollywood had a few drawbacks. It was a good fifteen minutes' drive to the nearest underground station, from where it was thirty to forty minutes into town, and the trains were packed during rush hour. Mr Cai could take the car, but the roads weren't much better. There were also high management fees to be paid. At one point he thought of renting the house out for a while, and moving back to the old shared family home. But it seemed hard to find a tenant, perhaps because of the transport situation. 'Still, wait a couple of years, this will be a great location,' he insisted. For the moment, though, they decided to stay in the house. And now that their daughter had gone away to study, most of the time it was just Mr Cai and his wife, alone in the 250 square metres of echoing marble rooms. At least it was quiet at night, away from the hubbub of the city – though inevitably there was now a new industrial zone just down the road, and more villa complexes were beginning to swallow up the surrounding farmland.

The Cais' lifestyle was hardly the mainstream, even in relatively wealthy Shanghai. But all over China, new developments were springing up, from the villa complexes for the rich to high-rise residential blocks of all kinds: basic ones for people being relocated from the city centres or young couples starting out in life; and more luxurious ones, with landscaped gardens, clubhouses and fitness centres, for members of China's growing middle class. The style of these compounds was often similar to that which had been popular in Hong Kong for decades now, and in fact many of the earliest developments were built by Hong Kong companies in southern China at the start of the 1990s – particularly in Special Economic Zones like Shenzhen where they received tax breaks and other incentives. Not all these early speculative investments worked out well: one region which saw massive construction in the early 1990s was Hainan, the large island off the coast of Guangdong which was designated a Special Economic Zone in its own right; but the slowdown in China's economic boom in the second half of the decade left Hainan's major towns pockmarked with the concrete skeletons of tower blocks and villa compounds abandoned halfway through construction; at one point the local government threatened to start blowing these up if the developers did not complete them – but many of the original investors had long since gone bankrupt.[8]

As the 1990s went on, though, such developments began to spread around the country, as home ownership began to catch on. Richard Li, who started out working for one of the biggest property developers in Shenzhen in the mid-1990s before becoming a real-estate consultant and media commentator, believes that one of the biggest factors in China's rush to home ownership is its importance as a status symbol, in a society which increasingly judges people by their material success. 'In China, especially in an immigrant city like Shenzhen, buying a home of one's own is an expression of someone's position and their acceptance by society, of how successful they are,' he says. 'At the beginning, no one had a house of their own. But the more capable people were able to buy one first, and the idea soon spread around the country.' So thoroughly has it caught on, he adds, that owning one's own home has, in the eyes of many, now replaced the 1980s standard of having a full set of furniture as a basic requirement for any man hoping to find a bride. 'In many towns now,' says Richard, 'if you want to get married you have to have a house, otherwise no girl will marry you.'

That certainly seems to be the case in Wenzhou, the once-small town on China's eastern coast a couple of hundred miles south of Shanghai, which has become one of the country's fastest growing cities, mainly as a result of embracing private enterprise back in the 1980s, long before most parts of China. In Wenzhou, with its ubiquitous billboards for local fashion brands and shoe companies and its profusion of gold-decorated restaurants, the idea of the planned economy seems far away, and the approach to life is straightforward and pragmatic. In the pages of local magazines it's common to find articles analysing the financial situation of young couples who are planning to get married, and giving them advice on how large an apartment they should buy. 'Putting aside romantic thoughts, getting married is an expensive business,' one such article reminded its readers, 'so don't forget to calculate the cost of the wedding photos, the banquet and the fleet of cars before you take out your mortgage.'

On one trip to Wenzhou, I met Mr Yan, a designer in his late twenties who worked for the family firm, and seemed to be the embodiment of the Wenzhou dream. On the day of his wedding banquet, he and his bride proudly invited friends and relatives to their new flat in a modern high-rise on the banks of the river. With its bare white walls, shiny white floor and minimalist furniture in black leather and tubular steel, the newly-weds' home had something of the feel of a contemporary art gallery. A projector on the ceiling beamed TV programmes onto a giant screen which filled one wall; almost the only decoration was a framed photograph of the young couple in tuxedo and wedding dress, staring optimistically into the distance in front of a famous local beauty spot. Mr Yan happily showed guests around the three bedrooms and open-plan kitchen. From the balcony in the master bedroom there was a spectacular view over a neighbourhood of old houses which were in the process of being reduced to rubble; a little further away the new

70

high-rises of the rapidly expanding city centre formed a jagged skyline. In Wenzhou, the love affair with a modern lifestyle was clearly spreading fast.

As the government had hoped, the growth of home ownership did help to stimulate demand in other sectors of the economy too. For many years, newly built apartments were generally sold by developers as little more than bare concrete shells, without even basic bathroom or kitchen fittings, and so decorating them became a major concern. It was not long before the giants of the international DIY world began to realise the opportunities this offered. In 2001, B&Q opened what was then its largest store in the world, in Shanghai's Yangpu district, a suburban area which had turned into a vast sprawl of building sites and high-density residential compounds. Within five years the company had ten stores in the city and some fifty across the country, had opened an even larger outlet in Beijing, and bought out OBI, the German firm which was its main competitor in China.[9] The concept of DIY, however, did require a little explanation in a society where many urbanites tended to see physical labour as something rather beneath them. Some of the firm's stores set up demonstration areas, where staff lectured shoppers on the joys of painting their own walls and installing shelves. And for those who were still not convinced, the company also provided a design and decoration service, with a team of workers who could go to customers' homes and carry out the job for them.

And so a nation which not many years before had resounded with calls for 'permanent revolution' was now in a state of what seemed more like permanent renovation. It became increasingly difficult to get away from the sounds of hammering and drilling in Chinese towns. One friend who lived in a small residential building in Beijing insists he was disturbed by construction noise from other flats in the same block every single day for eight years. Eventually the sale of new apartments as empty shells was banned, in theory at least, in an attempt to reduce the amount of work which needed to be done when people moved in to their new homes.

71

Not that this did much to dampen China's lifestyle boom, though. In 2003, when IKEA opened its new Shanghai store, there were said to have been 65,000 visitors on the first day. There were still some who found its prices too high, though they were significantly lower than in Europe, but this did not stop its designs catching on – not least since, in China, imitation is often the sincerest form of flattery. From the early days of the first Beijing IKEA, men in slightly dusty jackets with pencils behind their ears could often be found crouched over chairs and sofas, sizing them up with tape measures and making notes of the dimensions. 'You could say I'm in the design business too,' said one man, when I asked him what he was doing; 'we can learn a lot here,' he added, with a wink. Soon some remarkably similar furniture began to appear in other shops. Other furniture stores with strangely similar names also began to appear. According to Yan Mi, a lifestyle journalist, there was even a furniture workshop in Beijing dedicated purely to copying IKEA products. 'You just took your IKEA catalogue along and showed them what you wanted,' she recalls, 'and they made it for less than half the price.'

In Yan Mi's opinion, such copycat trends at least showed that people were becoming more aware of the idea of design. She too believes that IKEA's arrival played an important part in this process. 'You could say that was people's basic education,' she suggests. 'It helped a lot of people to start to know what style is.' She herself has played a role in the process too, as one of a new generation of writers on China's ever-increasing number of new 'lifestyle' magazines. 'The first of these magazines started in around 1997, just when the real-estate market was beginning,' she says over lunch in a cheerfully decorated Italian restaurant in Shanghai. 'Lots of people had bought their own homes and didn't know how to decorate them. So these magazines would draw a plan of a bathroom, tell them what to do, what kind of materials to use.' Magazines with names like *Colourfulness* and *Trends Home* quickly established a loyal readership; they have more recently been joined by the Chinese versions of foreign publications like *Elle Decoration*, for which Yan Mi now works, which offers articles on everything from space-saving tips for the kitchen to the latest in international architecture. Most of the readership, of course, comes from the wealthier sections of China's urban population, but Yan Mi believes that interest is growing fast.

'China is still in a stage where we want to absorb everything,' she says, 'everyone is very enthusiastic about new design.' It will take time for most people to move beyond IKEA and away from the mainstream, she believes, but she says the pace of change can't be underestimated. She compares the situation to China's fashion industry, non-existent fifteen years ago but now starting to make an impact internationally. 'I think everything from fashion to lifestyle has had to start from zero in China,' she explains. 'For example, if you look at girls in Shanghai now, they dress and make up not very differently from girls abroad, but it's been fifteen years since the first Chinese fashion magazines came out – these fifteen years have been a period of studying and then asserting our own individuality. In terms of lifestyle I think we're still in the period of learning.'

Inevitably, there have been some mistakes along the way, in Yan Mi's opinion, particularly the way that many people have simply thrown out their traditional Chinese furniture – sometimes including antique family heirlooms – in their desire to embrace a modern way of life. 'Some young people only want new things, and don't care about old things at all,' she says. 'A family who lived on the floor below me in Shanghai recently moved house, and they just threw away a lot of pretty old furniture. The older people didn't want to get rid of it – but the young man was telling them "these things are too old, they won't look good in our new place", so they just left them behind.' It's by no means an isolated phenomenon. In a small town in Zhejiang province, south of Shanghai, I once visited an enormous three-storey warehouse, each floor the size of a football pitch, stacked up to the ceiling with antique Chinese furniture of every possible shape and size. The company's owner, a canny local businessman, bought the pieces, usually for next to nothing, in towns and villages across China and brought them here to be renovated. He then shipped them to the US and Europe, where they sold for high prices. Ironically, according to Yan Mi, the popularity of classical Chinese furniture overseas has recently begun to influence some of China's young generation, who have been rediscovering an interest in such things – in part via the pages of foreign lifestyle magazines.

And in China's bigger cities there has also been a rapid increase in the number of shops selling home ware and living accessories of all kinds – from designer furniture to South-East Asian style and ethnic trinkets from around the world. Such details seem to matter a lot to many young people, who seem eager to redefine themselves in terms of new lifestyles and aspirations. 'Lifestyle literature' of all kinds has become popular; bookshops are filled with fashion and design books and guides to subjects such as café culture – indeed coffee itself has gone swiftly from being regarded as an unpalatable type of foreign 'bitter water' to a generally accepted symbol of sophistication. Chains like Starbucks have capitalised on the trend – the firm even opened a branch in Beijing's Forbidden City a few years ago. Cigars, golf, wine, all have become fashionable in certain sections of society. The aspiration of many for a sophisticated life was summed up by the revival of the once derogatory phrase 'petty bourgeois'. In 2002, a mere fifteen years after the 'Campaign against Bourgeois Liberalisation', one Beijing publishing house produced a book called *Petty Bourgeois Woman*, billed as a guide to a modern, upwardly mobile lifestyle. Society, explains its author, has now reached a level where many people are concerned about their individual well-being and quality of life – and to help them out she provides brief introductions to all the subjects a sophisticated young lady might need to know about: these, apparently, range from Cartier to Kafka, hip hop to Häagen-Dazs, and Issey Miyake to, well, IKEA . . .[10]

It can sometimes seem a little confused, but there's no doubt that Chinese society has recently been rushing to embrace labels of all kinds, as the modern generation seeks to differentiate itself from its stolid socialist predecessors. In the late 1990s, urban professionals proudly began to describe themselves as *bai ling* or 'white collar'. Those who have done especially well are known as 'gold collar'. Such people are also likely to include themselves in China's new *zhongchan* or middle classes. (For those who aren't quite certain what this involves, Wang Shouzhi, a prominent design professor based in California, has published a book called *Hello! Middle Class*, which analyses the differences between being lower middle class, middle middle class and upper middle class, based on his experiences in the US.)[11] Other categories have come and gone: yuppies, dinks, even bobos (bourgeois bohemians). One friend in Beijing told me, in slightly shocked tones, about what happened when he was interviewed by a young journalist from one of China's new 'style bible' magazines. 'She used scary vocabulary,' he said. 'She came to my flat and asked me if I thought I was "high class". Then she asked me whether I drank coffee,' he continued, 'so I said, "Yes, Maxwell House instant." She looked around my flat for a while,' he went on, 'then she turned to me and said admiringly, "Wow, you're really a bourgeois bohemian, aren't you?"'

The fascination with lifestyle has been fanned by the images on China's television screens, which now pump out not only imported soaps but also locally produced dramas often featuring characters living in the most luxurious surroundings: large mansions with chandeliers, modernist villas with spacious gardens and even domestic servants. One Chinese television executive once described the basic content of such dramas as 'good-looking men and women, living in beautiful houses and driving large cars'.[12]

And China's real-estate developers have gone out of their way to encourage this obsession with lifestyle and aspiration. The seemingly endless advertisements for new housing developments which fill the newspapers and hours of late-evening local television all do their best to appeal to the desire for the new, the exclusive, the exotic. Expensively dressed middle-aged men stare moodily out across manicured gardens and explain why this particular residential compound fulfils their dream of peace and sophistication. Indeed, China's real-estate advertising is, in general, an orgy of aspiration. 'Promote yourself to a better way of life' proclaimed the slogan on one luxury development in Shanghai – though few ordinary people would have been able to afford the cost of such an elevation. Another, built by a government-owned construction company, styled itself, unabashedly, 'Rich Gate', with the English slogan 'Wisdom Creats Wealth' [*sic*], its lack of concern for the niceties of spelling matched only by its utter disregard for the socialist society in which it theoretically existed. Another Shanghai project went by the name 'Block of Wealth Land'. In fact, respect for wealth, power and elitism sometimes seems to be the common language of the real-estate industry. Luxury villa projects stress they are 'only for outstanding people from the peak of the world' or 'dedicated to CEOs worldwide'. One development in Shanghai was surrounded by large hoardings proclaiming 'Boss and Winner' ('be a world boss, be a Shanghai winner'); another promoted itself with the slogan 'True Royalty by Blood and Right'; yet another residential complex suggested its residents would be able to 'stand aloof over Shanghai showing nobler sublimity' – though none could quite match the advertisement which announced simply, 'Divinity – a class above distinction'.

One of the major selling points of many of China's new residential compounds is the promise of an international lifestyle. From Venice Beach to Manhattan, Paris to Nice, Rome to Barcelona, somewhere in China there's a development named after it. Ningbo, on the east coast, offers the 'Oriental Louvre Palace' or, if you prefer, 'Riverside Pittsburgh'. Shanghai has the slightly less exotic 'Hyde Garden' and 'Windsor Island'. Sometimes the names can be a little confusing, as with Shanghai's 'De Oriental London', or the complicated-sounding 'Park Avenue: Greenwich (Creative Britain Phase 2)' in Kunming, the capital of south-western Yunnan province. Richard Li, the Shenzhen-based real-estate commentator, says this all fits in with the idea of selling lifestyles as well as bricks and mortar. 'It's like a model has been made for your life,' he says. 'The developers are telling you this is a blueprint, this is your beautiful life, the kind of Californian or British or Spanish life you should lead.'

The buildings which bear these alluring names also do their best to fulfil the desire for the exotic, with a dazzling – and sometimes baffling – array of imported architectural styles. Since the late 1990s China has been swept by a wave of what's known as *Oulu* or 'European continental' design: a combination of neoclassical

76

columns, moulded plaster decorations and decorative balustrades – often on buildings some twenty or more storeys high. Sometimes there's a French chateau-style roof, or a grand gateway modelled on the Arc de Triomphe. Neoclassical statues are common too: one high-rise complex in Beijing even has a pair of larger-than-life bronze Roman centurions on either side of its entrance.[13]

Some have raised doubts about whether this is a healthy direction for Chinese architecture. Shen Zhengchao of the Shanghai Construction Commission once explained to me that 'the developers think that European style means statues of Venus, big fountains, great big pillars at the front. But we look at some of these places and we think, "oh no!" I tell them that in Europe you might see these things in public places, but not on private houses or residential areas. But they think it's easy to promote: they can attract a lot of people who've never been to Europe and who think "oh, now I'm living in a European-style building".' The real-estate consultant Richard Li agrees that the reasons for the popularity of this style, which entered China via Hong Kong and Taiwan, are simple enough. 'In those days,' he says of the mid–late 1990s, 'the people who had just got rich wanted to show off their wealth, to be different from others. And because these things were rare at the time, they saw them as having more value – it was a way of saying I have money so I can have things which others can't.' Others see the trend in more negative terms, another indication of the damage done to China's traditional culture by the Cultural Revolution. 'Everything was broken,' says Yan Mi. 'In the Cultural Revolution we were told everything old was bad. And people like me who were born afterwards got a very western education, so young designers have grown up with a lot of foreign influences.'

But even these influences are changing all the time – at least, according to Richard Li, in places like Shenzhen, which has led many of China's recent architectural trends. Recent developments have included 'Spanish' fashion, with tiled roofs and decorative chimneys – on both low- and high-rise buildings – along with a fashion for 'southern Californian' style villas. Modernist, minimalist design has also started to become popular, says Richard

Li – and it's the very rich, the bosses of private businesses and leaders of industry, who tend to set new trends, he adds. 'They have very clear ideas,' he explains. 'To them real estate is a fashion, so they always want new things – if you can buy a certain kind of house it's a confirmation of you as a successful person.' And what's in fashion in coastal cities like Shenzhen, with their greater links to the outside world, has a big impact on the rest of China. Richard Li regularly receives visits from property developers and local government officials from all over China, some of the country's remotest regions included, all eager to visit new housing developments and see the latest Shenzhen styles – although in the end most of those from China's inland areas are more likely to play it safe and stick with the tried and tested 'continental' style.

Richard himself knows all about imported lifestyles, as the proud occupant of a flat in an upmarket compound which is, he insists, Shenzhen's 'first British-style residential development'. 'It's basically copying the English royal family's residences, that kind of luxury palace,' he explains, with a serious expression. Then his face breaks into a grin. 'Though actually the exterior was designed by someone from Hong Kong copying a French style, and the gardens were planned by an Italian. But everyone feels that high-class people in China now are seeking a British lifestyle,' he continues, 'so that's how it was promoted!' It can all seem a little absurd, he acknowledges, but the influence of these trends cannot be under-estimated – the big real-estate companies spend a lot of money studying what consumers want. Richard's luxury British compound includes indoor and outdoor swimming pools, a clubhouse, a gym and a supermarket for the four hundred families who live there. Only the fortunate few can enjoy such luxury, he agrees – but he believes that most members of the professional classes in cities like Shenzhen now expect a residential compound to have at least one swimming pool and a nicely designed garden, as well as decent transport connections and easy access to shops and schools. 'People know a lot more about houses now than they did a few years ago,' he says. 'They have a lot of basic demands.'

But the desire of so many of China's urban citizens for a more comfortable way of life comes at a price. The rapid spread of new residential areas has swallowed up farmland around the country's cities (some six million hectares between 1996 and 2003, according to official estimates),[14] while the dust from tens of thousands of construction sites has added to the nation's problems of air pollution. Soaring use of air conditioning – now installed as standard in most new urban homes – only puts greater pressure on China's already stretched energy resources. Shanghai's electricity consumption, for example, grew by 15 per cent annually in the first few years of the century.[15] And the building of so many new suburbs has also encouraged the growing desire of many of China's new middle classes to buy their own car. China's entry into the World Trade Organisation in 2001 fuelled the trend, since it brought cuts in the price of imported cars, which led to a similar fall in the previously high prices of cars made in China. Every time I visit a Chinese city, it seems, I am told that there are anywhere between two hundred and a thousand new cars coming onto that city's streets every single day. Young people's fascination with car ownership was underlined to me when I once accompanied a young manager from a Shanghai bank on a trip to a car showroom. A sober, earnest-looking man in a dark suit, he became highly emotional when he set eyes on a shiny black Audi A6. 'It's my dream to own a car like this,' he sighed. 'I just love it, I love the lifestyle, the freedom. If I have a car I can drive anywhere I like.'

And as with houses, car ownership has also become a status symbol. 'Everyone wants one now,' complained one driver in Shenzhen. 'For example, if you and I work in the same office, and you have a car but I don't, then I lose face. You may actually live very far away, while I live just round the corner, but I still have to buy a car,' he said. 'Everyone is more worried about face than a harmonious way of living.' Car manufacturers, not least the growing number of foreign firms which have set up joint venture factories in China in recent years, have been happy to promote such aspirations. Advertising for one popular brand, for example, stressed that its cars were 'a full indicator of their owners' elite positions'. One particular model promised 'leadership and aristocratic quality . . .

worthy of the Chinese leaders in the political and business worlds, who are themselves the embodiments of great minds, far-sightedness, power and wisdom'.[16] And in 2006, when Shanghai's state-run car manufacturer, Shanghai Automotive, launched its own brand, the 'Roewe', based on the technology of the Rover 75 which it had bought from Britain, its advertising emphasised the heritage of a brand in which, it noted, 'the British royal family have driven around for years'. Advertising for smaller cars, meanwhile, promotes images of happy families doing their shopping in comfort, or driving into the countryside for a weekend picnic.

Not surprisingly, the result has been worsening air pollution and growing traffic jams. Many Chinese cities have been building new subways and expanding their public transport networks, but this does not seem to have halted the trend towards ever busier roads and longer delays for drivers. Indeed, government policy often seems to encourage car use – in the past decade many of China's cities have removed the traditional cycle lanes and banned cyclists from main roads, and have also taken trams and trolley buses off the streets, to make more space for cars. The prevailing attitude was summed up in 2001 by the then mayor of Shanghai, Xu Kuangdi, who responded to a question about traffic congestion at his annual news conference by observing that 'our biggest headache now is not that we have too many cars but too many bicycles'. The urbane, British-educated former academic went on to startle many in his audience by adding that 'if we could halve the number of bicycles in Shanghai, then the car-flow rate would be very convenient because', he suggested, 'two bicycles take up the same road width as one car, but two bicycles can only carry two people, whereas one car can carry three or four people'. Such views perhaps also reflected the growing importance of car manufacturing to China's economy in recent years – and the fact that Shanghai has two of the country's biggest car factories. (In fact, Shanghai has imposed tougher restrictions than many Chinese cities on car ownership, limiting the number of new licence plates issued to 'only' a few thousand a month, and selling these at auction for prices as high as several thousand pounds each. Such measures have become increasingly irrelevant, however, since many people simply register their cars in other cities and provinces and then bring them to Shanghai.)

Some people undoubtedly remain blissfully unconcerned about China's traffic problems. 'Don't worry,' a taxi driver on one of Beijing's five ring roads told me, 'if these ring roads get too jammed there's plenty of space in between them to build some more.' But in general, public concern at congested roads and worsening pollution has grown, with articles in the Chinese media attacking the 'perverse' logic of 'car-centred development'.[17] And some officials do seem to have begun to at least reflect on the problems they are storing up. Several cities have experimented with car-free days in their city centres, while in 2006 China's Deputy Minister of Construction announced that his ministry was ordering cities to reinstate bicycle lanes, adding that rising car use was 'posing a grave challenge to the country's energy security and urban development'.[18] But he may have been fighting a losing battle. Official figures showed that bicycle use by urban residents fell by a quarter between 2000 and 2005, while sales of passenger cars quadrupled from 2001 to 2006, to some five million a year.[19]

Nor do such concerns seem to have had too much impact on the country's real-estate firms – said to number as many as 60,000 by 2005. The largest was estimated to have assets worth over three billion pounds, and pay a hundred million pounds a year in taxes.[20] Little wonder that, according to some observers, seventy of China's hundred richest people are property developers.[21] The power of such firms is emphasised by the type of promotional activities they organise. Bill Clinton in 2002, and Tony Blair in 2007, both received large payments for making brief visits to Guangdong at the invitation of local real estate firms. Another put on an exhibition of several hundred signed Picasso prints, reportedly the largest collection of the artist's works ever seen in China. One firm even succeeded in bringing the then manager of the England football team, Sven-Göran Eriksson, to Shanghai to promote a new residential compound in the city's suburbs, just a couple of months ahead of the 2006 World Cup Finals.[22]

The real-estate boom has been good news too for China's estate agents, another fast-growing sector of the country's economy. By the turn of the century big firms from Hong Kong, Taiwan and the US were competing with local companies in many of China's main cities. The windows of these estate agents' offices could be a surreal sight, since they were often filled with photographs of fifty apparently identical high-rise buildings. But their marketing practices were undeniably slick, with armies of young staff who were easily identifiable by their crisp white shirts, enthusiastic smiles and frequent use of phrases such as *nao zhong qu jing* – 'an oasis of calm in the bustle of the city'. Such people seem to have adapted well to the demands of the new market economy: an agent in Shanghai once showed me an old house which was for sale, before admitting that one of the residents, an elderly man who tended pigeons on the roof, didn't actually want to move out. 'You could buy the house first,' he suggested, 'then take the old man to court and have him evicted.' Where real estate was concerned, very little was sacred, it seemed. On another visit to an old lane house in Shanghai, I was shepherded out to look at another building further down the lane, where the estate agent and the owner insisted I would be able to get a better idea of the original interior of this type of house. It was with some surprise that I found myself being shown into the Museum of the Underground Bolshevik Printing Press – where China's future communist leaders once published a clandestine newspaper in the 1930s – and asked to admire the interior decor.

The booming property market of the early years of this century was boosted by the fact that some of the larger estate agents were authorised by banks to approve mortgages themselves, making purchasing easier and quicker. Houses certainly often sold extremely fast – in Shenzhen and other cities, there were frequent reports of people queuing overnight outside the offices of property developers to buy flats in new developments – sometimes before building work had even started. Estate agents also put pressure on clients to put down a sizeable deposit, giving them first option on a property, within minutes of seeing it; as a result many people went to look at houses carrying the equivalent of thousands of pounds in cash in a bag over their shoulders. It all added to China's soaring property prices, which increased by several hundred per cent in many big cities in the first few years of this decade.

And for those with the means or the connections, buying and selling houses in quick succession, often with little investment other than a sizeable mortgage, became a popular way of making money. The phenomenon became known as 'frying houses', a phrase derived from the popular description of speculation on China's stock market as 'frying shares'. It spread rapidly to cities all over the country. 'New money' from private entrepreneurs had a big impact. People from Wenzhou, where the private property market was longer established than in many other parts of China, began joining together and touring the country in what were known as 'house-buying groups' – each person often buying several apartments at a time if they liked a particular property. One Wenzhou resident once told me about a hundred middle-aged housewives from the city who pooled their savings to invest a hundred million yuan (around £7 million) to buy an entire apartment block in the capital of neighbouring Jiangxi province. Such people were often given a warm welcome by real-estate developers – one friend insists that, at a residential compound in one inland province, a big red banner proclaimed 'A very warm welcome to the Wenzhou house-speculating delegation'. But media reports of such activities stirred up significant unhappiness among ordinary citizens, who complained that property prices were being pushed out of their reach.

Indeed, so rapid were the price rises in the early years of the new century that some people became property speculators entirely by accident. A university professor once explained to me that he had bought a small flat for his mother-in-law, but had to resell it a few months later when she refused to move into it – and found that he had unwittingly made a 30 per cent profit.

There was also unhappiness among residents who moved into new housing compounds, only to find that they were almost the only people living there, since most apartments had been bought by speculators who were keeping them empty. At one compound in

Shanghai, the management company went as far as to reassure potential buyers that in order to avoid such problems, it would not be selling any of its apartments to people from Wenzhou. This in turn prompted anger from some Wenzhou citizens, who claimed that they were being unfairly made scapegoats for what was actually a national problem.

Foreigners contributed to the price rises too, particularly after the lifting, in 2001, of previously tight limits on where they could buy property in China. Many snapped up buildings in Shanghai or Beijing and other big cities, but others moved into less obvious regions too. In the seaside town of Sanya, on the southern island of Hainan, there was something of a boom in sales to Russians eager to escape to the south seas during the Siberian winters.

By the middle of this decade, public concern about real estate had become a major social issue in China. It was not only the fast-rising prices – though these were part of the problem. There have also been increasing numbers of disputes between residents and the private management companies which run many of the new estates and compounds. Some of these compounds are the size of small towns, with tens of thousands of residents, but management companies are often able to impose their own regulations and levy their own fees: disputes over such fees, and about issues like car parking and building noise, are common; there have also been frequent complaints that promised amenities have never been installed. Some residents have responded by setting up their own committees to protest against such problems – but there have been a number of reports of management companies responding with intimidation or violence against the organisers. In one Beijing housing compound, residents who refused to pay their management fees in protest at the way they had been treated found themselves dragged out of their homes in the middle of the night by court officials in riot gear, and carted off to the local court to pay up.[23] Real-estate problems have also led to protest marches against developers and management companies in several Chinese cities; in 2006 one Shenzhen resident even organised an Internet petition calling for a boycott of real-estate companies – within a few days he had collected 30,000 signatures – but he was soon warned by the authorities to end his campaign.[24]

It was a reminder of the pain caused by the transition to a commercial housing market – and there has been much anger at what many see as collusion between local officials and powerful real-estate companies, resulting in a market which benefits the wealthy but has left the poor struggling to keep up. 'I can't even afford to make the down payment for a mortgage now, and I could never afford the repayments anyway,' moaned Mr Liang, a truck driver in Shanghai, who lived in an old area due for demolition. Developers have been widely – and often correctly – believed to be hoarding land in order to push up prices: many old neighbourhoods have been demolished, and their residents forced out – and the land then left empty for two or three years. In 2005, the government finally began taking steps to address such grievances – banning the reselling of mortgaged flats and houses within two years of purchase and increasing taxes on property sales in an attempt to discourage people from buying property purely for speculation.

But by the following year, with prices continuing to rise, the government was forced to introduce a further set of measures, which were more drastic – at least on paper: they brought in strict limits on the sale of land for new villa complexes, increased the obstacles for foreigners buying property for investment purposes, and required developers to build more smaller apartments (70 per cent of the total area of any new development, it was announced, would now have to consist of flats of less than ninety square metres).[25] It was perhaps the first real step for many years aimed at ensuring that the housing market contained more property which would be affordable to ordinary people – or at least to ensure that the middle classes themselves would not be priced out of the market by soaring property values. (Some cities had continued to build a certain amount of so-called 'affordable housing' – but nowhere near enough to meet the demand.) But many people wanted the government to go further, and sanction the construction of new areas of public housing – or alternatively to specify not only the size of apartments which developers could build, but also to set maximum

85

price limits, to make sure that such accommodation really was low-cost. Some academics even called for all of China's real-estate developers to be closed down, and for homes to be built by the type of housing cooperatives popular in some western countries.[26]

Yet there's still little sign of a serious will to reverse the principle of allowing housing to be controlled by the commercial market. The actions of real-estate companies and local governments do seem to be coming under increasing official scrutiny. In Shanghai, for example, a senior official from the city's Housing and Land Management Administration was jailed for 15 years in 2007 for taking bribes and illegal approval of land requisition.[27] And China's Ministry of Land Resources announced that more than 60 per cent of land sales in some cities in 2004–5 were unlawful.[28] But if such revelations were designed to reassure the public, they were also a reminder of just how out of control the process sometimes seemed to have become, with increasing evidence of enormous amounts of bad loans to property developers and continuing warnings of a potential real-estate bubble in many cities.[29]

For all the official attempts to cool the property market, the aspiration for new and more luxurious lifestyles in wealthier sectors of society, which the government has tacitly encouraged for so long, seems unlikely to suddenly fade away. Soon after the government announced its second series of measures aimed at cooling the property market, I went on a trip to Shenzhen, the laboratory of new lifestyles throughout much of China's reform era. Shenzhen is above all a youthful city, attracting young educated people from all over the country with its high wages, proximity to Hong Kong and its relatively clean living environment. Many come specifically looking for a new way of life. 'I feel much less restricted by the attitudes of neighbours, family or friends here,' says one young professional who moved here from the north. The city is one of China's top three destinations, behind only Shanghai and Beijing, for graduates looking for a job. And with unskilled workers also flocking to work in its thousands of factories, Shenzhen has gone from little more than a small rural township to a city of some nine million people in just two decades. 'It's like something from *The Arabian Nights*,' one local told me, shaking his head as he described the city's development.

Wu Shixiong, a designer and artist who lives in Shenzhen, took me to look at one of the city's newest housing compounds in the hills outside the city centre. Known as 'The Village', it was built by Vanke, the Shenzhen-based real-estate company which has now become one of China's most influential property developers. Its masterplan, designed by Professor Wang Shouzhi, author of *Hello! Middle Class*, was an attempt to blend traditional Chinese architecture with the concept of the modern town house. A golf buggy took us on a tour through the lanes and culs-de-sac; the houses and low-rise apartment blocks drew their inspiration from the traditional architecture of the Yangtze delta region, with white-washed walls, black sloping roofs and gardens filled with bamboo; some looked out onto miniature canals or ponds. But inside, the show flats and houses were fitted with the latest expensive western-style kitchens and minimalist European furnishings. Eager well-heeled young couples were looking around them, clearly impressed. Mr Wu took me back to the little design shop he had been running in the commercial parade at the entrance to The Village; a few doors away a tiny B & Q showroom offered home-buyers free bus rides to the company's nearest store. 'Chinese design is getting pretty creative, eh?' said Mr Wu, with a chuckle. 'Now they're hoping that all these middle-class people are so interested in a different lifestyle that they're ready to return to their roots!'

Mr Wu himself had certainly experienced the changes in China's way of living at first hand. Now in his fifties, he had spent most of his childhood in Guangzhou. His mother had a job in a government agricultural unit, and so he had grown up in its dormitory block. He had had the opportunity to get a good education – at least until the Cultural Revolution, when he was first caught up in violent fighting between different factions of teenage Red Guards, and was later sent down to the countryside to 'learn from the peasants'. But he had been lucky: his family still had relatives in its ancestral village in the countryside not far from Guangzhou, and so he had been allowed to spend his rural exile there. As one of the few people in the village with much of an education – and a talent for art – he was quickly put in charge of propaganda, writing political slogans on giant banners and painting revolutionary pictures on walls. This led to him being made a delegate to the local 'Peasants' Revolutionary Congress' at the start of the 1970s. And when China's universities reopened in 1973, this ideologically sound status enabled him to be selected as one of the first batch of students admitted. He carried on studying art, and later moved into photography, soon becoming a university lecturer himself.

In 1984, shortly after the opening of Shenzhen as a Special Economic Zone, Mr Wu was offered the chance to move to the city, which needed qualified professionals. As a local government employee, he was entitled to a salary ten times what he had previously earned if he moved there. He thought he would be working on an art magazine; but in the end he was assigned to a new advertising agency set up by the local government. It was his first brush with the fledgling market economy – and it came as quite a shock. 'One of the first jobs we had to do was to send the first calendars with photos of Hong Kong film stars to companies in other parts of China,' he recalled. 'We had to drive to Guangzhou to post them, but when we got to the post office they told us to take them out of their boxes and pack them all into sacks.' He and a few colleagues had to unload the entire truckload in a car park and work all night to meet the deadline. As they were doing this, he had met an old friend. 'The last time I'd seen him, just one month before, I'd been the main photographer at China's first modelling contest,' he said. 'Now I was just like a manual labourer, a coolie. I felt like crying – I felt my status had sunk so low; now I was working for a business, with no guarantees at all. It was very painful, very hard to cope with.'

He had soon come to realise, however, that in Shenzhen's new society you had to stand on your own feet. 'It was a psychological turning point,' he said. 'I realised that with the economy opening up, everyone had to change their ideas if they wanted to survive – I had to start dealing with the market. That destroyed your sense of superiority in five minutes. It didn't matter who you were before – the key was now, how you could deal with the future. And so,' he said, 'I adapted.' So successfully, in fact, that he became one of the first batch of government employees to quit their posts under new rules announced in 1987, and 'jump into the sea' – go into business in their own right. Mr Wu opened his own advertising company, and had soon saved enough to buy his own apartment – long before most people in China had even thought of the idea. He carried on with his artwork too, setting up a studio and inviting other artists to work there; later he opened several lifestyle design shops, selling decorative items for the homes of Shenzhen's middle classes; sometimes he was commissioned to produce unique decorative tiles for the swimming pools of the rich. The rest of the time he carried on with his sculpture – mostly depicting abstract forms inspired by the naked human body.

Mr Wu seemed completely at ease in Shenzhen, though he acknowledged that some still found the highly competitive atmosphere hard to cope with – some of his artist friends had had enough, he said, and had gone back to their old homes instead. But for him, it was 'a good place for living', both for its natural surroundings, and for the opportunities it provided. 'If you do design here you can have an influence around the country,' he said. And he felt it was a good place for his daughter to grow up too: there were good schools, easy contact with the outside world, and plenty of options for the future. His daughter, who was just seven, was very much a product of the new China: always smartly dressed, she had been taught English by a foreign teacher since kindergarten, and spent her spare time at ballet classes or chatting to friends on the Internet. Her parents had given her a foreign name as well as a Chinese one, since they felt this suited the new era. They had chosen one which not only sounded a little like her Chinese name, but also, they thought, had a suitably contemporary feel to it. The little girl, as Mr Wu announced proudly the first time we met, was known as Ikea . . .

At the weekend, we went on a trip to Mr Wu's ancestral village. As we drove there in their 4×4, Ikea told jokes and tried to catch me out with Chinese puns. When we arrived, Mr Wu's mother, who was now in her nineties, was sitting up in her cane chair waiting for us. He had built her this house a few years ago, in the middle of the village opposite the pools where the locals raised their fish. 'This building looks a bit out of date now,' he said, as he showed me round. The house had a little courtyard, with a miniature pond with goldfish and a tiny bridge across it, and a roof terrace where you could sit in the evening, looking out towards the distant hills.

In the morning, Mr Wu's mother sat in her cane chair, telling stories of her early life as a child labourer in a silk factory and later as a coolie, carrying huge sacks of rice on her back across the hills of Hong Kong during Japanese bombing raids in World War II. Later we went for a walk around the village; the clan hall in the centre of the village had recently been restored with donations from Mr Wu and other descendants who had done well for themselves. But at the end of the village there was another ancestral hall which had not been renovated, where the farmers now dried their fishing nets. The faded outline of a picture of heroic-looking workers and peasants could be made out on one wall – it had been painted by Mr Wu himself, during the Cultural Revolution, along with the slogan 'Education serves proletarian politics'.

After Sunday lunch, we waved goodbye to his mother and set off to drive back to Shenzhen, along the new concrete roads now carving up the countryside. 'Last year I came here with a friend who had satellite navigation in his car,' said Mr Wu, 'and the system kept protesting; it was telling him all the time to turn right or turn left instead of carrying straight on – most of the roads weren't even on the map yet!' We stopped off in the local county town to drop Ikea at her mother's parents' home, where she was spending much of her summer holidays. While her mother took her inside, I went with Mr Wu for a stroll around the centre of the town. In the park in the middle of the main square, there were signboards featuring a picture of an ancient Greek statue, advertising a new housing development called 'Loftiness City' ('Step into Modern Noble City: New Vision, New Life'); a banner in the distance announced the opening of the 'Cannes Mall'. On the other side of the park, a wide, steep set of stone steps lined with palm trees led up a little hill, to an older building with large granite pillars. It was in a faintly Soviet style with a dated-looking sign on the top which read 'Hall of the People'. 'That's where I used to go for meetings of the Peasants' Revolutionary Congress,' said Mr Wu. 'Want to take a look? I haven't been inside since the 1970s.'

We climbed the stairs, sweating in the hot sun. A couple of dozy-looking security guards were lolling disconsolately on folding chairs in front of the entrance. 'You can't come in, it's shut,' one of them said. Mr Wu explained that he used to attend important meetings here thirty-five years ago, and just wanted to have a quick glance inside. Eventually one of the guards stirred himself and moved his chair out of the way. Inside it was almost completely dark; there was just enough light to see the high ceiling and the upper balcony filled with seats. We could faintly make out big dark shapes filling up much of the ground floor, and behind them a raised stage. 'That's where the revolutionary speeches were made,' said Mr Wu. We stood quietly, thinking of all that must have happened here in the past. Suddenly the security guard flicked on the lights – and we discovered that we were surrounded on all sides by display booths, each bearing the logo of a different brand of washing machine, air conditioner or fridge. They were, it turned out, part of a trade fair promoting household appliances which was due to open the next day. Even the Hall of the People, it seemed, was now serving the cause of lifestyle and the new market economy.

# 4

# Farewell to welfare?

The sun glinted on the white cherubs beside the ornamental pond. An early-summer breeze blew through the carefully manicured hedges. As he hauled himself out of his gleaming BMW Mr Pan took a breath of air and stretched his legs languidly. Straightening the sleeves of his tan leather jacket, he glanced around at the high-rise buildings of the exclusive residential compound which had been his home for several years and smiled. 'I used to do business,' he said, 'now I mostly just play the stock market.' Out here in the Shanghai suburbs on a glorious May morning, it seemed an almost perfect scene of new Chinese prosperity.

Only Wei Yuan looked a little out of place in such surroundings. Dressed in a scruffy blue overall, he had been standing on the pavement, watching the BMW as it approached. Now, with some trepidation, he crouched down beside one of the front wheels, took a tin of metal polish from his pocket, and began to dab a few drops rather gingerly onto the hubcap. His anxiety had perhaps been increased by overhearing Mr Pan complaining about the quality of car-cleaning in Shanghai. 'Normally when I have the car washed they don't do it well,' he grumbled. 'If the hubcaps are done properly it looks great – but most places can't get them clean.' Still, Wei Yuan needn't have worried – Mr Pan was confident he'd do a good job. 'I'm sure these people are going to do their best,' he said, watching the blue-clad workers going about their tasks. 'It's a new job for them, so they've got to work extra hard to protect their "rice bowl".'

A few minutes later, after a little stroll around the pond, Mr Pan returned to inspect the results. He seemed pleased. 'That's more like it,' he said, taking out his wallet to pay up. As he drove off with a jaunty wave, Wei Yuan wiped his brow with his sleeve and squatted down on the path beside the little garden. He certainly did want to make sure he kept his job. Like the other men and women from the car-cleaning service, he was one of the losers of China's economic reforms – a member of the country's long-term unemployed. Mr Wei had been out of a job, more or less, for almost a decade, since the state-run textile factory where he used to work closed down in the early 1990s. He had helped out running a tiny food stall in the lane where he lived, but he couldn't earn much money that way, and though he'd applied for plenty of other full-time jobs, he'd never succeeded in getting one. His local residents' committee had helped him to apply for income support from the district government. But the money wasn't much, and eventually his lack of a job had contributed to the break-up of his marriage.

'My wife used to love to go out dancing,' said Mr Wei, staring at the ground, 'and one day she met another man and left me. She said she didn't want to stay with me because I was too poor.' She had left him to bring up their son on his own; now the boy had grown up and was out of work too. So when Mr Wei heard about a new city government scheme to create jobs for older laid-off workers by supporting new small businesses, he'd rushed to sign up and had been offered this job cleaning and waxing cars. The income of around six hundred yuan (less than fifty pounds) a month was not so high, but it was more than he'd earned before.

One of the few consolations for Mr Wei was that he was by no means alone. While China's new middle classes have begun to enjoy the benefits of modern lifestyles and increasing opportunities, there are many urban residents for whom life has become an ever greater struggle. The decade from the early 1990s into the first years of the new century in China was not only a time of fast economic growth and broadening horizons; it was also, for many, the age of unemployment.

It was no coincidence that the two things came together. By the first half of the 1990s, many of China's traditional state-run

93

industries and businesses were facing fresh competition from the 'non-state economy' – the official euphemism for the new companies springing up in many parts of the country, which were actually, to all intents and purpose, privately owned. China was also starting to import more goods from abroad, adding to the challenge to its domestic industries. As the decade progressed, the authorities came to the conclusion that sweeping reforms of the state-run economy were necessary if the sector – and the nation – was to become internationally competitive.

It marked the start of an extraordinary upheaval in China's economic order – and in society in general. Right up to the middle of the 1990s, over a hundred million people – or close to half of China's urban workforce – were employed in state-run factories and units. Some forty to fifty million of them worked in manufacturing and production, in almost every area of the economy, from noodles to knitwear, bicycles to battleships.[1] In Shanghai, many of these enterprises were former private factories which had been nationalised after the revolution. But in other areas, particularly Manchuria in the north-east and some of the inland provinces, most of the factories had been set up in the 1950s, in the early years of socialist optimism. These included much of the country's heavy industry: oil refineries and coal mines, steel mills and car factories. And in practice, they were far more than just businesses. Most provided not only accommodation for their workers, but health care, education and pensions as well. In many cases they also found jobs for their workers' children too, or at least allowed employees to pass on their posts to their offspring when they retired. The largest state enterprises were virtually cities in their own right, with tens of thousands of workers and their own hospitals, schools, even radio stations. As one observer put it, 'You could be born, grow up, get married, live and die in an enterprise without ever needing to leave it.'[2]

A job in such an enterprise was a coveted position, since even in the socialist heyday of the 1950s and 1960s a sizeable proportion of the population, particularly in the countryside, did not enjoy such privileges. But the state enterprises had one problem: they were far from efficient. From the 1950s until well into the 1980s this was of

94

little importance, since China's businesses were insulated from competition; indeed it's been suggested that providing employment and social stability was at least as important a function of these enterprises as the revenue they generated. There's no doubt that many of these enterprises employed more people than were actually necessary to keep them running – and by the 1990s many of their jobs were becoming obsolete anyway as a result of new technology. A former factory worker I met in Shanghai spent twenty years in a state-run electronics plant, where her job consisted of making a note of the figures on an electricity meter every half an hour; the remainder of the time she spent in a small room, reading novels.

But by the mid-1990s, the new 'township enterprises', which had begun springing up in small rural towns during the 1980s, and the new privately managed factories of Guangdong in the south and Zhejiang on the east coast were proving themselves to be increasingly dynamic and flexible competitors, particularly in the fast-growing area of modern consumer goods. In many state enterprises, it became clear that things were no longer going quite as well as before. Mrs Li, who worked in a government-owned timber yard in Shanghai, observed this happening. 'At the beginning it was a really good work unit,' she says. 'The money they gave us was enough, and we often got extra food.' Their working methods were hardly advanced; Mrs Li remembers calculating the dimensions of tree trunks dozens of metres long using only a household tape measure. Still, business was steady; the yard, she recalls, 'was always full of such big, fragrant wood'. But during the 1990s this all changed. 'Gradually the whole place started going downhill, and by the mid-1990s business wasn't good at all,' she says. Soon her employers started quibbling over a tiny pay rise for which she was eligible. For Mrs Li, it was quite a shock. 'My father had worked there for twenty years before me,' she adds, 'and he never had any problems.' Not long afterwards, the company asked her to take early retirement. A few years later she went back to see what had become of the place – and found that it had simply disappeared. 'It had all gone,' she recalls, with a shake of her head. 'Even the woodcutting workshop had been demolished.'

The Chinese government did try to protect some of the state enterprises. In the early 1990s, it opened new stock exchanges in Shanghai and Shenzhen – China's first since the closure of the original Shanghai stock market after the communist revolution. One of the main aims was to give state businesses the chance to sell shares and raise funds to help them modernise. Even today, China's stock markets are still dominated by companies which began as state-run enterprises; relatively few of the country's new private businesses have been allowed to get a listing. But while this policy certainly benefited the thousand or so big state enterprises which were allowed to issue shares, many other state firms continued to struggle. Other ideas were tried out, such as selling stakes in such companies to private investors from China or abroad. Some firms were put up for sale for next to nothing.[3] But few investors were willing to take on the responsibility of their excessive numbers of staff, as well as retired employees and their family members.

Other makeshift solutions were tried, including transferring workers from one state enterprise to other more successful ones. This hardly helped in the long run, however. By the second half of the 1990s, many companies were asking staff to work shorter hours, or to stay at home on half-pay. Mrs Fu, a former employee at a state work unit in Shanghai, remembers being asked to stay at home for two months out of every four. 'During the months when I wasn't working I just had to try to find some other way of earning money,' she says. And there were more and more people like her, who were still officially employed by their work units, but who were not actually really working there any more.

Finally, the government began to face up to the fact that such enterprises would have to cut significant numbers of staff in order to survive – or, in many cases, would simply have to be allowed to go bankrupt. But in a socialist system, it was hard for the authorities to admit to the idea of unemployment. Back in the 1980s, when the first groups of school-leavers in China's cities began struggling to find work, they were euphemistically dubbed *dai ye qingnian* or 'youths waiting for work'. Now, as the government began to contemplate mass redundancies in the state enterprises, another new phrase was coined to avoid the dread word 'unemployment': *xia gang*. In English this was usually translated as 'laid off', but in Chinese it literally meant 'standing down from one's post'.

In one sense, this was just a way of massaging China's unemployment figures – since these did not include the *xia gang* workers. But it also reflected a curious reality. Because welfare in China had always been provided by work units, severing someone's ties with his or her employer was actually extremely difficult. As a result, most of the millions of workers being laid off from state enterprises during the second half of the 1990s were still living in housing which had been allocated to them by those enterprises; many of them were also receiving unemployment benefits paid by the same factories which had just made them redundant. It was a surreal situation – and the authorities themselves acknowledged this. 'It's a transitional stage,' one government adviser on social policy told me in the late 1990s. 'We don't have a complete social welfare system, so we can't immediately throw all the workers out – it could create social problems, especially where housing is concerned.' The ultimate aim though, he said, was to 'gradually push laid-off workers out into society', by creating a new social welfare system which was separate from the workplace. This would also have the advantage of increasing labour mobility, since people would no longer have to stay in a particular place to receive their welfare benefits.[4]

But in the meantime, these stop-gap measures not surprisingly created a number of problems. Many of the old state enterprises were on the verge of bankruptcy, and therefore struggled to keep up welfare payments to their laid-off workers. Public protests over unpaid unemployment benefits, pensions or back pay became increasingly common – particularly in cities in China's heavy industrial heartland in the north-east and some inland provinces. In some of these areas, a large proportion of state enterprises had gone bankrupt, placing a huge strain on the ability of local governments to subsidise their welfare payments. There were fears of serious civil unrest, and in a number of cases the leaders of such protests were arrested or detained.[5]

Still, millions of people continued to lose their jobs around the country – official figures, though hard to confirm, gave at least some sense of the extraordinary scale of what was happening: some 21 million people made redundant from state enterprises between 1997 and 2000, 12 million of them in 1998 alone.[6] China's state-run textile industry, for example, shed over a million jobs between 1998 and 2000. Soon job centres were opening around the country, and the government was talking of a leaner economy, with retraining for laid-off workers.

If it all seemed strangely reminiscent of Britain in the heyday of Margaret Thatcher in the 1980s, then that was perhaps no coincidence. The architect of many of China's most drastic reforms during this period was Zhu Rongji, Deputy Prime Minister in charge of the economy from 1992 to 1998, and the country's Prime Minister from 1998 to 2003. Mr Zhu was an unusual figure in Chinese politics – with a blunt manner, an apparent distaste for ideological slogans and a line in ironic humour. As a university graduate in the 1950s, he was labelled a 'rightist' after calling for less dogmatic economic policies, and was sent for 're-education' in the country-side as a punishment. Politically rehabilitated after the Cultural Revolution, he worked his way up to become mayor of Shanghai by the late 1980s, and played a part in pushing for that city to be given greater freedom to carry out economic reforms. He impressed foreigners with his command of English and his knowledge of financial theory. And perhaps because of the close attention he paid to global economic trends, it was Mr Zhu who, during the 1990s, became convinced that China would have to slash the size of the state workforce, and rely mainly on market forces and the private sector to create new jobs. His enthusiasm for China joining the World Trade Organisation – a deal struck under his leadership in 1999 – was widely believed to have been motivated in part by his belief that only the power of such an international treaty would be able to force greater reforms on often unwilling state enterprises, and indeed on parts of the bureaucracy too.

And while he also oversaw the beginning of attempts to set up a new nationwide welfare safety net, Zhu Rongji not only pushed for faster redundancies after becoming Prime Minister in 1998, but simultaneously introduced the housing reforms which forced many to buy their homes on the commercial market. And it was striking that on his first trip abroad as Prime Minister, to London for an international conference in 1998, he made a point of scheduling a private meeting with Margaret Thatcher, even though she had been out of office for seven years. The staunchly anti-communist Baroness, architect of Britain's mass lay-offs of the 1980s, subsequently referred to Mr Zhu as someone 'who has a formidable grasp of economics'.[7]

Thus the Zhu Rongji years were characterised by scenes which would previously have been unimaginable in socialist China. State television news began featuring reports of old state-run factories being physically taken apart – including memorable images of workers smashing up the old looms of bankrupt cotton mills with sledgehammers. It was a symbolic attempt to portray the collapse of these once-great industries in a heroic, socialist light. At the same time, official media began reporting heart-warming tales of laid-off workers who had set up their own small businesses and were doing well for themselves. Much coverage, for example, was given to a group of redundant women factory workers who were now doing a roaring trade selling 'laid-off' brand steamed buns.[8] China even had its first cinema film on the subject of unemployment. *The Red Suit* (*Hong Xifu*) by the female director Li Shaohong was a touching tale of a man who had been laid off from his job at a state factory but couldn't bear to tell his wife and family, and so still got up and went off to 'work' every morning as usual.

There was no underestimating the scale of the dislocation. In some cities in the north-east, as many as half of all workers lost their jobs. Even in ostensibly wealthy Shanghai, more than a million people were made redundant during the 1990s, the city having started its reforms early, while Zhu Rongji was still mayor. Several hundred thousand people lost their jobs in Shanghai's textile industry, which had once been so dominant in China but had been hard hit by new competition. Even those companies whose sales were still strong were making little profit because of their heavy welfare burden – as the director of one state-run shirt-manufacturer in the city lamented when I met him in 1998. Many textile factories simply closed down; others slashed their workforce or moved out of Shanghai to other parts of China where labour was cheaper. And other industries, notably electronics and chemicals, were similarly hard hit. The factories affected included some whose workforce had been at the vanguard of the uprisings which made Shanghai the heart of worker radicalism during the Cultural Revolution. Even some of the 'model' housing estates, symbols of the new socialist era, which were built for workers in the early 1950s, were now starting to be demolished to make way for more modern construction.

The government did, in 1998, begin to lay out plans for its new social security system. The basic principle was a welfare insurance scheme, which would provide some cover for unemployment, medical care and retirement pensions, and would, in some cities, incorporate the existing housing accumulation fund. Each person would have an individual account, into which they paid a proportion of their salary; employers would also contribute, and the government would top this up with money of its own. But to set up such a system from scratch would take time, and the authorities acknowledged that they urgently needed to find new jobs for as many laid-off workers as possible. They began to pin much of their hope on the rise of a whole new sector of service industries in the country's cities – in sales and promotion, telecommunications and finance.

Many new jobs were created in these areas. But for the laid-off workers from the state sector, adapting to this new economy was by no means an easy process. In 1998, at one of Beijing's recently opened network of 're-employment centres', the head of the city's labour bureau was blunt about the difficulties confronting such people. 'It's a question of their state of mind,' she said. 'In the state enterprises all their welfare was looked after for them. So when they're made redundant, they face all kinds of new day-to-day problems, and they're bound to feel pretty bad. They're not really accustomed to dealing with the realities of society,' she added, 'or the need to compete for work.'[9] Yet from the point of view of many laid-off workers, it was society which was rejecting them rather than the other way round. At the same job centre I met a woman in her thirties who made no attempt to conceal her anger as she described her attempts to find a job. 'It's so hard,' she said. 'All the employers want young people who look nice and have a university education. I don't think age should matter,' she went on, 'but the bosses think it does. There are plenty of jobs which I think anyone could do, but for some reason they don't agree.'

Indeed women workers, who made up the majority of the labour force in industries such as textiles, were particularly hard hit by the restructuring of China's economy. Not only were millions made redundant, but millions more were forced to take early retirement – sometimes extremely early. China's official retirement age was fifty-five for female workers and sixty for men. But as struggling state enterprises looked for ways of saving money, the retirement age for women in industry was lowered to fifty – and many firms actually pushed their female staff to quit when they were still in their forties. And in a job market where advertisements routinely called, for example, for 'attractive single females below the age of 25' – even for the most routine administrative posts – finding new employment could certainly be tough.

And the workers being laid off in the late 1990s – both male and female – often faced an additional hurdle. Many of them were of the generation which had missed much of its education during the Cultural Revolution, either because their schools were shut or because they were sent to the countryside. As Professor Liang Hong, a labour specialist at Shanghai's Fudan University, puts it, 'These people are a unique generation. When they should have been in education everyone was busy making revolution. Then they were sent home to work in the factories – but when the economy started adjusting, they began to lose their jobs.'[10]

Not surprisingly, many members of this generation felt as though they were being cast out onto the scrapheap. Mrs Li, who had watched the old Shanghai timber yard where she used to work go into such sharp decline during the 1990s, was effectively pushed into retirement at forty-seven. When I met her, five years later, she had not worked since. She spent her days pottering around at home, reading the paper, watching traditional Suzhou opera performances on television, or tending to her pet bird in the little courtyard of the old shared lane house where she and her husband lived (though it was soon to be demolished). Sometimes they went on day trips to the Shanghai suburbs, or took a stroll round one of the city's new shopping centres.

Financially, Mrs Li was not doing too badly – Shanghai's new social security system was now paying her a pension of eight hundred yuan (around sixty pounds) a month, far more than she had ever earned in her old job. But the years of heavy labour had left her with a bad back, and she was still upset about how her career had ended, particularly since she felt she had made many sacrifices. She had lost the last two years of her high school education during the political turmoil of the late 1960s, and then, at the age of twenty, had volunteered to go to the countryside so that her younger brother and sister would have the chance to stay in the city and carry on with their studies. (In those days, it was the policy in many cities that each family must send one member to work on the land.) Mrs Li had been sent far away to north-east China, near the Siberian border. 'I stayed in the countryside for ten years,' she said. 'We planted fields, fed pigs, harvested crops. It was so tough there, so cold in the winter.' It was beautiful too, she acknowledged, in fact now she sometimes even missed the place. But it had been so far away from her home in Shanghai, and she had been delighted when she finally got the chance to come back to the city and take over her father's old job in the timber yard. This was hard work too, though, and when she was passed over for the pay rise which she had been promised, in favour of a younger colleague, she was bitterly disappointed. 'I worked on the land, I was re-educated, I did everything Chairman Mao wanted me to do,' she said, still upset at the memory all these years later. 'And then who did they give the money to? Some young hooligan!' By the time her bosses asked her to take early retirement she was tired of fighting. 'What could I say?' she said. 'They didn't want me. They'd treated me so badly that I didn't want to talk to them again. So I just signed the piece of paper and went home.'

102

She had not thought it worth looking for a new job. 'I don't have any skills,' she said. 'We sawed wood and planted the land, who wants us now?' Her husband, a softly spoken man a few years older than his wife, nodded in agreement. He too had been asked to retire early from his job, and though he himself seemed to bear no grudge, he believed his wife's generation in particular had little chance of finding new work. 'Her generation had a very hard time,' he said. 'If you only have a middle school education, who wants you now? There are so many young graduates with university degrees.' He sighed. 'There's nothing you can do about it though,' he said, with a shrug of his shoulders, 'that's modern Chinese history.'

Some laid-off workers, women included, have of course succeeded in finding new jobs. In fast-developing cities like Shanghai, some at least have been absorbed by the new service sector. The super-market shelf-fillers, the roadside newspaper vendors and street sweepers, the cleaners in McDonald's or Kentucky Fried Chicken – many are former workers from the once-proud factories of socialist Shanghai.

Liu Yumei is one of them, prowling around the tables at a branch of one of the big fast-food chains in her jaunty uniform, clearing away the remains of people's meals and wiping the surface clean. 'I like working here,' she says, 'they're good employers. I only have to do seven or eight hours a day, and it's just round the corner from my house, so I can still cook dinner for the family.' It's something she wasn't able to do very often in her old job at a state-run chemical factory. Originally it had been close to her home – in fact it was one of the biggest employers in her crowded, inner-city district. But in the 1990s the factory was shifted out to the suburbs, as the local government tried to cut pollution in the city centre. The company provided transport to the new location, but the journey took nearly two hours each way – which didn't leave much time to see her husband and son. Still, working in the factory was a family tradition. Mrs Liu had taken over the job from her mother, who had started working there before the revolution. And she hadn't let her mother down: she had worked her way up from the factory floor to a place in the administration. But a few years after it moved to the suburbs, the firm was bought out by some of its managers and a group of foreign investors, and immediately began laying off many of the staff. Liu Yumei was one of them. She was forty-two, and had been with the firm for more than twenty years.

But, being a positive person, she immediately set about finding a new job. It helped to have personal contacts, she discovered, and appearance was definitely important, but she didn't find it too difficult. 'At least Shanghai's developing, not like some cities in the north,' she says. With her short hair neatly trimmed, and sharp-eyed, lively expression, Liu Yumei quickly impressed the manager of a new hypermarket, who gave her a job selling electrical goods. But the twelve-hour shifts, most of them spent standing on one spot, were hard-going. And, so with the help of an introduction from a friend, she found a job in the fast-food restaurant. She likes the fact that her shifts vary from week to week, she says, and she gets on well with her colleagues. In fact on Sunday mornings, when she's not working, she often meets up with some of them in a nearby teahouse, where they chat about their families and their lives over cheap cups of tea and saucers of melon seeds. All of them are women in their late forties or early fifties – and all have been laid off. One of Mrs Liu's friends used to work for the Phoenix bicycle firm, once one of the most revered companies in China, but a few years ago it moved its factory out into the suburbs; now it's employing cheaper migrant workers, she says.

Sometimes, the women are joined by one of their managers, with whom they've become friendly. Younger, in her early thirties, she is clearly imbued with the prevailing values of China's new economy. Surely, I suggest, with her cheerful personality and quick wit Liu Yumei would be ideally suited to taking orders and serving customers, rather than just cleaning the restaurant. 'Really?' says the manager, with an incredulous look. 'How would you feel if you came into a restaurant and found an older person serving behind the counter?' It's clear that no answer is required. It's a reminder of just why so many older people have found it hard to find new jobs. (China's traditional respect for older people may work against them too: anyone over fifty, it seems, may be referred to as an old person. On the one hand, it's a reverential description, but it also implies that they are someone to be protected and looked after, and more suited to a restful retirement than a challenging and energetic job.)

Liu Yumei seems none too bothered about any of this. 'It's all the same to me,' she says, with a diplomatic smile. 'They pay us the same whatever job we do.' In fact, since the fast-food chain has also adopted the same retirement age as China's state factories – fifty for women – she will actually have to give up this job too in a couple of years' time. But fortunately, since her former employer has not actually gone bankrupt, it still has to keep topping up her account in China's new social insurance fund, which means she'll be entitled to a reasonable pension, in fact slightly more than she actually earns at the moment.

And money is definitely her top priority these days. Her son is in high school and the family has to pay for him to have extra tuition at the weekends, to improve his chances of getting a place at university. If he succeeds, there will be the fees to pay too. 'Education is so expensive,' says Liu Yumei with a shake of her head. Her husband now runs a small clothes shop which brings in a little extra cash, but the family still often struggles to make ends meet. Sometimes, she admits, they have no choice but to borrow from her brother, a successful businessman. 'He's done much better than me,' says Liu Yumei matter-of-factly. 'He's got a car and a big flat. And he often helps us out.' She pauses, then lowers her voice, 'But it makes me feel really embarrassed, I don't like to be in debt to anyone, even my own family. I wish I could rely on my own labour.'

Not all laid-off workers, though, are as dynamic, as motivated or indeed as lucky as Liu Yumei. In Shanghai, when the weather starts to warm up in the spring, small groups of people cluster around little tables set up in the parks and the old lanes, or under the trees in front of the public housing compounds, playing cards or mahjong, or just watching the game. Others sit outside their front doors on rickety chairs, idling away the time gossiping with their neighbours, reading the paper or watching the world go by. Some are senior citizens, but many are in their late forties or early fifties. One energetic-looking man, who I often used to see sitting in front of the building where he lived, would always greet me with a friendly wave as I passed. I once made the mistake of asking him whether he'd been busy recently. 'Busy,' he said, with a slightly astonished laugh, 'what would I be busy doing?' He and most of his friends and neighbours had been laid off from old state factories, he said. 'I could take you on a tour of this neighbourhood,' he offered, 'and show you all the people who spend their days in the "chess and card rooms" in each lane. Shanghai looks like such a wealthy city – but there are hundreds of thousands of people like us.'

And he was right. According to official figures, in the early years of this decade, there were around 800,000 laid-off workers in Shanghai, most receiving some form of pension from the state, or, if they did not qualify for this, a subsidy from the city's 'Minimum Living Standard Fund'.[11] This scheme was set up in the late 1990s to help people who had slipped through the gaps in China's welfare safety net, while the old system was being phased out. Local citizens whose income was below a certain level, for whatever reason, could apply for a top-up to bring them up to the minimum living standard set by the local government – as Wei Yuan, the car-washer, had done in the past. In Shanghai, where more than 300,000 people were receiving this allowance as of 2005, the standard was fixed, in the early years of the new century, at around three hundred yuan (just over twenty pounds – or the price of ten cups of coffee in one of the city's smart cafés).[12] In less wealthy cities, the level was set far lower, at little more than a hundred yuan a month. It was barely subsistence level – and some cities struggled to pay it at all.

And even in Shanghai, with its fast-growing economy, supporting so many people was a drain on the government's finances. It was concerns such as this which, in 2001, led the city to set up the scheme which brought Wei Yuan and others out of their lanes and back onto the labour market after so many years. It was called the '4050 Project', because it was aimed at people in their forties and fifties, and it was one of the first attempts in China to tackle the problem of unemployment among 'older' laid-off workers. People

106

who set up small businesses and hired laid-off workers received tax breaks, loan guarantees and expert advice – and a small extra allowance for each person they took on. According to Professor Liang Hong, the labour specialist at Shanghai's Fudan University who was an adviser to the project, such people still had plenty to offer to society.

'All our feedback shows that these people take their jobs more seriously and are very loyal to their employers,' he said soon after the scheme started. 'They've been through the pain of unemployment, so they cherish having a new opportunity. Young people, on the other hand, are much more likely to jump from one company to another.' Laid-off workers, he acknowledged, were not always well qualified for the more skilled jobs being created in many of the city's new factories and businesses. 'Because most of them haven't studied much,' he said, 'they can find it hard to learn new skills quickly, even with retraining programmes.' But while they might not be computer-literate, there were other roles they could fill in China's changing society. 'Flower delivery, for example,' he said, enthusiastically, 'there's a growing demand for this now. Or chopping vegetables and delivering them to people's houses, making lunch boxes for office workers, recycling work.'

Another area the scheme was looking at, said Professor Liang, was the market for household cleaners and domestic servants. It might not sound very socialist, but it is in fact something the Chinese government has actively promoted in recent years. In 2000, China's Deputy Minister of Labour made a speech in which he stressed that this sector was an important potential source of new jobs in urban areas.[13] An ageing population, and the break-up of the traditional multi-generational family unit, means that more and more elderly people need caring for; and growing numbers of wealthy young urbanites are seeking people to do their housework and look after their children. Yet persuading city residents to take on such jobs was hard at first: many of the former workers of the big state enterprises, who had been told for decades that they were the elite of the socialist economy, saw doing someone else's chores as humiliating. In one survey in Guangzhou, for example, many laid-off workers said they would be embarrassed if their neighbours knew they were doing such jobs.[14] But according to Professor Liang Hong attitudes were starting to change. 'Now people think anything is OK, as long as they get paid,' he said. That certainly seemed to apply to Mrs Wang, a Shanghai resident in her forties who had worked for a now-bankrupt match factory. With the help of the 4050 Project, she had found a job with a local family, cooking their meals and looking after their young son. 'The project taught me ironing, washing, how to cook new dishes,' she said with a grin. 'I wasn't much good at any of this before!' She seemed genuinely happy to be back at work.

Other cities followed Shanghai's example and set up similar schemes to help older workers find new jobs. Some areas also set up specific programmes to assist women to start up their own small businesses. But some 20 per cent of those who were laid off between 1998 and 2003 did not find new jobs, according to official figures.[15] And some of China's laid-off workers still have no interest in seeking a low-paying job, preferring to live on whichever government subsidy they qualify for. As one Shanghai resident who was forced to take early retirement and now receives a small pension puts it, 'I get a few hundred yuan a month now. I could try to find a job, but I'd only get a little more – it's not really worth it.' Occasionally, he says, he does a bit of work for friends to top up his benefits; it's not strictly legal, but it's a common practice, part of China's growing 'grey economy'.

It all means that the Chinese government, despite the drastic cuts in the number of workers on the state payroll, still faces a heavy welfare burden. (Indeed, the authorities have specifically appealed to businesses and individuals to make donations to help support the payment of minimum living standard benefits.) In the early years of the new century, the government began to roll out its new national social welfare insurance scheme, with three separate funds covering unemployment benefits, health care and pensions – and, in some cities, a housing accumulation fund as well. But gaps in the system remain – not least because there are many millions of workers who retired from now-bankrupt factories too early to contribute to the new insurance scheme, but who still need to receive pensions.

Official media have reported a shortfall of several hundred billion pounds in China's pension system – and some commentators have suggested that forcing so many workers to take retirement in their forties or early fifties is only making the problem worse. The government has set up a special fund to invest money to help pay for pensions, but even official documents have admitted that the scheme will be under 'even greater pressure' in the future.[16]

Many ordinary individuals have likewise found the burden a heavy one. In 2002 the government extended the new pension scheme to cover private businesses and self-employed workers in the cities. But take-up has been slow – and it's perhaps hardly surprising: private employers have to contribute up to 20 per cent of an employee's salary to the scheme, while employees themselves pay 8 per cent; self-employed people, meanwhile, pay almost 20 per cent of the average local income. By 2005, only around 10 per cent of the estimated 120 million urban residents who were self-employed or working in the private sector had joined the scheme.[17]

Many citizens were perhaps saving up their money to offset the impact of another significant reform of China's social welfare system: the increasing expense of medical treatment. Over the past decade, the price of medical care has, with housing and education, become one of the biggest headaches for ordinary Chinese people. Some of the problems have been temporary, teething troubles of the reform process. But there's little doubt that, even with the establishment of the new medical insurance fund, the majority of people now have to contribute more to the cost of their treatment than ever before.

Just how far China has come from the virtually free medical care it once promised its citizens was brought home to me when I once went to hospital with someone who needed emergency treatment. An ambulance was called, and the patient was duly delivered to the accident and emergency department of a nearby hospital. Several members of his family swiftly arrived and clustered around him as he lay waiting to be transferred to one of the wards upstairs. Then, suddenly, most of them disappeared, leaving him lying there. It was only when they returned a few minutes later that I discovered they had been queuing up at the hospital's front desk, to pay the registration fee and cash deposit which were prerequisites for treatment in any Chinese hospital. Later, like most other families who could afford it, they hired their own private helper from the group of female migrant workers who were available at the hospital for this purpose. For a small fee, the helper would sit with the patient, help him get in and out of bed, and bring food if necessary – since the hospital's own staff were too busy to do this. Eventually, the family decided to transfer their relative to another hospital where the doctors were more expert – and once again had to pay an extra fee to secure an appointment with a top specialist. To them, it was all absolutely routine, in a medical system where little, it seemed, was now for free.

This state of affairs was another result of the government's decision to remove responsibility for the provision of welfare from the country's state enterprises. In the past, employees of state-run work units received almost free medical care. Some of the bigger units even had their own hospitals; others would send their workers to a designated hospital – often one which catered specifically for people from a particular industry. Shanghai for example had a Textile Bureau hospital, a Post and Telephone Bureau hospital, an Electric Power hospital. If people had to go to other hospitals for specialist treatment, they might have to pay for it themselves first, but they would be reimbursed later. But by the second half of the 1990s, some of the old state work units were struggling to make these payments. 'At that time, people were coming for treatment, then taking the bill back to their work unit,' recalls a consultant at one Shanghai hospital, 'but the units were telling them they couldn't afford to refund them, or they'd have to pay them back in instalments.'

It was clear that the old system was starting to crumble; at the same time, there were also increasing numbers of urban residents who worked for private companies or ran their own businesses and did not qualify for health care under the old set-up. Finally in 1998, after studying health care schemes around the world, the Chinese government announced plans for its new urban health insurance system. Once again, it was based in part on a model used in Singapore: workers paid about 4 per cent of their salary into their own health insurance 'account', their employers paid some more, and the government added its own contribution. But gradually, as the scheme was implemented around the country, it became clear that a fundamental change had taken place in China's health care. For all the new welfare system's impressive array of different funds and the smart computerised swipe cards issued to its members, it was undeniably the case that for many people, medical treatment was no longer completely free. Even after paying into the insurance scheme, patients would now still have to pay some of their medical expenses out of their own pockets if they went into hospital or if they needed long-term outpatient care.

Shanghai was one of the first cities to put the new system into practice. Since the mid-1990s it had already experimented with its own pilot scheme; in 2001, it moved over to the central government's new insurance fund. The following year I went to meet Xiang Siwen, the Deputy Director of the city's Medical Insurance Bureau. He seemed pleased with the progress. Downstairs in his building, people were queuing to register for their new medical cards; some seven million residents had enrolled in the scheme in little more than twelve months, he said proudly. But as he launched into a long and complicated slide presentation of how the system worked, it became evident that, as with most insurance schemes, when you read the small print there were actually rather a lot of exclusions. Patients could use the money in their personal insurance account to cover basic outpatient treatment and simple prescriptions. But once they had used up this money – which could happen quite quickly if they had only just joined the insurance scheme – they would have to pay a percentage of the remaining cost themselves.

And if they went into hospital, they would immediately have to start adding money from their own pocket. 'You pay the first part of the fees yourself,' said Dr Xiang, 'around fourteen hundred yuan.' This was, he explained, based on a calculation of one-tenth of the average annual salary in Shanghai. Patients then paid 15 per cent of any further costs – or 8 per cent if they were retired. If the total fees went beyond a certain limit – set at four times the city's average annual wage – they had to apply for 'additional assistance', which came from a separate fund, and again would have to pay some of the costs themselves. According to Dr Xiang, the patient's contribution was nevertheless only 'a relatively small percentage'. 'People who have jobs can cope with the burden,' he said. 'They may have to pay a little more than before, but they can accept these reforms.' For anyone who could not cope, he added, the city had another safety net – a separate 'medical aid' scheme, which the poorest citizens could apply for at the local Civil Affairs Bureau.

Still, he acknowledged that the insurance scheme did leave gaps. For this reason, he explained, wealthier employers and their staff were encouraged to pay into an extra top-up fund, which would give them more benefits. Other social organisations, such as China's official trades unions, also set up similar funds of their own which gave employees extra help in paying for hospital treatment or serious illnesses, for a small additional contribution from their salary. Beyond this, Dr Xiang pointed out, the authorities were also encouraging the development of private health insurance schemes, already being energetically advertised by China's big insurance companies. 'If you have these additional types of cover, the burden will be less when you go into hospital,' he suggested, reassuringly. Charitable foundations could also help out, he said, adding, 'And we hope that employers will give their staff emergency aid when necessary.'

For people used to the old days of reimbursement from their work units, though, it was dauntingly complicated and there was no doubt that many found it hard to adapt to the new system. Public anxiety about the cost of treatment under the new scheme was revealed when the Shanghai media began reporting stories of young people borrowing medical insurance cards from elderly relatives, in order to take advantage of the lower fees for retired citizens. Some employers too were reported to be less than enthusiastic at the size of their contribution – with many seeking ways to avoid paying the 8 per cent of their staff's salary into the fund. And getting refunds could now be a slow process too: in 2002, the then head of the World Health Organisation in China noted that 'even though they've contributed in advance through health insurance, people still have to wait for a long time [to be reimbursed]. In other words,' he said, 'they pay their money into the insurance fund, but they can't get it out immediately.'[18]

And Shanghai's medical insurance system had more resources and was more comprehensive than the schemes in many less wealthy parts of the country. During the 1980s and 1990s, the Chinese government had gradually shifted responsibility for funding health care from its central budget to local governments; in poorer areas, it was therefore inevitable that the level of support provided was lower and there were fewer resources for providing emergency help to the poorest people.

In Shanghai, at least, doctors insisted that under the new insurance scheme, no local residents would be turned away from a hospital if they needed emergency treatment, even if they did not have cash with them to pay the deposit – something which has often been reported as happening in other parts of the country. 'Now everyone has their medical card,' said one consultant, 'so even if they don't pay at the time we know how to contact them afterwards!'

Still, not everyone was convinced about the benefits of the reforms. One person who had plenty of experience of the workings of China's welfare system was Mrs Fu, a laid-off worker from a government enterprise in Shanghai. When I first met her she was bustling around in the lane where she lived not far from the city centre, chatting with her neighbours as she washed vegetables at the outdoor tap, apparently brimming with good health and energy. But when we sat down in the small room which served as her family's living room by day, and her eighty-year-old mother's bedroom at night, and she began to tell me the story of her life, it became clear that things might not have turned out this way.

Sipping tea at the table by the window, through which a tiny sliver of sky was visible above the high wall of the house opposite, Mrs Fu explained that she was a little girl when the communists took power in 1949. Her father, a soldier in the nationalist army, fled the mainland for Taiwan, leaving her mother to bring up three children on her own. In those early years of the revolution, she said, the socialist welfare system treated them well. 'The residents' committee gave us a letter with an official seal saying we couldn't afford our school fees,' she recalled, 'so we got our education free of charge. And in those days if you got ill you were well looked after – in the 1950s it was all free, serious illnesses too.' In the Cultural Revolution, however, she was sent to do agricultural labour in the countryside outside Shanghai, and when she eventually returned to the city she was not assigned a job, because of her 'bad class background'. Finally, after the end of the Cultural Revolution, she was given a menial post in a small government-run guest house. She was the most efficient of all the staff in her unit, she said, still proud of the fact, but by the mid-1990s the unit was in decline and she was asked to retire at fifty.

With only a tiny pension to supplement her husband's low wages, she decided to do some part-time work to cover her son's education costs, and found a job helping out in the home of a wealthy family. The family treated her well, but one day she slipped on a tiled floor and broke a bone in her thigh. 'When I got to hospital my blood pressure went down to forty,' she said, with a shudder. 'They wanted to give me an operation, but it would have cost so much.' It was the late 1990s, when Shanghai was still experimenting with its medical reforms, and Mrs Fu had to apply directly to her old work unit for support. 'They brought me some money,' she said, 'but I still needed another six thousand yuan for the steel pin they wanted to insert into my leg.' The pin was imported, she added, 'so you couldn't claim for that, you had to buy it yourself'. At the time, the family's entire savings amounted to just ten thousand yuan, which they had set aside to help put her son through university. 'And I didn't want to borrow money from anyone else,' said Mrs Fu. 'If I had, how would I have repaid it?' And so she told the surgeon she didn't want the operation. 'He said if you don't do it you'll be disabled,' she recalled. 'So I said if I'm disabled, never mind, I'm already retired anyway. So I just lay there and waited.' When she eventually improved enough to go home her son made her a crutch, and she began doing as much exercise as she could. 'Someone up there must have been protecting me,' she said, 'my leg got much better. Now I'm OK, in fact everyone says I look good for my age!'

Presumably, I said, she would have been able to afford the operation if the accident had happened after the new health insurance system was introduced. Mrs Fu, who, like many residents, seemed to have become an expert on how the scheme worked, was not so sure. 'Now if I had a serious illness like that I'd have to pay 8 per cent,' she said quickly. 'If you break a bone it normally costs about 40,000 yuan; you'd have to put down forty thousand yourself as a deposit, and you could probably only get about half of it back – the steel pin is imported material so it's still not covered.' Some people, she said, would borrow money from everyone in their family to pay the deposit. 'But I only have one son,' she continued, 'so it would be a heavy burden for him. If I had to put down forty thousand up front now I still wouldn't have the operation,' she said emphatically, 'forget it!' In her opinion, the best solution for such problems was to 'be careful when you're working'.

And a glance at the pages of local media makes it clear that there are still plenty of people who have fallen between the cracks of the new system. One report claimed that only around 20 per cent of people with Alzheimer's disease in China were taking medication for it – in part because of the cost of treatment. In Shanghai, for example, only domestic medicine for the disease was covered by medical insurance, while the most up-to-date foreign medication had to be paid for by patients themselves, at a cost of around eight hundred yuan a month – a month's wages for many.[19] And in the pages of the magazine of the local charities foundation, there are often appeals for assistance on behalf of people who cannot pay their medical fees – in summer 2006 these included a man with a brain tumour whose family had already spent 100,000 yuan (over £7,000) on treatment, and needed to pay another 15,000 every month. 'The company he worked for was newly established, and had not taken out major illness insurance for its staff,' noted the magazine. Another appeal was for a woman in urgent need of a kidney transplant. Her employer had already contributed

33,000 yuan, said the article, 'but this still can't cover the huge costs, and they hope for a noble person to come to their assistance'.[20]

Such stories have become increasingly common. In 2006, state media reported the case of a twelve-year-old boy in the north-eastern town of Dalian who spent his spare time playing his violin on the street to raise money for a classmate who had leukaemia and whose family could not afford to pay for treatment. Thanks to the boy's help, his friend survived, and the boy was given a special award by the local government. It was a heartwarming story – but a depressing reminder of the shortcomings of the medical system at the same time.[21]

And the public perception of health care as increasingly expensive – often prohibitively so – is not helped by the fact that hospitals have come under increasing pressure to make money out of their patients. Between the 1980s and the early years of the new century, China's spending on health fell from around 6 per cent of its total budget to around 4 per cent.[22] As a result hospitals now receive less direct funding and need to raise more money themselves. Their options have been limited, however, by government rules which have kept the fees for many basic types of treatment (including the price of a standard hospital bed) at relatively low levels, dating back years to the days of the planned economy. And so hospitals have had to look for other ways to generate income. Some have moved into luxury treatments, opening new wards to carry out cosmetic surgery – advertisements for which now fill the billboards of China's major cities.

Others have tried to increase revenue by using expensive new imported technologies (not covered by the old price list), or simply by raising the prices of medicines – sometimes to as much as ten times what they cost on the high street. In the early years of the new century, this provoked such an outcry that the government was forced to introduce price limits for commonly used drugs (though some drug manufacturers got around the restriction by simply changing the names of their drugs). And hospitals were also accused of prescribing treatments which were completely unnecessary. Xiang Siwen, the deputy director of the Shanghai medical insurance fund, acknowledged the problem. 'In our insurance scheme hospitals are refunded after they've provided services to patients,' he said. 'And in any such scheme, they're likely to increase the number of services they provide – so of course it's hard to prevent waste such as repetitive check-ups or over-prescription.'

Hospitals have also been criticised for wasting resources by building too many luxury wards, where they can charge high daily fees to wealthy clients. The hospitals, however, argue they have little choice since they have to purchase new equipment and pay for new facilities out of their own revenues. Doctors' bonuses – which many say are crucial to supplement their relatively low basic salaries – also come from this type of 'extra revenue'. And there have been frequent reports of collusion between doctors and medicine manufacturers, who offer them bribes to prescribe more of their particular brand of medicine. Dr Xiang in Shanghai chose his words carefully, but agreed that 'medicine producers will use all kind of methods to promote their products, and that does cause waste'. Steps were being taken to implement a system of fair tendering for medicine companies, he emphasised, but he accepted that China prescribed far more medicine per patient than in many western countries.

The situation has led to some startling stories of patients being handed enormous medical bills. In 2005, the family of a retired doctor, who had died in a Shenzhen hospital after four months of treatment, received a bill for 1.2 million yuan (more than £80,000), covering some nine thousand separate items and almost 150 types of medicine.[23] Later the same year, relatives of a teacher in north-east China were presented with a bill for 5.5 million yuan (some £400,000) after his death following two months of treatment for blood cancer. The news provoked an outcry in the media and an investigation by the Health Ministry, but one hospital official was reported to have claimed that the hospital's own investigations showed that the patient had actually been undercharged![24]

Little wonder, then, that health has become a major cause of anxiety for ordinary people in China. The high cost of medical care has long been cited by the old people who do their morning

117

exercises in China's parks as one of their main motivations for keeping fit; it was seen as one of the major reasons for the rapid spread of groups such as Falun Gong, the exercise-based spiritual movement which the government outlawed in 1999. The authorities insisted it was a dangerous cult, but most of its tens of millions of practitioners argued that its regime of traditional-style breathing exercises kept them fit and healthy. Fears about rising welfare payments have also contributed to the obsession of residents in cities like Shanghai with playing the stock market – many elderly people spend much of their time in the stockbrokers' trading houses which can be found on side streets all over the city, watching the movements of share prices on big electronic screens. Experts have described China's stock markets as so volatile that investing in them is little different from gambling. But for many they apparently offer hope. And the constant advertisements on Chinese television for health tonics – from chicken extract for the stomach to potions reputed to boost mental capacity – testify to the fact that concern about health, always a traditional obsession in China, remains very much on people's minds.

Worries about what some officials have termed 'soaring inaccessibility' of medical treatment for many people have become so widespread that they are frequently raised by delegates to the annual session of China's legislature, the National People's Congress.[25] In 2005 the State Council, China's cabinet, itself issued a highly critical report, describing medical reforms as having been largely a 'failure'.[26] Health Minister Gao Qiang, in a report by his ministry, announced that many medical institutions had been 'over-commercialised', and were now 'relying chiefly on exorbitant fees for their maintenance and development'. He accused some hospitals of 'putting profits ahead of health care' and of endangering patients.[27] There have been fresh pledges to provide more affordable health care, including the setting up of pilot 'fair-price' treatment centres – specific wards, or in some cases entire hospitals, which offer relatively cheap treatment to those who cannot afford standard fees. Such wards receive extra subsidies from the government – and the quantity of drugs they prescribe is carefully controlled; there has

118

been talk of using this as a model for the entire health service in the future.[28] By 2006 the government had also started to publicly name hospitals – including some very well-known ones – which had overcharged patients, in the hope that this would help to stamp out the practice.

But reforming China's health service is a daunting task: the system is a vast and unwieldy one, with some 17,000 publicly owned hospitals and much unnecessary duplication of function. At the same time, the best hospitals in China's cities are heavily oversubscribed. In the old days, many of these were exclusively for senior officials; now, in the free-for-all of the new system, people from all over the country flock to the best hospitals in Beijing, Shanghai or Guangzhou. Often they join the crowds of people waiting for days outside these hospitals for one of the limited number of consultants' appointments. Touts sell places in the queues, while some people hire others to do the queuing for them.

There's also evidence that the new medical insurance system, for all its failings, has actually increased demand, particularly for out-patient treatment, the costs of which tend to be covered under the scheme. This has added to pressure on popular hospitals, not least because China has never had a system of family doctors' surgeries, and so people suffering from nothing more serious than a bout of flu will often head straight for the nearest hospital. As a result, the waiting rooms and corridors of outpatients' departments can be a depressing sight, overflowing with people, some lying on beds, others propped up on chairs, many with their arms attached to precarious-looking drip tubes.

The heavy demands on doctors' time have contributed to a culture where patients and their relatives often feel they must ply doctors with expensive gifts or bribes to be sure of getting good treatment. In recent years the authorities have launched anti-bribery campaigns, and slogans in hospitals now remind doctors of their duty to be honest and fair. China's national Hospitals Association in 2006 called on its six million members to sign up to a pledge to refuse bribes, keep costs down for patients, and respect medical ethics. Nevertheless some doctors have argued they are so poorly paid that they have little alternative but to take bribes – while one Shanghai newspaper described the case of a doctor who tried to refuse such gifts, but found that this made his patients' relatives so nervous that in the end he had no choice but to accept them after all![29]

Patients' anxieties have been reinforced by frequent reports of arrogance, incompetence and malpractice on the part of China's hospitals. In some cases patients or their relatives have become so angry that doctors have been attacked or even murdered. In 2002 the authorities tried to calm such tensions by introducing new rules allowing patients to demand an independent investigation into their complaints. Hospitals, anticipating a flurry of new lawsuits, responded with some drastic measures: some installed cameras in operating theatres, so that they could keep video records of all surgery, while one hospital in Nanjing even invited people to watch their relatives' operations live on closed-circuit television.[30] Some doctors were said to be so nervous about being sued that they began refusing to carry out complex or high-risk surgery. And family members now often have to sign disclaimer forms absolving the hospital of any responsibility if anything goes wrong with their relatives' operations.

No wonder, perhaps, that some see the medical system as little short of a nightmare. Lu Youqing, a Shanghai businessman who wrote a widely read online diary detailing the final months of his battle against cancer in 2000, spoke for many when he described the process of treatment for the disease as an expensive but ineffective black farce.[31] In the years since, there's no doubt that the government has realised that change is necessary. It has recently announced plans to set up more community health clinics, in order to reduce the pressure on the country's hospitals, and has even talked about allowing more foreign investment in the health sector. But opinions remain sharply divided. Some Chinese media commentators have called for more radical reforms: one insisted that the country needed more private hospitals with fresh approaches to management.[32] Private institutions have been permitted in recent years, including a few with foreign backing. But they tend to cater to foreigners and wealthier Chinese citizens, since official restrictions prevent them from competing for patients funded by the national medical insurance system. And some fear that giving private hospitals greater freedom would only increase the divide between the haves and have-nots, and accelerate the siphoning-off of many of the country's best doctors from the public system.

The government is aware that such issues play into a wider public dissatisfaction about the direction of social change and the way in which the economic and welfare reforms of the past decade or more have altered Chinese society. Even on the relatively controlled Chinese Internet, it's not uncommon to read complaints about the cost of education, housing and healthcare, and worries about pensions too. Such bitterness is fuelled by the perception that the shake-up of society since the 1990s has left China far wealthier, but far more divided. In fact, the country's wealth gap, not just between urban and rural areas but between rich and poor in the cities, has been calculated as one of the highest in the world. Despite the establishment of the urban health insurance system, for example, some 20 per cent of permanent city residents were still not covered by the scheme by 2003, according to official estimates.[33] And even among those who have done reasonably well, many surveys have revealed an overall loss of a sense of security, in a society where life has changed so fast. As a commentary in one official newspaper put it, 'there are simply too many variables that kill our feeling of happiness'.[34]

The scandal over Shanghai's pensions fund in 2006, and the revelation that large sums of money had been illegally invested in projects set up by people with personal ties to some of the city's top leaders, hardly added to public confidence. In an attempt to show that it was addressing public concern about the fairness, or other-wise, of China's new society, the government in 2005 launched its national propaganda campaign promoting the idea of 'a harmonious society'. It also began to talk more about protecting 'vulnerable members of society' and 'putting people first'.

121

Still, many believe that turning such slogans into reality will require further investment in welfare – particularly as the pressures of an ageing population make themselves felt. The government has taken steps such as setting up a national welfare lottery to raise money for social projects. And in an attempt to replace the lost sense of security and social cohesion lamented by many, the authorities in Shanghai, for example, recently announced a scheme to set up new 'public service' centres. These would include not only community health facilities, but also old people's homes and other community and leisure services. The residents' committees found in every urban district in China, which as the lowest level of government organisation for many decades focused on political propaganda and spying out suspect tendencies among local residents, have now also been asked to take on a greater welfare role, including helping the poor apply for benefits, providing health advice and exercise facilities for the elderly.

But in an increasingly fragmented society, carrying out such tasks is not always easy. The head of one neighbourhood committee in a new Shanghai housing estate, for example, talked proudly of the craft workshops, dancing sessions and traditional opera performances which she organised for elderly residents; sometimes the committee arranged for volunteer lawyers to hold advice sessions for the locals too. But with several thousand families living on the estate, some aspects of the committee's welfare function had become more difficult, she acknowledged. 'In the past, in the old neighbourhoods, we used to send our staff to visit families who we felt might be having problems,' she explained, 'but in these new housing complexes, it's rare for neighbours to communicate with each other much.' It meant, she said, that 'it's very difficult for us to know what problems the families are having unless they come to us themselves'.

In an attempt to stress how much they care about people's problems, China's leaders frequently appear on national television news, visiting needy families in towns and villages. This phenomenon reaches its high point at the lunar New Year, when the President and Prime Minister themselves appear bearing gifts for and offering reassuring words to surprised citizens around the country. It's an old symbolic ritual known as *song wennuan* – 'delivering warmth'.

Yet at this time of year many ordinary people are more focused on activities such as letting off firecrackers or fireworks outside their homes, a traditional way of appealing for good fortune in the year to come. Over the past decade, local governments in many cities have tried to ban these fireworks as dangerous, but in the end most have had to accept defeat. In Shanghai massive explosions resound through every lane and neighbourhood in the city each night for at least a week – and if anything the practice has become even more widespread in recent years. Some see it simply as an expression of exuberance, others as a way for people to forget the pressures of everyday life. But some believe it reflects a sense too that good luck is all the more necessary in today's society – and there's no doubt that the smaller and poorer the lane, the greater the intensity of the firecrackers seems to be. Perhaps it's no coincidence either that the whole spectacular cacophony reaches its crescendo on the eve of the fifth day of the first lunar month – the day traditionally reserved in China for welcoming the God of Wealth.

# 5

# A half-open media

The man sitting opposite me in the city-centre coffee shop seems on edge, his eyes darting around the room as we talk. When his mobile phone rings he jumps a little but doesn't answer it. His assistant will take messages for him, he says, and let him know if they are urgent. 'I'm trying to keep a low profile,' he explains, a little apologetically, 'it's a difficult time.' Eventually he reveals the reason for his anxiety. 'I've just written a story which has annoyed some powerful people,' he says, 'so I've got to be careful.' In some societies, his cloak-and-dagger manner might feel a little exaggerated – but in China, being an investigative journalist can be a stressful way of life. The man is a reporter with a well-known Chinese newspaper, and the story which has made him so nervous has just appeared on its front page. The result of months of research, it accuses a prominent Chinese company of financial malpractice. The company's bosses were furious when they found out, he says, and immediately contacted influential local government officials in their home region, in an attempt to prevent the paper going on sale. Fortunately, his editors stood by the story – but he's still worried about the potential long-term impact on his career.

I wasn't actually intending to talk to him about such issues – our meeting was planned some time ago to discuss a completely different subject – but it's impossible not to be caught up in the drama of his situation: not least because the idea of a Chinese journalist being in such a position is something which would have been hard to imagine only a few years before. The reporter is one of a new generation of Chinese journalists who, in their attempts to keep in step with the requirements of a fast-diversifying society, are prepared to take risks to investigate social issues and problems which they believe the people – and the government – ought to know about. But it's an occupation fraught with difficulties and obstacles, in a society where the role of the media in the communist era has traditionally been clear-cut: to act as a propaganda vehicle for the party and the state.

It's a role which dates back to the time of the revolution, when all existing newspapers were either closed down or taken over by the state, and all media came under the control of the party's propaganda department. A veteran journalist on one of China's main newspapers once described to me his work during the highly politicised decades of the 1960s and 1970s. One of his most nerve-racking responsibilities, he said, was to ensure that each piece of political propaganda was given the correct amount of prominence, and that stories about the country's leaders were put in the right position on the page, and accompanied by photographs of the appropriate size, to reflect each leader's relative seniority in the hierarchy. Any mistakes could be disastrous. (It's a tradition which, in a modest form, still continues to this day on national television news, where stories about the Communist Party Secretary General still come before reports on the activities of the Prime Minister or other lesser leaders.)

The first hints of change came in the late 1970s and early 1980s, after the end of the Cultural Revolution, when some of the country's leading journalists and intellectuals began to write again, after years of exile in the countryside and, in some cases, persecution and detention. A number of writers sought to describe and make sense of some of the things they had experienced, and a few began to follow up individual cases of abuse and corruption. The journalist Liu Binyan, for example, who had spent years doing manual work in north-east China, wrote a searing exposé of a tyrannical local Communist Party boss in the region, which was published in the usually arid pages of the *People's Daily*, the party's main official mouthpiece. Others followed his lead, and a whole new style of writing known as 'reportage literature' was born. Many of the stories focused on social problems and

125

corruption, though they were often semi-fictionalised in order to get past the censors.[1]

But for some in the party's leadership, even this was too much. Liu Binyan and other senior journalists who had pushed for greater openness were among the main victims of the political campaigns against 'spiritual pollution' and 'bourgeois liberalisation' of the 1980s. After the second of these campaigns, Liu Binyan effectively went into exile in the US, where he remained until his death in 2005. But by the late 1980s other Chinese journalists started to take up the cause. Newly established papers, particularly in some of the new Special Economic Zones in the south, experimented with a livelier style and greater coverage of entertainment and social issues. In the year preceding the Tiananmen protests of 1989, there were unprecedented debates on politics and philosophy in the Chinese media – some of the most outspoken in the pages of a Shanghai newspaper, the *World Economic Herald*. And journalists from Chinese newspapers and television were prominent among those carrying banners demanding greater freedom and openness on the streets of Beijing in spring 1989. Not surprisingly, many journalists were fired from their jobs during the conservative back-lash which followed the resulting crackdown, and liberal papers like the *World Economic Herald* were closed.

As a result, the Chinese media of the early 1990s was again dominated by political propaganda campaigns, the dull grey front pages of many newspapers echoing the turgid articles calling for ideological correctness which filled their inside pages. The liveliest content in those days was likely to be a campaign eulogising a newly nominated 'model worker', or reviving the memory of some old revolutionary hero. These were years when journalists kept their opinions to themselves, and writers 'submitted their best stories and articles to their desk drawers', as the saying went at the time.

And so the appearance of the Chinese media a decade and a half later can come as quite a surprise. News-stands on the pavements of China's big cities groan under the weight of newspapers with colourful front pages and eye-catching headlines, and glossy magazines of all kinds. Fashionable young presenters grin from television screens. Even the staid national television station now sets its news bulletins against a contemporary-looking backdrop of an open-plan newsroom, with banks of TV sets and people working in the background. It still broadcasts the official line, of course, but it has the air of an organisation struggling to keep up with a media world which is changing fast.

One factor in this transformation has been the increasing commercialisation of China's media – a process which, ironically, also dates back to those tense days of the early 1990s. And like so many of the country's reforms, it was down south, in Guangdong, that the experiment began.

Shang Jiu Lu – Upper Ninth Road – is the heart of old Guangzhou, a mile-long pedestrian strip of typical old south China-style shop-houses, recently spruced up and repainted, their colonnaded frontages now home to the brightly lit stores of fashionable clothing chains. On a Sunday afternoon, the street throngs with families and young people out for a stroll; shop assistants line the pavements chanting and clapping to attract their attention; the pumping pop music pouring out of the shops only adds to the hubbub. And clothes stores are not the only kind of business trying to lure new customers. In the middle of the street there's a line of stalls manned by young people in colourful T-shirts, who call out to the passers-by with special offers of free gifts and attractive discounts. They are the representatives of local media groups, doing their best to sign up new readers for subscriptions to their newspapers and magazines. 'We can deliver to your door, no extra charge,' an eager young woman tells me. 'You live in Shanghai? No problem, we can deliver there too,' she insists. 'Here, have a free copy. This is our hotline number if you need more information.'

In Guangzhou, media and marketing are closely linked. It was here, in the 1990s, that the idea of the media operating without direct government subsidy, and instead paying its own way through advertising revenue, was pioneered. The city was also one of the first in China to bring together its many separate newspapers to create three big media groups. The aim was to stimulate

127

competition, and increase efficiency – and revenue – so that they could invest more in technology and pay more into the coffers of the organisations which controlled them (which in Guangzhou included the Provincial Communist Party and the local branch of the Communist Youth League). Within a few years, the city's papers were battling it out for readers and advertising revenue, with the most successful generating tens of millions of pounds a year.[2]

It was a far cry from the traditional approach of the *People's Daily*, which has never advertised itself and is rarely even sold on newsstands, instead relying for customers on the government work units around the country which have always been required to subscribe to it. And when I went to visit Yang Xingfeng, the editor-in-chief of the *Southern Daily* group, one of Guangzhou's big three, in its concrete high-rise headquarters in 2002, he certainly seemed to talk the language of the new era. 'Papers are a product,' he said, 'so they must get closer to the market – we can't ignore income, a loss-making paper is no good!' Mr Yang, who was in his early fifties, admitted that it had taken a while to get used to this way of thinking. 'At the beginning we had no concept,' he said, 'we never thought that news was an industry too and you could run it like that.' He seemed happy about the situation now, however. 'We can run our advertising, distribution and management along the lines of the market economy,' he explained, 'so we can develop fast.' So fast in fact that his group now had eight newspapers, one magazine and its own publishing company, and was the main shareholder in a provincial news website.

Mr Yang was quick to stress that 'we still have editorial guidelines', but he acknowledged that the need to attract readers, and with them the advertisers who were now so important, had also contributed to a change in the style of the papers. 'In the past, I only considered the situation from my point of view,' he said. 'I had things I wanted to publicise, but I didn't consider whether or not you'd be interested in them. Now,' he went on, 'I must continue to promote the policy direction of the party and the state, that can't be changed – but at the same time I must also consider whether you want to read my reports.'

And the media in Guangzhou faces another kind of pressure too, as a visit to almost any bar or restaurant in the city makes clear. At lunchtime in the old Guangzhou Restaurant on Upper Ninth Road, for example, famous for its dim sum and roast duck, the television in the corner of the room blares out the latest news – from Hong Kong TV. Guangzhou's location, less than a hundred miles from the Hong Kong border, means it has always been within reach of the former British colony's television and radio broadcasts. Up to the 1970s, the Chinese government used to do all it could to stop people tuning into these, both by jamming the signals, and by giving harsh punishments to anyone caught listening to foreign radio stations. But in the 1980s these controls were relaxed, and people in Guangzhou and other nearby cities only had to set up a simple aerial to pick up Hong Kong broadcasts.

What they found if they did so was a very different style of media: with fast-paced, lively presentation, and colourful, sometimes sensational news reporting – to say nothing of an often rather different perspective on events in the Chinese mainland. For those born in the 1970s and 1980s, these have become part of life: as one young media student in Guangzhou puts it, 'Everyone watches Hong Kong channels, we grew up watching them – we'd turn to Hong Kong TV instead of our own stations.' In fact, he adds, 'if you weren't watching those programmes, people would think you were unfashionable and they wouldn't want to talk to you'. Living between two such different types of media can be a little confusing at first, he agrees, but he says you soon get used to it. 'It's like Chinese grammar and English grammar,' he explains, 'you just learn to adjust from one to the other.'

For Guangzhou's own newspapers and television stations, the growing popularity and influence of Hong Kong media also became impossible to ignore. At the *Southern Daily* group, Yang Xingfeng did his best to put a brave face on the situation. 'We couldn't stop it coming in,' he said. 'But we looked at it as a challenge, something which could force us to speed up our own reforms and give our readers better service.'

And so, during the 1990s, the style of the Guangzhou media began

129

to undergo a significant makeover. Newspapers actually started trying to make their readers feel included, focusing on issues which affected their daily lives, such as environmental pollution, traffic problems or dangerous building sites. They published surveys of people's opinions on local issues such as plans for new roads. They even introduced news hotlines, which members of the public could call if they had stories which they thought should be investigated. The *Southern Daily*, which Yang Xingfeng edited, was one of the first to do this, he said proudly. 'We published the reporters' phone numbers and pager numbers,' he explained, 'and said, if you have any tip-offs – for example if you see an accident or you see someone about to commit suicide by jumping off a tall building – then just call us and our reporters will rush to the scene to report it.' Now the paper's newsroom received a couple of hundred calls a day, he said – not just about suicidal citizens but also with reports of illegal construction or cinemas showing banned pornographic movies, even rumours of bombs. It was a big change from the old days, he added, when 'our reporters got most of their information from government departments. If they left the office, they didn't know what was happening!'

So successful was the hotline idea in building up public interest – and trust – that it has been widely copied around China; indeed, it can sometimes seem that, in an emergency, many citizens prefer to call the media rather than the police or government; one Guangzhou newspaper once published a front-page photo of a drug addict lying dead on a city street: it had been tipped off to the story, it said, by a call from a reader.

Of course there were still many issues which went beyond minor local problems and which newspapers found too sensitive to investigate. But as the 1990s went on, some within the Chinese media began seeking to push the limits. Another paper in the *Southern Daily* group, the *Southern Weekend*, led the way. It began life as an entertainment newspaper in the 1980s, but in the first half of the 1990s it was relaunched as perhaps China's first serious broadsheet-style paper. It provided thoughtful analysis of current social issues – homosexuality, prostitution, street children – many of which had previously been taboo. And it also published in-depth investigations into individual cases of corruption or abuses by local government officials around the country. It was a significant development, since local leaders tended to wield so much power over the media in their own areas that it would never dare to publish such critical articles. As Yang Xingfeng put it, 'If we find something we need to criticise, we do. The paper is influential now,' he added, 'so writers from all over the country will offer us stories. If we think something is representative, or has relevance for the country as a whole, then we'll publish it.'

The *Southern Weekend* sometimes ruffled feathers nationally too. In 2001 the Chinese police, after a much-publicised manhunt, arrested a man suspected of a series of bombings in the northern city of Shijiazhuang, which killed more than a hundred people. State television proudly announced his arrest and reported his confession. But the *Southern Weekend* took the unusual step of insisting that he should be presumed innocent until a verdict was announced, and that even if he had confessed, evidence was required to prove that his words were genuine.[3] It was typical of a paper which often seemed to be doing its best to put the government's slogans about promoting the rule of law to the test. And its cultural coverage could be bold too. In late 1997, the year that Deng Xiaoping died, the paper compiled a list of important people who had passed away that year: alongside Mr Deng, it included not only Princess Diana and Mother Teresa, but also the controversial beat poet Alan Ginsberg and the radical writer William S. Burroughs.[4]

Not surprisingly, the *Southern Weekend* quickly became the most talked-about paper in China. It was the first regional newspaper to win a national readership, and inspired many imitators. It certainly sometimes still published stories which echoed the government's official line, particularly when it came to issues of 'patriotism' or foreign policy – journalists said this was necessary to enable the paper to keep printing other types of stories. But the fact that it was challenging the official limits was proved by the fact that over the years several of its editors were suspended, moved to other jobs or sacked for publishing stories deemed too sensitive. These punishments would usually be followed by a period when the paper was a little less daring – but, for many years at least, it always seemed eventually to return to more critical reporting. According to some observers, the fact that such papers made so much money put pressure on the authorities to continue to allow them greater freedom – in order to gain the benefits of the revenues they generated.

And as the idea of commercially driven newspaper groups spread around the country, other innovations were introduced. The *Southern Daily* group, for example, set up a successful business newspaper aimed at China's growing commercial and financial communities; it acquired a sports paper from another publisher and rebranded it, helped by promotions such as its 'football babes', photos of scantily clad, football-scarf-wearing women, which it published in the run-up to the 2002 World Cup finals. And it also introduced a colourful, brash, tabloid-sized daily paper, the *Southern Metropolis News*. Yang Xingfeng described this as a 'city paper', dedicated to modern urban life. It still had to include the important political stories sent out to all China's media by the official Xinhua News Agency, but it did its best to keep these on the inside pages, and filled its covers with photographs and colourful headlines about corruption, lurid crimes and social problems too. Its popular entertainment section echoed the style of many Hong Kong papers, with stories about the private lives of top Asian film stars and pop singers, but also cast a sometimes critical eye over China's own entertainment scene.

The *Southern Metropolis News* quickly became a best-seller, not only in its home town of Guangzhou, but in other nearby cities too, causing so much concern among the publishers of papers in those towns that some were reported to have tried to ban it from being sold in their area. Its modern methods extended to its marketing team, which promised to be at your door within minutes if you phoned to take out a subscription. And most of the paper's journalists were young, with an international outlook – as demonstrated after my visit to the group's headquarters to talk to Yang Xingfeng. I was told that the staff of the *Southern Metropolis News* were too busy to meet me themselves – but that didn't stop the paper from publishing a colour photo of my interview with Mr Yang on its front page the next day with the headline 'The BBC pays attention to our paper!'[5] The implication was clear: interest from the foreign media was something to be proud of. It would have been hard to imagine a similar newspaper headline in Beijing, where official attitudes to large international media organisations were often tinged with suspicion.

Gradually the reforms introduced in the Guangzhou media were mimicked, to a greater or lesser degree, across China. By the start of the new century, most cities had a range of lively, small-format daily papers which combined a focus on local issues with sometimes sensational social stories and pages of colourful entertainment news. The investigative tradition of the *Southern Weekend* was echoed in the growth too of an in-depth serious media, with a number of new financial newspapers, and several national weekly and fortnightly news magazines which often took a relatively liberal – and critical – stance on social issues of all kinds.[6]

The transformation was encouraged by another development which was to have a profound impact on China's media: the growth of the Internet. In 1997, when I began working in Beijing, the country had barely a million registered Internet users. Few people, even in the cities, could afford to own a computer. Talk of the Internet posing a challenge to authoritarian governments worldwide seemed, in this particular case, far-fetched. But soon after I arrived in the country I met a journalist from the *People's Daily*, the Communist Party's official mouthpiece. 'Don't waste time reading the paper,' he said, 'look at the website.' That, he insisted, was where all the interesting stories were to be found. And it did soon become evident that the extra space provided by the Internet, and the relative lack of rules controlling it at the time, was allowing for the publication of stories which would never have made it into the pages of China's newspapers. Such stories were not necessarily politically daring, but they often provided fascinating insights into crimes, corruption and other strange goings-on in all corners of the vast nation.

133

The Internet also brought new media players: Sohu.com, established by Charles Zhang, a young techno-wizard who had returned to China from the US, started out as a search engine, but soon set up its own news channel, as did another new website, Sina.com. This had a more official background, but the style of writing, headlines and use of pictures on both these sites was far closer to the lively atmosphere of the media of Hong Kong or Taiwan than to the staid old mainland model. The flexibility of the Internet also undermined China's traditional censorship system, under which nothing sensitive would ever be published without approval from officials at several levels, and events such as disasters would often not be reported until long after they actually happened – if at all. As local newspapers and official news agency branches around the country began to set up their own websites and news channels, all seeking to compete with each other, there was now far more pressure to respond quickly to local events. It meant that news of earthquakes or accidents, even photographs of explosions on buses, could often be found on the Internet soon after they happened.[7] And the new websites quickly began to attract a loyal following, even among those who did not own a computer: by the late 1990s, Internet cafés were springing up in towns all around the country – the largest, in the university district of Beijing, had more than a thousand terminals. Some people simply used them to play computer games, but more and more people were surfing the Net: by the early years of the new century there were over a hundred million users – and all the surveys showed that the majority of them were people in their teens and twenties.

Soon China's official media organisations began trying to catch up, in order to gain a slice of this growing market. In 2001, for example, I met the editor of Eastday.com, a new site set up by one of Shanghai's main newspaper groups, at its headquarters in a shiny modern office tower. Xu Shiping, an energetic former sports journalist in his early forties, seemed enthusiastic about adopting a fresh approach. 'If Internet news is just the same as the traditional media, then to me it loses its fundamental meaning,' he said. 'Young people pay to get online, they spend time getting on your site – if

134

you just give them some kind of stern lecture they won't come back,' he explained. 'You need a relaxed atmosphere, so they'll feel some kind of connection.' It meant there were certain types of story he would not be highlighting, he said. 'Which city leader has held a meeting with whoever, and what they said, there's no way we're going to make that a headline. People can get that from the TV news in the evening and they're not interested in it anyway!'

In a country where photos of government leaders greeting distinguished visitors from every nation, large or small, had dominated front pages for decades, it was an almost radical comment. But according to Mr Xu, news on the Net had to be lively, faster – 'and bolder too'. 'Lots of media very rarely publish really striking social stories,' he said. 'Either they don't report them at all, or they give you very little information, or they actually cover up the details so you can't really work out what it means!' Now, he suggested, the spread of technology meant people were less easily duped. 'If you don't tell them, they're going to find out from somewhere else; you can't treat the readers the same as in the past – you have to move with the times.' He took me for a walk around the website's open-plan office, with its view across the highways and high-rises of the city centre. Teams of young staff huddled over computers, editing content for the site's various channels: not just headline news but sport, entertainment, a children's channel, online dating. A stake in the site was held by a state-owned advertising company, it turned out, no doubt adding to the pressure to attract these young consumers. Mr Xu picked up some local papers from a desk. 'If you look at these now, they look closer to websites,' he said excitedly, pointing to the colourful, menu-style lists of headlines on the front pages, designed to draw readers to the inside sections. 'And I think if there are changes in form, there will also be changes in concept. The Internet is bringing challenges: how to run the media, how it responds. It may all lead to enormous change.'

It's not always easy to see the changes in the Chinese media in quite such spectacular terms. The official media remains firmly under the control of the Communist Party, and newsrooms still receive directives from 'above' giving them guidance on the coverage of sensitive issues, or telling them not to report particular stories. In 2005, Zhao Ziyang, the Communist Party's reformist Secretary General of the late 1980s, who was removed from office for showing too much sympathy to the student protestors in Tiananmen Square in 1989, died in Beijing. State television made no reference at all to his passing, while the next day's newspapers carried only a terse two-line report from the official news agency. Mr Zhao, who had been under house arrest for the previous fifteen years, remained a non-person, even in death. A less predictable case came in 2000, when the writer Gao Xingjian won the Nobel Prize for Literature. Initially Chinese television and websites reported the news – not surprisingly, since the dream of a Chinese author winning the award had been a national obsession among intellectuals since the 1980s. Yet within a few hours the government ordered the media to stop covering the story. Editors were informed that Mr Gao, who had found fame as a playwright in China in the 1980s before moving to France, was not really a Chinese writer at all, since he now held a French passport. The real reason, however, was thought to be the fact that the authorities did not like his politics – and so this brief outburst of national pride came to an abrupt end.

Such control means the media can of course be mobilised to promote official policy at important moments. In 1999, for example, the Chinese government decided to ban Falun Gong – the Buddhist-inspired exercise and meditation practice, established by a former low-ranking civil servant, which had attracted many millions of followers around the country, mainly older people seeking to improve their health. The round-ups of leading practitioners which followed were accompanied by a propaganda campaign denouncing the movement which lasted for many months, and was of a shrillness and vitriol not seen in the Chinese media since 1989. In cases like this, editors were simply ordered to toe the line. At other times, such as the bombing of the Chinese embassy in Belgrade by NATO in 1999, the wave of patriotic outrage which swept through the media was undoubtedly more spontaneous – but the authorities continued to channel this in a particular direction, instructing editors to revive phrases such as 'US and British imperialism' which had not been heard for many years. The tension was fuelled by the fact that in the preceding months, the Chinese media had already been ordered to depict the NATO campaign against the Federal Republic of Yugoslavia over the Kosovo issue as the illegal bullying of an innocent sovereign nation by the arrogant governments in Washington and London. (The continuing ability of the Chinese media to edit events to fit the official line had been highlighted a couple of years previously, when the then President of Yugoslavia, Slobodan Milosevic, paid an official visit to Beijing. As was traditional with visiting dignitaries, state television broadcast a five-minute biography of Mr Milosevic, which listed his career in some detail but made no reference at all to the years 1991 to 1995, the period of the Balkan War.)

On many social and domestic issues, however, there's no doubt that the Chinese media has generally become more open in its coverage – within limits of course. No editor would dare to criticise a central government leader, for example, but they might be willing to expose corruption or mismanagement involving officials at the local level. This was the case in the central province of Henan, where officials for years covered up a scandal involving the illegal collection and selling of blood from local farmers, leading to a devastating outbreak of HIV in villages in the area. The story eventually emerged in the Chinese media, as did revelations about cover-ups of the scale of the SARS epidemic in 2003. On many such occasions, the authorities intervened after the initial reports were published, and ordered other media to stop discussing these subjects. But by then the stories had been followed up by journalists from Hong Kong, Taiwan, and abroad, and had thus effectively entered the public domain, making them harder to deny and conceal in the future.

And on less sensitive subjects, relatively outspoken debate is often possible. Sport, for example, seems to be an area where the media is free to be quite critical. The national football team, and its success – or lack thereof – has become the subject of an ongoing and sometimes angry discussion. In 2006, after China's failure to capitalise on its first appearance in the World Cup Finals in 2002 by qualifying for the finals in Germany, the Chinese football authorities came in for much criticism for selecting a coach, the former Dutch international Arie Haan, who had not previously worked as a national team manager. In the words of one official report, 'The strategists made mistake after mistake – and the team has paid a high price for this "experiment".' The situation was, it said, 'embarrassing'.[8] Corruption in the Chinese professional football league, and a number of scandals involving referees, have also provided the nation's press with plenty of colourful material over the years. By 2005, even the once revered Chinese National Games – a mini-Olympics involving sporting teams from each province and from organisations such as the army too – had become the butt of scathing criticism. The official *China Daily* newspaper dismissed the contest, dogged by failed drug tests, controversies about refereeing decisions and allegations of match-fixing, as 'farcical'. It suggested that 'while Chinese society moves away from the old planned system, the sports sector is still managed largely in outdated ways' and said the games had left fans feeling 'cheated and outraged'.[9]

Improved communications and the growth of well-known media groups in different parts of the country have also contributed to greater openness, by making it harder for local authorities to impose news blackouts on awkward stories. Journalists who uncover a local scandal or abuse and can't get their reports published in the local press now have the possibility of sending the story to a paper in Guangzhou or a website in Beijing or Shanghai. It was a Shanghai paper, for example, which first published information about a major mining disaster more than a thousand miles away in south-west China in 2001, after local officials tried to cover it up.[10] At the same time, cities such as Shanghai still retain close control over coverage of their own affairs. When the head of the city's pension fund was arrested in 2006, the Shanghai media gave the story much less coverage than media from other parts of the country – until the detention of the city's Communist Party Secretary as well made the whole thing harder to keep quiet.

The nervous investigative journalist I met was a reminder, though, of the potential risks involved in bolder reporting. Journalists who offend local leaders can find themselves in trouble. A reporter in the northern province of Shanxi, Gao Qinrong, uncovered a case of corruption involving officials in the region in 2001, which attracted national media attention. But while the officials involved in the case were given limited disciplinary reprimands, Mr Gao soon found himself arrested, accused of bribery and using prostitutes, and given a twelve-year jail sentence at a closed session in the local court. The *Southern Weekend* newspaper in Guangzhou described the evidence against him as dubious and unsatisfactory.[11]

And in a society where money increasingly equals power, journalists following up stories of corruption may find themselves treading on the toes not only of unscrupulous local officials, but of powerful local business interests too. Two reporters who wrote critical reports about a company in Shenzhen in 2006 suddenly found their assets frozen by a local court, after the company filed a suit against them. It was later reported that a judge at the court had taken bribes to take action against the journalists.[12] And sometimes reporters find themselves on the receiving end of physical violence. Journalists covering accidents or disasters have been beaten up by local police or security guards – as local governments try to prevent bad news about their areas from being published. And in 2005, the editor of one local paper in Jiangsu province was reported to have been attacked in his office by members of the local police force – after publishing an article accusing them of extorting illegal fees from people applying for driving licences. The editor suffered liver damage and later died in hospital.[13]

Political risks also remain, of course. In the old days, the limits as to what Chinese journalists could report were clear-cut. But the partial opening of the media has left the lines blurred; reporters are now more likely to have to test the limits for themselves – and in some cases they discover that they have gone too far. One example of this came at the *Southern Metropolis News* in Guangzhou – the popular tabloid of which the *Southern Daily* group's editor-in-chief

Yang Xingfeng had spoken so proudly in 2002. The following year the paper scored what many saw as a major victory for the Chinese press in its attempts to establish its credentials as a social watchdog. Reporters at the paper were contacted by the family of Sun Zhigang, a young graphic designer from Hubei province, who had been detained by police in Guangzhou for not carrying the right identity papers. His employer and others subsequently brought the correct documents to the police station, but were ignored; Sun Zhigang was sent to a detention centre where, at the instigation of one of the supervisors, other inmates beat him to death. The police insisted he had died of natural causes, but an independent autopsy carried out for the family confirmed that his death was the result of his injuries. The *Southern Metropolis News* ran the story, though its editors knew this would infuriate the police. The report quickly spread around the country, aided by the Internet, and eventually led to the jailing (in one case for life) of those responsible for Mr Sun's arrest and death. And after a campaign led by prominent academics, it also resulted in a change in China's law, reducing the decades-old powers of the police to detain people simply because they were not carrying the right documents.[14]

The *Southern Metropolis News* won widespread praise for its actions. And it continued to report sensitive stories: later the same year it revealed the discovery of a new case of the SARS virus, before it had been officially announced by the government. But its activities had clearly upset the authorities: investigators descended on its offices and its general manager, Yu Huafeng, was accused of embezzling 100,000 yuan (around £7,000), and of making an illegal payment to a former colleague. Staff at the paper said this was a legitimate bonus, but the two men were arrested and jailed for twelve and eleven years (though their sentences were later cut, and they were released in early 2008 and 2007 respectively). The paper's young deputy editor, Cheng Yizhong, was also detained on bribery charges; eventually, after six months, he was released, but he lost his job and was expelled from the Communist Party. Many of the paper's staff left in protest. In 2005 Mr Cheng was awarded a UNESCO World Press Freedom Prize. He was not permitted to leave the country to attend the ceremony, but posted a defiant statement on the Internet, encouraging journalists to keep telling the truth.[15]

There is undoubtedly an ongoing, though usually unspoken, struggle in China between those who wish to promote greater press freedom and the forces of the status quo. In recent years, there have been clear signs of official alarm at the increasingly outspoken stance of some of the country's most popular newspapers. In 2005 the *Southern Metropolis News* was again in trouble, after reporting on a rebellion by villagers in Guangdong against their local leaders. Its recently established Beijing sister paper, the *Beijing News*, reported on a case where hired thugs attacked farmers protesting against the construction of a power plant, and killed six people. Local officials were eventually punished – but the paper's editor was also sacked later the same year.[16] It was almost as though, for every small victory for press freedom, a price had to be paid – a reminder to journalists that they did not have a completely free hand.

And such warnings have become sharper and more frequent through the middle years of this decade. In 2005, the editor of a popular weekly supplement to a national paper under the auspices of the Communist Youth League was also replaced, apparently because of articles challenging official interpretations of Chinese history and the status of Taiwan. Zhao Yan, a Chinese journalist working as a researcher for the *New York Times* in Beijing was arrested – initially, it was thought, on subversion charges, though he was eventually jailed for three years on a lesser charge of bribery. And the following year Ching Cheong, a Hong Kong journalist with Singapore's *Straits Times*, was jailed on charges of spying for Taiwan.[17] These punishments were interpreted as a warning to those who work with the foreign media, and to Hong Kong journalists, who do not have the protection of a foreign passport. Non-Chinese journalists have generally been less at risk than local reporters: surveillance of their activities and in a few cases expulsion from the country are usually the worst they face – but the increasing numbers of locals who work for them, or provide them with sensitive information, are more easily punished.

Official concern that the media was becoming unruly was emphasised in 2006 by proposals, later watered down, for fines of up to a hundred thousand yuan for any media organisation which reported 'sudden events' without first getting permission. This seemed designed to rein in the new, more reactive media culture which had evolved following the spread of the Internet. And the Internet's rapid growth was also provoking anxiety. It was bringing unprecedented ease of communication between people in all corners of this vast country, with online communities of all kinds, catering for everyone from pop fans to pet lovers, poets to pregnant women, and allowing ordinary people to express views and spread information. When Qiu Qingfeng, a female student at Peking University, was raped and murdered in 2000, for example, the university authorities tried to hush the case up – but students quickly posted the information on their Internet bulletin board. The authorities closed this down, prompting days of protest marches by the students until, eventually, the officials relented and held a memorial for the young woman.[18]

Even bulletin boards set up by the official media, which were usually closely monitored, sometimes allowed unwanted opinions to see the light of day. The official *People's Daily* newspaper group, for example, joined the Internet boom with a bulletin board – and later a blog – known as the Strong Country Forum, focusing on China's international relations and national security. It was designed to provide a platform for expressions of patriotism and denunciations of the Japanese or Taiwanese or American govern-ments, or whoever else the Chinese authorities happened to be annoyed with at the time. But sometimes the postings veered into criticism of China's own government itself, for being too weak in its foreign policy; occasionally there was dissent from a more liberal perspective too. Such remarks were quickly deleted by the site's 'webmasters' – but usually not before they had been read by at least a few people, who sometimes posted their own messages com-plaining about their deletion.

And so the Internet began to attract ever closer official scrutiny. In 2000 the government issued rules aimed at controlling news websites: these would now require a special licence from the government, would not be allowed to publish news from foreign sources – as some had done – and would either have to appoint state-approved editors or simply republish stories from official media. The authorities also sent other warnings: in 1998 they jailed a Shanghai man whom they accused of providing thousands of email addresses to dissident groups overseas. And scrutiny of the country's ever-growing millions of Internet users was increased too. Internet cafés were ordered to apply for licences and anyone using their terminals was now required to register with their identity card before going online – making it harder to use the Net anonymously. The authorities had some other weapons in their armoury too . . .

In a quiet Shanghai side street, near the city's old Jesuit cathedral, a young man emerged from an unassuming office building and ushered me inside. Friendly and softly spoken, he led me upstairs and into a small office where a number of staff sat at their computers. Everyone was rather busy at the moment, he explained a little apologetically. He had only recently returned to China after studying abroad, but he was finding plenty of demand for the services of the new business which he had set up with a friend. Their focus was Internet security – mainly helping big companies to protect themselves from hackers and information theft. But now they had a new role too. The Chinese government had recently decided that all Internet cafés would have to install software linking them to local police stations – enabling the police to keep tabs on the websites people were visiting, and the messages they sent. His company had won one of the contracts to design this software.

Of course the government could simply block access to specific websites, the young man acknowledged, since it controlled the servers which people used to get online. But there were so many of these sites, he said, and new ones were appearing every day. The software his firm was writing would scan the pages being viewed on each computer in every Internet café for keywords programmed in by the authorities. If it found them it would set alarm bells ringing at the local police station – almost literally in fact. 'Beep beep beep,' said the young man, explaining the sound it would make. 'It's like a trigger,' he said. 'If you breach the database or keyword, a record will be sent to the police, showing them which computer in which café is on which website.'

Part of the aim, he suggested, was to block access to pornography – something which was reportedly causing considerable concern among the parents of young Internet users. But the software could of course also be set to search for any other material which the government considered threatening, political content included. It was, the young man said with a shy smile, a situation 'rather unique to China'. But with such software due to be installed in tens of thousands of Internet cafés around the country, it was clearly also an advantageous sector of the economy to be in. 'It's given us a very good commercial opportunity,' he agreed, before seeing me off with a friendly wave.

The new software was part of a growing operation by the authorities to control the Internet. In the years since its introduction in 2001 there have been reports of more and more people joining the ranks of the country's 'cyber-police', not just supervising Internet cafés, but monitoring online discussions, in some cases joining in the debates with carefully timed expressions of patriotism too.[19] And as the big international Internet companies have begun to move into the Chinese market, the government has increased the pressure to ensure that they play by its rules. Companies which want to operate with a Chinese-registered domain name – seen by many as a way of attracting more local users – have been required to sign up to the authorities' restrictions on providing news content, and to monitor discussions on their bulletin boards. (Websites, it was announced, would be held responsible for the expression of opinions the government did not like – thus increasing the pressure on them to carry out their own censorship.) In one notorious case, Shi Tao, a journalist who posted a list of subjects which the media was forbidden to cover on the internet, was jailed for ten years after Yahoo! China provided information about his identity to the authorities. Yahoo! was later sued in the US by relatives of Mr Shi and another jailed dissident, and eventually agreed to an out-of-court settlement

Restrictions have also been imposed on search engines like Google, meaning the company's Chinese site, Google.com.cn, filters out search results from banned sites. Yet at the same time, its international site, which does not have the same restrictions in place, can still be accessed from China. It's an example of what many experts describe as the Chinese government's targeted approach to controlling the Net: the authorities focus their efforts mainly on limiting access to information which is easily available and in the Chinese language, and pay less attention to foreign sites in other languages. The theory seems to be that the relatively small number of Chinese citizens who speak fluent English will be able to get access to information from other sources anyway.[21] Thus over recent years the authorities have removed the blocks on access to many foreign media websites – but have retained restrictions on those, like the news pages of the BBC website, which include links to news stories in Chinese.

Some people are of course expert enough to get round the restrictions, but the government's strategy appears to be to concentrate on making it sufficiently difficult for the average user to access such information; at the same time, it seeks to offer enough lively-looking sources of information of its own to dissuade people from taking the trouble to seek out foreign news sources. This is one reason for the colourful appearance – and huge number of stories – of the average Chinese news website. As one Internet specialist put it, the government knows it can't control everything, but it wants to limit what's easily available, provide alternatives which will satisfy most people, and occasionally take a tough line against individuals it sees as particularly threatening, as a warning to others (international media groups estimate that at least sixty people were jailed for Internet-related offences by 2005).[22]

Yet for all the restrictions, many of those involved in the growth of the Chinese Internet still insist that it is bringing significant change to the nation. Fang Xingdong is one of the believers. A gangly former science student with a friendly manner, he talks of the Net with the passionate intensity of one who has followed its development closely since the early days, in the mid-1990s. As one of China's first commentators on the Internet, Mr Fang caused a stir with an article criticising Microsoft's domination of the Net in the country. When he found that this had been deleted from various websites, he decided it was time to set up his own space so that he could express his views – and in 2003 he founded China's first website dedicated to blogging, to allow others to publish their thoughts too. When we met in 2005, the site, Bokee.com, was signing up 50,000 new users a day, according to Mr Fang. By late 2007 there were estimated to be over 47 million bloggers in China; soon it became a rarity to meet a university student who did not have a blog.

Mr Fang was the first to admit that, in practice, much of the content of these blogs was 'pretty boring actually', made up of the trivia of people's daily lives. But some people did use their own patch of cyberspace to write about social issues. Mr Fang also encouraged well-known journalists to publish their articles on blogs on his site – some used the opportunity to post stories that they were unable to publish in the conventional media. Inevitably, one or two such blogs were eventually closed by the authorities for going too far, but others continued. And Mr Fang himself remained convinced that there was 'far more space' for people to express themselves than in the days when there was no alternative to the traditional press. 'In terms of bringing social change in China over the past decade, I think nothing can compare to the Internet,' he insisted eagerly. 'In allowing interpersonal communication and the flow of information, in bringing more outside ideas into our society, I think it's led to a fundamental change.'

He acknowledged that his site had to filter out any particularly outspoken attacks on the government – but claimed that these are rare anyway. 'The things that you really need to control are very few,' he suggested. Perhaps, I said, this is in itself a sign that the authorities have cowed people into self-censorship. Well, said Mr Fang, there's plenty of critical comment on other subjects. A cursory search of his website suggested there was some truth in this – and in fact

Mr Fang argued that it was in the government's interests to permit this. 'During the process of moving to a market economy, there are a lot of social problems,' he said, 'and I think that if you can express your views or your anger through blogging, it will relieve a lot of the tensions in society, people's psychological tension in particular.'

This may be a slightly optimistic way of looking at the situation, not least given Mr Fang's argument that such postings are unlikely to cause much trouble because only a couple of thousand people would see them – when in fact the ability of obscure postings to spread rapidly to millions of users around the country seems to have become one of the features of the Chinese Internet. In late 2005 for example, Hu Ge, a young advertising designer in Shanghai, emailed a few friends a video he had made, satirising the film *The Promise* by the director Chen Kaige. Within days it had become one of the most talked-about topics on the Internet around China, and Hu Ge soon found himself the object of mass public admiration and endless media articles – to say nothing of the threat, later retracted, of a lawsuit from Mr Chen himself. And official nervousness about this fast-growing realm of self-expression was made clear by the announcement, in 2006, that all China's bloggers would have to register with their real names at the sites which hosted their blogs, enabling the authorities to trace them more easily if they wished.[23] Tighter controls on websites which allowed users to post video content were also announced in early 2008.

Still, many observers share Mr Fang's view that, in the age of the Internet, the government will have little choice but to accept a wider range of different voices, at least up to a point. And the authorities have proved themselves quite capable of making use of greater openness when it serves their own ends. Down south in Guangdong, for example, state-run television stations have, in recent years, actually started to rebroadcast Hong Kong television channels, watched unofficially by many via their TV aerials in the past, on their own local cable networks. They didn't bother to sign contracts with the Hong Kong companies, but simply picked up the signal and routed it through their own networks. In the process they took the opportunity to cut out the commercial breaks from the Hong Kong broadcasts and resell the advertising space to local companies. It's a lucrative business, since the Hong Kong channels remain popular. And the arrangement has another advantage for the authorities: if the programmes touch on any particularly sensitive subjects, they can simply cut the signal. I first realised this while watching Hong Kong television in a Guangzhou hotel: I was surprised when the newsreader suddenly vanished mid-way through a bulletin, and was replaced by a photograph of an attractive sunset, with an accompaniment of gentle piano music. Three minutes later, the newsreader reappeared, still reading the news – and I realised that he had been halfway through the introduction to a story about the banned Falun Gong movement when he was cut off.

In a sense, this seems to sum up China's media policy. On the one hand, showing Hong Kong television channels keeps many viewers happy; it might give them some information they would not otherwise have received, but the authorities can black out anything they are particularly worried about – and they can make money too. Of course people can still rig up their own aerials and pick up the uncensored signals direct from Hong Kong if they want, but the assumption is that most people living in new apartment blocks, where almost all television is delivered by cable, will be too lazy to do this. And it's an approach which seems to have worked, at least up to a point. 'When they first saw this kind of blocking, people got really frustrated,' says one Guangzhou resident. 'But as it went on, they got used to living with it – and I think they don't really care too much because they get so much information every day.'

The result is that many in China would now say they have relatively free access to information – yet the authorities have been able to control, up to a point, what people know about certain key issues. Few in China, for example, would recognise the image, so well known around the world, of the man standing in front of a tank close to Tiananmen Square on the day after the crackdown of June 1989 – it has quite simply never been shown by any Chinese media outlet. And while a few foreign TV companies have been licensed to broadcast into Guangdong in recent years, they have only been allowed to show approved entertainment programmes, and have so far not been permitted to move further into the country. Even Phoenix television, a joint venture between Rupert Murdoch's News Corporation and mainland Chinese partners, set up in Hong Kong in the 1990s, and whose programmes – a blend of slick presentation and a news agenda which does not diverge too far from that of China's own official media – have been targeted largely at the Chinese market, has never been formally approved by the government, though it has tolerated it being shown by some local cable operators.

Still, control these days is far from watertight. Reception of foreign satellite television, for instance, is in theory only permitted in big hotels and luxury residential complexes inhabited by foreigners. But in a number of cities it's common to see satellite dishes on ordinary people's balconies; in Shanghai, for example, Taiwanese television is widely available to those with the money and the interest to watch it. In rural areas, meanwhile, many farmers simply put dishes on their roofs and see what they can pick up – I once visited a village in central Jiangxi province where the locals were clustered around a TV set showing Indian pop music videos. And on the south-east coast, in Fujian province, many people can easily receive broadcasts from Taiwan – since the nearest Taiwanese-controlled islands are just a few miles across the sea.

Increased public awareness of the international media and its methods does seem to have added to pressure on China's domestic broadcasters to move with the times. China Central Television, the powerful national TV company, was widely criticised for its slow response to the events of 11 September 2001. Switching on CCTV, as it's known, some forty minutes after the first plane hit the World Trade Center, I found it was still showing normal programming. When the scheduled news bulletin did begin a short while later, it devoted the first few minutes to reports of meetings between top Chinese officials and various visiting dignitaries; only after this did it make a brief reference to the events in New York. Channels like Phoenix, meanwhile, immediately switched to rolling news coverage, and Chinese websites responded far more rapidly too. It was seen as a wake-up call for CCTV, one of the most tightly controlled media organisations in the country – and led, eventually, to the modernisation of the appearance of its news programmes, with tentative steps to introduce more live reports – something previously seen as dangerously unpredictable by the authorities.

CCTV is still capable of producing out-and-out propaganda, of course: remarks by senior government leaders are rarely introduced as anything less than 'an important speech'. And the openings of Communist Party congresses, or announcements of new ideological theories or economic plans, are routinely accompanied by scenes of 'ordinary' people in all corners of the country – from nomads on the Inner Mongolian grasslands to workers on oil rigs at sea – expressing their heartfelt support and admiration, often in uncannily similar forms of words.

CCTV's traditional monopoly of national television in China, and of the advertising revenue which goes with this, has made it immensely wealthy in recent years. But growing commercialisation may yet threaten its absolute dominance. Since the late 1990s, the government has allowed local TV stations from each of China's provinces and regions to broadcast one channel of their own across the country via satellite. These local channels initially made little impact – but in recent years a few have begun to shake up China's television world. The satellite channel from Hunan province in the south, for example, has broken many taboos with frank chat shows on subjects such as homosexuality, and has lured viewers with fashionable soap operas, many from Taiwan or South Korea. In 2005 it proved that a local channel could win both a significant share of the national ratings, and large amounts of advertising income too, with *Supergirls*, a *Pop Idol*-style singing contest which became the talk of China. In Shanghai, meanwhile, various local TV stations were merged into a single group in 2001, significantly boosting their financial strength; the company now operates one of China's most modern-looking national satellite channels, Dragon TV, along with stylish music and fashion stations, a thoughtful documentary strand, and a business news channel in cooperation with the US company CNBC.[24] Most of these are of course currently only available in Shanghai, but the group seems to be positioning itself to exert a greater national influence if the restrictions on nationwide

150

broadcasting are ever relaxed. China's rush to embrace new technology may also undermine CCTV's monopoly: regional TV companies have already been given greater opportunities to compete for contracts to provide digital television channels around the country, and to operate IPTV (Internet protocol television) and mobile phone programming as well.

All of this means that the Chinese media in the first decade of the twenty-first century is a sometimes bizarre combination of the modern, the intelligent, occasionally even the controversial – and the highly conservative too. Surfing the fifty-plus television channels which are available to the average viewer can be a surreal experience. You can flip from a patriotic propaganda gala in CCTV's daily viewing slot dedicated to the military – with young women in short skirts gyrating onstage before an audience of politely applauding soldiers – to a hard-hitting investigation of the abduction of children in the countryside, or a thoughtful documentary on Shanghai television about people whose homes are to be demolished for urban reconstruction – and then back to the city's lifestyle channel's fashion makeover show, where a breathlessly trendy presenter in a puffa jacket with a woolly hat pulled down over his ears encourages nervous-looking young men to try putting a miniskirt over their jeans for a more up-to-the-minute look. On the country's news-stands, almost any newspaper features at least a few eye-opening stories about social issues, while the popular daily, the *Global Times*, focuses on international news with a strongly nationalistic line on foreign policy. Next to it you might well find one of a new wave of glossy tabloid-style celebrity magazines, featuring salacious headlines and intrusive paparazzi-style shots of Hong Kong pop stars changing out of their bikinis or caught crouching down to reveal their thongs, along with speculative articles on their love lives.[25]

Some are alarmed at this latter phenomenon and the tendencies it reflects. 'It's all about the commercial pressure for competition,' says one Chinese media executive. 'The unique thing about China's media,' he adds, 'is that ideological and political things are very tightly controlled – but this is actually quite a limited area. There are just a few things you can't discuss, but other things are very open.' As a result, he says, 'in my opinion some of the things in the media now have real problems, particularly in terms of their moral judgements, but nobody cares about that!' It is, he suggests, the result of China's media embracing what he sees as the American model, in which television stations, like newspapers, rely on increasing sales and attracting advertising in order to survive, rather than following the public service model of some European countries. 'It's a very strange phenomenon,' he says. 'For a country like China to want to do things which are both so political and so commercial is contradictory – that's why you have these problems.'

Others have highlighted the existence of a bribery culture, in which some companies offer gifts of money to journalists who come to their press conferences. Still, the media environment in China is undoubtedly changing. A popular Chinese television drama series in 2006, for example, featured a fashionable young actor in the role of a fearless crusading journalist on a local newspaper, whose determination to uncover the truth in a case of wrongful imprisonment eventually led to the downfall of the powerful and corrupt deputy mayor of the city.[26] It was a reflection of a growing public perception that the media should be a more independent voice – and a reminder too of the increasing role in the media of a new young generation. 'I went with a delegation of Chinese journalists to France,' says one young reporter, 'and the French media people, who were all middle-aged, were shocked to find that we were all only in our twenties!' And with more and more young journalists getting a chance to study and work abroad, the push for a more open media seems likely to continue. This impulse will of course continue to find itself at odds with the government's desire to control such development; but it's a balancing act which is likely to become an increasingly complex one for the authorities.

# 6

## The 'me' generation

Outside there were crowds in the street and the sunshine was bright and sharp, as befitting a May Day holiday afternoon in Shanghai. But as I made my way down the long corridor into the recesses of the upper floor of the shopping centre, the light grew fainter and fainter, the people fewer and fewer. By the time I reached the entrance to the Starlight nightclub there seemed to be no one else around. A security guard appeared from the shadows, checked my name on a list, and waved me inside. As the doors closed behind me, the sense of dislocation from the real world became even stronger.

A shrill screaming filled my ears. In the semi-darkness, I could faintly make out a crowd of people, pushing and jostling, apparently trying to surge towards a stage in the centre of the room. On the stage a young woman, illuminated by a spotlight, raised her hands above her head and began to clap rhythmically. A chant rose from the crowd, which judging from the sound seemed to be made up mainly of teenage girls. It was in a language I couldn't recognise, but as the voices reached a crescendo, I was able to pick out what sounded like three letters, repeated again and again: 'NRG, NRG, NRG.'

Eventually the chanting faded, and a girl in the crowd turned round. 'It's so emotional,' she shouted. 'I fell in love with it the first time I heard it.' Her friend nodded. 'It really moves you,' she yelled; 'it's so different, it gave me a real shock when I first heard it.' At this moment, a group of young men with spiky yellow hair bounded on-stage and launched into an energetic, tightly synchronised dance routine, to the accompaniment of a blaring electronic beat. The crowd began to cheer and wail. For many of them it was the nearest they would get to seeing their idols in the flesh. The South Korean pop band N.R.G. were not able to come here today themselves, the MC had announced apologetically, but this new Chinese boy band would mime and dance to South Korean sounds. For most of the audience, members of an online club for fans of Korean pop, it seemed to be good enough.

'Korean music has a lot of soul, we feel it's really close to us,' said one of the girls, her voice quavering with excitement. 'Most Chinese music is just love songs, but in Korea they have all different kinds of styles,' she explained, 'it's really inspiring. They even have music criticising the government!' Her friend waved a leg in the air. 'Korean style is the best,' she shouted, pointing to her baggy jeans, part of the uniform of the Korean music fan. 'These jeans are very big,' she said; 'they're very "hip hop", very "in"!' Her friends all laughed as she used these English words.

Another girl, slightly older-looking, emerged from the swaying crowd. 'I've seen the real N.R.G., and they're better than these guys,' she said, pointing dismissively at the boys onstage. 'N.R.G. came here once, and we talked to them,' she went on, 'they were great, they didn't act like big stars.' Today she had come because she was planning to set up her own band. 'I like to dance,' she said, 'and I can learn a lot from the Korean bands.'

Their favourites, they all agreed, were N.R.G. and H.O.T., the first rawer and more radical, the second slicker and perhaps a little cuter. 'We all like male singers,' said the older girl. In fact, she added, she wasn't just a fan of Korean pop culture, unlike most of the audience – it was Japanese bands she liked best. 'Japanese and Korean music are similar,' she said, 'but the Koreans are really just copying, the Japanese are more alternative.' The bright lights illuminating the stage flickered across the audience, picking out her pastel eye make-up and her outfit of miniskirt and leg-warmers. It was a style perfected by millions of Japanese teenagers. 'I got the idea from the Internet,' she said. 'I like their fashion, their make-up, it's really avant-garde.' She was seventeen, she said, and went by the name of Kira. 'Sounds Japanese, right?' she added, proudly.

I asked how it felt to be a fan of things Japanese in a nation where there was still so much bitterness towards Japan for its invasion of

China in the 1930s. 'Some of the older generation might not like it, because of some previous historical reasons,' said one of the girls. 'My parents don't mind, but my grandfather's generation can't really accept these things.' For her and for her friends, though, it all seemed perfectly normal. 'If you like Japanese pop bands, it's not because they're Japanese,' said one of the others, 'it's because you like their music. China doesn't have many of these kind of bands – if it did we'd like them too.'

The older girl took out a notebook and asked me to write down my name. She was thinking of becoming a DJ when she left school, she said, though she didn't want to be too famous. 'If you're in the public eye you don't have any privacy these days,' she said, with a worried look. She took the book back and closed it, revealing a picture of a Taiwanese pop star pasted on the cover. '*Arigato*,' she said, thanking me in Japanese, as she turned to leave.

It was not always quite like this. While studying in the central city of Xian in 1986, I was invited, for reasons which still remain obscure, to give a talk to the students of the North-Western University on the development of western popular music. The lecture theatre that Friday evening was packed with young people dressed in their smartest brown flared trousers and baggy green Mao jackets, wrapped up in several layers of home-knitted jumpers against the winter cold. Equipped with a cassette recorder, some home-made tapes and a translator, we began with the birth of the blues, jazz and rock 'n' roll, before moving, via Elvis and Bob Dylan, to the Beatles and the Rolling Stones and on to Motown, soul and disco. The audience smiled slightly awkwardly, shifted a little in their seats, betraying not a flicker of recognition. Psychedelia, punk, new wave, none of it elicited the slightest reaction. It was only when we reached reggae, and an early version of 'Rivers of Babylon', culled from an ancient compilation tape, that the students were suddenly transformed, swaying in their seats, clapping along, grinning with excitement. In the entire history of western popular music of the previous half-century, it seemed, the only thing they had heard of was a tune made popular around the world by the 1970s German disco band Boney M.

155

The 1980s was in fact the time when western popular culture first began to make inroads into China, after the decades when the country was effectively cut off from trends of all kinds. But in those early years, the arrival of such influences was, to say the least, somewhat hit and miss. Many seeped in through the back door from Hong Kong, bringing the songs of the Taiwanese crooner Teresa Teng and the films of Hong Kong stars like Leslie Cheung and Chow Yun-fat to mainland audiences. At the same time, China began tentatively importing western movies – by definition the oldest, the cheapest, and the least controversial in content. Whistle a song from *The Sound of Music* to a Chinese person over the age of thirty-five and they're highly likely to start singing along. Indeed, such is its enduring popularity that a stage version performed in Beijing in the late 1990s, with the lyrics translated into Mandarin by a top university professor, was so successful that it was later staged again, by special request, for delegates to the advisory body to the Chinese parliament during its annual session.

For people starved for so long of anything other than earnest official culture, almost anything foreign seemed like a breath of fresh air. One Beijing musician, who later became part of the city's rock scene in the 1990s, still speaks with awe of the first time he heard what he took to be western popular music. 'When I heard "Jingle Bells",' he says earnestly, 'it was like discovering an entirely new form of music.' Other popular arrivals included Czechoslovakian animation and ageing Donald Duck and Mickey Mouse cartoons. And the early 1980s saw the opening of what's now credited as China's first disco, when the Dongfang Hotel in Guangzhou held a series of what it described as 'dancing tea parties' – though the public staging of dances was not formally permitted until several years later. A few western pop albums were eventually imported for release by state-run publishing houses, or turned into cover versions by Chinese singers, making Abba and Bananarama household names in the People's Republic. And China even had its first performance by a major foreign pop group in 1985, when, after much negotiation, George Michael and Andrew Ridgeley brought their band Wham! to a slightly bemused audience in Beijing – with the result that songs like George Michael's 'Careless Whisper' featured prominently in several Chinese films of the late 1980s, as symbols of all that was modern and sophisticated.[1]

But another brush with western culture the following year only served to confirm continuing official suspicions about the impact of such foreign imports. It's a slightly curious footnote to the history of contemporary China that one of the most significant student protests of the 1980s was provoked, in a small way, by a concert by the US 'surf music' duo Jan and Dean. The band's star had faded somewhat since the 1960s, when they vied with California neighbours the Beach Boys, and topped the charts with songs like 'Surf City', but in late 1986 Jan and Dean were invited to give six shows in China as part of an American–Chinese cultural exchange programme. They began at the Shanghai Gymnasium, where 10,000 people witnessed what the official *China Daily* newspaper described as 'the heavy rhythms, sensuous melodies, wailing electronic instruments, dazzling light displays, and energetic contortions of the musicians'.[2] Some in the audience found it so overwhelming that they ignored warnings to remain in their seats, jumped onto the stage and began to dance; one fan even climbed on top of a loudspeaker. They were quickly detained by the police, and later that evening rumours spread that several students among them had been beaten up. A few hundred of their classmates immediately took to the streets, marching to the police station to demand their release. By the time they were set free a few days later, there had been protest meetings and banners in several Shanghai universities, fanned by news of other student protests in another city, Hefei, against bad living conditions and official corruption.[3]

These various grievances quickly merged into a protest movement which spread to major cities around the country, and eventually provoked the official ideological backlash known as the Campaign against Bourgeois Liberalisation. One of its major targets was western culture and its impact. Yet the interest in such things was hard to stem, as the young generation of the late 1980s continued to seek out new ideas. In intellectual circles, the French existentialists, and later the works of Gabriel García Márquez and

157

Milan Kundera, were all the rage. And in Beijing, which always had an edgier, more rebellious streak than many other cities, a few daring young people started to experiment with rock music – inspired partly by tapes brought in by the foreign students now studying in the city's universities. These fledgling rock bands were usually only able to stage small-scale 'underground concerts' – but by the late 1980s they had produced China's first bona fide rock star, Cui Jian. The waifish former trumpeter in a local orchestra put together a band including a foreign guitarist, and released China's first rock album, *Rock 'n' roll on the New Long March*. His music conveyed a sense of lost ideals and a desire to break the boundaries of a controlling society, most famously in the song 'Yi wu suo you' – 'Nothing to my name'. ('How can he say he has nothing – doesn't he have the Communist Party?!' one old general is said to have fumed.)[4] And his songs struck a chord with many young people, notably the students occupying Tiananmen Square in spring 1989, for whom Cui Jian performed live.

In the aftermath of the crushing of the 1989 student protests, the authorities were in no mood to tolerate this kind of popular culture. Cui Jian was never actually arrested, but he was effectively banned from playing large-scale concerts in Beijing over the next decade. He did begin a nationwide tour in the early 1990s, but it was called off before he reached the capital. In the next few years, rumours of underground Cui Jian concerts, followed almost inevitably by the news that the police had intervened to call them off, became a feature of Beijing life. By the end of the decade Cui Jian was able to play low-key shows in small bars and clubs; he carried on producing albums for other musicians, occasionally made his own, and was acknowledged as the 'godfather' of the Beijing music scene. But there was no doubt that, throughout what should have been the prime of his career, his impact was blunted by the official restrictions. By late 2005, when he was finally permitted to stage a large solo concert in the capital, he was still able to draw a large crowd to Beijing's Capital Gymnasium, but the mood was more one of nostalgia and regret at what might have been, than the cutting edge of contemporary youth culture.

Yet for all the government's attempts to focus young people's minds on politics and patriotism in the years after 1989, China continued, after a slight blip, to become increasingly connected to the outside world, and access to foreign popular culture gradually became easier. Video technology soon made foreign films and music far more widely available, while Hong Kong pop stars also began performing in the mainland, and found enthusiastic fans among a generation seeking new idols. (The intense reaction in China to the death by suicide of the singer and actor Leslie Cheung in 2003 was proof of this – with a sense almost of national mourning among the younger generation.) Beijing's underground culture continued to defy the censors too – in the early 1990s, many of the city's artists and musicians formed their own colonies in decrepit old courtyard houses in the suburbs, before the city's real-estate boom made such cheap accommodation harder to find; some artists began experimenting with video, contemporary dance or experimental theatre. By the middle of the decade, Beijing had a thriving, though small-scale, music scene, with bands influenced by hard rock, reggae and new wave. There was an all-women group, Cobra, and by the late 1990s China's first punks were performing in bands such as 69 and Brain Failure. To some of their elders, these young people became known as the *kuadiao yi dai* – the 'collapsed generation' – seen as selfish and lacking in belief or morals, in contrast to the more idealistic youth of the 1980s.

Such music rarely reached a mass audience, however, and was seldom played on state-run radio. And though a number of western pop stars did perform in China in the 1990s, all imported music had first to be approved by the government – which meant the selection on sale in official shops was very limited. It was only later in the decade, as pirate CDs became widely available, and some people got the chance to watch Hong Kong and Taiwanese music TV by cable or illegal satellite, that the influence of popular culture began to spread. China's own radio and television stations were finally starting to modernise too: they began to play more contemporary foreign music, and to import soap operas from Japan, Korea and Taiwan, which attracted many young people with plots which were

159

more romantic, offbeat or witty than China's own equivalents. By the late 1990s China's first pop music magazines had begun to appear. The arrival of the Internet had a big impact too, bringing websites filled with entertainment news. By the turn of the century, as interest in Japanese and Korean stars grew, you could buy self-help guides on how to dress like a Japanese teenager in Chinese bookstores. There was a sense that pop culture was finally becoming a major part of young people's lives.

Suddenly the older generation began to wake up to the idea that China's new 'teenagers' were developing new interests of their own. While many young people were still dreaming of getting a good job or a place at a foreign university, some were also becoming fascinated by things which their parents found rather hard to understand. In 2001, for example, Shanghai newspapers reported that local school teachers were concerned that many of their pupils were obsessed with a Taiwanese rap singer called MC Hot Dog, whose songs had titles like 'Dad I want Money', and 'Everybody's Sick', and who described his life as being 'fucked up'.[5]

Young people were doing their best to make themselves look different too. In the late 1990s, the Shanghai artist Shi Yong produced a work featuring images of himself wearing a Mao jacket, with blond hair; at the time it seemed amusing but absurd, since hardly anyone in China dyed their hair. But within just a couple of years, young people with hair dyed peroxide blond, light brown or even orange were a common sight on the streets of big cities. In 2002 the headmaster of one Guangzhou high school became so alarmed about his pupils' hairstyles that he stationed teachers at the school gates armed with scissors, and gave pupils arriving for that day's classes the choice of going to the nearest barber's shop to get their hair trimmed, or having their teachers cut it for them.[6]

And it was in the same year that the growing popularity of youth culture really began to make waves across the country. It all started when local TV stations, keen to attract a new generation of viewers, began showing a drama series from Taiwan called *Meteor Garden*. Inspired by a Japanese cartoon, the programme told the story of the four sons of Taiwan's wealthiest families, who attended an elite

160

university, and spent most of their time driving around in large sports cars, breaking girls' hearts, laughing at poor students, and beating up people they didn't like. Only one girl, a student from a poor family, refused to be impressed; the story followed her on–off romance with the most arrogant of the four boys, and his conniving mother's attempts to destroy their relationship. It was hardly profound, but it was slickly made, blending mawkish sentimentality with comic characters and dramatic plot lines. Its four young, floppy-haired stars – collectively known as F4 – soon won the hearts of teenagers around China. Some schoolteachers reported that almost all the students in their class had watched the series, some as many as six times.[7]

Its success was such that the older generation began to pay attention too – and many didn't like what they saw. 'It was disgusting,' the mother of a sixteen-year-old boy told one Chinese newspaper. 'The university had no atmosphere of studying. It was full of rich playboys fighting, bullying, and showing no respect for their teachers.' Another mother described the series as 'electronic heroin', saying her daughter had become 'weird and crazy' since watching it, and was now infatuated with one of its main characters. Newspapers fumed that its characters 'give up everything for love, as though that were all that being young was about'. There were warnings that such programmes were 'poisonous' and would lead young people to 'blindly copy problem idols' – in fact, wrote one journalist in shock, some had already done so, by 'forming gangs, fighting and chasing girls'.[8]

Amid headlines like 'Is F4 a virus?', and demands from parents for the programme to be banned, China's broadcasting authorities finally stepped in, ordering local TV stations to axe the series halfway through its run. But what happened next only seemed to confirm how much Chinese society was changing. F4's fame continued to grow: pirate video stores did a roaring trade in DVDs of the TV series, books and magazines about the stars filled newsstands, and their new pop album became a bestseller. Big businesses were quick to cash in on their popularity too. Soon the boys they tried to ban could be seen on billboards and television screens all over China, even in the heart of Beijing, advertising Pepsi and many other products.

And when the band themselves arrived in Shanghai a couple of months later, there were scenes of near hysteria. A Chinese computer manufacturer had organised a personal appearance by F4 at a local nightclub on a Saturday evening. By the morning, thousands of teenage girls were queuing outside the venue; some had flown in from other parts of the country to catch a glimpse of their heroes; others were reported to have bought new computers just to have the chance of winning a ticket for the event. Inside the venue, security guards struggled to control the crowds, and the band's appearance had to be delayed. When they finally did make it onstage the screaming was so loud that it was impossible for them to sing; after just a couple of songs they had to be escorted off again.[9] And the band's planned appearance at a concert in a Shanghai sports stadium a couple of days later was also called off: the official reason given was that the event did not have formal permission, but some insiders suggested that authorities were actually scared they would not be able to control the screaming teenagers. Fans wept at the news of the cancellation.

Something akin to Beatlemania was sweeping China. And despite official reservations, China's own TV companies soon began doing their best to repeat the success of *Meteor Garden*, making youth dramas of their own, sometimes with actors who bore an uncanny resemblance to the members of F4. The plots were slightly toned down to pass China's TV censors, but the general themes were similar: rich families, poor students, aspiring rock singers and basketball stars. And the streets of Chinese cities too suddenly seemed to be full of F4 lookalikes with tight shirts and floppy hairstyles.

Some found this all a little hard to accept. At the annual meeting of the National People's Congress in 2002, some delegates raised concerns about the growing fashion for such TV dramas, and the popularity of what they described as cute, dumb-acting comic characters.[10] It was further evidence of what seemed to be a rapidly expanding generation gap between China's new youth and those who had grown up in more sober and austere times. Many of the parents of F4's fans, for example, had been in their teens in the later years of the Cultural Revolution, a time when the idols were all political, and romance was virtually a taboo subject. And since many had missed much of their own education due to the political upheavals of that era, they seemed to assume that their offspring would be grateful for the chance to study, and would dedicate themselves to this wholeheartedly.

This growing clash of values was underlined to me when I met Mr Chen, a man in his forties who appeared to have adapted well to the changes in Chinese society. He spoke good English, had studied abroad for a few years, and was successful in his career. But he was in a state of shock after discovering that his son, who was in his second year at senior high school, had a girlfriend. 'I just can't believe it,' said Mr Chen, shaking his head. 'I'm so worried about him.' He simply didn't know how to deal with the situation, it seemed. He couldn't talk to his son, he explained. 'I don't know what to say to him.' The only time he had raised the subject they had had a furious row; now they had barely spoken for several months. For Mr Chen the idea of teen romance was completely unimagin- able. 'What will happen?' he asked forlornly.

Many parents of Mr Chen's generation had grown up too with the traditional belief that children should obey their elders, making it even harder for them to come to terms with the growing individualism of the younger generation. Xiao Jun learned this the hard way. He was a softly spoken university graduate, born in the early 1980s in a small town in eastern China. His parents, who came from the countryside and had had little chance to study themselves, were obsessed with his education. 'Even before I started school my dad made me learn lots of things in advance,' Xiao Jun recalled. 'They always wanted me to come straight home after class, and they never gave me much time to play.' In fact they had taken some extreme measures to force him to concentrate on his studies. 'Sometimes they would even rip up my non-school books and smash my toys,' he said. It made him unhappy and disobedient, and he often fought with his father. He hated the way his parents came into his bedroom unannounced to check up on what he was doing; later he discovered that they had secretly read his diaries. 'In China a lot of parents have this habit,' he said. 'They'll poke their noses into a lot of your private things or suddenly pounce on you.' He took to barricading himself in his room to keep them out.

And when he got older and became interested in Japanese cartoons, and began drawing his own, his parents were even more upset. 'These things were new in China,' said Xiao Jun, 'and my parents didn't understand them at all. They themselves didn't read things like that when they were little, and so they thought they were a waste of time.' He joined the school cartoon society, but his parents tried to stop him going to its evening meetings. So he started sneaking out of the house when they weren't looking, and often stayed the night at friends' houses instead of coming home. 'We had lots of really serious clashes,' he said. Only when he won a place at university to study animation did his parents begin to see that his hobby might not be such a waste of time after all. 'Now they support me,' he said. 'If they have any decisions to make they always ask me for my advice.' He seemed to bear no grudge, simply accepting that his parents had been struggling to adapt to the fact that society had changed. 'I think my parents really love me,' he said. 'It's just that their methods were, well, different!'

His experience was an extreme one – but it does reflect some of the difficulties which some young people face in dealing with their elders. Traditional family values are one aspect. 'I think the power of Chinese parents is generally pretty great,' said Xiao Jun. 'Children don't get enough respect in the home; it was only by struggling that I was able to get a little bit of respect.'

But the historical factor – with so many parents having lost out on their own education – is clearly significant too. 'Most parents didn't have the chance to go to university because of the Cultural Revolution,' says Professor Yang Xiong, director of the Centre for Youth Research at the Shanghai Academy of Social Sciences. 'Instead they went down to the countryside. When they should have been starting their career they were still coming back to the cities – and by the time they got a job they'd missed out on the chance for promotion.' As a result, he suggests, many feel 'it doesn't matter if I suffered, if I'm just doing a very ordinary job, if my life is basically a failure – they put all their hopes on their children's shoulders, pass their ideals and their dreams onto them'.

There's no doubt that this adds to the pressure which some parents put on their children. That's certainly the case for Wang Yi, a university student in Shanghai. 'My mother couldn't go to university, because she had to go to the countryside in her second year of senior high school, and never finished her studies,' he explains. 'She's always regretted it. She says if she had been to university she would have become the governor of the province!' And so she passed her high aspirations onto her son. 'She always urged me to go to university, and she gave me the task of completing a PhD to compensate!' says Wang Yi, with a grin which may be not unconnected to the fact that he has lived up to his mother's ambitions, having just secured a place to begin postgraduate studies.

The fact that so many families now have only one child has also added to the pressure on many of today's younger generation. China's one-child policy was first introduced in 1978, with the stated aim of reducing the country's booming population growth by several hundred million over the next few decades. Urban families would only be allowed one child; most rural families would be permitted two. The actual implementation of the policy has varied: in some rural areas people have continued to have several children, while in others there have been reports of brutal enforcement of the policy. In urban areas, women are expected to register with family planning authorities, which often have a quota for the number of births they will permit in their area in one year. There are steep fines for those who break the rules – and the prospect of a second child not receiving the normal social welfare benefits such as a free basic education. A few richer families have more recently been willing to pay this price to have another child – and children of the only-child generation are in theory themselves allowed a second child if their spouse is an only child too. But the combination of strict rules and the rising cost of living means that most urban citizens have basically accepted the policy, though some may grumble about it.

And so, as Yang Xiong of the Shanghai Academy of Social Sciences puts it, parents 'have to put all their dreams onto one child – they can't say if this one doesn't do well I'll put my hopes on another'.

The policy has only increased the desire of many Chinese parents to train their children to become as successful as possible. 'They want them to learn the piano, practise calligraphy and study foreign languages even before they go to primary school,' says Yang Xiong. At the same time today's children are also far more likely to be pampered. 'Parents give them everything,' he adds. 'Even if they're unemployed, they borrow money to give them things to satisfy them.' Grandparents, many of whom have retired early because of economic reforms, now tend to have more time, and in some cases more money too, to lavish on a smaller number of grandchildren. And urban parents, who are likely to be working longer hours than in the past, often simply leave their child with its grandparents in the years before it begins school. According to Professor Yang this makes it even more likely that children will be spoilt. 'Now in Shanghai there are even cases where the two sets of grandparents are fighting over the child and arguing about who should be looking after it this week,' he says. 'It can get pretty heated!' He gives an example of one of his own friends who has a small grandson. 'My friend told me, "When my wife and I are taking care of him we look after him very well. But when he's with his other grandparents they give him whatever he wants. They let him stay up as late as he likes. If he wants a pizza at 11 p.m. they order him one – there's no order or regulation."' As a result of this type of treatment, he says, some children now start primary school armed with all kinds of advanced knowledge – but unable to tie up their shoelaces or go to the toilet on their own. 'Many primary schools have to keep lots of pairs of clean pants for their pupils,' he says.

Some worry too that so much attention – and indulgence – may encourage these children to become self-obsessed and selfish. When I visited Mr Wu, the former peasant revolutionary turned lifestyle designer in Shenzhen, his daughter Ikea, at the age of seven, was self-confident and charming. But she was also demanding, bossing around the lady who looked after her grandmother when she tried

166

to brush her hair in the morning, and insisting I took her to buy an ice cream at the local shop. 'Hurry up, uncle,' she said after we'd bought it, 'we've got to get home quickly so we can put it in the freezer to eat after lunch.' And her mother, Yan, said she did sometimes worry that the little girl had a selfish streak. 'For example,' she said, 'I wanted to give away some of her old clothes which she doesn't wear any more – but she just refused to do it.' She thought for a moment. 'I do think this generation are different. They have so much, and they have it all to themselves. It was different for me when I was young – I had a brother, we shared things.'

Certainly members of the young generation seem to be growing up with a heightened sense of their own individuality. They are much more likely to have a bedroom to themselves – and are increasingly prepared to demand their privacy. 'Kids in Shanghai now have their own room and they can lock the door,' says Professor Yang Xiong. 'If you try to look inside they know they have the right to complain about your behaviour.' Indeed, some experts fear that today's young children are more solitary than their predecessors from previous generations. They may spend time with their grandparents when they're very young, but once they're older, children are increasingly likely to be living on their own with their parents, at least in the cities, where China's tradition of the extended family unit residing together is rapidly breaking down. And with parents likely to be working longer hours than in the days of the planned economy, children are often left to their own devices. As an official at the Child Protection Department of the Shanghai Education Commission once told me: 'During the process of modernising, people's way of life, the pace of life, and the way they communicate their feelings are all changing. And the exchange of ideas between parents and children, for all kinds of reasons, is not as great as it used to be.' It was important to organise more out-of-school leisure activities, he said, 'to fill in some of the gaps in terms of loneliness or lack of interpersonal contact which have been created by rapid modernisation'.[11] By 2006, Chinese state television started showing public service announcements calling on parents to spend more time with their children.

167

Professor Yang Xiong thinks the problem may diminish as a new generation of better-educated young people moves into parenthood. But he agrees that young children tend to be more isolated from the community than in the past. 'When we were young we didn't have any games to play at home,' he says, 'so we played in the street all the time. Now the living conditions are better: the kids have their own room, they can get online or play computer games – and so they spend more time alone.' Parents are also more worried about letting children play outside these days, he adds, because 'they don't think it's safe. In these new residential areas families are much more separate – so the children are bound to be more solitary and lonely.'

There's no doubt that many of the young generation do spend a lot of time online. It's hardly surprising, given that the education system often encourages them to do so. In Shanghai, for example, by the early years of this decade every nine-year-old was, in theory, being taught to use the Internet. And it's not only the well-off youth in the big cities: in almost any medium-sized town in China there are Internet cafés packed with young people until late at night. For some the net provides a chance to communicate and make new friends. But others have become hooked on online games (perhaps it's no coincidence that the world's largest online gaming company, Shanda, is Chinese). In recent years youth organisations and hospitals in several Chinese cities have opened treatment centres for teenagers addicted to the Internet. And youth experts worry that excessive introversion among the young generation is contributing to a growth in delinquency, even violence. These are still less common in China than in many western societies. But a couple of years ago, in a Beijing backstreet, I stumbled on a sight which did make me start to wonder about the young generation. An old shop dummy, the torso of a woman, was lying on the ground beside the remains of a demolished row of buildings. Two small boys, probably no more than seven or eight years old, and neatly dressed in brightly coloured school tracksuits with little Mickey Mouse rucksacks on their backs, were picking up the largest pieces of rock they could find among the rubble and hurling them at the dummy, apparently determined to smash it into pieces. It was

168

probably just harmless fun, but there was still something faintly sinister about the whole scene, and the two boys' evident pleasure in what they were doing.

Parents' worries about the behaviour of their children, and the inability of the generations to communicate, were highlighted in 2001, when the Chinese media reported that some parents had started hiring private detectives to follow their children – in an attempt to try to understand them, or at least to find out what they did in their spare time. According to the head of one such detective agency, more and more parents felt that their children behaved in 'mysterious ways' – receiving text messages from unknown people, going out late at night, and rarely telling their families what they were doing.[12]

In response to such concerns, many schools and social organisations have in recent years planned holiday activities in which urban school children are taken to rural areas for summer camps, in order to learn more about nature and experience something of the realities – and hardships – of rural life. One enterprising company even started a series of 'boot camps' for parents who wanted to instil some military-style discipline into their offspring. Yet those involved often say that today's city children find it hard to give up their pampered way of life. The organisers of one summer camp for Shanghai middle school students, for example, complained that more than half the participants broke the rules and brought extra snacks, cash to buy more food, and mobile phones so they could call their parents (though one twelve-year-old girl said she would have been quite happy to cope on her own – it was her parents who'd insisted she brought her phone so they could keep in touch).[13]

In the opinion of Professor Yang Xiong, whose own teenage years were during the Cultural Revolution, today's young generation are often intellectually precocious – but not well equipped for the challenges of the real world. 'When I was very young I'd already been sent down to the countryside, and then I was in the army,' he says. 'But now parents just wrap their children up – they're always protected.' He puts this down to the 'three excesses' – 'excessive parental hopes, excessive protection and excessive spoiling'. It all means, he says, that 'their eyes are wide open, they understand everything, but they're like people who've grown up in a garden: they haven't experienced the difficulties of life, so their level of socialisation is low. Their ideas are mature but their behaviour is not.'

Many young people, however, complain that the stereotype of today's only-child generation as spoilt, selfish and unable to look after themselves is a misunderstanding. As one student born in the mid-1980s puts it, 'We're not selfish, we just need more private space than the older generation.' Others say they spend so much time with their cousins that there's little difference from having their own brothers and sisters. And Carolyn, a university student in Shanghai, believes that the reality is often the opposite of the stereotype: 'I think that because we have no brothers or sisters we actually learn to be more considerate of others,' she says. 'From a very early age, in kindergarten, we're always in contact with all kinds of people, and we have to learn to get on with them. With your own brothers and sisters you have no barriers,' she adds, 'you don't worry about asking them to do things for you, or to play with you. But with your classmates or your friends, you have to take care about how you get on with them – you have to respect each other, consider their feelings. It's a good test of character.' Indeed, some argue that the only-child generation particularly cherish their friendships, as a respite from the pressure which their families tend to put on them. And some young people believe they become mature sooner, because they spend more time in the company of adults from an early age. Still, it's striking that if you meet a young Chinese person who does have a brother or sister, they're often quick to emphasise how fortunate they feel. 'I'm really lucky, I have a sister who's four years older than me,' says Wang Yi, the student whose mother insisted he studied for a PhD. 'Actually, when we were little we were always quarrelling,' he admits with a grin, 'but now I feel very happy – if I'm upset or depressed I have someone to talk to.'

What few dispute is that today's young people have more

educational opportunities than most of their elders – and a far greater access to information and new ideas. Many believe the result is a more imaginative generation of youth, and there's no doubt that young people seem increasingly keen to throw themselves into activities and create worlds of their own. This may be partly a way of escaping from the increased pressures of daily life, but the results can certainly be eye-catching – though, once again, they may not always be fully understood by the older generation.

In the summer of 2005, while China's leaders were busy promoting a campaign to remind people of the Communist Party's leading role in society, fifteen-year-old Luna was sitting at a trestle table in a Shanghai exhibition hall, with a pair of furry rabbit ears on her head. Spread out in front of her was a selection of pictures of Japanese cartoon characters which she had drawn. A teenage boy in a bright pink wig and black eyeliner was flipping through them. Not far away Alan, a finance student, was presiding over a stall piled up with alarmingly real-looking metal swords. 'Don't worry, they're not sharp,' he said. Dramatic music swirled around the room: on a stage at the end of the hall a boy dressed all in black, with a cartoon-like spiky black hairstyle, was waving a cardboard sickle above his head; in front of him, a woman in a leather catsuit and a red wig was doing battle with a white-faced young man with long grey hair. As she plunged her sword into the man's chest, the watching crowd sighed with admiration.

It was the third annual Shanghai Comic and Animation Expo, and more than a thousand young people had come, some from far away, to indulge their love not only of cartoons, but of Cosplay (costume play), a type of performance invented in Japan, in which people dress up and act out stories involving their favourite characters from cartoons or computer games. Cosplay had first arrived in China a few years before, and was now sweeping through many of the big cities. Most of the cartoons were fantasies: romantic tales, gothic melodramas or science fiction. Like many of the teenagers taking part, Luna was an expert. 'We all grew up with these things,' she said. In fact, she added, she was the head of the animation society at her high school, and was hoping to go into film directing. Did she think many of the others here shared such ambitions, I asked. 'Definitely,' she said, 'lots of them want to be famous!'

Certainly many of the participants seemed keen to attract attention – there were luminous wigs and weapons of all kinds; girls in wedding dresses; broomsticks and surfboards, miniskirts and platform heels. There were vampish-looking women, and coy girls wearing childlike clothes with cute blonde curls, who were known as 'Lolitas'. One couple in their early twenties were dressed as a sinister-looking doctor and nurse, armed with a giant syringe and a claw hand. Many were waiting their turn to go onstage. And it was a competitive business – the leaflet handed out to all participants in the event asked them to refrain from 'loudly criticising other people, just because they're acting one of your favourite characters and you don't like the way they've done their make-up'.

Some of the audience, aged twelve or thirteen, were there simply to watch in awe – though many of them had attached furry animals to their heads too, just to look the part. There were a few parents there as well, with even younger children, looking slightly bewildered. One young student said the parents probably did not really understand what was going on, but they realised their children needed an outlet for their imagination. 'I think parents know that kids now have more stress than in their time,' she said. 'They have to learn English from kindergarten, they have so much homework, and they don't have much time to play.' She was in the middle of helping a friend who was arranging a Japanese-style kimono on a rather embarrassed-looking fifteen-year-old boy. 'It's a girl's costume,' giggled the student. 'We wanted to make him walk around dressed like this – he looks pretty cute, right?' It was a playful, relaxed scene which would have been hard to imagine in China even a few years earlier. And walking round the exhibition hall, with its stalls where young people were busy selling each other home-made wigs or fans decorated with their own paintings, or signing up new members for their cartoon societies, it felt as though they had created their own little world where they could define the rules of behaviour – and their own identities too.

There were others for whom Cosplay had become even more of a way of life. One of the performers in Shanghai that summer was a twenty-three-year-old known as 'Easy', who had brought his Cosplay group with him from Guangzhou for the occasion. With their long black hair, black eyeliner and velvet jackets, they looked a little like a Glam Rock band of the 1970s; one girl was wearing a punky tartan miniskirt and a T-shirt with the word 'Spunk' written across it. Easy had been one of the first Cosplay performers in Guangzhou, and had no intention of giving up as he got older. 'It's a chance to make the most of your imagination,' he explained. 'You can put all your daily life, your problems and pressures, to one side and forget about everything, transform yourself into a different image.' He grinned. 'I call it the "psychological suicide cure",' he said. 'Sometimes I'm Spiderman, sometimes I act the part of a girl – you can really feel it releases the pressure.'

And Easy believed Cosplay was ideally suited to the new generation. 'Young people now all like to express themselves,' he said. 'They want to show their creativity, to perform; they feel they have talent, but they may not have a chance to express their artistic abilities at school or college.' In Guangzhou in particular, he said, Cosplay had become so popular that some of the city's many roadside tailors now specialised in making costumes for the performers. Of course, not everyone approved. That was one reason why his website carried a warning that anyone who disapproved of things like homosexuality should not enter, he said. 'You really do need to say that,' he explained. 'There are still people in China who can't really accept this – for example, if I wear women's clothes, in some inland parts of the country there are people who'll think, "a transvestite, how disgusting".' And the fact that so much of the content was inspired by Japanese cartoons could also be controversial, he added. 'Once we took part in a competition organised by a TV company and we won first prize – but in the end the programme was never shown,' he said. 'It was a traditional Japanese story, so our clothes were very Japanese style. And someone must have looked at it and said, "What's this – a bunch of Japanese people winning the competition, how can that be acceptable?"'

Still, it seemed that even the authorities were starting to realise that Cosplay was here to stay. The next time I met Easy he was working in the offices of the Guangzhou Youth Cultural Palace, the city's official activity centre for young people, organising a cartoon and animation festival which was to take place during the next school holidays; some 50,000 people were expected to attend. 'Now the government has recognised the power of the animation industry,' said Easy, 'so they basically support it.' The city was even building what was described as 'Asia's biggest animation-themed shopping-mall' just round the corner. This wasn't to say, though, that there were no restrictions on performances in the Cosplay competition. 'Pornographic or violent things are forbidden,' said Easy, 'so you're not allowed to see any blood. We used to like using tomato ketchup, but the parents didn't approve.' This didn't seem to have cramped his style too much, though. On my way out of the Youth Cultural Palace I passed a poster of the previous year's Cosplay competition, featuring photographs of Easy and his group in action. Black-clad snipers in combat gear took aim from the stage with semi-automatic weapons, while Easy himself reclined on a giant motorbike . . .

Not all of China's youth go as far as the Cosplay fans, but these days many do seem more confident about expressing their individuality. Take a walk around any big city and you'll find young people sporting an ever-growing array of different fashions, apparently oblivious to the often disapproving glances and comments of the old people who watch them go by. Crimped hair, thick black 'retro' glasses, beatnik-style berets, trousers with one leg rolled up, anything goes – in fact these were what I saw in a fifteen-minute stroll around a quiet neighbourhood of Shanghai one Sunday afternoon. And young people's search to define their own identity can cover more than just appearance. Most students now give themselves 'English' names, something unknown back in the 1980s. These are often rather creative ones: a glance at the staff list of one youth magazine revealed that it was edited by a team of people by the names of Archer, Arbiter, Rain, Summer, Eleven and Crayon. Some people take on not just a foreign first name but a family name too. Perhaps it's a good way of being remembered: I certainly won't forget Jerry Tom, Jason Keys or the estimable Demon Still in a hurry.

And there's no doubt that this confidence to be themselves reflects the increasingly important status of young people in a society where they are generally acknowledged to be better educated, more technologically advanced and more connected to the outside world than their parents and elders. It's a change which can be visible within individual families. I was talking to Mr Liang, a private businessman in Guangzhou one day, and we got chatting about his teenage son. Young people these days, he believed, had less respect for authority figures. 'When we were young, if we saw our father coming we would hide,' he said. 'Nowadays kids are more likely to mock their parents.' What's more, he added, 'when we try to teach them about our views on things, they're not interested'. But unlike many in China, he didn't necessarily see this as a bad thing. 'Society's changing so fast,' he went on, 'young people need more advanced ideas to survive. So now we're the ones who have to learn from the kids about all the new fashionable ideas.' It simply meant, he explained, that parents had to get used to a different role. 'I just treat my son like my brother – or my friend,' he said.

Surveys have backed up this sense of a changing balance of power in Chinese families. Victor Yuan, who set up Horizon, one of China's first opinion polling companies, in the early 1990s, and has followed social trends closely ever since, recently produced an analysis of conversations within Chinese families. This showed that children did 47 per cent of the talking, their parents 20 per cent each, while the grandparents could barely get a word in. 'Grandparents say it's hard to discuss things with their grandchildren,' he explains. 'They feel they're always likely to be proven wrong. The kids spend more time online, they know more.' Sometimes it can seem that the younger generation are taking control. It's not uncommon to see families out shopping, with the child making decisions. I once saw a girl of around ten walking round a furniture warehouse with her mother; she was busy talking on a mobile phone to someone back home, discussing what to buy, while her

175

mother stood beside her saying not a word. And the influence of these junior consumers can be quite significant, according to Victor Yuan. The Chinese electronics maker Haier has become one of the country's best-selling brands partly because it uses a logo featuring a cartoon of a child, he suggests. 'This attracts the children – and so they demand that their parents buy these products!'[14]

The young generation certainly do tend to be far better informed than many older people about the new technology now arriving fast in the country – in fact they have embraced it at a remarkable speed, considering China's relatively backward technological state just a dozen years ago. For many urban young people, the Internet, the latest mobile phones, MP3 players and PSPs are an indispensable part of life, while many have become hooked on making their own digital video films, or creating computer graphics and flash animation. It's a state of mind which is encouraged by the education system: the Chinese government is determined to boost the development of science and technology – and even primary school textbooks promote the vision of a hi-tech future. In Shenzhen, Mr Wu's daughter Ikea showed me one of her school books, which featured a story called 'A-De's dream'. It was a cartoon strip in which the young A-De imagined a future world: just before setting off in his spaceship to visit his family on Mars, he made a call on his video phone to his grandmother, who informed him that the latest model eco-friendly solar-powered car was now on the market. So A-De pulled up the online shopping centre on his hand-held computer and ordered one, to be waiting for him when he got back.

The interests, attitudes and fashions of the young generation are also becoming increasingly influential in mainstream Chinese society. A whole new vocabulary has spread rapidly, much of it inspired by cartoons, the Internet, computer games and other aspects of youth culture. Phrase such as 'interactive', 'alternative', 'accessories', and 'marginal' have all entered the Chinese language. Some teenage slang has become widely used – for example the Japanese phrase *kawai*, meaning 'cute', or 'PK', a phrase used in computer games, derived from 'Personal Kill', which refers to a victory in a one-on-one battle, and which is now sometimes used in mainstream advertising. Many young people will tell you that their dream is to *zuo xiu* – to put on a show or a performance (or indeed simply make a spectacle of themselves). Those who get the chance to do so in public are likely to acquire their own *fen-si* – which literally means 'rice noodles', but is a punning transliteration of the English word 'fans'.

Big businesses have been quick to recognise the power of this new youth culture, as they seek to attract young consumers. The lovable old ladies and trustworthy-looking middle-aged men, earnestly recommending products, who used to dominate Chinese advertising, have been replaced by an array of trendy, sometimes witty advertisements featuring new young pop stars and images inspired by computer games, cartoons, even punk fashion. Spiky-haired teenagers promote mobile phones; Cosplay characters are used to advertise McDonald's. Nike meanwhile has run a series of 'counter-culture' advertisements, shot in grainy black and white: a young female basketball player practises hip-hop dancing and talks about her struggle to be accepted in a man's world; trendy youths skateboard through old Beijing, with the catchline, 'What I'm seeking can be summed up in one word: pleasure.' (And without the influence of the youth market it would certainly have been hard to imagine a Japanese star being used in an advertising campaign in China, given the continuing underlying political tensions. But that's exactly what one soft-drinks manufacturer did a few years ago with the Japanese singer Ayumi Hamasaki, who had a big following in China at the time.)

Youth culture has also become increasingly influential in the Chinese media in general. The popularity of television programmes from Taiwan, for example, has made the island's softer, southern-style Mandarin pronunciation all the rage among young TV and radio presenters – in sharp contrast to the more clipped, formal northern speech traditionally heard on Chinese television. By 2005 the central government – along with some parents – had become so alarmed at this development that it issued an order demanding that 'standard' Mandarin be used in all TV and radio programmes.[15]

The impact of youth is also visible in the types of programme now shown on Chinese TV stations, with an endless diet of Taiwanese, South Korean or Japanese dramas, many focusing on young romance and yuppie lifestyles. And as Chinese-made programmes seek to catch up, some producers have imported Korean stars to act in Chinese drama series, in order to boost the ratings, and simply dubbed their lines into Mandarin. Chat shows and comedy quiz shows, featuring all manner of joke sound effects and cartoon-style graphics, have also been widely copied. By 2006, even the official New Year's Eve gala on national television was including hip-hop performers.

The startling success of the *Supergirls* singing contest, produced by the satellite television station of Hunan province in 2005, was further evidence of the power of the youth market. It drew up to a hundred million viewers, many of whom voted for the winners by sending text messages from their mobile phones. The result astonished many too, with viewers choosing the tomboyish, spiky-haired Li Yuchun and Zhou Bichang as their favourites, in sharp contrast to the more conventionally beautiful, 'feminine' stars who usually dominate Chinese television. The pair, along with several other of the show's contestants, were soon among the most talked-about people in China: they appeared in countless advertisements; made pop albums and movies; the Chinese Post Office even issued a set of Li Yuchun stamps. And every TV station around the country, it seemed, rushed to mimic the success of *Supergirls*: by the following year China had an estimated five hundred reality shows of all kinds.[16]

According to Bao Xiaoqun, the energetic, French-educated head of the research department at the Shanghai Media Group, which now combines all the city's TV stations, the success of *Supergirls* and its clones is a sign of changing times. 'In the 1980s, youth culture was mainly seen as underground, alternative,' he says, 'but since the 1990s, and especially in the twenty-first century, the things which young people like have gradually become the main-stream, and have influenced mass culture. So now you have national state television copying things like reality shows from the grass roots!' The importance of attracting a young audience is evident in the Shanghai Media Group's own programmes. Its education channel features an hour of news about pop singers and film stars every evening; its fashion channel is known in English as Channel Young, while another called Channel In broadcasts non-stop pop videos. There's also a channel aimed at children and teenagers with a very trendy, pop look, and yet another dedicated purely to cartoons and animation. Bao Xiaoqun is blunt about the reasons for this. 'Young people are our most important audience,' he insists. 'If a programme doesn't have any young viewers, only old people, we probably wouldn't do it – we need the young to be watching.' Of course, he adds quickly, 'we also hope that on this basis, older people will watch too'.

Attracting young people – so prized by the TV station's all-important advertisers – inevitably means adapting to the different mentality of the young generation, according to Mr Bao. Young people, he says, now generally watch less television than before. 'They're all online or playing games machines, and as new media evolves this will get more serious.' And so, he believes, to keep them watching television requires a fresh approach. 'They don't want to just sit there and watch television, like a "couch potato",' he says, 'they need interactive things.' As a result, many of Shanghai's TV channels now encourage viewers to participate wherever possible, by sending in text messages, however frivolous, which scroll along the screen during everything from debates about romance to live English Premiership football matches. The Shanghai Media Group's biggest hits of 2006 were a series of reality shows – including a celebrity dancing contest and two star-search programmes: *My Hero* and *My Show*. The latter used the slogan: 'I put on my own show – anything goes.' Once again these produced some unexpected winners – the *My Hero* champion was an ethnic Tibetan, one of the runners-up a deaf and dumb dancer. In Mr Bao's opinion it was another sign that the young generation are keen to assert their own taste and choose their own idols. 'Young people want a different kind of image,' he says. 'It's a kind of rebellion against all the beautiful stars on television.' The winners might be young and trendy, he says, but 'in the viewers' eyes, they are more like their

179

neighbours or their classmates – so they can relate to this. It makes them think if someone from a normal background can become a star, they can do it too.'

And the desire of young people to be close to their heroes has been underlined by the rapid spread of 'fan culture' – the millions of young people who have mobilised their own support groups for the *Supergirls* and other reality TV show contestants, or started online communities devoted to their favourite stars. In 2002 China was even reported to have had its first fan suicide, when a young man killed himself in Fujian province, allegedly out of grief at his failure to get to see a concert by the pop star and actress Zhao Wei. Some have criticised the new fan culture, seeing it as excessive and abnormal: 'When I see this I can't help thinking of the hysteria of the Cultural Revolution,' says one middle-aged Beijing intellectual.

But it's clear that many of the young generation are seeking to define their own world. One of China's biggest hits of 2005 was a TV series called *Wulin Waizhuan*, an irreverent comedy which mixed historical costume drama with science fiction, time travel and surreal references to twenty-first-century advertising slogans. Chinese television had never seen anything quite like it; not least the fact that one of the stars of the show was a fourteen-year-old girl who continuously proved herself to be cleverer by far than the adults. Similarly, many of the heroes of the young generation are people who have done things their own way – not just Li Yuchun and the other *Supergirls*, but also Han Han, who first caught the public eye as a teenager in 2000 when he dropped out of his Shanghai high school and published a novel expressing his dis-satisfaction with China's education system. He later pursued his dream of becoming a racing driver, and became one of the first of a new generation of celebrities to write their own blog on the Internet. Other popular figures include the rebellious, hip-hop-influenced Taiwanese pop star Jay Chou, and the Shanghai athlete Liu Xiang, who rose as if from nowhere to win the gold medal in the 200-metre hurdles at the 2004 Athens Olympics, and quickly became one of China's wealthiest and most marketable sporting celebrities – all the while maintaining a careful distance from China's rigid sporting bureaucracy. Even the Flowers, who could hardly get played on the radio when they started out as a teenage punk band in Beijing in the late 1990s, are now deemed sufficiently mainstream to headline concerts sponsored by big international brands.

And the tastes and fashions of China's young people seem to be evolving faster and faster – adding to a sense of rapid generational change. It's only a few years ago that the '1970s generation' – the phrase used to denote people born in that decade – were hailed by the Chinese media as the new face of the nation. But they have been rapidly overtaken by the '1980s generation', with their greater openness to the outside world, obsession with the Internet and love of Asian pop culture. According to one fashionable magazine, people born in the 1970s are already out of date and 'as nostalgic as a bunch of old people'.[17] Now the '1990s generation' of tech-savvy teenagers are making their mark too. 'I call them the fifth generation,' says the sociologist Yang Xiong. 'Their time and space have shrunk, their values have shrunk.' Next, he suggests, it will be the turn of the 'millennium babies'! Bao Xiaoqun of the Shanghai Media Group agrees that the pace of change is breathtaking. 'The generation gap is bigger than ever,' he says. 'Things which would take twenty or thirty years, even fifty years to happen in the US are happening here in five or ten years, even one or two years!'

There are some who feel that, beneath its glossy surface, much of the new youth culture remains fundamentally conservative: that Cosplay, for example, is an escapist fantasy, and that South Korean soap operas tend to reinforce the more traditional Confucian values of that country. Bao Xiaoqun agrees that the kind of idealism seen among China's youth in the second half of the 1980s is no longer so obvious. 'In the 1980s, things like rock 'n' roll were about looking for freedom,' he says, 'about political demands – there was a kind of anger at social or moral repression. Now it's totally individualistic – the kids want freedom, but the freedom to express themselves, to perform, because that makes them happy.' Indeed, one Chinese magazine has summed this up as the change from the 'we' generation to the 'me' generation.[18]

Not everyone sees this as apolitical. Every now and again there are reminders that the authorities still remain nervous about the impact of youth culture and of foreign ideas: in 2006 they suddenly ordered a halt to showings of the film *The Da Vinci Code* – when it was well on the way to becoming China's best-selling foreign movie ever – claiming that this was in order to give more opportunities for home-grown Chinese films to be shown in the cinemas. In the same year they also ordered TV companies to stop showing foreign-made cartoons during peak viewing time in the early evening, a move which provoked much criticism in the Chinese media.[19] In 2007 the government announced limits on the airtime given to TV talent shows, and sought to restrict voting by viewers. But there's a growing sense that it will be hard to turn back the clock. Certainly many feel that youth and its fads will continue to become increasingly important. 'I think China is now a youth society,' says Yang Xiong. 'In the past we used to talk about how society could influence young people – by making them learn lots of social rules and regulations, for example. Now it's the other way round – it's the youth who are influencing society!'

# 7

# Unsentimental education

At dinner in Shenzhen, real-estate consultant Richard Li was fretting about his daughter's education. 'There was one kindergarten we really wanted to send her to,' he said. 'It was called Victoria – like your English Queen.' It was popular, he added, because it was run by an education group from Hong Kong and used Hong Kong teaching materials – and it wasn't too expensive. But his daughter had been too young: she was just two and a half and the school didn't take children below the age of three. Richard felt rather frustrated. 'Most parents in Shenzhen want their children to start kindergarten before three,' he said. 'Some children start when they're just one if their parents are busy working.' Fortunately he'd now found an alternative. 'It's a bilingual kindergarten,' he said proudly, 'they have teachers from Canada and Australia and New Zealand – so the children have a couple of hours of English teaching every day.' Was his daughter at the kindergarten full-time? I asked. Richard's definition seemed a little different from mine. 'Oh no,' he said, 'we still have to take her there at eight in the morning and fetch her at five in the evening.' It didn't come cheap: the monthly fees were equivalent to about a fifth of the family's income, but Richard felt it was worth it. 'There's a problem, you see,' he explained. 'Now, with the one-child policy, everyone's worried that their child won't be able to keep up with the others – so you have to invest a lot in education.'

Education, like health care and housing, has become a national obsession in China over the past decade and a half – yet another area of life where, for the lucky ones, the choices are greater than ever, but for ordinary people, the pressures and the costs are growing all the time. Before the 1990s, education in China was a straightforward affair. Children went to their local primary school, followed by junior high school, and, if they were academically good enough, three years of senior high school too. If they were fortunate – or their families well connected – they might get into one of their city's top schools, which tended to cater for the offspring of officials and civil servants. And a very privileged minority would then get the chance to go to university. Not that the undergraduate life was an easy one – students usually lived eight to a small dormitory, with very basic facilities. At the university where I studied in the 1980s many of these dormitories had window panes missing, even in midwinter. Students were given limited choice in the subjects they could take – and even less choice upon graduation, when the government would simply allocate them a job, which might well be a thousand miles away from their home town, and have nothing at all to do with the subject they had studied.

And so when the authorities stopped allocating jobs in the early 1990s, leaving students to compete in the employment market, there was much relief. The reforms came as the government began to turn its focus to other areas, in particular promoting nine years' compulsory education – up to the age of fifteen – for all students, including those in the countryside. This was supposed to be free of charge; but to help the system pay its way, the authorities announced that students at senior high school and university would now have to pay tuition fees. Some privately funded schools and colleges were also allowed to open as a way of lifting the pressure on the state's resources. Universities were gradually given the freedom to set up links with colleges abroad, and to introduce courses such as MBAs and other postgraduate business qualifications, for which they were permitted to charge higher fees.

It has all meant new opportunities – and new challenges. Families now pay more for their children's education, and university tuition fees in particular have risen rapidly, from just a few hundred yuan a year in the mid-1990s, to some six thousand yuan a decade later. The new job market also quickly became increasingly competitive, as the growth in educational opportunities meant there were more well-qualified people looking for work. In the late 1990s anyone with an MBA was virtually guaranteed a well-paid job as soon as they graduated – but within just a few years the wages being offered to people with such qualifications fell sharply, as they became more common. It only added to many parents' conviction that they must give their children the best possible start in life.

That means not just attending kindergarten from an early age, but also private tuition and classes of all kinds, in order to help children gain admission to the best primary schools. As youth sociologist Yang Xiong puts it, 'If parents want their children to get into a good primary school they have to teach them maths and lots of things at home first. Everyone else is doing it, so you have to compete.' It means, he says, that 'children of five or six are doing all kinds of maths problems which in most parts of the world you wouldn't do until you were much older'.

One school for such aspiring geniuses in Shanghai even offered what it described as MBA courses for kindergarten pupils.[1] And the obsession with producing precociously brilliant children has become increasingly visible in Chinese society. TV advertisements for powdered baby milk (of which there are many) stress, for example, that they contain substances found in Einstein's brain, and will therefore help to produce more outstanding babies; television programmes feature prodigies such as 'the six-month-old boy who can recognise a thousand Chinese characters'. Some parents start even earlier – I met one couple who were expecting a baby and had invested in a set of CDs to play to the foetus. The product went by the name of the Unborn Baby University.

The desire of parents to get their children in to the top schools (which are clearly designated by an official system which ranks certain establishments as 'key schools') has also made education very much a 'seller's market'. There have been many stories of popular schools demanding sizeable 'donations' from parents anxious to secure their child's place. 'We had to pay 30,000 yuan [around £2,000] to get our son into his school,' said the father of a six-year-old boy from Zhejiang province. Such payments were technically illegal, but, like many parents, he had felt that he had no choice but to pay up. 'What else could we do?' he asked. 'We had to get him into that school.'

The pressure put on children does not let up once they get into primary school. Back in Shenzhen I went to meet my friend Mr Wu. His seven-year-old daughter Ikea insisted on coming out with us for dinner. We had to wait for her to be dropped off by her friend's mother, who was collecting the two little girls from their after-school music lesson. When Ikea got out of the car, she was accompanied by a violin case as tall as she was. Her father stowed it in the back of his own car, but as we set off to walk to the nearby restaurant I noticed that Ikea was wheeling a shiny pink Princess Barbie suitcase along behind her, which came up almost to her waist. What was in it? I asked. 'My schoolbooks,' she said. 'I can do my homework during dinner.' In fact, it turned out she had several hours of homework every night. I mentioned that I'd never done any work after school until I was twelve. 'Waaah!' she shouted in astonishment. 'You didn't have homework?! You were so lucky!' Tonight, she said, she had four separate books to look at; the school took it so seriously that her teacher sent a text message to her mother's mobile phone every afternoon, listing the work she was expected to do that night. According to her mother, this was by no means one of the most demanding schools in Shenzhen – in fact they'd intentionally chosen a relatively 'normal' school, rather than one of the city's more coveted establishments. These were commonly known as *guizu xuexiao* or 'aristocrat' schools, famous both for their demanding teaching standards and for the large cars which waited outside their gates at the end of the school day; reports of pupils arguing about whose parents were richer were common. 'Lots of my friends try to get their children into those schools,' said Ikea's mother, Yan. 'Everyone said we should too. But I think the demands they place on the children are too high – I don't think it would be fair on her.'

Still, whichever school children attend, there's no doubt that China's education system has for many years been oriented towards getting them to memorise large quantities of information, in order to pass a series of exams. The most important of these looms over young people's lives like a dark cloud: the *gaokao*, or higher education examination, which every would-be university student has to sit at the end of their final year of high school. The gruelling three-day exam takes place in June each year, provoking a state of frenzied anxiety among parents and pupils alike. Local governments divert traffic to ensure that students arrive at the exam halls on time; building sites near schools are ordered to close in order not to disturb the candidates; some parents even hire hotel rooms so their children will not have to make too long a journey, and to allow them to do their final preparation in air-conditioned comfort. Crowds of parents wait for their children to emerge from the exam halls, ready to ply them with snacks and drinks, or to fan them against the summer heat. The excitement is understandable, since a student's hopes of getting into university usually rest on this one exam, and it may therefore have a defining effect on their lives. The fear which the *gaokao* strikes into the hearts of students and parents was until recently heightened by the fact that many good students failed to get into university each year, simply because China did not have enough places to satisfy the demand. In 1999, for example, some five million people took the exam – but only around one and a half million places were on offer.

The exam system means that the final years of senior high school leading up to the examination are a particularly stressful period for China's youth. For Shirley Li, a student of English literature at one of Shanghai's top universities, it's an experience she will never forget. 'My high school days were really the toughest of my life,' she says, over a cup of tea in a café near her university. Nowadays she seems relaxed, chatting away in fluent English. But the mere mention of those days makes her look anxious. 'It was very stressful,' she says. 'There were so many students, all preparing for the university entrance exam – the competition was really fierce.' As one of the top students in her school, she admits that she put pressure on herself too – not least since she knew her parents and teachers had high expectations of her. But the system hardly encouraged her to take it easy: in the city where she grew up, all schools required their pupils to stay behind until nine o'clock at

187

night doing homework or reading. 'It was pretty tiring,' says Shirley. 'I got up at six a.m., went to school at seven and worked until nine in the evening. When I got home all I could do was watch a little TV or listen to some music, then fall asleep.'

And it wasn't only on weekdays. For three years, summer and winter holidays excepted, Shirley went to school every single day. 'We had classes every Saturday morning and afternoon, and on Sunday we had to spend the morning at school too,' she says. 'After that,' she recalls with a sigh, 'we could go home and relax!' She was a dedicated student – she used to enjoy spending her spare time challenging friends to science tests – and despite all retains positive memories of her schooldays. 'It was still wonderful,' she smiles. 'We could play with our classmates too, read books, do our own studying.' But even she feels the system was too rigid. 'I think that kind of exam-oriented education is not very good for students to develop a very all-round kind of personality and talent,' she says – though she sees signs that things are beginning to change. 'I think now they're starting to realise that students have to be educated like a person, not a machine.'

There's certainly evidence that a young generation which is growing increasingly aware of its individuality is starting to find the rigidity of the system hard to accept. In one survey of middle school students in Beijing in 2006, more than half complained that teachers had told them that they were 'stupid' or 'idiots'.[2] The strict approach of Chinese schools was highlighted by the slogan which traditionally hung in school playgrounds, which instructed students to be *tuanjie, jinzhang, yansu, huopo* or 'unified, tense, serious and lively', a collection of requirements which perhaps only a contortionist would have been able to fulfil. In recent years, however, more and more teachers have reported having to deal with disruptive pupils; even some primary schools have had to ban mobile phones to stop children using them during lessons.[3] And at one school in Chongqing in the south-west in 2004, students rebelled and held a demonstration outside the school gates, in protest at being forced to attend extra classes at the weekend. It later emerged that the local education department had previously ordered an end to these weekend lessons – but the school's head-master was quoted as saying he had no choice but to continue with them, due to pressure from parents. The parents, he explained, feared that without these extra classes their children would fall behind pupils from wealthier families, who could afford to hire private tutors.[4]

And the issue of overworked children has become the subject of a growing debate in recent years. Educationalists have warned that many pupils are not getting enough sleep – a subject which was raised at the annual session of China's legislature in 2006. 'Chinese urban children sleep for less time than adults,' says the sociologist Yang Xiong. He and some of his colleagues in Shanghai even called on the local government to ban homework in primary schools. The proposal was not fully implemented, but the quantity of work given to younger pupils was slightly reduced: in 2006 the city education department announced it was cutting the number of Chinese characters that children were expected to learn in the first two years of primary school by 20 per cent; officials said the excessive pressure was reducing pupils' interest in learning. As a result, according to Yang Xiong, 'the sleep time of children in Shanghai has gone up by one hour'.[5]

Some believe, though, that there's a need for far more drastic reforms of China's education system. Guo Sile, a professor of education in Guangzhou, has spent years developing a whole new approach to learning, from primary school onwards, which he calls 'student-centred teaching'. He talks about it with a missionary zeal. 'The problem in China now,' he explains, 'is that education controls your life, when it should stimulate your life.' In his opinion the solution is simple. 'If we remove pressure, give back freedom, and rely on children's own motivation, they'll create their own ideas,' he insists. In his method, which has been piloted in a number of schools in Guangdong, there are far fewer exams, but a greater emphasis on helping children to become interested in reading, by encouraging them to write down their feelings about what they read; this he believes, inspires them to learn the difficult Chinese writing system. 'Other people have exams all the time,' he says. 'They want to grow a flower every month, but that doesn't bring good results in the long term. We don't have exams, but in the end we grow a good flower!'

Such experiments are still in their early days. But the Chinese government has in recent years tried to tackle at least one of the causes of the pressure on the nation's schoolchildren: the shortage of places at university. Around the turn of the century, it announced a massive expansion of the country's universities, as part of its new emphasis on education, science and technology. Small universities were merged to form big ones, others were allowed to expand, and many new institutions were set up too. Several of China's biggest cities now have brand new 'university cities' in their suburbs – entire districts of new campuses, which are sometimes home to as many as a dozen different universities. In Guangzhou, for example, a new university district was built on an island in the Pearl River, capable of accommodating 100,000 students. In the nearby city of Zhuhai, preferential land prices and an attractive seaside environment have attracted colleges from Guangzhou and as far away as Beijing to open campuses in another new zone.

In Shanghai, too, many universities have moved out to a new university city, while others have developed their own separate campuses in the suburbs, enabling them to expand rapidly. The Shanghai Normal University, the city's teacher training college, once had only a cramped downtown facility, but can now house as many as 20,000 students in a state-of-the-art campus. 'It looks a bit like Stanford University now,' says Zhang Minxuan, a professor of education at the university and recently also deputy head of the Shanghai government's Education Commission. The key to this rapid development, he says, was the fact that universities were given more commercial freedom to raise funds. 'We were under a lot of pressure,' he explains. 'Everyone was asking us to develop higher education, but we had no money, so we allowed the public universities to take out bank loans – and they all did.' Professor Zhang, a scholar of the development of Britain's education system, is proud of the results. 'In the history of education around the world, nowhere have universities developed with loans,' he says – adding an English idiom to reinforce his point: 'I think we've solved the problem of which came first, the chicken or the egg,' he grins. 'We didn't have any chickens, and we didn't even have a place to raise chickens. So we went to the bank to borrow an egg. And now we have more and more eggs!' Indeed, Shanghai created around 20,000 extra places at university between 2003 and 2005, and the number is still growing, according to Professor Zhang. By 2005, he says, the city had just over half of its college-age population in higher education, compared to only 2 per cent in 1980.

Across the nation the expansion has also been spectacular. The number of high school students who were able to get a place at university after taking the entrance examination rose from one and a half million in 1999 to more than four million in 2006. Yet experts say this has not necessarily made life so much easier for China's high school students. According to Professor Zhang Minxuan, 'We thought if there were more university places the pressure would be reduced, but now we see that it's still very great – because everyone wants their children to get into the best schools.'

The expansion does mean, however, that there are now alternatives for students who fail to get into the top college of their parents' dreams. Out among the last few fields in a remote corner of Pudong, Shanghai's new district, a freshly paved concrete road leads to a collection of new white buildings. Here, on what was agricultural land a few years earlier, helpful staff point the way to the library, the sports stadium, the teaching blocks, and the new dormitory buildings on the other side of the grassy compound. In the café-style canteen, students pay for their meals with electronic swipe cards and watch TV as they eat, before heading off for afternoon classes. The atmosphere is fresh and energetic, a world away from the sleepy environment of China's traditional universities. It's a source of satisfaction to Zhou Xingzeng, as he overlooks the scene from his large office in the administration building. Mr Zhou is the president of the Jianqiao Institute, one of China's new generation of privately run higher education colleges. A softly spoken, thoughtful man in his forties, he made his money doing business in Wenzhou before getting together with a group of friends and investing some 300 million yuan (around £20 million) to set up this college. Their intention, says Mr Zhou, was not to earn lots of money – they have enough already – but to make a contribution to society, by helping to provide some of the extra education places which China so badly needed. Mr Zhou knows all about the difficulties of getting an education: he was the first child from his village near Wenzhou to go to high school – and later university.

But he also believes that colleges such as Jianqiao can offer something else too: a different approach to teaching. Having worked as a university lecturer himself before going into business, he believes China's higher education system has not done enough to stimulate creativity. 'Often students spend four hours just listening to their lecturers,' he says, 'without any chance to ask questions or raise their own views. It's not good for encouraging them to think or for encouraging individuality.' Nor, he suggests, does traditional teaching always do much to equip students for dealing with the real world either. 'I studied accounting,' he says, 'but when I graduated I didn't even know how to write a cheque. I'd never seen one, even though all businesses use them!' As a result, he adds, 'graduates get to a company and they don't know how to fit in. And the employers think, these kids know all this theory, but if you try to get them to do something practical, they can't!'

And so his college (which does not have full university status yet, but has been approved to offer full undergraduate degrees) insists on sending students on work-experience placements. 'Teaching needs to get closer to society, to the market, to international style,' says Mr Zhou. The college has also broken with tradition by looking beyond exam results when it selects students. 'We take the ones who seem special and have a lot of ideas,' explains Mr Zhou, 'not necessarily the ones with the highest grades.' Students are also encouraged to broaden their horizons by joining clubs and doing voluntary work, such as teaching children in nearby villages.

It is an approach which seems to appeal to some of the younger generation. 'I think a place like this helps us to know more about society,' says one student, who left her home in northern China to

192

come here to study for a degree in Business English. 'It's funded by businessmen, so we have more chance to come into contact with companies and business people and learn about the world of work.' She found the college on the Internet, she says, and was attracted by its promise of using different teaching methods. 'In our society we have to do something new, do something special, not just follow the old ways,' she emphasises. And as she sits chatting cheerfully in English to one of her lecturers, it seems she has benefited from the experience.

The fees for such private colleges are usually higher than those of traditional universities – but some parents are clearly willing to pay. 'My parents aren't very rich, but they support me,' says Beibei, a tall, athletic nineteen-year-old, as he sits in his comfortable shared room, with a view over the fields and a poster of the Backstreet Boys on the wall. 'I think I've made great progress here,' he adds with a smile. 'We pay double now but I think we'll also make double money in the future!'

Private colleges are still seen by some in China as a second choice for those who fail to get into a good state university. But their numbers are growing fast: Shanghai alone had more than twenty such institutions by 2005 – some set up by professional associations or businesses, others by individuals – accounting for around a tenth of the city's higher education places.[6] Some have complained about official restrictions on the amount of profit which investors can take from such private colleges. But the founder of the Jianqiao Institute is convinced that institutions in the philanthropic tradition of some of the great American universities will eventually develop in China. 'There's not yet a famous private university in China, but there are many in other countries,' says Mr Zhou, adding a little shyly, 'I think it's quite possible that this college could become a world-famous university in fifty years.' I ask whether that's why he chose the name Jianqiao, which sounds rather similar to the Chinese translation of 'Cambridge'. Mr Zhou gives a slightly embarrassed smile: 'I wanted to choose this to show that our generation and the next can catch up.'

*

Yet for many people, just keeping up with the rising costs of education in China is a struggle. Mr Zhou himself acknowledges that the fees charged by his college – and even those for state universities – are hard for many families, particularly those in China's poorer, western regions, to cope with. His college does offer some scholarships, but in general it's an issue which has caused growing concern in recent years. Fees of five or six thousand yuan a year (some £400) may not sound especially high – but they're equivalent to several months' wages for many Chinese citizens. Indeed, one official newspaper calculated that in 2004 the combined tuition fees and living expenses for a university student were higher than the annual income of the average urban resident.[7] The burden on parents was made worse by the fact that until recently Chinese students were not allowed to take part-time jobs while studying to help pay their way.

For rural families, the pressure is greater still. 'One student's fees alone may be a year's income for a peasant,' acknowledges Professor Zhang Minxuan of the Shanghai Education Commission, though he notes that the government is doing its best to keep prices down, in the face of pressure from many universities which want to raise them. Stories of rural families struggling to cope with the cost of education have become increasingly common in the Chinese media – there have been a number of reports of parents who have committed suicide after learning that their children have won a place at university, out of fear and shame that they will not be able to afford to pay the fees.[8] China's state-run universities do offer scholarships for some poor students – according to official figures, some four and a half million in 2003, worth around 3.3 billion yuan (some £240 million).[9] Yet this worked out at an average of little more than £50 for each scholar. In the same year, poor students were also, for the first time, given the chance of doing some work on campus to earn extra money.

In the late 1990s, as concern about the costs of education rose, the Chinese government decided to follow the example of other countries and introduce a system of student loans. These allowed students to borrow money and repay it interest-free while they were

194

studying, or at low rates after graduation. But implementation of the system has been anything but smooth. Many people, particularly the families of rural students who are often in the greatest need, are still unaware of its existence, or simply find the application procedures too complex. In some areas loans have only been made available to the very poorest families, excluding others who also need assistance: official figures suggest that while some 800,000 people took out loans during the first five years of the scheme, the number who needed them was three times higher.[10] China's banks, meanwhile, have complained that many students do not repay on time: in some provinces the banks have refused to join the scheme altogether. The authorities have responded by offering extra guarantees to the banks, and threatening non-paying students with exposure in the press; at the same time they have extended the repayment limit. But some believe the loan period is still too short, forcing many students to accept low-paying jobs in order to keep up with repayments, instead of taking time to look around for better opportunities. Education officials also acknowledge that some local governments have been slow to implement the loan scheme, and in some cases have misused funds set aside for it.[11]

Even among those who can afford the fees, some have in recent years begun to opt out of China's state education system and seek alternatives, either out of a sense of dissatisfaction or simply a desire for new horizons. Some parents have sent their children to privately established 'international' high schools, which promise more emphasis on foreign languages; some of these are joint ventures between foreign investors and local partners. It can be a costly experiment, however. 'I earn around 60,000 yuan a year doing this,' said a taxi driver in Shanghai, tapping his meter, 'and it all goes on my son's education.' His fourteen-year-old son was at a Singapore-invested establishment, he explained. 'The teachers are very good in those schools, they take their job seriously.' His son even had a native speaker teaching him English. 'Now my son's teaching me English,' he grinned. (China also has a number of fully foreign-operated schools, but so far they have only been permitted to cater for the children of foreign citizens working in the country.)

Others are looking a little further afield. Over afternoon tea in a Beijing café one day, a Chinese friend suddenly announced her plans for her son's future education. 'I've put him down for Eton,' she said, 'he'll probably be in the same class as Madonna's son.' The subject of this dramatic piece of news was barely one year old, and could do little more than gurgle in response. But his mother was adamant. 'I want him to learn to be independent,' she insisted, 'and be in an environment where they still have traditional values, and good discipline.' Wasn't discipline one thing for which Chinese schools were famous? I asked. 'Well, yes,' she said, 'they can control their pupils, but what they teach is so utilitarian, it's all about exams. And there's too much competition,' she added. 'Everyone's just competing to learn the most knowledge so they can get a job.' A British public school, she believed, would offer something more. 'Education should include social values, life concepts, knowledge and moral issues all together,' she said.

The fact that she had a successful career and could afford the fees helped a lot, of course. But there are plenty of less privileged parents in China who also dream of sending their children abroad to study, both to give them an advantage in the future and sometimes to escape the pressures of China's own education system too. It's a fashion which has developed rapidly since the 1980s, when the first groups of Chinese students began to go abroad. In those days, most were postgraduates who were sent by the government to study engineering, or other scientific and technical subjects. By the end of the 1980s, a few people began paying their own way, particularly to study in the US, the dream of many at the time. But it was only in the second half of the 1990s that more ordinary Chinese families began to think of sending their children abroad – as some grew wealthier, and as a gradual easing of once tight restrictions began to make it relatively simple for the average Chinese citizen to apply for a passport. At first these students were again mainly postgraduates, but soon people were going abroad for undergraduate degrees too. And before long, some families were sending their children over-seas even earlier.

In a spacious apartment in a new residential compound in the suburbs of Shanghai, Mr Hua was helping his daughter prepare her luggage before she set off on her trip. She needed to make sure she took the right things with her, he said, since she was going to be away for a long time. A pair of umbrellas in her luggage hinted at her destination: his seventeen-year-old daughter was soon to depart for England, where she was to study for A levels, before hopefully going on to win a place at a British university. She was a student at one of Shanghai's top high schools – but the family believed it was worth her dropping out a year early to go abroad. 'I've researched this,' said her father. 'I've heard that if students come over to Britain later they won't get into the best colleges. But those who do A levels there can normally get into good universities if they get good results.' Part of the motivation, he explained, was frustration with the state of education in China. 'We think our education system puts a heavy burden on the students,' he said. 'There aren't so many opportunities to develop individual imagination. Of course they're trying to change it now – but it's hard with the current exam system.' A western education, on the other hand, would be different, he believed. 'I've heard that teaching in the West puts more emphasis on analytical skills, which will be important when she's working in the future,' he said.

Some of his friends thought his daughter was too young, Mr Hua admitted, but he was sure she could cope. 'I think going abroad young will help her to grow up, to become a full member of society,' he insisted. 'If you go at this age your ideas will be more open, and your English will definitely be better too!' His daughter, who had already been on a month-long exchange to the US the previous year, agreed. 'I think it's good for me to have the chance to meet so many different people,' she said, 'and maybe it's easier for me to accept foreign ideas when I'm young.' Having a foreign degree was also likely to give her the edge when it came to applying for jobs in China, she believed. 'Big companies will need people who've studied abroad,' she said, 'so I think I will have a good future and get a job more easily.' Her father, who was in his fifties and worked for a local trading company, acknowledged that the cost of sending

197

her abroad was a significant burden. 'Basically we're spending years of our savings,' he explained, 'we've been preparing for this for years.' But he emphasised that it was no sacrifice. 'Responsible parents make education their first priority,' he said. 'In China we see our children's education as the most important thing,' he added with a smile, 'even more important than ourselves.'

By the early years of this century, many families were following suit. Books by parents describing how they had succeeded in preparing their children for a place at Harvard or other famous foreign universities became bestsellers. Education fairs promoting study abroad attracted huge crowds, not only in the wealthy cities on China's east coast, but in inland areas too. By 2004, Chinese students accounted for one-sixth of the foreign students at British universities, some 50,000 of them in total.[12] In a Shanghai bar that year I met several students, all the children of well-off local families, who were home on their holidays from universities in Europe. One was taking a business studies degree at a university in the south of England – she was a bit disappointed, she said, because at least half the other students in her class were from China too. In Guangzhou, local media reported that one in every five families had at least one member studying abroad, and that many parents worked so hard to pay for their children's education costs that they ended up having to be treated for exhaustion. Others had apparently become so depressed and lonely after sending their children overseas that they had set up support groups with other parents in order to discuss their problems.[13]

But there was also growing opposition to this 'blind rush' to go abroad. Critics not only complained that children were being sent away too early and would struggle on their own, but also that their 'cultural values' were at risk of being eroded. Others felt that the practice was draining China of much needed resources: in 2005, for example, the cost of sending a child to study in Britain was estimated at some 300,000 yuan (around £20,000 pounds) a year.

At the same time, the rapid development of China's domestic economy also began to focus people's attention on events back home as well as abroad. Many felt that China was now changing so rapidly that anyone who left the country for three or four years would be out of touch when they returned. This was thought to be one reason why the total number of students going abroad actually fell slightly for the first time in years in 2004 – though others believe this was also the result of the availability of greater choice and more university places at home. As Professor Zhang Minxuan of the Shanghai Education Commission puts it, 'First we went abroad because we had no chance at home, then we went abroad if we got a cheap chance to go – now we only need to go abroad if we get a quality chance.' There is also the fact that, as the country becomes more closely linked to the rest of the world, 'abroad' is increasingly starting to come to China.

On the outskirts of Ningbo, the famous old trading port a couple of hours south of Shanghai, lies one of those new university districts which have sprung up all around the country in recent years. It boasts wide roads, a shopping mall, an imposing central library and, in between, green fields, though their numbers are decreasing rapidly as they are converted, one by one, into new universities and colleges. In one of these campuses, alongside a man-made lake, sits a very wide building, four storeys high, surmounted by an imposing clock tower with a bell that chimes on the hour. If it looks a little out of place in this part of eastern China, that could be because it would be more at home in the English midlands. It is, in fact, a replica of the main building of the University of Nottingham – and the centrepiece of that institution's recently opened Chinese campus.

Since the second half of the 1990s, many Chinese universities have opened courses and programmes taught in conjunction with foreign universities, or at least using their names and their endorsement to attract students. But this is something different – the first attempt to transplant an entire foreign university, its culture, teaching methods and curriculum into China. The University of Nottingham, Ningbo, was set up with the aim of offering an entirely British education to local students: they would study for full British undergraduate and postgraduate degrees, with all teaching carried out in English by lecturers sent out from Britain. It opened in

2004–5 with a relatively limited range of courses – in areas such as business, communications and international studies – but the plan was to add to these, and attract Chinese people who were looking for something different, but felt it was too expensive to send their children abroad. As the university's first Provost, Professor Ian Gow, puts it, 'I tell parents you can have a degree from Nottingham, or you can get the same degree here and buy a car.'

In the Yummy Café on the university's central 'high street', nineteen-year-old Jiang Weibo tucked into an ice cream with a friend, before going back to spend the rest of the evening writing essays in their shared room. She had just completed the university's first year, a foundation course designed to train Chinese students to do academic research and write essays in English, and now she was in the first term of an accountancy degree. She and her friend had not expected to be studying so much British business law, she said, but overall they were happy with their new environment. 'I think it's better for me to stay in China at the moment,' said Jiang Weibo. 'If I just go abroad maybe I won't know what's happening in China, and I want to work here in the future. But we need to know about the foreign situation too, and here I can get some foreign knowledge – so this is ideal.' Nor would her parents, who came from the countryside and now ran a shop in a small town nearby, have been able to afford to send her abroad for three or four years. Here they already paid some 50,000 yuan (around £3,500) in fees – ten times the cost of a state university – and a few thousand more for accommodation and living expenses. They could afford it, said their daughter, but it was a lot of money for them, especially because she had a younger brother who needed educating too. Still, they had been willing to let her try this new university, after she missed out on a place at her first choice, a top university in Beijing.

And Jiang Weibo felt it was bringing her the new experience she had hoped for. 'It's a challenge for me,' she said; her English had had to improve fast, and there had been other new skills to learn too. 'Here we are asked to do more reading and study by ourselves, it's quite different from the Chinese method,' she explained. But she liked the fact that she had a personal tutor who she could talk to if she had any problems, and she was impressed with the practicality of the course. She and her friend had also been struck by the university's rigorous approach: they had to work hard from the first day, they said, and there were strict warnings against copying other's work, something often cited as a problem in Chinese universities.

It was just the kind of comment to inspire Xu Yafen, one of the prime movers in bringing Nottingham to Ningbo. At first sight, she seems an unlikely figure to be the main investor in a multimillion-pound international education venture. The headquarters of her Wanli Education Group is not exactly glamorous either – it's located in a slightly decrepit two-storey building, the paint peeling from its outside walls, squeezed between a primary school and a row of stalls selling steamed dumplings on the banks of Moon Lake, in one of Ningbo's last surviving old neighbourhoods. When I finally find my way in, Ms Xu, a diminutive woman in her late forties, dressed in a simple jacket and short skirt, springs up from behind the desk in her cramped office and bounds across the room to greet me. 'I can't speak English,' she announces with a throaty chuckle. 'If I tried, it would come out sounding more like German! Ha ha ha!' In fact she didn't get too much education herself at all, she says, since she grew up in the countryside near Ningbo during the Cultural Revolution. But after becoming the secretary to a local official, she started paying more and more attention to management skills, and began reading books by the American management guru Dale Carnegie. Soon she was giving lectures on the subject to local civil servants; eventually she was put in charge of a crumbling local training college for state enterprise staff, which she revived by slashing the bureaucracy and introducing tougher competition for qualifications. Then, in the early 1990s, as reforms of China's education system began, she set up her own education group. Little more than a dozen years later, it has eight schools and colleges, including a university-level institution with 16,000 students. All the profits, Ms Xu emphasises, go back into the schools. 'We're running them for the nation,' she says. 'I wanted to do something for education and my home town.' She gives another chuckle. 'That's why our office is so decrepit, I want to sort out the schools first.'

Despite her group's rapid development, Ms Xu says she became increasingly convinced that the reforms of China's education system needed an external stimulus – particularly where management was concerned. 'Our universities are not so well organised,' she says. 'They're full of bureaucrats, one for every two teachers. And that wastes teachers' time – so things move slowly.' Nor is the system good at motivating those who use it, she believes. 'I've been to universities abroad,' she says. 'Students write a lot of papers, they have to do their own research, ask their professor's advice. In China you don't do so many essays,' she continues. 'We give you a thick book, and you just have to be a good kid and work hard and you can find the answers. In China lots of kids leave university without ever getting to know their teachers.'

Some Chinese academics might disagree, but Ms Xu produces what she sees as conclusive evidence of the problem. 'Chinese people aren't stupid,' she says, 'but we haven't had any university in the top two hundred in the world. And with a population of 1.3 billion, nobody in China has won a Nobel Prize,' she adds. 'Chinese people living abroad have won prizes, but no one at home has. So we felt that one of the biggest problems must be our university education.' It was this which led her to start looking for a foreign model to bring to China. 'We felt that higher education in China needed to import the principles of first-class universities from around the world,' she explains. 'Our system of education needs to change, and this can push it along. If we have a university with very advanced principles on Chinese soil, we can observe it carefully, and study the management methods,' she says. 'The important thing is to show our parents and officials and university heads that we can run our education according to a different model.'

Ms Xu's choice was partly inspired by the fact that two Nottingham graduates won Nobel Prizes, for medicine and economics, within two days of each other in 2003. 'How could they get two Nobel Prizes in a matter of days?' she asks. 'It's all about good management and structure.' And so she and her group set up this joint-venture under a new law on education partnership, introduced in 2003. The Wanli Group has invested more than £30 million to build the infrastructure, while Nottingham is responsible for the teaching side. As to whether the university's teaching on, for example, international relations might raise any awkward political questions, Ms Xu is quick to stress that all the courses have been quickly approved in advance by the education authorities – and according to Provost Ian Gow there will be no taboo subjects. Under Chinese law, the university still has to teach China's compulsory courses on ethics and politics, though students get most of these out of the way in their foundation year. But Ms Xu is convinced that the new set-up is already starting to stimulate students' creativity. 'Our students come here and say, "Aiya, it's harder than final year in high school,"' she says. 'But they don't complain, they're happy: they interrupt the teacher in class, they want to ask questions – because it's all very fresh to them. In most Chinese classrooms no one will interrupt the teachers.' And she's happy too, she grins, because the university is offering a new choice, while at the same time 'saving a lot of money for China's mums and dads'.

And such 'foreign choices' are likely to increase in China: the University of Liverpool has also opened a new institution, as a joint venture with a Chinese university in Suzhou. The Chinese government is undoubtedly paying careful attention to how such institutions develop, but already a number of other colleges from Europe, the US and Australia have either set up shared degree courses, or are considering opening their own facilities, regulations permitting.

Of course, many students are still going overseas to study, but the growing preference for a China-based degree is seen by some as a sign of changing times – and in particular of a shift in the mentality of today's young generation. 'In Shanghai now, lots of kids don't want to go abroad,' says the sociologist Yang Xiong. 'It's very strange,' he frowns, 'it would have been impossible to imagine when we were young! When I was eighteen it was a dream to go abroad, to study modern western experience, see advanced systems.

If you didn't want to go abroad everyone thought there was something wrong with you. Now young people tell me they don't want to go!' Yang Xiong acknowledges that this can be seen as a positive development, a sign that this generation has more confidence in China and its future, and so sees foreign experience as less vital. But he's also concerned that it may reflect a lack of adventure among the pampered only children of the modern era. 'They say to me it will be hard if they go abroad,' he says. 'They ask, why should we spend all that money just to suffer? I think this generation has been spoilt,' he continues, 'life's too comfortable, at least in the big cities, so they're scared of suffering.'

He's not the only one to have expressed concern about China's young generation and its attitudes towards the education on which so much money is lavished. University lecturers, particularly those working at prestigious, foreign joint-venture colleges, where many of the students come from wealthier families, frequently complain that students don't take lectures seriously, and are more interested in looking good and impressing their friends than in acquiring knowledge. The Chinese media often publishes stories about students who spend most of their time on the Internet or playing computer games. According to one report, as many as 80 per cent of students who drop out of university do so because they've become addicted to such games and spend little time on their studies.[14]

In the past few years, there have also been articles by shocked journalists in the Chinese press about students from top universities who don't seem to be in any hurry to look for a job after graduation – either because they're waiting for a good offer or a place on a postgraduate course, or simply because they feel like a rest after years of studying – and are quite happy to let their parents support them for a while. Such people have been dubbed the *ken lao zu* – people who 'feed off the older generation'. According to Zhang Minxuan of the Shanghai Education Commission, the phenomenon has been exaggerated by the media – but he agrees that there are sometimes 'gaps in expectation' between the high aspirations of many of the new young generation and the types of jobs on offer in the labour market – leading to disappointment for some. But it's something he sees as inevitable. 'It's part of the development process,' he says. 'It's like in Britain, if you graduated from university two hundred years ago you might expect to be a government minister or a university chancellor,' he suggests, 'but now maybe you'll be a taxi driver. Over two hundred years the expectations have been reduced generation by generation, so you've got used to it – but the problem here is we've only had one generation.'

Certainly there's plenty of anecdotal evidence to suggest that many young people's hopes for themselves are every bit as high as those cherished for them by their parents. Yang Xiong cites a survey he carried out comparing the ambitions of young people in China and France. 'It's very strange,' he says, 'the French children all wanted to become guitarists or sports stars when they grew up, but in China very young children wanted to be the CEO of a company, or a manager, and to have money and social status.' It was perhaps a reflection of the values of a society where such people are now widely respected and increasingly influential. This may also explain the case of the primary school in Sichuan province where, in 2001, it was reported that children aged ten or eleven were using their pocket money to set up their own 'businesses'. They reportedly insisted that other pupils addressed them as 'managing director', and hired classmates to work as their staff – the girls as 'secretaries', and the boys as 'bodyguards'. One 'managing director' even hired another boy who he called the 'taxi', whose job was to pick him up when he arrived at the school gates in the morning and carry him into the classroom on his back. A local education official suggested that such children had been influenced by television dramas, and had thus acquired what he described as 'a superficial understanding of the market economy'. The large sums of pocket money some children now received also played a part, he noted.[15]

According to Professor Yang, such stories have added to doubts about the ability of the young generation to adapt to the realities of life. 'Lots of old and middle-aged people look at them and say, are this generation any good?' he says. 'Our generation worked hard for this world, we struggled for half our lives to create good living conditions for the young. We went down to the countryside, so we know how to battle and suffer. But these kids grew up in a pot of honey!' As a result, he adds, some fear that China's young generation will simply fritter away the economic achievements of the past decades. 'Many of my friends – older people, officials – often discuss the next generation and ask, "Will they be OK, can we hand the country over to them?"' says Yang Xiong. 'All these "aristocrat kids", we say they're "enjoying luxury before the nation has really got rich".'

Professor Yang himself still believes that, in the end, the younger generation are sufficiently attached to the trappings of the modern world that they have a vested interest in ensuring that China continues to develop. But others remain doubtful about the qualities these young people bring with them when they enter the world of work. Xu Yafen, who set up the educational partnership with Nottingham University, is typically blunt. 'I think the values of our university students have gone downhill a lot compared to ten years ago, or before the Cultural Revolution,' she says. 'Chinese students aren't stupid, but some of them won't lose sleep if they get something wrong. Before they may not have had so much knowledge,' she suggests, 'but they were very strict in their behaviour. Now graduates just want to get a salary – if you give them a task they don't really take it seriously.' As a result, she says, many employers soon become disillusioned with the young people they take on. 'They think they lack a sense of responsibility – and the problem is the young people themselves feel they've done really well.'

Ms Xu has her own ideas of how to deal with this – she insists, for example, that the primary and high schools run by her education group should drill some discipline into pampered children. 'I tell parents they shouldn't spoil their kids too much,' she says. 'They want their children to realise their own dreams, but they don't control how they behave or how they treat others. In our school you can't tell the difference between children from rich families and those whose parents are workers. You can't eat snacks, you have to wash your own clothes, you have to scrub the floors, so in life you'll be able to do things for yourself and not waste people's time,' she adds with a determined look. A lot of parents find this hard to accept, she admits, but she insists it's an approach she's applied to her own son too. 'He was going to England on a school trip, and I told him to pack everything himself,' she recalls. 'He had everything he needed, just no socks. But I didn't tell him. And when he got back he said, "Oh Mum, it was so hard, I didn't have any socks and it was very damp, and there wasn't time to buy any, and they were expensive anyway." So his feet were bleeding,' she says, adding: 'He had to pay the price of not having done his work well, so after this he never forgot anything!'

But not all members of the younger generation accept that it's more discipline they need – or that they're not capable of looking after themselves. Many feel they are coping well under heavy pressure – both from schoolwork and parental expectations. 'I think my parents expect me to be a successful woman in the future,' says one university student, 'so I've always felt a heavy burden. Actually I want to choose my own life, and do something creative. But they just want me to study harder.' And some university students say that, despite the stereotypes of taking it easy, many have to work twelve hours a day to keep up. 'I tried relaxing for six months in my second year,' says a student at a university in Shanghai, 'I wanted to test whether I was good enough. But I soon realised I'm not so clever – I had to work really hard to catch up, and I never did as well again as I had in my first year.' There have been stories too of students committing suicide because they felt they had let their parents down by not doing well enough in their studies.

And other issues add to students' burden. One is the growing competition for jobs. The number of new graduates, nearly five million a year by 2007, is expected to increase by between 700,000 and one million each year for the rest of this decade. The number of students who leave university without a job to go to has also grown rapidly. Job fairs attract thousands of well-qualified graduates, all vying for a few posts: a public examination for 10,000 places in the civil service in 2006 was reported to have received a million applications.[16]

The pressure on young people is intensified by demographic changes: partly as a result of the one-child policy, and also because of longer life expectancies, some of China's big cities are already showing clear signs of an ageing population structure, a phenomenon usually seen in developed countries. In Shanghai for example, 20 per cent of the population was over sixty by 2006 – almost double the national average. As the trend becomes more pronounced, there are official predictions that China could have 400 million people over the age of sixty-five by 2040 – by which time the ageing population problem could be more acute in China than in the United States.[17] And with the national pension fund still not fully implemented throughout society, the burden on members of the young generation is likely to grow. As Yang Xiong puts it: 'I worked out that in the future my son might have to look after twelve old people when he gets married – his parents and grandparents, and his wife's too. So we're already starting to save money for the family in the future. We can't just rely on him – he has to work, he will have his own child to look after; he won't have enough energy and he won't have enough money either!' It's a particular concern, he says, since, in his opinion, the young generation 'spend an amazing amount of money – which will be a problem as the only children become parents'.

Professor Yang is not alone in being concerned about this issue. In recent years, greater publicity has been given to the clause in China's family planning regulations which allows a married couple who are both only children to have two children of their own. In 2006 the local government in Guangzhou publicly urged young people to have a second child, in order to 'reduce the pressure on younger members of society', as one city official put it. But he acknowledged that the cost of living and stresses of modern life actually meant that more couples were now starting to choose not to have children at all.[18]

It all adds to the challenges for China's education system – which now has to balance the urgent need to produce graduates equipped to find jobs in a fast-changing labour market with the demand to make teaching more stimulating, and retain the interest of a young generation with different expectations. It's a difficult task. Some academics have already warned that expanding student numbers, and the pressure on universities to generate income, do not leave staff with enough time to spend with students. And while teaching methods and textbooks have been modernised to some extent, students are still weighed down with, for example, requirements to take political studies courses. These courses have been revised in recent years too – but they can still give rise to some curious combinations: one English literature student I met was studying basic Marxism and Deng Xiaoping theory, while simultaneously researching feminist ideas in the writing of Margaret Atwood.

Some experts insist that teaching is improving – and becoming more relevant. Professor Zhang Minxuan says universities in Shanghai are adapting their courses each year to suit the changing demands of the labour market – and he says they are budgeting higher salaries to attract young academics who have studied abroad. 'These people might not all be good,' he says, 'but at least they've learned some modern advanced things.' And some older academics agree that many of these young lecturers are more willing to express their own opinions and challenge the old ways.

Certainly there's a growing recognition that a more flexible and imaginative education system will be vital in the future – as China attempts to move on to the next stage of its economic development. Many believe this will not only involve a shift away from cheap labour to a more educated, skilled workforce, but will also require greater creativity and original thinking – in order to enable the country to become an innovator rather than just a supplier and manufacturer.

Professor Zhang warns, however, that while it seeks to give students the chance to be more creative, China must not allow the education system to lose all its rigour. 'This nation still has a very high expectation of education,' he says. 'I think Chinese teachers put higher demands on their students than any in the world, and the demands placed on them by their parents are even greater! So the pressure is too high,' he agrees. At the same time, he insists, 'If we don't have high expectations, then we have a problem; if Chinese people don't want to study, what does China have? We don't have so much in the way of resources – we only have people! So we should release a bit of pressure on the students, but I don't want to have none – then there'd be no hope!'

It's no easy task – but striking that balance, and meeting the fast-evolving needs of the younger generation, is one test the Chinese government itself will have to pass in the years and decades to come.

# 8

# The great proletarian sexual revolution

The young couple strolling hand in hand out of the old concrete government housing block and along the tree-shaded pathway hardly looked like the vanguard of a social revolution. Fresh-faced and not very tall, they seemed even younger than their twenty-two years. The girl was wrapped in a thick padded jacket against the winter cold; her metal-rimmed glasses and delicate features gave her a rather bookish air. The boy by her side had a round, friendly face under a fringe of shiny black hair; he greeted me a little shyly and we made our way to a nearby coffee bar. On a Sunday afternoon it was crowded with students from the nearby university, where the girl herself had studied until recently. At one table a trendy young Japanese couple were deep in conversation, chain-smoking all the while; opposite them, a hippyish young woman was hunched over her laptop, complaining to the manager that the wireless Internet wasn't working. When a waitress came to take our order, the boy seemed slightly embarrassed: 'I don't really like coffee,' he said, as though it were a shameful admission.

His girlfriend laughed and teased him a little. The warmth and understanding between them was obvious – and it was hardly surprising. They had been a couple for six years now, ever since their high school days in a small town north of Shanghai. And they had kept up their relationship despite being apart for most of the last four years, while she was at university in Shanghai and he went to art school nearer home. 'It was tough being separated all the time,' the boy admitted with a sigh. He had come to see her whenever he could, staying the weekend or longer, sometimes missing lectures. In fact he spent so much time in Shanghai that his classmates thought it must be his home town. He'd done some part-time work to pay for all the travel: he couldn't ask his parents for money since they didn't really know about his girlfriend – and anyway his relationship with them had been quite difficult since his teens, when they'd thought he was spending too much time on art and not enough on his other schoolwork.

Now he and his girlfriend had finally graduated. She had already found a job, with a foreign company in Shanghai. The boy, on the other hand, had decided to take a year out and prepare for entrance exams for a prestigious university in Beijing, where he hoped to study for a PhD. It was a rare chance to spend more time together, and so he had moved to Shanghai to be with her. 'The last few years have been hard,' he said. 'A lot of our friends split up because they were apart for too long. We managed to stay together, but I don't think it was good for either of us.' They had rented a little flat in the residential block – it wasn't big, just one bedroom and a small living room, but the landlord, a young Shanghai man, was kind and had given it to them at less than the market price. The boy had decorated the place with pictures and craft works which he'd brought from home, and spent his days studying and doing the housework; he often had dinner waiting for his girlfriend when she got home from the office. 'I enjoy cooking,' he said, with a note of pride. 'There's something quite artistic about it.' 'Don't boast,' his girlfriend chided him. 'It's true,' he smiled. 'She's always complaining that when I cook I'm more concerned about the colour of the food than the taste!' 'He's so full of himself,' she laughed. 'He waits for me to come home and praise him!'

The boy grinned. Behind the banter, he was obviously happy with life at the moment. 'This period is very precious for us,' he said. 'Next year I may be away again.' It seemed the most natural thing in the world that they should take this chance to be together after all these years.

And yet what they were doing was something which would not only have shocked many people in China, it would actually have been virtually illegal just a few years before. For decades, Chinese people were effectively forbidden from living together unless they were married. In the extreme years of the Cultural Revolution – and even in the early years of the reform period – such couples could have been accused of the crime of being a *liumang* or 'hooligan', a word used for anyone whose behaviour was considered harmful to the good of society, and could have found themselves locked up in a young offenders' institution. By the 1990s it was less common for such draconian punishments to be imposed, but living together before marriage was still widely known as *feifa tongju* or 'illegal cohabitation' (though in theory the term applied only to a married person who lived with another partner). This reflected the values of a society in which young people had traditionally been expected to concentrate on their studies and not allow personal matters to distract them; indeed, it was only in 2005 that a ban on university students marrying was lifted – and even now some universities still threaten to expel students caught having sexual relationships.[1]

Such attitudes meant the boy and girl had had to keep their relationship secret during their high school years. For him, concealing it from his parents had not been too difficult. 'I think they were a bit embarrassed about things like this,' he said, 'so they never asked me. The first time they actually asked me if she was my girlfriend was when I was in my third year at at college!' But for his girlfriend it was harder. At first she was helped by the fact that her parents had always seen her as *guai* – obedient and well behaved – something seen as a prime female virtue in China. They never imagined that she would be so bold as to have a boyfriend. But during her second year at senior high school she had left the diary she kept lying around in her bedroom, and her mother had found it while tidying up. 'They'd always trusted me and never really checked up on me,' she said, 'so I got careless. My mother was furious. She criticised me, told me I had to break off all relations with him immediately.' As a result, her boyfriend, who had played at her house with other friends when they were younger, was never invited to her home again.

But they had stayed together. At school they took care that their teachers didn't notice anything – though all their classmates knew, indeed many were in similar situations themselves. 'There were seventy people in our class and perhaps twenty were having relationships like this,' said the boy. 'Yes,' his girlfriend agreed, 'it's very normal. We know that abroad people of seventeen or eighteen are basically considered to be adults.' Their cautious approach had paid off, helped by the fact that the girl, hard-working as ever, continued to do well in her studies. 'When my parents saw that my grades were still good they assumed we must have stopped seeing each other,' she said with a smile. 'When I passed the university entrance exam my mum said to me proudly: "You see, I told you to split up with him, and now you've got into a good university!"' It was only later that her mother realised they were still together after all. During her university years, the girl had done her best to win her parents round. She introduced her boyfriend to some of her cousins, and he got on well with them. He even met her parents again; they admitted that he didn't seem so bad, but they were still doubtful about his career prospects. 'My parents are quite traditional,' said the girl. 'They can't understand how studying art can be of any use, they don't think he can earn a living from it. So they want to wait and see whether he can make a success of it.'

Still, for all her family's doubts, they had had no hesitation about moving in together now. 'While you're young you should make the most of being together,' said the boy. Anyway, he said, they were only doing something which was quite normal among their age group; in fact, he added, some of their friends found it strange that they'd been a couple for so long before actually moving in together. 'A lot of my university classmates met their partners at college and started living together after just a year,' he said. During his time at art school he'd shared a flat near college with three male friends: one had his girlfriend living with him, and the girlfriend of one of the others was there most of the time too. 'I was really envious of them,' said the boy. 'They could be together every day, cook their meals together.'

Such 'cohabitation' has become more common in recent years, in part as a result of the changes in China's education system. Traditionally, almost all students were required to live on campus, in tightly segregated single-sex dormitories. The rapid expansion of

214

China's universities from the late 1990s onwards, however, has left some colleges without enough space to accommodate all their students. At the art college which the boy attended, for example, students generally had to rent their own flats after their first year. And even at universities which do have enough space, many students have begun to move out too; it's still not always officially permitted, and so they often have to keep paying for their college dormitories, but many universities now no longer check so carefully whether all students are in their beds at night. But while it has become possible for couples to live together, few of them dare to admit it to their families. 'Their parents might know that they have a girlfriend or boyfriend, but they couldn't tell them they're living together,' said the girl, matter-of-factly. 'I think there are very few parents in China who could accept this.' Her boyfriend agreed. 'My flatmates at university asked us to lie for them,' he said; 'if somebody phoned, we never said who they were with.' Once he'd been woken up very early in the morning by an urgent knocking on his door. His flatmate's mother had just phoned to say she was visiting town and was coming to see him in ten minutes' time. 'He had to throw all his girlfriend's things into my room,' the boy grinned, 'and his girlfriend had to get dressed really quickly and go out!'

Such experiences had clearly stood the couple in good stead for their current lifestyle. Their parents did not know they were living together – and they took care to keep it that way. The boy always spoke to his family on his mobile phone and never answered their home number. 'She has the usage rights for that,' he said with a smile. His girlfriend had told her parents that she was renting a flat alone, and that the boy was still studying in another city. She wasn't sure whether her mother actually believed her, she said, 'but there's nothing she can do about it really. She knows he must come to Shanghai a lot anyway, and she often asks whether he stays with me – but I just lie and say no!'

It was, added the boy, a necessary subterfuge. In recent years he'd actually taken his girlfriend to visit his parents a few times; they liked her, thought she was a nice, reliable girl, even hoped they might get married one day. But still there was no question of

215

admitting that they were already living together: his parents were from the countryside, he said, their values were still old-fashioned. 'If we don't tell them it's because we don't want to hurt them,' he insisted. At the same time he thought they weren't so concerned about him now, at least they didn't ask too many questions anyway. 'I think they don't worry about it so much because I'm a boy,' he said. His girlfriend, however, had to cope with her mother's constant anxiety. 'My mum will often say things,' she said, adding, 'I'm a girl after all . . . My parents are terrified of what others might say; they care a lot about their face, and they worry that my reputation could be damaged.' It was a reminder both of the fact that Chinese society still tends to give men more freedom in terms of what is considered acceptable behaviour – and also of the influence which the opinions of friends, neighbours and society in general have long held over the lives of individuals in China. (This reached a peak, of course, in the Cultural Revolution, when a complaint from a neighbour that someone was behaving in an unconventional way could create serious problems for their family.)

But though such attitudes still exist, some things have clearly begun to change. The young couple were now looking at life through the prism of their own happiness, and, for all their enforced caution, were still basically living as they wanted to. Nor were they in a hurry to think of marriage. 'That's something for the years ahead,' said the girl. In fact, she said, her parents did not want her to rush into marriage either – they were keen for her to study more, ideally abroad, before tying the knot – whoever it was with. 'They hope I'll get married when I'm twenty-seven,' she said. This in itself was a sign of changing times, since in the past most families would have been very worried if their daughter was unmarried at this age. Some of her classmates were planning to get married soon after graduating, she said, but now that she had left home and was more financially independent, she felt freer to live her own life. 'My parents may give me pressure, but I always feel that it's my right to choose,' she said, smiling at her boyfriend. 'If I want to do something I will.'

*

Two decades earlier, university students could have attracted censure just for holding hands. At the student dance parties of the 1980s, men would waltz with men and women with women, and the words 'boyfriend' and 'girlfriend' were hardly heard. The expression most commonly used at the time was *duixiang*, which literally meant an 'opposite number' or partner. If people said they were looking for a *duixiang*, it was generally assumed that this was with a view to marriage. The word smacked of a functional union – of finding someone with a good enough job, a large enough room in their work unit's accommodation block and all the requisite household items to make a suitable partner. In those early years of the reform era, the idea of romance was still frowned upon by many as a bourgeois indulgence. Couples getting married had to fill in a form which included a section where they were asked to explain their 'reasons for getting married'. 'We wrote that we wanted to pool our revolutionary ideals,' said one friend who married his university sweetheart in the early 1980s. 'It seemed like the right thing to say,' he added with a grin.

And once people got married, it was not a state they were expected to think of altering in a hurry. The communist government's first marriage law, passed in 1950, gave women equal rights for the first time, and made it relatively easy for them to divorce brutal or errant husbands – leading to a flurry of divorces in those early years. But during the highly politicised decades which followed, divorce became far less common: any action which suggested that someone was overly focused on their own feelings could lead to accusations of suspect bourgeois, individualistic tendencies. People married, had children, and got on with their jobs. The hints of feminist liberation which had been evident among a minority of educated women in China's big cities in the 1930s and 1940s – when some even defied the restraints of marriage – had also faded. And so, even after the end of the Cultural Revolution, the prevailing values seemed to be a stifling combination of socialist rigidity, traditional peasant attitudes and a smattering of Confucianism, which decreed that a woman's duty was to her husband. Any couple wanting to get divorced had to go to the civil authorities and provide proof that

217

their feelings for each other were damaged beyond repair. And to do so would be to invite widespread disapproval. According to one woman whose parents divorced in a north-eastern city in the mid-1980s, 'It was pretty difficult – when my parents told people they were getting divorced everyone criticised them. My mother moved out of our home town and went to live in Beijing because she couldn't face talking about it any more.'

Extramarital affairs, and sexual relationships before marriage, were even more taboo. It was not that they never happened, of course, not least in the Cultural Revolution when many people were sent to the countryside, far away from families, spouses and convention. But the penalties for those who were caught could be stiff. As the British journalist David Bonavia put it at the start of the 1980s, 'such activities are frowned upon and may even bring legal sanctions'. Indeed, he added ominously, 'the death penalty for repeated extra-marital sexual liaisons is not unknown'.[2]

But as the 1980s progressed, and the controls on many aspects of life began to loosen a little, attitudes and social norms started to evolve. Imported films and popular love songs brought the idea of romance back into society; the 1970s Hollywood movie *Love Story* packed cinemas around China in 1986–7 (though the person sitting in front of me when I watched it in a cinema in Xian spent most of the film commenting on the curious western food which the characters were eating). Slowly but surely, the divorce rate began to climb too. And by the late 1980s, the first Chinese academics were starting to carry out research on sex and sexuality; the female sociologist Li Yinhe even began work on a book on homosexuality together with her husband, the popular author Wang Xiaobo, which was eventually published in 1992.[3] Greater social and geographical mobility – as more people began to travel on business or to seek work – also resulted in more freedom for some, from their spouses if they were married, and from the watchful eyes of their elders if they were not. And changes in the welfare system eventually meant that the once all-powerful work units began to lose some of their influence over an individual's private behaviour. People were also starting to have more living space of their own. Strict controls in hotels, where couples had to show their marriage certificate to rent a room together, began to fade too, as such institutions became more interested in people's money than their morality. By the end of the decade, a few novelists caused sensations by including references to sex in their writing, even if these were often euphemistically phrased.[4]

But it was in the 1990s that China really saw the beginnings of what Li Yinhe has described as a 'silent sexual revolution'.[5] A new generation, which had grown up after the Cultural Revolution, was coming to maturity, with more foreign influences and new role models, and old taboos were starting to break down. The mainland-born, Hong Kong-educated pop star Faye Wong inspired controversy and admiration in equal parts by becoming pregnant by her rock musician boyfriend before they were married. By the late 1990s, a wave of books describing true stories of ordinary people's love lives began to appear in the shops, covering subjects such as one-night stands – though the stories told were often rather sad ones.[6] The number of divorces rose to a million a year by the end of the decade – still not a high proportion compared to many other countries, but triple the number at the start of the 1980s. Divorce remained a sensitive subject, however: while the 1993 film *A Man at Forty*, by the female Beijing director Li Shaohong, depicted the life of a split family, it took more than a decade before the country saw its first major television drama series on the topic. *Divorce Chinese Style* became a huge hit in 2004, with its painfully realistic presentation of the unravelling of the relationship between a young doctor and his increasingly neurotic wife, and its impact on their young child. Now many television series seem to feature divorced characters, or disaffected teenagers blaming their personal problems on their parents' divorce.

There's no doubt that a significant shift in values has been under way. But, for some, it has been a painful process. In the mid–late 1990s, some older women began complaining that their husbands had made the most of the chances afforded by greater wealth and a more open society to find themselves young mistresses. It was a problem which was most pronounced down south in Guangdong, where wealth was growing fast, and where many young women were moving from other parts of China, in search of a job and a better life. By the second half of the 1990s one of the most talked-about phenomena in the area was that of the married men – some from Hong Kong but others from the mainland – who took a young woman as a mistress, set her up in a flat, paid her living expenses, and visited her whenever they could. The practice became known as taking an *er nai* or 'second wife'; in some areas around Shenzhen, close to the Hong Kong border, there were so many such women that entire neighbourhoods became known as 'second-wife villages'.

Scholars attacked such behaviour, branding it the return of traditional 'feudal' values, a throwback to the old pre-revolutionary days when it was common for men to have one or more concubines as well as their first wife. The backlash was strongest in Guangdong, where the local branch of the All-China Women's Federation, a government-backed body charged with representing women's interests, led the calls for such men to be punished. Their appeals coincided with a debate in the late 1990s on plans to revise China's marriage law, which had last been updated in 1980, and was generally acknowledged to be increasingly out of step with the changes in society. The most controversial of the proposals from Guangdong was a suggestion that all adultery should be made a criminal offence punishable by a jail sentence. It was an extreme response, but it reflected the pain which many women felt, explained Yang Jiezhi, Vice-President of the Guangdong Women's Federation, when I met her a few years later. 'The women we talked to were very vocal in calling for this issue to be included in the new marriage law,' she said. It was, she suggested, an attempt to 'preserve traditional Asian concepts of marriage', and protect China from what she saw as foreign values. 'We didn't want a marriage law which was too free,' she insisted. 'Our women feel very strongly about this. We don't want to learn from the West about sexual liberation, sexual freedom, all those things. Besides,' she added, perhaps a little optimistically, 'haven't people in Britain and other countries also started realising that sexual freedom and living with anyone you please is not so good after all?'

The proposals received immense coverage in the Chinese media – in fact rarely had a piece of legislation been subjected to such public scrutiny. Pressure for tougher measures was fuelled by stories in the press highlighting the fact that many of the government officials caught up in corruption scandals (of which there were many in the late 1990s) were men embezzling money to spend on their mistresses. But there were opposing voices too. Li Yinhe described the idea of criminalising adultery as 'seriously wrong-headed'. She sympathised with the pain of abandoned women, she said, but she believed the best response was to strengthen education on moral matters, and at the same time to clarify the rules on compensation for couples who divorced. To jail people for their relationships, she argued, amounted to 'oppressing ourselves', by inviting the state back into people's private lives just as it had begun to retreat a little. Anyway, she claimed, extramarital affairs were so common that the policy would be completely unworkable. 'If the police suddenly had to deal with 30 per cent of the population that would be pretty stupid,' she said at the time, 'the prisons would be full!'[7]

Other aspects of the new law were more generally welcomed. For the first time, it gave clear definitions of domestic violence, which would now be accepted as grounds for divorce; in the past, according to Yang Jiezhi, the police had often been unwilling to intervene in what they saw as a 'domestic issue'. The new marriage law also clarified the rights of the 'innocent' party in a divorce case to damages and compensation, as well as increasing protection for children and setting out rules on parental visiting rights after a divorce – which had not existed before.

In the end, the proposal to criminalise adultery was rejected by China's legislature, which also threw out a suggestion that couples should be separated for three years before they would be granted a divorce. (Indeed, divorce actually became even easier a few years later, with the abolition of a rule requiring a letter from an employer or local official explaining why a couple wanted to separate.)[8] But in a concession to the appeals from Guangdong, the revised law did strengthen the powers of the courts to jail people found guilty of bigamy, the definition of which included not just people who were actually married twice at the same time, but anyone found to be living, de facto, as 'man and wife' with a partner, while officially still married to someone else.[9] It was not everything the Guangdong women had called for – but it provided them with some useful ammunition nonetheless.

Mrs Lau cut a disconsolate figure, as she sat hunched up in a chair in the Women's Federation office in Guangzhou. When she spoke she kept her eyes focused on her lap, her voice so soft I could barely make out what she was saying. The tale she told began as a new Chinese success story. She had met her husband when they were working in the same factory, at the start of Guangdong's economic boom in the 1980s. Soon they married and had a daughter. With help from her father, the couple were able to set up a small factory of their own, which did well. But in the mid-1990s, on a business trip to another city in the province, her husband met another woman, and began an affair with her. Soon he was staying away from home for a day or two every week.

At first, Mrs Lau did her best to accept the situation, since she wanted her daughter to have two parents. But her husband's absences grew longer and longer, and he saw the little girl less and less – even at weekends. Then one day, suddenly, he left home completely; soon he bought another house and moved in with his mistress. 'He wouldn't come back even when our daughter asked him to,' she said. The following year he asked for a divorce, but on terms his wife considered so unreasonable that she refused. 'It was you who did wrong,' she told him, 'not me!' Her husband took her to court and sued for a divorce, but his case was turned down twice – because of his wife's refusal to cooperate, and perhaps also because the law, as it stood at the time, still sought to preserve marriages wherever possible. In his fury at the verdict, her husband cut off the money he had been giving her for their daughter's upbringing. He had even come home and taken away many of their shared possessions. 'He wanted to force me to accept the divorce,' said Mrs Lau.

She tried taking legal action of her own: she contacted the Women's Federation, and was told she could try to have him charged with bigamy, but this was before the revision of the marriage law, and the court said there was not enough evidence to bring the case to trial. And so she had carried on trying to bring up her daughter alone; at her age it had not been so easy to find work, and she had had to borrow money from her parents. Her daughter had taken part-time jobs to help pay for her own education. 'She's such a good girl,' said Mrs Lau. But, she added, the little girl had been hit very hard by the separation. 'Her classmates used to ask her why they'd never seen her father,' she said. 'She used to tell them he was away on business, but after they came to our house a few times and never saw him they stopped believing her.' Above all, it was the loss of her father's love which had hurt her daughter the most. 'He used to love her so much,' Mrs Lau went on, 'he would give her anything she wanted. Now he doesn't even talk to her any more! No wonder she finds it hard to accept.'

Finally, after the revised marriage law was introduced, Mrs Lau and the Guangdong Women's Federation tried again. Now the police were willing to investigate her allegations of bigamy. Her husband was caught living with his mistress, who was by now pregnant; he was charged, and sentenced to eight months in jail. It was less than Mrs Lau had hoped for. 'To be honest I don't think the punishment is enough for him,' she said, her voice almost a whisper. But it was better than nothing. 'This is the price he ought to pay for what he did,' she said. 'He should take responsibility for his actions.' It was in fact one of the first such verdicts under the new law – which had also given her the opportunity to file for a divorce on her own terms. She didn't want everything, she said, just a share of the money they had made together from their factory. 'It's impossible for him to get nothing,' she emphasised. Even after such a long time, she was still clearly perplexed by what had happened. 'Could it have been because he became wealthier? Perhaps people change when they get rich,' she wondered aloud, as though searching for an answer which would make sense of it all. 'I suppose as we open up the market economy, people's ideas change,' she continued. 'Maybe they've been influenced by foreign TV series or movies – I just don't know.'

Yang Jiezhi, who was sitting next to Mrs Lau as she talked, gave her a reassuring pat on the shoulder. She hoped, she said, that the changes in the law would reduce the number of similar cases in the future – and improve the compensation given to women who did get divorced. The publicity given to another local case, in which a husband had been jailed for a year and a half for bigamy, had helped – and the number of complaints received by her organisation had recently fallen a little, she said. But she knew too that many people would not call the Women's Federation if they had such problems. And she felt there was an urgent need to try to change the attitudes of young women, to urge them not to become mistresses. Some young women these days were very bold, she said – she'd had cases of mistresses asking her to help them claim property rights, after their married lovers left them or died suddenly. It was, she suggested, a sign of the times. 'Under the market economy now there are lots of different views,' she said. 'Lots of young women think it's better to marry well than to work hard – they have a sense of dependence.' In an attempt to influence their thinking, she and her colleagues often spent the weekend driving what she described as their 'propaganda van' out into Guangzhou's poor suburbs, where many migrant workers lived. They showed videos, held photo exhibitions, had competitions, she explained. 'Lots of these young women come to the city to work and don't have a family yet,' she said, 'so they're looking for a stable life in Guangzhou – or they may just be greedy for money. But we encourage them to look after themselves, to work for a living, not just rely on their looks for money. We want to tell women comrades, "respect yourselves, don't become a mistress, follow the law" – if they learn about the law then they'll realise that it's a horrible thing to be someone's mistress,' she added with conviction.

There's little doubt that, as Ms Yang herself admitted, the attitudes of China's young generation have been in a state of flux in recent years. Compared to many other countries, they may still seem relatively conservative – in 2005, for example, a poll carried out in seven big cities found that the average age of first sexual experience among people in their twenties was 21.9 years. But the same poll also suggested that things were changing fast – among fourteen- to twenty-year-olds, it suggested, this figure had fallen to 17.4 years.[10] Not everyone is convinced. The youth sociologist Yang Xiong, who surveys young people's sexual attitudes every five years, agrees that the percentage of high school students who have sex has increased – but only from 2 to 5 per cent over the past decade. 'The media like to stir things up,' he says. 'Of course it's gradually getting younger, but the rate is pretty low compared to the West.'

Still, few questioned the results of another survey carried out in Beijing, which found that the proportion of people who admitted to having had sex before marriage rose from 15.5 per cent in 1989 to between 60 and 70 per cent in 2004.[11] The fact that more people now got married later was one factor – but changing morality was undoubtedly a reason too. One study of university students in Shanghai, for example, found that, while some still believed in remaining virgins before marriage, they would now talk openly about sex. Others disapproved of sex among students in their first or second years, but would 'consider it quite strange if someone was still a virgin in their final year', according to James Farrer, the American sociologist who carried out the research. In his opinion, the young generation has succeeded in merging imported ideas of sexual openness and romance with traditional conservative values. The sentimental love songs of Cantonese pop music from Hong Kong, so popular in China, symbolise this mixture, he suggests. 'This is a sexual revolution,' he says, 'but one that's still largely driven by ideals of romantic love.' There is, for example, he believes, still an emphasis in many people's minds on concepts such as 'purity'. 'But the difference now,' he adds, 'is that many young women will tell you that being pure means only sleeping with someone if you love them.'[12]

There is no doubt that, publicly at least, China remains a society in love with an idealised vision of marriage. On high streets around the country, Taiwanese-run wedding chain stores peddle dreams of the perfect western-style wedding – offering the romantic wedding photographs, with flowing white gowns and beautiful backdrops, which have become a prerequisite for most young couples. But in practice, more families do now seem able to accept their children living together with their partner before they actually marry, as long as they are more or less engaged. Dr Sun Zhongxin, a sociologist at Fudan University in Shanghai, and co-author with James Farrer of a number of studies, believes that a generation of young people who are more focused on their personal fulfilment are increasingly interested in, as she puts it, simply 'having fun'. 'Economic development has made these people feel optimistic,' she says. 'A few years ago people did not have that kind of mentality. The rise of the middle class is another factor: this class stresses personal happiness and their own life quality. And they think sex is a basic right, connected to their happiness.'[13]

And the younger the people, it seems, the greater the change. The sight of teenagers kissing in the street is now commonplace in big cities, and researchers say that young people are now becoming sexually mature four or five years earlier than in the 1970s – sometimes as young as twelve or thirteen.[14] Parents, not surprisingly, are concerned. 'I'm pretty worried about my son,' said the forty-something father of a teenage boy. 'You know what teenage girls are like these days!' It seemed an exaggerated reaction – but it had no doubt been partly inspired by stories in the Chinese media. One case which attracted much attention was the arrest in 2002 of a group of high school girls in the south-western city of Kunming. They were accused of operating a prostitution racket involving more than fifty of their classmates, some as young as thirteen, who met wealthy clients in luxury hotels. What caused the greatest shock was the fact that the girls did not seem to have been driven into the trade by poverty, or forced into it by pimps – in fact many of them were doing well at school, and appeared to have been motivated mainly by curiosity and by the money and gifts which their clients gave them. One newspaper described the case as 'having brought pain to the whole of Chinese society'.[15]

It was an unusually extreme case, but evidence of a new morality is not hard to find. I recently met a university lecturer, a worldly

226

man in his early forties, who seemed to be in a state of shock – he had just received a text message from one of his students, he said, saying that she wanted to sleep with him. And some sections of the Chinese media seem to delight in reporting stories of university students either becoming the mistresses of rich men – who wait for them outside their college gates in large cars – or even working as prostitutes in their spare time. Such reporting has angered some, however, who believe it gives an unfair picture. In late 2005 there was uproar when the Chinese media reported a 'survey', published on the Internet by a group of male students at a Beijing university, which claimed that only 15 per cent of the female students at another university in the city were virgins when they graduated. Women at the university in question defended their virtue, producing their own research which showed that 88 per cent of them remained virgins. Yet they in turn were criticised by feminist academics who suggested that women ought not to be influenced by a male-dominated society's 'obsession with virginity'. 'What does it matter whether a student is a virgin or not? As long as it's a voluntary act, I don't see any problem with it,' said one.[16] And advertisements outside some campuses, offering post-abortion care to students who become pregnant, suggest that not everyone is so concerned about such attitudes.[17]

China's young generation are clearly caught in the middle of a significant transition, trying to navigate between what remains of a highly conservative traditional morality and fast-evolving new lifestyles. And they are often doing it with relatively little guidance. China's schools have in recent years begun to teach more sex education classes, and most city schools have introduced more modern textbooks on the subject. But experts say some teachers are still too shy to go into much detail; many parents, meanwhile, are reticent about talking to their children about something which was still more or less a taboo subject during their own youth. The situation may be starting to improve a little – one high school in central Hunan province recently set up a website offering expert advice on sex to its pupils – in order to reduce the embarrassment of face-to-face discussion for both students and teachers.[18]

Nevertheless, ignorance remains high, and has contributed to a rise in the frequency of such problems as teenage pregnancies. There are few reliable statistics on this issue: Shanghai, for example, reported just 140 such pregnancies in 2004, out of a population of 17 million, though officials acknowledged the figure was 'incomplete'. Yet at the same time, alarm about the problem was serious enough that, at Chinese New Year 2006, Shanghai newspapers carried a warning from experts at one hospital in the city, urging parents to pay attention to their children's behaviour during the holiday week. 'Young people's attitudes to sex may become rather relaxed during the vacation period,' they noted, adding: 'with the holiday atmosphere, it's easy for them to get carried away and have sexual relations.' The hospital, which reported a 30 per cent rise in the number of teenagers seeking advice – and abortions – during this period, was keeping its 'Teenage Girls' Accidental Pregnancy Assistance Hotline' open twenty-four hours a day for the duration.[19]

At the same time, China remains a society where family planning rules still, in theory, require women to have permission to have a child, and where the idea of being a single mother is still considered highly shocking by many. One bold young professional woman did announce on her blog in 2006 that she was going to become a single mother, and was proud of it, and a few similarly minded people were reported to have set up a single mothers' forum on the Internet.[20] But for teenage girls who become pregnant through ignorance or by accident, the consequences can be tragic. Chinese media have reported a number of cases over recent years in which teenagers have tried to conceal their pregnancies, or have abandoned – and in a few cases even killed – their newborn babies, out of shame or terror at what will happen to them.[21]

Some experts have also expressed concern that continuing reluctance to talk about sex openly means that a growing number of people lack awareness not only of practical details, such as contraception, but of issues of morality as well. As one educator in her thirties put it, 'Society doesn't give too much idea about what they should really think about sex, so it all depends on the individual families. If the family's morality is very strong it will influence the kids; if not, the kids just have to work things out for themselves.' Among the young people she worked with, she said, more and more had parents who were divorced, or unhappily married, and she felt that this was affecting their attitudes. 'For some of these people the family values are completely gone,' she said. 'The kids see their parents having affairs, and they don't trust marriage or traditional values any more – they just think about what will make them happy now. In the past, if a relationship wasn't quite satisfactory people would try to work it out. Now if it doesn't work then it's over – let's try another!' A rising divorce rate, reaching almost 1.8 million a year by 2005, may have added to such cynicism.[22] And certainly in recent years more young people, particularly the well qualified and professionally successful, have chosen to wait longer before getting married – causing much alarm among their relatives, and leading to the curious sight of anxious parents congregating in parks in major cities, exchanging photos and information about their children, in the hope of finding a suitable match for them.

The difficulties which the government itself has had in facing up to changing attitudes to sex and relationships have been made clear by the way it has responded to the threat of HIV/AIDS. Throughout much of the 1990s, Chinese officialdom was largely in denial about the problem, associating it with the kind of decadent lifestyle assumed only to exist in the West. As late as the turn of the century, China, with more than a fifth of the world's population, claimed to have only somewhere between ten and twenty thousand cases of HIV, and still portrayed the disease as something which mainly affected intravenous drug users, and, to a lesser extent, homosexuals. The authorities did begin making some gestures, marking events such as World AIDS Day, for example, yet the activities they organised usually consisted of handing out leaflets – rather than condoms, as in some other Asian countries. Even in a nation with a strong interest in promoting contraception to keep the population down, it seemed that traditional taboos were hard to overcome.

And when one branch of government did start facing up to reality, it sometimes encountered resistance from others which were less enlightened. In 1999, for example, China's Family Planning Commission made the country's first ever public information film promoting the use of condoms. It was a cheerful cartoon showing smiling condom superheroes defeating villainous-looking viruses, broadcast on a health education programme on national television on 1 December, World AIDS Day. The next day, however, before it could be repeated, it was banned by China's commercial regulation body, which said it infringed rules on the advertising of products connected with sex.[23] There were a number of similar incidents around this period – health workers trying to promote condom use among sex workers were detained by the police and accused of encouraging prostitution, for example; while activists handing out condoms on university campuses found themselves denounced for promoting promiscuity. An official at one Beijing university announced that undergraduates were too young to be the targets of such campaigns – after all, she pointed out, they were 'only eighteen'.[24] And in general, the availability of contraception was limited in a country where condoms had traditionally been issued to married people by health officials in their work units, and were otherwise only available from the stern assistants in state-run pharmacies.

Yet little by little, attitudes began to change. Even as the commercial authorities in Beijing were banning the cartoon about condoms, the local government in Shenzhen, in the south, became the first in China to install condom vending machines on its city streets. When I met the man who initiated the project, Wang Zhiqiang of the city's family planning department, he seemed not in the least embarrassed. In fact, he marched into the room laden with an armful of brightly coloured boxes, deposited them on the table in front of me, and announced proudly: 'These are our condoms!' Mr Wang was blunt about the need for the service: Shenzhen had a lot of young migrant workers, he said, who were far from home and family – and the restraints these imposed. And so they had installed many of the condom machines in areas of the city where migrant workers lived. 'In the inland areas, people can collect condoms from their work units each month,' said Mr Wang, 'but here a lot of people have no fixed work unit and we don't have very many people in charge of family planning, so this makes sense.'

Mr Wang, who said he often appeared on local television talking about such issues, admitted he had come in for some criticism. 'At the beginning some people said, "Hey, Old Wang, if you put all those condoms out on the street people will get confused." But I said, no they won't, is that what happens when people see women's bras and knickers in shops? You think we shouldn't sell them either?' People needed to face up to changing times, he said. 'Some people think this could make it easier to have sex outside marriage,' he went on, 'but our view is that this will happen anyway, whether or not you have the condoms. And as a family planning department, we feel our duty is to help people who need condoms, to reduce STDs and reduce unplanned pregnancies.' Greater openness, he added, was inevitable. 'It's like in the Cultural Revolution,' he said. 'You never saw anyone wearing a swimsuit then – if you wore one everyone would say you were disreputable. Now we have people wearing swimsuits in beauty contests – attitudes have changed. That kind of closed attitude wasn't normal. Now people are becoming more rational!'

Out on the street in front of Mr Wang's office, one of his condom vending machines stood next to a little stall selling snacks and drinks. I asked the couple behind the counter whether they thought people would be embarrassed to use the machine. They laughed. 'How could people be embarrassed in a place like this?' said the man. 'Now Shenzhen is an open place, even women come here in the daytime to buy them. There should be more of these machines.'

In the intervening years, Mr Wang's ideas seem to have caught on – to a degree at least. Condom vending machines can now be found on the streets of many Chinese cities, and even in some university campuses. The new 24-hour convenience stores which have opened up around the country often have a rack of condoms prominently displayed in front of their counters. Indeed, in 2005 one chain of such shops in Shanghai marked World AIDS Day by handing out leaflets to customers promoting a new 'vibrating condom', illustrated with a picture of a pneumatic drill on which was written, in English, the word 'romantic'. Quite what elderly shoppers or parents of young children made of this was another matter, but some of the taboos have undoubtedly begun to break down. Hotels in some parts of China, such as Yunnan in the southwest, which has one of China's highest incidences of HIV, now provide condoms in all guest rooms, and some hotels and office buildings in Shanghai were even reported to be offering free condoms in 2005.[25]

This greater openness has been boosted by the arrival in China of the major international condom manufacturers, with their more direct approach to HIV awareness. And the government too has begun to take a more down-to-earth approach to the problem. In the early years of the new century, for example, it suddenly raised its estimate for the number of cases of HIV sharply, to more than eight hundred thousand.[26] The well-known actor Pu Cunxin, star of, among others, the film *Shower*, showed considerable courage in agreeing to become China's first celebrity AIDS ambassador, and sought to break down prejudice by being filmed meeting and touching people with HIV/AIDS; it was not long before China's President and Prime Minister followed suit. And in 2005 Guangdong province was reported to have taken the bold step of appointing a young unmarried woman – Zhou Bichang, one of the winners of the *Supergirls* TV singing contest – as its own AIDS ambassador, in an attempt to get the message across to young people.[27] There was, inevitably, still some criticism of this move, but it reflected a growing realism – though health experts still have concerns about the implementation of anti-AIDS campaigns in remoter parts of the country. As one AIDS campaigner puts it, 'I think the central government is quite serious and their attitude is genuine, but if you come down to the local level there's still a lot of resistance because of stigma. Local officials may not want to be labelled as an area of high AIDS prevalence, because they're afraid of losing foreign investment, or that it might affect their political career.'[28] And while government health departments, such as the Centres for Disease Prevention and Control (CDC) which work in every province and city, have tended to take a more pragmatic approach – promising to promote condom use among gay men on World AIDS Day 2006, for example – they can still find that their work brings them into conflict with other parts of the system. CDC officials who organised safe-sex lectures for local prostitutes in the north-eastern city of Harbin, in 2006, were again reported to have been warned by police that they were encouraging an illegal trade.[29]

This combination of growing openness and continuing resistance from some quarters is echoed in attitudes to sex in China's media and publishing industries. China is a country which, after all, now produces the majority of the world's sex toys. Yet depictions of sex on television or in movies are still more or less banned. A Chinese television series, *I really really really want love*, widely hailed as the country's answer to *Sex and the City*, attracted many viewers in 2004 with its depiction of the love lives of a group of women in Beijing, but avoided any sexual detail. And while writers who discuss sex, such as the Japanese novelist Haruki Murakami, have become popular in China, translations of their works often cut out some, though not all, of the details of the sex scenes. (Similarly, when the Rolling Stones played their first concert in China in 2006, censors at the country's Ministry of Culture banned them from playing songs such as 'Let's Spend the Night Together'.)[30]

And while tales of extramarital affairs are now seen on television, it was reported in 2006 that these had provoked official disquiet, and the government was planning to impose restrictions on such stories.[31] Indeed, one TV screenwriter suggested that there already were guidelines for scripts on such subjects: 'No television series will ever take the side of the other woman or man,' she said. 'Either they'll be shown to be a bad person, or something bad will happen to them; according to traditional morality, they can't be the winner.'

Nevertheless, although pornography is in theory illegal in China, pirated pornographic movies are often on sale in the country's DVD shops, and foreigners visiting tourist markets in places like Shanghai have long been harassed by men offering 'sex movies'. And in 2006 China's Ministry of Information Industry announced that around half of all spam text messages sent to the country's mobile phone users were pornographic.[32] Even in the realm of official culture, some attitudes seem to have relaxed a little. In 2001, an exhibition was held of the winning entries in China's first official nude photography competition. Most of the photographers were men; most of the pictures were of young women, many of them sprawled naked on large rocks, in deserts, or against other scenic backdrops. The exhibition toured several major cities, attracting large crowds wherever it went. In Shanghai, where it was held in the somewhat unlikely setting of the official 'Workers' Cultural Palace', I was shown around by a middle-aged woman from the company which had promoted the event. The fact that it could be staged, she said, was a sign of 'the progress of Chinese society in the twenty-first century'. And certainly there were plenty of older men and women looking at the pictures who said they saw no harm in them. But as we gazed at the picture of a young woman emerging from the ocean, the sunlight shimmering on the drops of water on her breasts, I asked the promoter whether some might not see this as a kind of 'soft' pornography. 'Certainly not,' she replied, offended. 'This is "human body photo art". It reflects the aspiration of photographers to express the beauty of the human body.' So why were almost all the pictures of young women? I asked. 'The beauty of women is an eternal theme of art,' she responded quickly. She pointed at the picture in front of us: 'This isn't pornography. Look, it's the expression that makes the difference, these are the expressions of models, very shy, natural and beautiful. In pornography the expressions are wanton and unhealthy. And,' she concluded triumphantly, 'these are all natural backgrounds; they're very lovely.' The model who appeared in the winning photograph had even come to the opening of the show, she added, and signed copies of the exhibition catalogue. 'The public reaction was very enthusiastic,' she assured me.

Indeed, so enthusiastic was society's reaction to this type of 'photo art' that the exhibition seemed to give a green light to numerous collections of similar photographs, which soon appeared in bookstores around the country. The popularity of nude

The quiet life: an old *hutong* neighbourhood in Beijing

Out with the old, in with the new: Shanghai lane-houses awaiting demolition

Blueprint for a new life: customers at a real estate fair, Shanghai

Fanning the dream of wealth: Shanghai residents watch share prices
in a side-street brokerage

Indulging the one-child generation: families at McDonald's, Guangzhou

Driving ambition: Auto Shanghai car show

Youth under pressure: anxious parents wait for children to emerge from
the annual university entrance exam, Shanghai

Fighting for freedom: Cosplay fans display their individualism, Shanghai

New idols: Li Yuchun (centre) and the other finalists in Hunan TV's
*Supergirls* contest, 2005

National pride: military training for Shanghai university students,
part of their 'patriotic education'

Women for hire: customers choosing a masseuse at a Shenzhen massage parlour

On the move: migrant workers at Shanghai station on their way home to their villages for Chinese New Year

Hard lessons: children of migrant workers at an unlicensed school in the Shanghai suburbs

The price of poverty: a farmer in Henan province lies dying of AIDS, contracted after repeatedly selling his blood

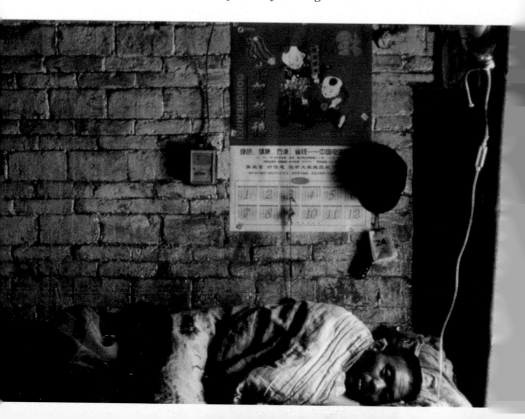

Undying faith: a funera[l]
procession of rur[al]
Catholics in the hills [of]
Yunnan provin[ce]

Praying for fortune:
making an offering to mark
the lunar New Year at a
Taoist temple in Guangzh[ou]

photography has also extended to photo studios, which are often reported to be catering for customers, particularly young women, who want such portraits taken of themselves, in order to 'preserve their youth', as the head of one studio put it.[33] More prudish attitudes do still remain: in 2006, several well-known actresses took part in a publicity campaign to promote breast cancer awareness, in which they were photographed topless, with their hands covering their breasts. But this provoked a storm of controversy and one of them later issued a public apology for her 'mistake'.[34]

Overall, though, there's no doubt that the Chinese media have become more comfortable in covering issues relating to sex and the human body. The arrival of Chinese editions of foreign magazines like *Cosmopolitan*, *Marie Claire* and *FHM* has played a part – these have brought with them their own types of stories and surveys on relationships and sex, though toned down a little compared to their editions elsewhere. Chinese publications too have risen to the challenge: even the most timid-looking magazines can sometimes contain sex tips and advice which the country's sex education teachers might blush at. 'Can I contract STDs through oral sex?', 'Does size matter?' and 'Is the protein in semen good for the complexion?' were just three of the questions fielded by a doctor in an issue of one Shanghai-based women's magazine, alongside recipes for soup and photographs of kitchen units. A psychological test in the same magazine assessed readers' responses to such dilemmas as whether they would go home with a 'very tasty man' they met in a bar, and whether they would look if they found a folder on a colleague's computer entitled 'naked photos of my husband'. (Multiple-choice answers to the latter included: 'Pay no attention, it's just a man's bare buttocks, nothing to get excited about', and 'Look at each one carefully, maybe you'll get a glimpse of some rare "jewels".')[35]

All such women's magazines are still subject to censorship by the publishing houses to which they are affiliated. But according to one former magazine editor, the attitudes of these publishers vary. Her magazine, for example, was not allowed to use the Chinese word for sex on its cover, she said, but it was able to use the word in English, since the person who did the censoring 'didn't know any English'. Other publications, she said, dared to be bolder, since they were backed by more powerful publishing companies with influential connections. As if to prove the point, her mobile phone rang while we were talking: it was an editor from another magazine, asking whether she could write an article about having sex in cars, by the next day. And in the past few years it has become less surprising to find stories such as that published by one Guangzhou magazine, in which a young woman described her dream in life – to open her own shop selling sex toys.[36] The media's changing values have also been highlighted by the success on Shanghai television of a programme called *Soul Garden*, which features couples (sometimes wearing masks to conceal their identity) discussing problems in their relationship in front of a panel of experts.

The Internet too has had an influence on China's changing sexual mores. Websites offer tips on sexual health, and sometimes seem to smuggle in semi-pornographic pictures under headings such as health and fitness. The Net has also been seen (and criticised by some) as providing a whole new way for people to meet and find partners, not only for long-term relationships, but also for one-night stands and casual sex. And it has provided a platform for some of the young generation to talk about issues still unimaginable in the mainstream press on their websites or blogs. The most famous young blogger is Muzimei, a former journalist from Guangdong, who in 2003 began posting details of her sex life and stories about the men she had slept with. She quickly attracted the attention of China's mainstream media, and soon so many people were trying to access her website that the server crashed, while her name reportedly became the most searched-for word on Chinese search engines. Eventually the authorities closed the site, but she later reappeared with another – and other writers have since followed suit.

If the changes in Chinese society have provided new freedoms for some, there's a downside too – not least in the dramatic revival of the country's sex trade, which has brought exploitation and suffering to many others over the past decade and a half. Abolishing prostitution was one of the communists' proudest boasts after they came to power in 1949. The refined courtesan or 'sing-song girl' was a long-established part of Chinese tradition, and in cities like Shanghai existed, alongside less elevated practitioners of the trade, until the time of the revolution. The re-education of these prostitutes and their reintegration into society in the early years of the communist state was heralded as proof that the bad old days of capitalist exploitation had been swept away and a more humane society created.[37]

Yet since the late 1980s, when the first large-scale waves of migration of peasants to China's cities began, prostitution has re-emerged with a vengeance. A plentiful supply of young rural women seeking a better way of life, urban unemployment, and the emergence of a large number of men with the money and inclination to pay for such services, have all contributed to the phenomenon. It's a trade which has become increasingly visible. In the less upmarket areas of many Chinese towns you will find 'hairdressing salons', complete with revolving barber's-shop poles, which are often almost empty in the daytime. In the evening, though, they're illuminated, usually with a pinkish glow; inside, groups of bored-looking young women loll on chairs, watching television or playing cards, occasionally darting to the door to beckon to passing men. Their miniskirts, low-cut tops and late working hours suggest they are offering something more than just a short back and sides. In one small town in central China I counted some fifty such 'hairdressers' in a single street.

And while some of these venues may offer little more than 'erotic massage', it's well known that full-scale prostitution is common in venues such as saunas, karaoke lounges and some hotels. Hotel guests often receive phone calls in their rooms in the middle of the night, from young women offering them a massage. Sometimes these women have simply rented rooms in the hotels as a base from which to work – one hotel where I stayed in southern China cut off the room-to-room call service after 8 p.m., in order to prevent this kind of harassment. But some hotels operate their own saunas or massage services which are little more than a cover for prostitution;

in one hotel in the south, guests who booked a traditional Chinese massage reported finding a pair of smartly dressed young women arriving at their door, offering them a range of expensive alternative 'services'. When they turned these down the women left and the 'real' masseuse arrived. Such practices are apparently not uncommon – even an anti-corruption movie made by the Chinese government in 2000, which senior civil servants and party officials were ordered to watch, included a scene where a local Communist Party boss was taken to a karaoke bar by corrupt business associates, and asked whether he wanted a girl. When he asked, in the interests of research, what the price was, the boss held up one hand: 'This much for one girl,' he said; then he held up the other hand as well. 'And this much,' he said, 'for two!'[38]

In theory, prostitution is still illegal in China, and those involved in the trade run the risk of being jailed or sent to detention centres for 're-education'. One of the most notorious recent cases occurred in 2003, when an entire hotel in the southern city of Zhuhai was reportedly booked by a group of Japanese tourists, and hundreds of local prostitutes were brought in to serve them. This provoked a wave of outrage on the Internet, fuelled in part by the fact that it had occurred on the anniversary of the start of the Japanese occupation of northern China in the early 1930s; arrests were made and two of the organisers jailed for life.[39] Local governments sporadically launch highly publicised 'clean-ups' of sleazy hairdressers, saunas, karaoke bars and nightclubs.[40] In one case in Shenzhen in 2006, police detained around a hundred prostitutes and their clients in one district, and paraded them through the streets in an attempt to shame them (though the action was widely criticised for infringing their civil liberties). Yet the trade never quite seems to go away. The exact relationship between such venues and the local authorities is hard to establish; one Chinese researcher who investigated the trade said he was told not to write about who operated these venues. But it's widely assumed that they either have good connections with, or pay money to, local officials or police, or that these authorities lack either the will or the capacity to close them down.

One factor may simply be that such establishments provide

employment in a society where it is badly needed. A number of tragic cases have been reported, of women and young girls who have been forced into prostitution, sometimes after being raped and threatened, sometimes after being tricked by people they know; and there have been instances of the 'human traffickers' responsible being jailed or executed. Yet other young women undoubtedly take the step 'voluntarily', believing it can offer a quicker route to relative prosperity than other forms of employment for those who lack educational qualifications or social connections.

One man who has seen the trade from the inside is Zhao Tielin, a writer and photographer from Beijing. 'Old Zhao', as he's known, spent much of the 1990s in Hainan, the island province off China's southern coast which was designated a 'Special Economic Zone' in the late 1980s. The plan was to turn it into both a tourist paradise and an industrial powerhouse; at the time, the anticipated economic boom never quite happened (though tourism has developed since), but it did attract young rural migrants from all over China to the island in search of work. Old Zhao himself arrived in Hainan in the early 1990s, having decided to quit his research job in Beijing to start a new life in the south. But the business he set up in the provincial capital Haikou did not last long, and so he decided to try to make a living from his hobby, photography. Many of the clients who came to him for portraits were young women who worked in a strip of 'hairdressing salons' near where he lived on the edge of the city. Most were from Sichuan, Guizhou and other poor inland areas of south-west China; some were still teenagers, few were older than twenty-one or twenty-two. Some wanted to use Old Zhao's photographs for promotional purposes, to help them achieve their dreams of success or stardom; others simply wanted a memento of a youth which they were fast using up.

As he got to know the women better, Old Zhao decided that he should do more than just take portrait photographs. Their world, he felt, was one which deserved to be recorded, in all its harsh reality. He was inspired in part, he says, by the English writers who had documented society in the early decades of Britain's Industrial

Revolution. 'You know *The Pickwick Papers*?' he asks. 'Those writers really cared about people, about how they lived.' And most of the women from the Midnight Cowboy Hair Salon and the Jenny Beauty Parlour were only too happy for their lives to be dignified by the 'professor from Beijing', as they called him. Soon he was spending most of his time with them, photographing them in their spare time and while they were waiting for customers, negotiating with clients, with friends and family. He even accompanied some of the women back to their home villages to visit their families. By the time he left Hainan, at the end of the 1990s, he had taken some 20,000 rolls of film.

The pictures form a remarkable archive – from images of happy, smiling young women, posing for the camera, shopping for clothes, or burning incense in a temple, to pictures of a girl badly bruised after being beaten by a client, having an operation to treat her wounds, and of another woman on a drip tube after being diagnosed with VD. The women had no medical insurance, says Old Zhao, and many could only afford to go to the doctor in the nearby village. 'Some of those doctors were really just quacks,' he says.

There are photos taken in the cheap rented concrete rooms where the women lived, and where they sometimes brought their clients. Some had boyfriends who lived with them, who would go outside if a customer came home. According to Old Zhao, though, such relationships were never stable. 'Most of those guys were good-for-nothings,' he says. 'When they found a girl they would stop working and try to live off her earnings.' Occasionally some of the women did find the wealthy boyfriends they dreamt of, he says, 'but it never lasted'.

As he flips through the pictures, Old Zhao gives a matter-of-fact commentary. 'This woman had just had thirteen clients in one day,' he says, 'she could hardly put on her trousers.' He points to a smiling young girl. 'This child is dead,' he explains. 'She took drugs then drank alcohol.' Of another happy-looking young woman he says, 'This one killed her boyfriend. He had another girlfriend, and she found out and got angry – now she's on the run.'

But of the lifestyle the women chose he makes no criticism.

'Everyone follows their own path,' he says. 'Of course the majority of people would never do this; some would rather die of poverty. But most of these girls felt they had no alternative. They didn't have any work skills, they didn't have urban residential status and they weren't well educated.' In fact, he says, some of them had never finished primary school. Many had previously worked in the factories of Guangdong in the early 1990s, when, according to Old Zhao, labour conditions were generally worse than they are today. 'Some of these places were like Manchester in the Industrial Revolution,' he says, 'blood and tears, people working sixteen hours a day for six hundred yuan [forty pounds] a month.' He pulls out some photographs of a very young-looking girl. 'She was a child labourer,' he says. 'She started working in a factory at thirteen.' When she was sixteen, earning five hundred yuan a month, she had heard from other women of the money to be made in the 'hair salons'. By the time Old Zhao met her, she was eighteen and earning more than 20,000 a month. 'So how do you think she felt about this issue?' he asks.

And it seems that others were able to accept their choice of profession too: there are photos of the women chatting happily with their neighbours. 'The neighbours don't mind, in fact they rely on them, they earn their living by renting these rooms to them,' says Old Zhao. And in their home villages it's a similar story. He points out pictures of the large houses some of the women have built for their families back home. 'The old clan structures in the countryside have gone now,' he continues. 'In the old days, if a girl had gone away to work, she'd lose the respect of all her family. Now if they come back with money people will understand what they've been doing, but no one will look down on them. They have money, they can build a house, that's better than anything else.' Most of the women he knew did manage to improve their financial situation, he says. Some put their children through school, others paid for younger brothers to get married or even go to university. And most moved back home within five years. 'For them this was just a primitive way of making enough money,' Old Zhao emphasises. 'When they got to a certain age they wanted to go home and get married.'

Some of these pictures and stories appeared in a book he published, one of the first on the subject to appear in China. Old Zhao says he was lucky to get it cleared for publication; the officials, he believes, 'accepted that I genuinely cared about China's social problems'. When it came out, he gave copies to the women he had written about. Most were already married with children, living 'normal' lives, he says – but they were not ashamed to be reminded of their past, on the contrary in fact. 'When I gave them the book, they cried,' says Old Zhao. 'Some who had children told me: "If my daughter doesn't treat me well when she grows up, I'll show her your book, so she'll know what a hard life her mother had in the past"'.

And despite the harsh nature of this way of life, Old Zhao believes that other women will have little alternative but to follow the same path in the future. He has been criticised by some for such views, he says, but he argues that 'if you took this trade away, these people would have nothing, no food to eat'. And in his opinion, the huge number of male migrant workers living alone in Chinese cities means the existence of the sex trade is inevitable: 'I think if there's not a legal channel for these people's sex drive, it will cause social unrest,' he says. If the trade cannot be legalised, he suggests, 'the government should at least allow it to exist in a semi-open way – for example, they could set up a special area of town for this, make them pay tax'.

His views are shared by many of those involved in the fight against AIDS in China, who believe that the illegality of the trade contributes to the spread of the disease by hindering attempts to provide health education and information to prostitutes. Indeed, even those who see the sex trade – and the way it turns women into a commodity – as a worrying reflection of women's status in Chinese society increasingly seem to agree that it should be put on a more official footing. 'Women who have already fallen to the status of sex slaves need legal protection,' says Ai Xiaoming, an academic and outspoken member of China's fledgling feminist movement. 'That way their labour rights can be protected, they can have health checks, and they won't be harassed so much. At least it's better than keeping it a crime, which only makes it easier to force people to sell sex.' In her opinion the real issue is the need to find alternative ways for such people to make a living. 'Otherwise large quantities of rural women from undeveloped areas will continue to become sex slaves,' she says.

For Ai Xiaoming, the sex trade is just one of a number of areas of life in China where women are in need of greater protection. An open-faced, friendly woman in her fifties, she started her career as a comparative literature specialist. Later, on a study trip to the US in the late 1990s, she came into contact with the rapid development of gender studies in the West. It was an eye-opening experience, she says. When she returned home, to Sun Yat-sen University in Guangzhou, she set up courses on feminist theory and literature, and eventually established a sex and gender education forum to stimulate debate on such subjects. And here, on the leafy campus of the famous old university – first established by American missionaries in the 1880s, and later renamed in honour of the Nationalist leader of the early twentieth century – she and her colleagues have found themselves drawn, as if by an irresistible force, towards some of the darker aspects of life for women in China.

In Professor Ai's opinion, women in China face a double challenge. On the one hand they are vulnerable to some of the more brutal aspects of the new market economy – not just the exploitation of workers in factories, or the dangers of working as prostitutes, but other hazards too: when I last met her, she was enraged about a case in which a hospital carrying out cosmetic surgery had caused serious injuries and suffering to many women. It came soon after another incident in which tens of thousands of women were exposed to the risk of disease through the use of dangerous cosmetics. To Professor Ai, such incidents were alarming signs of a lack of regulation in this industry – as if the pressure on women to conform to society's ideas of beauty were not enough in itself. 'Women's status is low and so they have to think of every kind of way to increase their opportunities in the labour market,' she says.

At the same time, she and her colleagues believe that many

attitudes which date back to China's traditional, male-dominated culture remain prevalent in society today. It's a conviction which was reinforced by an event which happened on their own doorstep in 2004, when a twenty-one-year-old female student at Sun Yat-sen University was murdered by a male student from another university in the city. Students immediately began to post reactions to the news on the university's internal Internet bulletin boards. Many expressed shock and sadness – but others were less sympathetic. 'Some people's immediate reaction,' according to Professor Ai, 'was to ask whether the murdered woman had done something wrong.' Many assumed that because the girl knew her killer it was a 'crime of passion', she says, as though this 'somehow made it less serious'. Others suggested that the girl may have been sexually permissive, and therefore, by implication, brought her fate upon herself. 'People love to speculate on her relationships, and her sexual relations with her boyfriend,' said Ai Xiaoming during a meeting soon afterwards, which was captured on film by one of her colleagues. 'Many people say, "Only a certain type of person will encounter a certain type of problem." ' In fact, she stressed, there was not a shred of evidence that the girl had been in any way 'promiscuous' or cheating on anyone – and even if she had been, she insisted, 'that would be no reason to judge her as right or wrong. At worst she only broke a "man's law", that women should be possessed by men.'

Ai Xiaoming and her colleagues responded by calling a public meeting on International Women's Day, soon after the student's death. Professor Ai made an impassioned speech: she was not angry with the individual students, she said, but their comments reflected the influence of 'thousands of years of patriarchal society'. 'It's the culture and public opinion which support such violence,' she added. Men at the meeting were asked to wear white ribbons (a symbol of mourning in China) and make a public pledge against violence towards women. The campaign spread rapidly: the university promised to improve safety for its female students, while a number of local officials signed up to a public declaration calling for an end to violence against women. And the following year China passed its first law against sexual harassment. Nevertheless,

Professor Ai says the way such laws and regulations are actually implemented still often reflects traditional attitudes and prejudices.

When she and her colleagues tried to take the debate on the status of women in society to a wider audience, they again encountered some of the limits which persist. In 2003, Professor Ai and her students organised the first ever Chinese-language performance in the mainland of *The Vagina Monologues* – the American play by Eve Ensler which focuses on women's bodies and others' perceptions of them, covering issues such as menstruation, childbirth, sexual pleasure, oppression and violence. It was a radical step, in a country where many of these subjects are still rarely discussed in public – and reference to this particular part of the anatomy has been more or less taboo. Female students and some of the staff of the gender studies programme eventually overcame their embarrassment to participate in the performance: one young teacher acted out a scene about enjoying making love; three others performed a sketch about the sounds they made while having sex. Professor Ai was also keen that the play should reflect some of the specific realities of China, including what she sees as a lack of education for young girls about the onset of puberty and menstruation. 'We need to make parents realise how bad it is to let girls enter puberty with no information,' she explained at the time. The performance also incorporated stories of female babies being abandoned, as has sometimes occurred in rural areas where some people retain the traditional attitude that only a male child can preserve the family line. And to highlight what one participant called 'society's fantasies that women like to be raped', two students performed a hip-hop song which stressed that 'my miniskirt is not a provocation or an invitation'.

The play was performed once, in the theatre of the local art museum in Guangzhou. Some students brought their parents to watch it – and despite some initial embarrassment, it was rapturously received. But when some of those who saw the performance attempted to stage the play in Beijing, as a benefit for a local anti-violence network and women's counselling centre, the performance was called off at the last minute by the police. The official reason was that the venue – an art gallery – was not licensed for such an event, but the organisers noted that such rules tend only to be invoked when an activity does not meet with official approval. Attempts to perform the play again in Professor Ai's university were also frustrated. And although in Shanghai permission was initially given to stage the play in a local theatre, this was later suddenly revoked (though one student group did manage to put on their own performance in a university in the city in 2004).

The first performance did, however, attract much coverage in the Chinese media. The male presenter of one television discussion praised those involved for making 'a good start to break through the silence'. But in a documentary made by one of Professor Ai's colleagues about the various attempts to perform the play, one female academic made the point that China's women were still waiting for what she called 'a revolution of desire'.[41] Students quoted in the film described advertisements posted near the hostels where they lived, for operations to restore women's hymens – a reminder of the continuing prevalence of the belief that women should be virgins when they marry. Indeed, one staff member described the case of a female academic who became pregnant by her boyfriend, only for him to refuse to marry her because she was no longer a virgin!

Professor Ai calls such attitudes 'cultural violence'. There's little doubt that they reflect the pressures which women in China are often under to conform to various stereotypes. These are reinforced to a large extent by the media. Advertising has for years been dominated by slim, beautiful women, and newspapers and television carry frequent advertisements for cosmetic surgery, and for creams and potions which claim to enlarge women's breasts. In television dramas, women are frequently portrayed as beautiful accessories to successful men, as long-suffering wives or mothers, sacrificing all for their husbands or families, or alternatively as scheming villains. It's only recently, with the arrival of more youth-oriented dramas from Taiwan and other parts of Asia, that strong-willed, independent female characters have become more common on Chinese television. The *Supergirls* phenomenon of 2005, in which two spiky-haired, less 'feminine' contestants were chosen as winners of the TV singing contest, seemed to be a sign that some young women were indeed looking for fresh role models and new images. The youth sociologist Yang Xiong notes that the winners were much less popular with male viewers, but sees their victory as a sign that 'the feminist movement will be very strong in this generation'. For the moment, he says, women have a high status 'on the surface', but 'still tend to look at themselves through the eyes of a male-centred society'. For example, he suggests 'there are still many female university students who think getting married is better than getting a good job – it's very sad!'

One person with a particular insight into the status of men and women in China is Jin Xing, one of the country's leading contemporary choreographers and dancers, and also China's first open transsexual. Born the son of a military family in the late 1960s, Jin Xing trained as a dancer in a military academy from an early age before moving to New York as a nineteen-year-old to perform and study. After returning to China in the mid-1990s, Jin Xing underwent gender reassignment in a Beijing hospital, and now lives with her husband and adopted children. In Jin Xing's opinion – and her opinions tend to be forthrightly expressed – 'people want girls to be cute and pretty. Smart is OK too, but if you have less education that's fine – your goal is to find a rich man.' Chinese society, she believes, is still 'eighty-five per cent male-dominated. Women can do a lot of the second-tier jobs,' she suggests, 'and they may be more efficient, but for major decisions it's still a male-dominated society.' Jin Xing herself has been successful since her sex change, running her own dance company, and choreographing and appearing in major performances in official theatres in both Beijing and Shanghai. But even after more than a decade as a woman, she admits she still often reverts to a more 'masculine' approach to get things done. 'When I'm working I still talk like a man,' she says. 'I live in a man's world, I know the mentality, how to talk about work,' she adds. 'I have to have strength so that people will take me seriously; if I take a woman's approach then they may just ignore me.' Some women are starting to become more assertive, she agrees, but she feels that, when they do, society encourages them to behave in similar ways to men. 'In the past you could just be pretty and find a rich man,' she says, 'that was OK. Now it seems you should be pretty and nasty too if you want to get something for yourself: if you can't be a princess, be a bitch!'

Still, Jin Xing says society has been generally quite accepting of her since she became a woman; after a few years when the media were cautious about discussing her story, she now finds herself held up as a role model. 'Now they talk about what I've achieved,' she says. 'I think they're trying to encourage young people, because young Chinese people now talk so much about individuals, about who's successful – so they've used me as an example. Some young people, students for example, actually call me China's Statue of Liberty,' she continues, arching an eyebrow, 'because I came from such a background and did something completely against the mentality of traditional society.' Nevertheless, Jin Xing believes that if she had been less successful in her career she might not have received such a positive response. 'If I was really struggling, maybe everyone would criticise me,' she says. 'I knew society's mentality – so the moment I came out of the hospital I said I need to continue chasing my dream, make myself successful, then you can convince people about the kind of life you have.'

Jin Xing's openness – and perhaps her success too – has helped other Chinese transsexuals to face the challenges of choosing their own life; at least a thousand such operations are reported to have been carried out in the past decade. But they are far from being the only group in China seeking more tolerant attitudes towards issues of gender and sexual identity.

On the pavement in a Beijing side street, a few dozen young people milled around in the gathering gloom, stamping their feet against the cold of the early-winter evening. There was a sense of anxiety in the air. A few people darted in and out of the crowd, apparently passing information backwards and forwards; others craned their necks and peered towards a small door set a little way back from the road; the neon lights above it were turned off, but they suggested it was a bar. Just inside the doorway it was possible to make out a few dark blue jackets with white reflector strips, bobbing around. The police had evidently arrived. Eventually a young man emerged from the door, with a message which quickly spread through the crowd: it was time for everyone to leave. Many of the young people made their way across the street to a nearby restaurant, half nervous, half annoyed. The first All-China Gay and Lesbian Cultural Festival, it seemed, was not going to be taking place today after all.

It was hardly a complete surprise. The organisers had already shifted the venue of the event once, from a large gallery in Beijing's popular art district to this small gay bar in an obscure side street, after being told by the police that they did not have the necessary permissions required to stage the event. But for those behind the idea, it was a disappointment. They had felt that attitudes towards the gay community had changed enough in recent years for them to stage something like this, an entire weekend of performances, exhibitions and debates on the status of gays in China. People had come from across the country to take part; Professor Li Yinhe, the pioneering sexual sociologist from the Chinese Academy of Social Sciences, was due to speak.

The festival's main organiser, Cui Zi'en, gave a shrug; perhaps it was just the local police being overzealous, or perhaps the declaration which he had publicised in advance had been just a little too blunt. Generally, he said, the government's attitude to gays now was 'intentionally ambiguous, they don't oppose and they don't support. Normally they just don't get involved,' he said, 'don't even talk about it.' Cuizi, as everyone called him, knew more about official attitudes to the gay community than most. A big, jovial-looking man, whose round face and red-tinted hair made him look younger than his forty-something years, he bustled around, giving instructions to the young festival volunteers with the air of a concerned hen keeping an eye on its chicks. For him, this was nothing very new. Cuizi had been closely involved with the trials and tribulations of Beijing's gay community since he moved to the capital in the mid-1980s from his home town in the north-east. In those days, he said, there certainly wouldn't have been any gay bars for the police to close; the nearest he and his friends came to organising community activities was to hold meetings in people's homes. It was only in the early–mid 1990s that they began getting together a couple of times a week in bars in Beijing. Not all the bar owners liked it, but eventually one decided it was good for business and turned the place into a gay bar full-time. Now, in 2005, there were perhaps five or six in the city – and more in other cities around the country.

That it had taken a long time for China's gay community to emerge into the light of day was perhaps not surprising, considering that the country had included gay sexual activity on its list of behaviour which could be labelled as 'hooliganism' until 1997, when the relevant law was repealed. And it was another four years before homosexuality was removed from the nation's official list of psychiatric disorders.[42] It was an ironic situation, said Cuizi: there was plentiful evidence that throughout Chinese history homosexuality and bisexuality were not only common but at times considered quite acceptable, at least among the country's educated elite. In his view, their demonisation in more recent decades showed the influence of ideas from abroad – and the Soviet Union in particular – on the communist state. 'This type of thinking was not part of Chinese culture,' he said, 'we didn't delineate so clearly.' But it had meant that gay men had had to hide their sexuality. The vast majority married and had children; those who tried to meet furtively in parks could face harassment and arrest if caught.

Cuizi himself said he had been sure of his orientation since he was a small child, and had never felt any shame or doubt about it. Coming to Beijing as a student had helped too, since it was easier to find like-minded people among intellectual circles in the big city. And when he was assigned a job in the Beijing Film Academy after finishing his postgraduate studies, he felt confident enough to express his feelings about the status of China's gays, writing articles and fiction, and starting to make a series of underground gay films. But his activities did not endear him to his bosses at the Film School, and in the early 1990s he was barred from teaching. The official reason, he said, was that he had made films without permission, and shown them abroad without submitting them for approval by China's official censors. Cuizi, though, was sure that his gay activism was a major factor. 'Lots of others are doing underground films, even now,' he said, 'but they don't have the same kind of hassles as me.' Yet in a curious example of the workings of China's bureaucratic system, he was never actually sacked from his post. He kept his flat at the university, and still received his salary, he just hadn't actually been allowed to give lectures for all these years. Over lunch in the college restaurant, where he exchanged friendly greetings with various 'colleagues', he seemed remarkably sanguine about the situation. It was all the result of the vague status of gays in society, he said. 'By not letting me teach, the bosses can show their superiors they don't really support me,' he explained. 'But if they kicked me out and then the government decided they were wrong to do it they'd have problems. So they just don't want to do anything to make people talk about it.'

And so he spent most of his time getting on with his writing and film work as best he could. Yet despite his years of advocacy for the gay movement, Cuizi admitted that he himself had not felt comfortable about telling his own family about his sexuality until just a few years ago. The occasion was his appearance on a discussion programme about homosexuality, made by the pioneering satellite television station of Hunan province. Cuizi was joined by the sociologist Li Yinhe and a lesbian writer from Beijing, in what he says was the first open debate on the subject in China. He had realised that it would be a high-profile event, and decided it would be wrong to keep concealing the truth from his parents – so he had simply asked them to watch the programme. His mother's initial reaction was disapproving, but she eventually changed her mind. Cuizi said this was in part down to the efforts of his two older sisters' teenage children. 'They were very open-minded about this,' he said. 'My niece would even phone other members of the family and argue with them quite strongly about this issue.' Her action had initially provoked scorn from some relatives. 'People think, you're a kid, what do you know? Can you really talk to us

251

about homosexuality?!' said Cuizi. But in the end they were won over, and had accepted the reality.

And in Cuizi's opinion, the more open attitudes of the young generation were playing an important part in helping to change the situation for gays in China. Showing support and interest in the gay community had become quite fashionable among students, he said; and media coverage was improving too. 'A lot of journalists working in the media now are only in their twenties,' he explained, 'so they don't have too many prejudices. They just want to report on things that interest them.' Not long before, he had even been interviewed by CCTV, the national television station – though he believed the producers had only been able to include him because the topic of the programme was AIDS. 'Normally if a programme's just about gays it can't be shown,' he said, 'but if it's about AIDS then they can talk about homosexuality, that's the attitude of their editors.'

It was a reminder of the impact of AIDS in forcing a greater openness with regard to sexual issues in China. And this combination of continuing restrictions and fast-changing attitudes had convinced Cuizi that the planned Gay and Lesbian Cultural Festival was the right moment to make his outspoken appeal, in a statement issued in advance, for society to put ambiguity behind it and formally grant gays equal rights. 'I want society to reflect on itself,' he explained. 'I'm proposing a new standard for society: you tell us that this is the new China, a new society. We're asking, is it really new, or is it old? You can't just look at whether society has money or not – you should look at equality between men and women, whether homosexuals can love each other openly.' He didn't expect that his appeal would have an instant impact, he said, but he hoped it might encourage others to speak out. His dream, he added, was a society where gays could hold hands or kiss in public, and would have the confidence to appear on television without their identity being concealed, as was still often the case.

But he knew it wouldn't be easy. He himself still faced prejudice from people who looked at him and asked out loud whether he was a man or a woman, he said. 'Sometimes they bet with each other about it.' And he also had to make a point of keeping out of the way of 'middle-aged women who look very concerned and friendly', since he knew that as soon as they discovered he wasn't married they were likely to start trying to introduce him to prospective brides. It was a common problem for gay men, who were still under intense social pressure from the traditional assumption that everyone ought to get married and have children. Cuizi said more gay men were starting to refuse to marry – but the majority still bowed to convention. And he believed that perhaps only 5 to 10 per cent of gay people had been able to tell their families about their orientation, though a larger number were now likely to be open with their friends. Things would change, he was sure, and he hoped that fewer of the generation born in the 1990s would have to get married against their will. But, he added, 'in my opinion, it will take a generation before these things disappear: when one generation dies off and another new generation is born, only then can these things be thoroughly changed'.

In China's cities there's no doubt that many gays are now finding it easier to live their own lives, with thriving scenes of gay bars and clubs – and some catering to lesbians too – in cities like Shanghai, for example. The Internet has helped too, providing information, dating opportunities and a sense of community – with an estimated three hundred gay websites in China by the middle of the decade. And in some circles, such as the worlds of fashion and culture in Beijing, Shanghai or Guangzhou, many young gay people now seem able to be open about their sexual identity with their colleagues. Yet even among these relatively privileged groups, there are still very few who are prepared to follow Cuizi's example and 'come out' in a very public way. And if it's still so hard for the urban elite, how much more so for gay people growing up in China's vast rural hinterland?

Mr Sun knows all about the prejudices of the older generation, particularly in the countryside, not least because he used to share them himself. 'It's very hard to understand, and very difficult for most people to accept,' he says. 'I didn't understand at all, I didn't sympathise.' His feelings were provoked by the discovery that his own son, who was in his early thirties, was gay, and had been living

253

with his boyfriend for three years. For Mr Sun it was a stunning blow. 'I was very shocked,' he says. 'It was a real struggle. I had to go through a long process before I could accept it.' A handsome, craggy-faced man in his late fifties, Mr Sun still looks a little out of place in the big city, sitting very upright at dinner in an urban restaurant. He retains the blunt but courteous manner of the north-eastern Chinese countryside, where he grew up – and where attitudes remain highly traditional. 'In the countryside we put a lot of importance on the family line,' he explains. 'You can't not get married.' He gestures to his son, who is sitting across the table. 'All the people of his generation had kids running around, but he still hadn't got married.' His son had moved away from home to a city a couple of hundred miles away, and his visits home became rarer and rarer. Now Mr Sun knows why. 'In fact he was trying to hide,' he says. 'He was afraid that when he came home people would try to introduce him to a marriage partner.' When he finally found out that his son was not only gay, but that the bar he ran was a meeting place for the local gay community, Mr Sun initially had murderous thoughts. But he was persuaded to see sense by his wife, and his son's friends too. 'Once you get over the shock, you can come to terms with it,' he smiles. 'You can't not have a son!' Now, several years later, they all get on well again. 'On Sundays he and his boyfriend normally come home for a family gathering,' Mr Sun adds. 'And all his gay friends are very good to me, they call me "old dad", because they know I understand them. We're very close – they tell me everything.'

But not everyone is so understanding, he says; in fact, after discovering the truth about their son's life, he and his wife decided they should leave their home village, because they felt it would be too difficult to explain to friends and relatives. 'Our relatives would ask, how come your son still hasn't got married, what kind of wife is he looking for, what's going on?' he explains. 'In the countryside people take this so seriously. Very few of them have any idea about homosexuals, they don't know the word, they couldn't even imagine it. And,' he continues, 'if you explained it to them you'd become a laughing stock. They'd be saying, "See his son, how did

254

he become a homosexual?!"' He sighs. 'Everyone would have been talking about it; I couldn't stand that.' Now, with a new home in Dalian, the city where his son lives, things have become a lot easier, he says. He and his wife don't have too many friends there, and mainly keep themselves to themselves in their little flat. But Mr Sun has plenty to do – he's decided to use his experiences to help others, and has set up China's first telephone hotline for other parents of gay children. 'There are many parents who don't understand their children,' he emphasises. 'The children are really suffering. I want to help parents to understand the gay community – and to understand and love their children a bit more, that's my ambition.' So far, he admits, most of the calls have come from gay people themselves, asking him for advice on how to explain the situation to their parents. It seems as though he's facing an uphill battle. But Mr Sun is convinced there's hope. 'Society will keep developing,' he says. 'We've already made so much progress.'

Most in the gay community would say there's still a long way to go – but despite the ambiguity of official attitudes, there have been some surprising developments. The sociologist Li Yinhe, who is also a delegate to the advisory body to China's legislature, has made several attempts to table a motion calling for the legalisation of gay marriage. She has yet to win much backing from other delegates, but her appeal has received growing coverage in the media, and she was able to write about it in detail on her official blog on the *People's Daily* website during the legislature's annual session in 2006. The country's first recognised gay society was also approved in 2006, at Sun Yat-sen University in Guangzhou.[43] And in recent years, Chinese health officials have finally started to face up to the existence of the gay community, with local governments in several cities now supporting outreach programmes to promote the use of condoms.[44] It's a reflection both of changing attitudes and also of the fact that a relatively more open atmosphere for gays has brought with it some urgent new challenges: there are still few complete statistics on the spread of HIV in China's gay community, but the official surveys which have been carried out show an incidence of

255

between 3 and 5 per cent in some areas, enough to set alarm bells ringing – and there are fears that many still lack awareness of the threat of the virus.[45]

'I'm concerned that China could repeat the disaster of the US in the 1970s,' says Chung To, the head of the Hong Kong-based Chi Heng foundation, which promotes AIDS awareness in China among gay and bisexual men. Chung To grew up in San Francisco in the early 1980s, where he saw many friends – and his high school teacher too – die of AIDS. He believes there are parallels between the response to the delisting of homosexuality as a mental illness by the American Psychiatric Association in 1972 and the similar move in China in 2001. Among China's gay community, he says, 'people felt really empowered by this change, and so now you see a lot more gay bars and saunas. And in the past few years we've also seen the institutionalisation of the gay sex trade.'

At the same time, he points out, condoms are still less easily available in more remote parts of the country, while in the big cities gay saunas are often reluctant to provide them, according to Chung To, 'because they don't want to be seen as a sex venue'. As a result, he says, there are people driving to these venues at the weekend from different cities – 'like they did in Chicago or San Francisco in the 1980s, driving to the city to have fun for the whole weekend' – but not taking precautions. 'I spoke to a guy in one sauna who said he had had sex seven times that night, all without a condom,' he recalls. 'So the social acceptance has increased, and the sexual activity has increased – but the safer sex practice is not there.'

The spread of HIV may be speeded up in China, he suggests, by the fact that bisexual behaviour is relatively common: not only are more gay men married, but he says there are now a significant number of young men who may be heterosexual in orientation, but who work in the gay sex trade because they can earn more this way. 'People have a more relaxed attitude to sex in general these days,' says Chung To. 'For some people, as long as you can make money and get rich, the way you do it is less of a concern.' And his organisation's attempts to do outreach work promoting safe sex among male sex workers are sometimes frustrated by the police, he adds. 'They don't always understand why we care so much about sex workers, and about gay men,' he says, 'because to them such people may not need so much attention or sympathy.' Often the only way he can get them to understand, he notes, is to explain that such people will spread the virus to their clients, who might include 'entrepreneurs, wealthy people – the engine of China's economic growth'. Such attitudes on the part of officials are another reason, he believes, for the urgent need to decriminalise the sex trade in China. And another reminder too that China's uneven sexual revolution not only still has some way to go, but is bringing with it new challenges.

# 9

# Floating people

It was a rainy evening, and the Shanghai subway was even more crowded than usual. Commuters in heavy coats were pressed up against the windows of the carriages; among them, a few young women in the smart suits of office workers clutched bunches of red roses, holding them up at head height to protect them from the crush. It was 14 February, and the city's young middle classes were celebrating Valentine's Day. When the train stopped and the doors opened, the well-dressed throng surged out on to the platform and up the escalators, heading for home, or to meet loved ones in the shopping malls and restaurants of the city centre. As they went, another group of travellers was heading in the opposite direction, a straggling line of men pushing their way down the stairs as they rushed to catch the train. Their scruffy clothes and outsize luggage set them apart from the crowds around them: an old man with a weather-beaten face, a round-faced teenage boy wearing a suit jacket a couple of sizes too big for him, a couple of men in their thirties with holdalls over their shoulder; one carrying a toolbox, another clutching a portable electric fan.

These were people whose lives were dictated not by imported western consumer festivals, but by the rhythms of China's own calendar. It was the second week after the Lunar New Year, the time when China's vast army of rural migrant workers returned to the cities, after spending the holiday week in their home villages and townships – for many, the only time in the year they saw their families. Now, from all corners of the country, they were flocking back to Shanghai, back to the menial jobs – as waiters and waitresses, chefs and shop assistants, workers in the factories and on the building sites, roadside cobblers and backstreet tailors – which kept life comfortable for the city's residents. Some had no fixed job: for them, urban life might mean sifting through the rubbish thrown away by the local residents for things to sell for recycling, or a fresh search for work – like the men who sometimes squatted on the pavement in the remoter Shanghai side streets, with little cardboard signs laid out in front of them advertising their services: 'carpenter', 'plasterer', 'labourer'.

It was a scene repeated around the country – perhaps a hundred million people were on the road this week, and the trains and buses were full, even though ticket prices had been raised to cash in on the holiday rush. The queues at the stations were horrendous. For Mr Liu, as he fought his way through the crowds on his way back to Shanghai, it was a reminder of why he usually avoided travelling at this time. In fact, this was the first time he had been back to visit his family in central China for years. He had been happy to see them, of course, but getting back to the city was actually quite a relief after the long journey – even though it meant returning to a small shared room in a decrepit house out on the fringes of town, where the last pockets of the city's old rural areas intermingled with the new suburban developments of modern Shanghai. Mr Liu rented the room together with three other friends, who had all come from their home village hundreds of miles away to work as painters and decorators in the city. They weren't usually all there at the same time – fortunately, since there wasn't enough room for them all to sleep there; they had also rented another similar place, in a village on the other side of the city, and took it in turns to use one or other, depending which was nearest to the part of town where they were working at the time.

Not that these rooms were exactly convenient: sometimes Mr Liu had to get up by five o'clock in the morning to reach whichever apartment block or luxury villa he was working on, travelling two and a half hours by bicycle and bus. When there was no alternative he took the underground, though it was more expensive, and the prices had just gone up again. 'These days a ticket might cost you five or six yuan,' he complained. 'When you add the bus fare, plus

259

two or three for a snack, and a packet of cigarettes, you can easily get through twenty yuan or more a day – it doesn't leave too much left. But you've got to make a living, haven't you?' he added. At least the rent was cheaper out in the suburbs, and he was happy to be with his old friends, it made the bare rooms feel a little bit more like home.

For many of the migrants returning to the cities, there was no such comfort: many did not even have a place like this to call their own; for those working in factories, accommodation was usually just a dormitory shared with their fellow workers. And others had nowhere even that permanent.

'I'm basically "floating",' was how Xiao Yang described his life. After several years in Shanghai, he had no fixed address; most of the time he lived in a hut on the building sites where he worked as a labourer – and often this was a pretty makeshift structure. 'You don't have a real door,' he said, 'just a wooden board to cover the entrance, so in the winter it can be pretty cold.' There wasn't much space for personal possessions either. 'I only have one bag, with a toothbrush, toothpaste, and a few clothes,' he said. When one job finished and he was waiting for the next one he would stay with his friends, a young couple he knew from back home, who'd rented a place in the centre of the city. That's where I found him, in an old house at the end of a narrow lane, not far from one of Shanghai's most popular shopping areas. The neighbourhood was due for demolition soon, but for the moment his friends still had their room on the top floor, up several flights of twisting stairs. Inside, a ladder led up to a platform under the eaves, where they'd put a mattress for Xiao Yang to sleep on. This evening they were all there, a group of friends from home, sitting on the floor around a low table, where a hotpot of mutton and vegetables was bubbling away. The badly fitting windows let in a constant draught, and the steam from the hotpot billowed white and thick in the cold air.

As Xiao Yang tucked into the meat and stewed vegetables, he began to tell his story. He had once had dreams of a more glamorous life, he said. As a teenager, he had been accepted by the Shaolin

Temple, China's most famous martial arts teaching academy, which was not far from his home in the northern province of Henan. For three years, he lived the life of a trainee Shaolin monk, practising *wushu* for hours every day. It was a tough existence, but he loved it. But in the end he decided it was becoming too expensive for his parents. 'My family are real peasants,' he said, with a self-deprecating smile. 'They only earn a couple of thousand yuan a year, so they had to borrow money from friends to pay the cost of my training. I felt the burden on them was too heavy, so I quit and went to look for work.'

Since then, like so many of China's migrant millions, the wiry twenty-five-year-old with the ready grin had roamed from north to south and back again, trying to find a foothold in the uncertain tides of the new market economy. When he started out, back in the mid-1990s, he had headed first for Guangzhou, where he got a job as a security guard in one of the city's upmarket areas. But he only stayed for a few days. 'I felt really bad there,' he said. 'I didn't know the place, I didn't have any friends there, and the cost of living was so high.' In despair, he phoned one of his friends, who suggested he should try Wenzhou, the capitalist boom town on the east coast, where private industry had already started to flourish. He got a job in a tiny restaurant, selling breakfast to workers on their way to start their shifts in the factories, and dumplings and other snacks for their lunch and dinner. But he had to start at four thirty in the morning and work until seven at night, for just three hundred yuan a month – little more than twenty pounds. Soon he'd had enough. He decided to go to Shanghai, where his brother was already working. Here his martial arts skills came in useful, and he found a job in the local film studios as a stunt man and extra. In fact, most of the time the job consisted of being kicked around by others: 'the dangerous bits', said Xiao Yang with a smile. And in weeks when there was not much filming to be done, he received only a very minimal salary.

And so he had finally taken the path trodden by millions of young men from the countryside before him, and begun working on the building sites of the big city. It was easy to get started: friends from his home province introduced him to their boss, who ran his own 'work team' – a gang of labourers which he hired out to the big construction companies, often for months at a time. At the beginning, building work had come as quite a shock to Xiao Yang, even though he was pretty fit. It wasn't just the eleven-hour days he had to work in his first job, it was more the sheer physical demands of the manual labour involved. 'We had to carry concrete blocks,' he said, 'and I'd never done that before. They weigh over a thousand pounds each, so it takes a few people to lift one. And if the truck can't get into the building site you have to carry them in from the road.' He was able to laugh about it now, but it had been a painful introduction to the trade. 'At the time I just felt like crying,' he said. 'The skin on your hands gets worn off, my fingers were bleeding and blistered – I didn't even have a pair of gloves for the first couple of months.' Often he had to work high up on tall buildings too. It wasn't as dangerous as you might expect, he insisted. 'Now in Shanghai the safety precautions are quite good – if you don't wear a safety helmet you get fined, and if you're working high up you have to wear a safety harness.' But it didn't mean it was easy. 'Sometimes in the winter, when you're up on the twentieth floor of a building at six thirty in the morning, it can be absolutely freezing,' he went on. 'Even if you feel like slacking off a bit you don't dare – it's better to work up a sweat.'

Now, several years later, Xiao Yang earned about nine hundred yuan a month, more than in his previous jobs. But usually he put aside about a third of this to send home to his parents. Life in their village had become a little easier in recent years, he said, but if there was a drought or the crops failed, they'd need his support. He also had to keep some money to tide him over when he wasn't working, since he sometimes had to wait a few weeks or longer between jobs. It meant he had to be careful what he spent: he took the bus because it was cheaper than the underground, and at the moment he didn't have a mobile phone either. Occasionally he went rollerblading with a few friends, at the rink under one of the big department stores, but he couldn't afford to do it too often. 'It's ten yuan an hour,' he explained. 'On my income you can't go skating every day, can you?' Shanghai was an expensive place to live in general, he said, and it could be hard not having much to spend. He rarely went to places like the Huaihai Road, Shanghai's most fashionable shopping street, even though it was not far from his friends' place, because it could be a depressing experience. 'It's no fun seeing everyone dressed up so smart, wandering about the streets looking so casual, buying lots of things,' he said. He looked thoughtful. 'It's hard to express,' he carried on, after a moment. 'It's like wanting something that's out of reach, like when you see those big business-men spending a few thousand yuan on one meal on the Huaihai Road – we wouldn't even dare to walk through the door of the restaurant,' he said. 'Or when you see people buying one item of clothing for a few thousand yuan and you think what that much money means to you, how long you'd have to work for it.' Xiao Yang gave a little sigh. 'It doesn't seem fair. You work hard every day and you can't even afford nice clothes,' he went on. 'So I have a lot of feelings about all this. Sometimes it makes you feel really bad about yourself, like you're really worthless, a real country bumpkin.'

But as he looked round the room at his friends, he quickly laughed these feelings off. Anyway, he said, there were some good things about life in Shanghai: it was safer than back home, where the law and order situation was not always too good; and sometimes he could at least content himself with a kind of reflected glory, from the glass walls of the buildings he had once worked on. 'Sometimes I feel a sort of pride,' Xiao Yang smiled. 'I look at one of those tall buildings and I think, hey, there's a bit of my labour, my contribution, in there. There's a building near here which I worked on,' he continued, 'I often go past it on my bike. And when I see it I feel kind of close to it, it's weird!' His friends started to chuckle at these sentimental remarks, but Xiao Yang hadn't finished yet. 'Now they wouldn't let me in there, of course. I worked on the place, but I can't go in.' He started looking a little sad again. Mr Zhang, one of his friends, who ran his own business delivering vegetables to restaurants, gave him a reassuring slap on the back. 'Yes,' he agreed, 'you feel bad because you've made such a lot of effort, but you can't enjoy the results – that's not fair to anyone. Still,' he added, 'that's reality.' Xiao Yang nodded. 'True,' he said. 'It's a harsh reality – but what can you do?' Then he smiled and took another ladle of hotpot.

One day, said Xiao Yang, his dream was to put a bit of money aside so that he could move back to his home province and start a little business of his own. 'When you're in Shanghai you're always a migrant,' he explained. 'At home you know the people, you have friends and family.' He wouldn't be able to continue in the construction industry forever anyway, he added. 'Once you get past forty there aren't many jobs you can do on the building sites,' he said. 'So you have to look after yourself – because there's no welfare to take care of you. Either you have to go home, or look for some lighter work in Shanghai.' Most people he knew, he said, chose to go home.

But that was for the future. At the moment he was just waiting for the next job, and trying to keep himself in shape. Every morning he got up early and went for a run in the park. 'You have to do something to stay fit,' he said, 'or you can't hope to do the job.' It was particularly important to stay healthy, he added, since there was no medical insurance to cover him if he got sick. 'If it's a work injury they'll still give you your salary,' he said, 'but otherwise they won't pay you – no way!' What's more, he added, 'if you're really ill and don't want to get sacked, you need to get a medical certificate, which is expensive too – otherwise, it's goodbye!'

Xiao Yang's concerns were understandable, since the lack of a welfare safety net is something which casts a shadow over the lives of most rural migrants in China's cities. While permanent urban citizens fret about what percentage of their medical fees they might have to pay for themselves under the new social welfare insurance scheme, for most migrant workers the picture is all too clear: they are not entitled to a single yuan for medical treatment, nor are they eligible for social security payments if they lose their job – and there is certainly no pension fund to tide them over when they reach retirement age.

This is a reflection of one of the great fault-lines running through contemporary Chinese society: the officially enshrined divide

264

between urban and rural citizens. It dates back to the earliest days of the communist state, when the party, in its desire to control the nation and the lives of its people down to the minutest detail, set up a system known as 'household registration'. Every member of each family had to be registered with the local police in the town or village where they lived; the details were recorded in a booklet which listed their address, names, relationship to each other, and the identity of the designated head of the household. This booklet, known as a *hukou*, became a crucial part of one's identity – not least because any welfare benefits to which a citizen was entitled were only available in the place where they had their *hukou*. And to change any details of this household registration was extremely complex – with the result that people became tightly bound to their home towns or villages. For several decades after the 1949 revolution, it was quite rare for people to move around the country at all (unless they had been sent by the government to work in other areas, or mobilised as part of one of the mass political movements of that era).

And just as significantly, the *hukou* system also divided China's citizens into two separate types – rural and urban. Someone from one city, for example, might occasionally get permission to move to another city, by swapping their *hukou* with someone who lived there and wanted to move in the opposite direction. But a rural resident would never be able to change their household registration to an urban one and move to the city. One reason for this separation was the fact that the authorities had, in the early years of the revolution, made a point of setting aside significantly greater resources for the welfare of urban citizens, partly in order to guarantee that industrial output was maintained, and had invested much more in their housing, medical care and education than was the case for rural residents. At the time of the revolution, urban citizens made up only around one-fifth of China's population; the authorities had no desire to see the size of this privileged group swollen by an influx of rural people to the cities.

It was a system which was most certainly not designed to encourage the free movement of labour. And so in the early 1980s, when the first economic reforms in Guangdong began to create a demand for more workers than were available locally, there was some uncertainty over how to deal with the situation. Eventually, in 1984, the rules were relaxed to allow people to move to other parts of the country and apply for a temporary residence permit in their new place of work, though they had to get it renewed by the local police every month. This marked the beginning of what became a massive surge of people heading for the big cities, particularly the new Special Economic Zones of Guangdong, looking for jobs and a new life. By the later years of the 1980s, China's railway stations were clogged with peasants on the move, dressed in cheap blue or green Mao jackets, their possessions bundled up in big red, blue and white striped bags. By the middle of the 1990s, this phenomenon had spread to towns and cities around the country, and the 'floating population', as it was known in China, was estimated at anywhere between 50 and 100 million.[1]

Not everyone welcomed the change, however. Many urban residents blamed migrants for rising crime rates. Already in the early 1990s a few city governments began expelling migrants, or tried to ban them from moving to their areas. Some cities imposed regulations restricting them to the most menial jobs; others raised the fee for temporary residence permits to a prohibitively high price.[2] Even the standard monthly rate of some five to fifteen yuan was a significant sum for people who were earning just a few hundred yuan a month. The migrant workers were effectively paying for the privilege of working long hours for low salaries. Yet their temporary urban residence permits did not entitle them to any of the welfare benefits available to permanent city dwellers; if they were sick or out of work, that was their own problem. Even at the turn of the century, China's plans for a new urban social security system made no provision at all for rural migrants in the cities – even though their numbers were now estimated to have reached some 130 million. They were, after all, still only 'temporary' residents – effectively second-class citizens.

Most of the migrants were relatively young, in their late teens, twenties or early thirties, and, initially, most travelled to the cities on their own. But as the years passed, some began to bring their families to join them, while others married and had children in the city. This created a further headache – since their children were not entitled to attend urban schools. Under the 'household registration' system, the money allocated by the government for the education of each child was tied to the place where that child was registered as a permanent resident – meaning that children born in rural areas were only entitled to go to school in the local village or county town; and since children born to migrant parents working in the city still officially had to be registered in their parents' home village, they were excluded from China's urban schools.

Gradually a few schools in the cities did begin to relax the rules to accept a few migrant children but, when they did so, they usually charged steep extra fees which few migrant workers could afford. With no solution to the problem in sight, some migrants began to take the situation into their own hands, and set up their own schools for these marginalised children. Such schools were not legally registered, and were constantly at risk of closure by the local authorities; they usually occupied cheap rented premises in poor suburbs; their staff often lacked formal teaching qualifications, and the curriculum was thrown together as best they could. But they provided some kind of education for the children – and allowed parents to concentrate on their work during the daytime too.

For people like Yu Xiaomei, these schools were more or less the only choice. She had grown up in a village in Anhui, the land-locked province which runs down to the banks of the Yangtze River and which is one of China's major exporters of migrant workers. She was barely twenty when she first left home with her new husband, to find work in the nearby city of Nanjing. But after a short time she became pregnant and returned to her village, where she gave birth to a daughter. But the need to earn a living was pressing, and when the little girl was just a few months old, they took her back to the city. Once she was able to walk, though, they found it too hard to look after her and work at the same time, and so sent her back to live with her grandparents. Then Yu Xiaomei and her husband moved to Shanghai, where he got a job in a factory. She worked in a laundry, then as a waitress in a Taiwanese-owned café; later she started doing housework, going to the homes of local elderly people and helping them with their cleaning and cooking.

When she and her husband had been in the city for a few years, they decided they wanted to bring their daughter, who was now nine, to live with them too. They were quite prepared to spend all their savings to send her to an official Shanghai school. But it wasn't that simple. The city schools had different standards from those in their home province, where the little girl had already spent three years at primary school. She had never learned English, for example, whereas the children in the city had studied it since their first year. One school was prepared to admit her – but only if she retook two years of classes. Yu Xiaomei and her husband decided this would be too expensive and waste too much time; in the end they had no alternative but to send her to one of the schools set up by migrant workers. 'It wasn't the best,' said Xiaomei, 'but it was all right. At least they could give her lunch, and they had a school bus to pick her up and bring her home too.' It was an important consideration, since both she and her husband were out working until early evening. But the school was located in a distant suburb, which meant the little girl had to leave home very early to get there on time, getting up at five in the morning to be at the bus stop by six.

And having their daughter living with them wasn't always ideal. She got home before her parents and had to get on with her homework alone. In the school holidays she was on her own a lot too – her classmates were scattered all over the big city, and her parents didn't feel happy about letting her go out alone. So she spent a lot of time at home watching television. One summer, a big typhoon hit the city, and the roof of their rented single room leaked badly; they all had to pack up and look for somewhere else to live in a hurry.

And after a couple of years the school fees suddenly doubled: the Shanghai government had begun restricting vehicles with out-of-town licence plates from using major roads during the rush hour, and so the school decided it would have to replace its cheap old bus with a new one rented from a city company. It was much more expensive, and the school had no choice but to pass on the cost to the parents. It meant Yu Xiaomei and her husband now had to pay around three thousand yuan a year for their daughter's education. It wasn't impossible, but it still amounted to several months' wages. They also discovered that the school would only be able to teach students up to the age of fifteen – after which their daughter would have little chance of getting into a Shanghai senior high school, even if she had done well, and it would be too late for her to transfer back to a school in the countryside. So when the little girl was twelve they decided, with heavy hearts, to send her back to their home village, to live with her grandparents again. Here she was still able to get into the local school, where there were no fees to pay, only a little over a hundred yuan a year in expenses for school books. The teaching wasn't the best, said Yu Xiaomei, 'you know how little they pay teachers in the countryside' – but at least she might have a chance of studying until the age of eighteen. 'I miss her a lot,' she frowned, 'but we want her to have the best chance possible.'

The problem of education for the children of migrant workers eventually became so serious that it became increasingly hard for the authorities to ignore. In Shanghai, for example, there were 320,000 migrant children of school age by 2003, in Shenzhen some 400,000.[3] UNICEF estimated in the same year that around 10 per cent of such children were not attending school at all, because their families could not afford even the fees of the migrant schools, or because there just weren't enough such places available.[4] The authorities have now begun to talk about allowing migrant children to attend local schools, and reducing or waiving the extra tuition fees which they used to have to pay. According to official figures, fifty-seven per cent of the migrant children in Shanghai had been admitted to government-run schools by 2007. But the policy also risked putting local schools under immense pressure: in Beijing, for example, a number of city schools refused to accept more migrant children in 2006, after class sizes expanded rapidly to forty-five or more.[5] As an alternative solution, some cities have also started giving some of the existing migrant schools licences to operate legally – though some which have applied for such licences have found that they are still at risk of being closed down if they fail official safety inspections.[6] In wealthier cities such as Shanghai, the local authorities have, in the past few years, given financial assistance to some of these schools, providing them with better equipment or help with building new classrooms.

I once went to look for one of the few officially licensed migrant schools in Shanghai's downtown area. It lay on a winding lane in the old city, a poor neighbourhood where many migrant families live in cheap rented rooms. But even here, there was a visible divide. Just next door was a high school for Shanghai children, with smart modern buildings, a big tree-shaded playground, and a freshly laid basketball court. It was the end of the afternoon, and children in blue tracksuits were assembled for brass band practice, parading up and down in neat formation. Around the corner, the migrant school occupied much humbler quarters, with a small concrete yard and a row of nondescript buildings. But the parents waiting in the narrow street outside to pick up their children seemed pleased to have it, nonetheless. 'At least my son gets some good teaching here,' said a father from Chongqing, leaning on his bicycle. 'He can even sit the entrance examination for a Shanghai high school – you wouldn't have the chance in most migrant schools.'

And many children whose parents have moved to the urban areas still never have the opportunity to study in the city at all. Most migrant workers still find it simpler – and cheaper – to leave their children at home with their families. Mr Liu, the painter and decorator who lived in the Shanghai suburbs, had a twelve-year-old son who lived with relatives in his village. The boy had been on visits to Shenzhen where Mr Liu used to work, and where his wife was still working – but they usually only saw him a couple of times a year. They just didn't have the time or the money for him to live with them in the city, Mr Liu explained.

Such divided families are seen by many of China's migrants as completely normal. As they sat around chatting during a lunch break in a flat they were renovating in Shanghai, Mr Fan, one of Mr

Liu's friends, said that he had a wife and two sons back home in his village in Hubei province. His wife didn't like the city, he explained, and preferred to keep the children with her, to help her grow rice in their fields. Mr Fan had been working around the country for almost a decade now, but the two boys had never visited him. His eldest son would probably enjoy a trip to Shanghai, he said, puffing on a cheap cigarette. 'He's in junior high school now, he's thirteen – but he already wants to leave. At that age all kids care about is having fun.' But he laughed off suggestions that the boys might have lost out as a result of their father being away for so much of their childhood. 'It's no problem,' he said, 'I still go back to see them three or four times a year.' His younger brother, who worked with him, looked a little more doubtful. 'Young Fan', as they all called him, was a quiet, thoughtful man in his thirties, who spent a lot of his spare time reading the newspaper – when he wasn't folding its pages into little hats to protect his hair while he was painting. He had a son back home too – but his wife was with him, working in the city, so the little boy was being brought up by his grandparents. 'He's only six now,' said Young Fan. 'He's quite happy, and they look after him well.' He too insisted that his son didn't lack for family contact – at weekends he often went to play with his two cousins in the next village. But, as he talked about him, Young Fan's eyes were downcast, and he seemed to be close to tears.

And experts have become increasingly concerned about the impact of so many children being left behind by their parents. One survey in 2003 claimed that 85 per cent of migrants had left children at home. Other estimates are lower – but various official bodies have put the number of children in this situation at between 10 and 20 million.[7] And the majority, according to researchers, are being looked after by ageing grandparents. Professor Yang Xiong, the Shanghai youth sociologist, agrees that it's a far from ideal situation: 'Many of these grandparents are illiterate peasants, so they can't do much to help these children if they have problems with their studies'. And according to the 2003 survey, unhappiness, personality disorders and delinquency were more common among such children. The headmaster of one school in Hubei province was quoted as saying that almost half his pupils had at least one parent working away from home – and that these children tended to have more problems at school.[8]

After another study found that the majority of such children were planning to quit school at fifteen, and almost 70 per cent complained they had no one to help them with their homework, the Chinese government announced, in 2006, that it would set up a thousand training centres around the country to give advice and education to the grandparents and other relatives who were bringing up such children.[9] Still, worries remain that these children are more likely to join China's growing number of street children or 'floating youths' – teenagers who leave home without a job or a place to go. Some become part of wandering gangs, or join the ranks of the *ka wa* – the gangs of teenage boys who earn money by thrusting advertising cards into the hands of passers-by on the streets of big cities, at stations or on underground trains. Often they aggressively force these cards onto people who don't want them – I once saw a gang of these teenagers harassing passengers emerging from Shanghai's domestic airport for almost an hour, until the police finally arrived, sending them scattering in all directions. 'They're all over the place now,' says Professor Yang Xiong. 'There are adults organising the trade – but there are millions of wandering children in our cities now.' Concerns have been raised too that children who have grown up without a parental presence may be more naive and easily tricked – and that the criminal gangs which sometimes kidnap young women and force them into prostitution may be specifically targeting teenage girls from such families.[10]

The migration phenomenon has placed all types of family relationships under pressure, with many married couples living apart for years. Often husbands go away to find work and leave their wives at home to look after the children – in some cases, both parents migrate to look for a job – but the pressure to go wherever work is available can lead them to split up and move to different parts of the country. It's a source of great unhappiness, which can make extramarital affairs more likely and lead to marriage break-ups. And, as many experts have observed, men working alone far from home are a major clientele of China's sex trade. (It's noticeable, for example, that in the poor areas of town where migrant workers live, the walls are often plastered with advertisements offering treatment for sexually transmitted diseases.) However, one survey found that although many migrant men wanted to visit prostitutes, they could not afford the cost, while China's Ministry of Health has reported that over 80 per cent of male migrants suffer from 'sexual depression'.[11]

Even when husbands and wives are both working in the same town, the migrant lifestyle can challenge the most harmonious of relationships. Many factories insist that staff live on the premises, and do not provide individual rooms – so husbands and wives who work together either have to sleep in separate single-sex dormitories or, in some cases, in special rooms shared by five or six married couples. Even those who rent places of their own sometimes share with other couples because of the cost. In 2005, one group of migrant workers in a Shenzhen factory became so frustrated with the situation that they wrote to a local newspaper demanding 'the right to a family life'. They all had spouses living elsewhere in the city, they said, but they were only allowed to spend one night away from the company dormitory each week to be with them. A few towns are reported to have built short-term, low-rent apartments for migrants to enjoy conjugal visits. Nevertheless, one Chinese newspaper in 2005 described 'the sexual oppression of migrant workers' as a 'social cancer'.[12]

Migrant workers often have to cope not only with difficult personal lives, but with the discrimination of a society which is eager to make use of their labour but not always so happy to have them bringing their rustic ways and manners to the streets of its cities. Over the past decade or more, urban incomes have grown more rapidly than those in the countryside, making the wealth gap between city residents and new arrivals from rural areas bigger all the time (in 2004, the average urban income was more than three times that in the countryside). And many of China's newly rich urbanites have little time for the scruffy, less sophisticated migrants in their midst.

Rural workers continue to be blamed for much of the crime committed in China's urban areas; there is evidence that many crimes are indeed committed by rural migrants down on their luck (in 2006, for example, Guangzhou announced plans to ban motorbikes from the city's streets, because of frequent cases of gangs of motorbike-riding youths from out of town stealing pedestrians' bags, and sometimes slashing them with knives as they did so). But at the same time, there's no doubt that the majority of China's migrant masses are honest, extremely hard-working, and demand very little from society in return. That does not exempt them from prejudice, however. In 2005 a luxury tourist resort in Zhejiang province, not far from Shanghai, put up a sign saying, 'Entrance forbidden to people in rustic-style clothes'; it was aimed specifically at migrant workers, who had been blamed, apparently without evidence, for a number of crimes in the area.[13]

Suspicion of migrants has also opened up regional divisions within Chinese society – with people from certain parts of the country particularly stigmatised. In the manufacturing boom town of Wenzhou on the east coast, which by 2006 was home to some two and three-quarter million migrants, people from Jiangxi, the next province to the west, have faced particular discrimination. 'I wouldn't hire anyone from Jiangxi,' one local factory boss once told me. People from the province, one of China's poorer areas, were seen as unreliable and often dishonest, he explained. There were even reports that companies had put up signs at labour recruitment fairs saying, effectively, people from Jiangxi need not apply. One group of workers from Jiangxi responded by writing to the local press to complain about such treatment. Finally the local government appealed to citizens to show more sympathy to these people who were making such a contribution to the local economy – though it slightly undermined its message by urging local residents to help educate migrants in what it described as 'the moral restraints of modern civilisation'.[14]

The objects of such prejudice seem to vary in different parts of the country. 'Shanghai people look down on us, but they still treat us better than people from Anhui,' a worker from neighbouring Jiangsu province once told me. 'Anhui, Sichuan, Jiangxi – all the poorer places, they like them the least,' he added. In Shenzhen, meanwhile, a local police station caused anger in 2005 when it put up a banner warning of the danger posed by gangs of criminals from Henan province in the north. Two Henan residents took the police station to court and won a public apology. But the following year local leaders in another suburban area of Shenzhen instructed residents not to rent rooms to people from Henan – and one researcher who studied migrant workers in the city said such prejudice was 'very strong'. It focused on people from Henan and a couple of other regions, he said, but added, 'it's mainly a prejudice towards poor people'.[15]

China's system of dividing its citizens into urban and rural categories has also served to institutionalise the notion that people from the countryside are somehow different. The bureaucracy has, over the years, even put a different value on their lives. In 1999, for example, a bridge collapsed in a suburb of the south-western city of Chongqing, killing forty people. The news was greeted with shock in the nation's media. But there was equal shock when it was announced that the families of urban citizens killed in the disaster would receive more compensation from the government than relatives of victims who came from the countryside. The calculation was based on the different average incomes for urban and rural residents – something which no doubt seemed perfectly reasonable to officials who had grown up with China's *hukou* system, but which led to some (at the time) rare soul-searching in the Chinese media about discrimination against rural citizens.[16]

Such divisions even exist within individual cities. Many of China's municipalities include large suburbs, which are – or at least were until the urbanisation of recent years – basically agricultural areas, made up of fields and villages. People from these districts are also classified as 'rural residents' – Shanghai, for example, had more than two million 'rural Shanghai citizens' in 2005.[17] Such 'urban peasants' receive greater access to social welfare than most Chinese farmers – but are still sometimes treated differently from downtown citizens.

One family who knew all about this were the Zhongs, who hailed from a rural part of Pudong, the area of Shanghai which now includes its new financial district. In the 1990s, Zhong Guoshan, the older brother, put his rural past behind him and became part of the new Shanghai, opening a hairdressing salon, and paying for his daughter to attend high school and then university. But in 2004, when he was tragically killed in a road accident near his home, the family discovered that there were limits to their acceptance as urban citizens. Mr Zhong's household registration, which he'd had since birth, still labelled him as a rural resident, and so the family was offered compensation based on the average rural income in the area – around half of what the relatives of an 'urban' dweller would have received. Mr Zhong's family challenged the decision in court – but lost the case. It was sad, one of the defence lawyers admitted at the time, but he said rural citizens had other benefits, such as a piece of land on which they could build a house – and anyway, that's just how the law was.[18]

There's no doubt that China's media has begun to pay far greater attention to such cases in recent years, amid rising concern about how the country treats its migrant workers. One notable example was the outcry, led by Guangzhou's *Southern Metropolis News*, over the beating to death of the migrant designer Sun Zhigang in 2003, after he was detained by Guangzhou police because he was not carrying his residence documents with him. The paper's powerful reports and the public appeals (by, among others, the feminist Professor Ai Xiaoming) eventually led to a change in the law, limiting the powers of the police to detain people or have them removed from urban areas simply for failing to carry local residence papers. The *Southern Metropolis News'* reporting was thought to have been one of the reasons for the subsequent detention of several members of its staff, two of whom were later jailed. But for many migrant workers, the change in the law was a significant breakthrough.

Young Fan, the painter and decorator from Hubei province, who worked in Shanghai and had left his son at home in the countryside with his grandparents, was all too aware of the changes. He had read about them in the paper, he said, and heaved a sigh of relief – not least because of his own previous experience of the law. 'I was riding my bike out in the suburbs one day,' he said, 'and I was pulled over by the local neighbourhood security guard. He asked for my papers, but I hadn't got them. How can you carry all your documents around with you when you're working on a building site?' he asked. He was detained and sent to a local holding centre. Luckily, he had his mobile phone with him, and before it was confiscated he managed to call his boss, who rushed to the detention centre and brought him some money. But he couldn't save Mr Fan from being 'deported' from the city; nor could the husband of a relative, a university lecturer and permanent Shanghai resident, who also tried to help him.

Mr Fan was driven away in a bus and deposited hundreds of miles away in a detention centre in Henan province. After a week he was set free – but only after paying a few hundred yuan in fines. 'They basically wanted to make money,' he said. 'They detained so many people, they had to let some go to make room to detain the next batch.' Mr Fan had to pay his own way back to Shanghai, though at least his boss had kept his job for him, which was more than could be said in many such cases. Now, after the revision of the law, he was no longer so worried about being picked up by the police. 'I feel more confident when I go out now,' he said. One of his colleagues nodded in agreement. 'Even if they stop you now and you don't have your ID card, you can just give them your name and address and they'll check it in the computer,' he explained. Some people, he added, were not bothering to renew their temporary identity cards at all any more, even though in Shanghai they no longer had to pay a monthly fee to do so.

The changes in the rules were certainly seen as something of a watershed in the attitude of the state to China's 'floating population'. And in recent years there have been some hints of reforms of the household registration system itself. Many experts have advised the government that such changes are necessary, since the flow of people from the countryside to the cities is now a fact which is unlikely to be reversed. Some cities, like Shenzhen and Shanghai, have, since 2004, begun to offer new basic welfare insurance schemes for migrant workers, covering accidents and some minimal health care – though many employers have resisted joining such schemes, since these require them to make a contribution.[19] A few smaller urban areas have also taken steps to allow migrant workers to apply for the same welfare benefits as local citizens, and sometimes even permanent urban residence rights, once they have been living there for a certain number of years and have a stable job. But in several cases, these relaxations of the rules led to such a rush of migrants into the urban areas that the authorities quickly reverted to the old system.[20]

And attempts to make it easier for migrant workers to become permanent urban residents do not always meet with approval from urban citizens, fearful of seeing their cities' already overstretched social welfare systems put under even greater pressure, and the character of their cities changed still further. In Shanghai, for example, where the number of migrants rose from some three million in 2000 to almost 4.4 million in 2005, elderly residents often look askance at these people with their regional accents and different living habits, who now do so many of the city's menial jobs.[21] Some Shanghai residents have also been alarmed at the increasing number of beggars and hustlers on the city's streets – another apparent side effect of the change in the law which reduced police powers to remove people from the city.

In 2005 the Shanghai government even issued a guide to help citizens distinguish real beggars from fake ones.[22] Such people certainly increased in number around that time: from the organised groups clutching small children, who they thrust in front of foreigners or wealthy locals, to the shabbily dressed families wandering around quiet backstreets asking residents for money, and the old men, their heads wrapped in cloth, in the style of the peasants of north-west China, who knocked on car windows at traffic lights. It was as though the poverty of some of China's remotest areas had suddenly been transferred to the streets of the big city. Many locals were unimpressed. 'We should kick all these people out and send them far away, back to their homes,' said one resident. 'There are lots of people who have arms and legs and could work,' he added, 'but they don't want to.' But it was getting harder to remove such people, he said, 'because of human rights – if we kick them out the Americans will start criticising us!' Others, however, are adamant that there should be no going back to the old ways of detention and expulsion. According to Professor Ai Xiaoming, who played a part in getting the powers of the police curbed, 'countries around the world have all kinds of ways of controlling their population – you don't have to kidnap people on the street!'

Despite the change in the law, there's no getting away from the fact that migrant workers remain among the most vulnerable members of Chinese society. They do many of the lowest paid jobs: in 2004 their average income was estimated at around 6,500 yuan (less than £500), barely two thirds that of a permanent urban resident.[23] Many earn significantly less: in the same year, in the south-western province of Yunnan, one of China's poorer regions, a survey of eight hundred migrants in local towns and cities found that less than a third earned over six thousand yuan a year. And many of these migrants had spouses, children or parents with them in the city – by the time their salaries were divided among these dependants, the average income per head, according to the survey, was around or below the local 'minimum living standard' (even the level used in the poorest urban areas, where the standard tends to be set particularly low). The survey, for the local Poverty Alleviation Bureau in conjunction with a German development agency, also found that three-quarters of the migrants worked seven days a week; one in six worked more than twelve hours a day; and almost two-thirds worked more than eight hours a day. Working conditions for women were significantly worse: almost 30 per cent worked more than twelve hours a day, while nearly two-thirds earned less than three hundred yuan (just over twenty pounds) a month.[24]

Migrant workers' chances of protecting their rights are not helped by the fact that many are poorly educated. In the Yunnan survey, for example, over 40 per cent of migrants had only a primary school education, and only a third of them knew the officially specified minimum wage for the type of job in which they worked. In the bigger cities of the south and east, the average educational level of migrants tends to be higher – but they remain vulnerable. In extreme cases, migrants can fall victim to abuse, violence, sometimes even rape, by employers or supervisors. And more generally, there's a sense that such workers are often treated as little more than cannon fodder by their employers. In industries such as construction, they are sometimes used as human beasts of burden, given back-breaking tasks, and shouted at and ordered around by their bosses. In some factories workers have to stand in ranks singing company songs at the start of every day to inspire them to work harder. Restaurant staff, meanwhile, can often be seen lined up outside on the pavement at the start of their shifts, and forced to stand to attention while their boss shouts instructions at them, and they chant responses in quasi-military fashion.

I once watched half a dozen migrant workers, most of them women, hammering out small trinkets from big pieces of metal on the floor of a factory courtyard in Zhejiang province, south of Shanghai. It was late at night and the centre of the yard was picked out from the surrounding gloom by bright lights. As the shadows of the workers flickered in and out of the light, it was hard not to think of scenes from Dickens. China is undergoing its own industrial revolution: the technology is often more modern, but the scale is bigger by far than anything seen before in Europe – and many of the issues relating to the rights of workers remain the same.

In recent years, there have been some official attempts to catch up with the rapid growth of private industry by tightening labour laws and stepping up monitoring of working conditions – at least in comparison with the Wild West atmosphere which prevailed, particularly down south in Guangdong, in the early years of economic opening. Big factories are usually required to have a branch of China's official labour union, which may sometimes provide a certain amount of protection for workers' rights. But the vast majority of migrants are employed by small, privately run businesses, where there is often little control over working practices, and where they lack any form of representation. And though they are among the lowest paid workers in China, they are particularly vulnerable to being cheated out of even this meagre income. A government survey in 2006 suggested that at least 20 per cent of migrants had had wages unfairly docked, or delayed by an average of four months – some were owed years of back pay. In the construction industry alone, official estimates have put the amount of unpaid wages at some 10 billion yuan – more than half a billion pounds.[25]

It's a problem which becomes most obvious in the months leading up to Chinese New Year, when there are frequent reports of strikes by workers who are owed money, and now need it more than ever in order to go home and see their families. In local newspapers around the country, it's not uncommon to read about migrant workers threatening suicide in protest at not being paid; one such migrant, who threatened to jump off a bridge in Guangzhou in 2005, was arrested and sentenced to a year's detention for disrupting traffic.[26] Others have gone further still. In May the same year, a migrant worker from Gansu province in the north-west murdered his boss and three of the boss's relatives after an unsuccessful five-month campaign to obtain his unpaid wages; both the courts and the local labour department had failed to help him.[27]

In the past few years, the government has repeatedly pledged to tackle the problem, recognising its potential to create social instability: action has been taken against some companies which have failed to pay staff for long periods, and there have been proposals that companies awarded government contracts may be required to put wages into deposit accounts in advance to prevent defaulting on workers' salaries. But many migrant workers in smaller companies do not even have formal employment contracts – making it hard for them to defend their rights. And if they try to fight back by staging protests, they run the risk of detention or, in some cases, of being attacked by thugs hired by their employers.[28]

In response, migrants in some areas have resorted to forming their own organisations, frequently of people from the same home province, to try to protect their rights. These organisations are technically illegal, however, and some have apparently turned into little more than protection rackets, extorting fees from vulnerable workers.[29] In the past few years, some cities have begun offering legal aid to migrants, and giving them more education on their rights. In 2005, for example, the Shanghai government sent professors out onto local building sites to lecture some of the city's half a million construction workers on their legal entitlements and what to do if these were infringed. In some areas there have been experiments with setting up official unions for migrants; China's new Labour Contract Law, introduced in 2008, also held out the prospect of greater protection for workers – but it remains to be seen how much impact it will have.

For all the problems, the phenomenon of migration to China's cities shows no sign of letting up. Many are lured to the cities by success stories – like that of the woman I once met from Anhui province who lived with an elderly couple in Shanghai, caring for them day and night, and had succeeded in putting her three children through university. Migrant workers can now be found in towns and cities all over the country, the total number estimated at some 150 million by 2006.[31] But the phenomenon is still arguably most pronounced down south in Guangdong province, where the number of migrants dwarfs that of even Shanghai or Beijing. It becomes apparent as soon as you leave the provincial capital Guangzhou on the train line which runs down through the Pearl River Delta towards Shenzhen and the Hong Kong border. As the train approaches the neighbouring city of Dongguan, the fields and fish ponds of the remaining rural areas are replaced by the first workers' dormitories, ugly square buildings with clothes drying on the balconies, and occasionally a worker peering out of a window. The signs of factories flash by – thermal products, LED lamps, leather goods – many announcing proudly that they have been awarded 'ISO 900', the international quality standard. Soon there are advertising billboards promoting new luxury housing developments, perhaps some of the neoclassical towers on the city's skyline, which can now be seen in the distance. Dongguan was a largely rural area until the mid-1980s, when it became one of China's first Special Economic Zones. It quickly began to draw in migrant workers: 150,000 by 1986, half a million by 1989. And since the 1990s, its expansion has taken on staggering proportions: in 2004 the city had almost five million migrants; just one year later the number had risen to nearer six million.[32] Now, as the train announcer proudly reminds passengers, Dongguan has thirteen five-star hotels, no doubt catering to the bosses of some of its 20,000 factories, which make 40 per cent of the world's computer parts and much of its furniture too. The city has the biggest Nokia factory in the world; and recently opened what claims to be the world's largest shopping mall.[33]

But soon all this fades into the distance. The train passes Zhangmutou, a town hardly known outside Guangdong but now another fast-growing industrial area. Finally it approaches the out-skirts of Shenzhen, where the densely packed, grim-looking tower blocks of the city's first wave of development in the 1980s are gradually being replaced by modern luxury residences. Shenzhen is another migrant city: only one and a half million of its total population of more than 10 million are permanent residents. The city centre has wide tree-lined avenues and shiny shopping centres, but factories still lurk behind them. At lunchtime, workers in matching factory overalls spill out onto the pavements and head for the cheap restaurants and convenience stores. On the street, in the subway, people are talking about business deals and orders from clients.

And you don't have to go far before you are in a world far removed from the surface glamour of the city centre. In one of Shenzhen's remaining downtown industrial zones, on a grimy side street, lies a tall, decrepit building incorporating various workshops and ware-houses, as well as small dormitory apartments where migrant workers live as many as ten to a room. It's here that you will find Liu Kaiming, in the rented office where he runs the China Labour Research and Support Network. Wiry and energetic, Mr Liu is a former academic who worked as a journalist in Shenzhen, until he became so concerned at the plight of migrant workers that he decided to set up his own organisation to study their problems – and try to find solutions. The figures he reels off explain his concern. Shenzhen has more than six million people working in manufacturing, but 30 per cent of them, he says, still receive less than the official minimum wage (officially set, in 2006, at between six hundred and eight hundred yuan a month, depending on whether they work in the central part of the city or in its more distant suburbs). Four million of the workers live in group dormitories, and Liu Kaiming says many still work long hours in contravention of labour laws. Disputes over unpaid wages are common here too.

Mr Liu believes one of the biggest causes of problems for migrant workers in the area is straightforward – a lack of management skills. Hundreds of thousands of factories have sprung up in Shenzhen and the surrounding parts of Guangdong in the past decade and a half, the majority owned by domestic or Hong Kong firms, but, Mr Liu suggests, few of those in charge have ever studied how to run a business. 'Most of the managers of China's factories have never worked in management before, they've never studied for an MBA, they don't know the value of workers,' he says. He and his colleagues, with backing from several international organisations, have launched their own education campaign – both for workers and managers. 'Empowerment of workers is a key thing,' he explains, 'but you have to make the bosses feel there's some practical advantage for them too. Some are worried that we just want to protect the workers and they're scared that once the workers start understanding their rights there'll be clashes.' And so his organisation offers training for all, management included, and emphasises that a satisfied workforce will bring greater efficiency – and greater profit. Many companies refuse to get involved, says Mr Liu, but he believes those which have taken part in the scheme have seen the benefits. He gives the example of one clothing factory where he and his colleagues advised the staff on how to set up a committee of workers. As a result he says, 'the workers' salaries went up from four yuan an hour to five, and now they only work forty-five hours a week, instead of ten hours a day'. At the same time, he emphasises, 'the bosses' income has gone up too'. Almost all the company's orders

284

are now completed on time, he explains, saving the firm large sums of money which it used to have to spend on shipping delayed orders to its clients by air.

His organisation also runs training courses for individual workers who contact them: workers are becoming better informed these days, he believes, and more concerned about their rights; some even volunteer to use their limited spare time to help educate other workers. 'Lots of workers come to look for us now,' he says, 'and they have a lot of ideas. They're all young people, and they're more in contact with information – newspapers, TV, the Internet. It's different from in the past – their awareness of their own rights is very different.' And in a place like Shenzhen, where the majority of migrants have at least a junior high school education, Mr Liu says more and more of them now come to the city not just to earn money, but because they are looking for a different way of life. 'From around 1997,' he says, 'we've seen more and more people coming out to work who were born in the 1980s; they're better educated, and their main aim is to change their lives. It's not just about survival,' he stresses, 'they want to be urban citizens.' However, he says, society hardly makes it easy for them. 'Seventy per cent of Shenzhen's tax revenue comes from manufacturing, and much of this is created by migrant workers,' he explains, 'but we spend almost none of it on their welfare.' What's more, he adds, it has actually become increasingly hard for migrants to win permanent residency rights in the city.

In Mr Liu's opinion, this kind of harsh treatment of migrant workers is to blame for a growing labour shortage which has affected many factories in Shenzhen and other parts of Guangdong over the past few years. 'This system doesn't encourage them to stay here and become stable permanent workers,' he insists. 'Your kids can't go to school here, your whole family can't be here together, you don't have any social welfare. We always tell you you're a worker from outside, a temporary worker, a labourer – and your home is in your native place,' he continues. 'All voices are telling them they should go back, so they won't see this place as their home in the long term.' And because workers feel unwanted by the city, he says, they're more likely to vote with their feet and head for other parts of the country – such as the Shanghai area, where wages have tended to be slightly higher, and where they may have more chance of joining an employment insurance scheme – or simply return home. This exodus of workers is particularly common among young women, who come to work in the factories but soon leave to get married. 'They get to twenty-three and then they go back home,' says Liu Kaiming. 'Actually they could have carried on working until thirty, but because we don't have the social welfare provisions, they have to go back home to marry or have kids. And so all our factories lack experienced workers.'

Shenzhen's government, like many others in China, is seeking to respond to these shortages by trying to encourage a shift towards less labour-intensive industry. But for the moment it still needs the workers, and so in 2005–6 it introduced a series of rises in the local minimum wage. According to Mr Liu however, these did not seem to achieve their aim of making the region more attractive to migrant workers. He believes it's a problem which will only become more pronounced in the coming years, as China's exports continue to grow and the number of workers required continues to expand.

The lack of opportunities for migrants to become long-term urban citizens is creating other problems too, he says, since, in his opinion, many of them are no longer really suited to returning to a life on the land. 'It's harder and harder for them to go back to their homes,' he suggests. Some of China's migrants do still go back to their villages once or twice a year to help with the harvest, but Mr Liu believes that the new generation has ever weaker ties to the traditional ways of the countryside. 'More and more of them don't know how to plant the fields,' he says. 'They left home as soon as they graduated from junior high school, and now they don't suit the rural way of life. So there's a very low chance they'll want to go back to plant the land.' In fact, he notes, an increasing number have no land to go back to anyway – since it has either been swallowed up by urban development, or, with all the young people having gone away to work, their families have leased it out to others for the foreseeable future. And Liu Kaiming sees the millions of children of migrant workers who have grown up in the cities with only limited access to education as a further cause for concern. Some experts have warned such people will be filled with bitterness towards society; he himself is more cautious, but says with a sigh, 'this will be a problem which will have a big impact in the next decade'.

Such worries are one reason why the Chinese government has in recent years announced a series of policies aimed at creating more medium-sized towns and cities in rural areas around the country. The aim is to absorb some of the 'surplus rural workforce', as they're officially known, and prevent them all from heading to the big cities. The authorities have also tried to attract more industry to the west of China, in an attempt to spread wealth – and population – more equally around the country. But so far, these strategies seem to have done little to stem the flow of migrants into the cities of the south and east. In the immediate future at least, industry in many eastern provinces will continue to require migrant workers, while rural provinces in the hinterland will continue to export them; in fact, many of China's poorer regions are only too happy to see their workers move to the richer big cities, since the money they send home provides a major boost to their economies. In Anhui province, one of the main sources of migrant labour, for example, I met the head of a local government bureau which organised rural workers from Anhui to move to other parts of the country; the province even had its own office in Shanghai, responsible for its migrants there. And in one mainly rural area of south-west China, I heard a local academic tell a conference on migrant labour that his province should strive to forge a 'brand identity' for its migrant workers, stressing their honesty and diligence, in order to export more of them and increase its income.

Attempts by the government to make life better in the countryside – such as recent steps to cut the tax burden for farmers – may encourage some to stay at home. But many migrants, having grown up with idealised images of city life on their television screens, are now clear about their desire to become urban citizens. It seems China may simply have to get used to the idea that, as in the European Industrial Revolution of the nineteenth century, rural people will continue moving to the cities – and once they arrive, the majority will remain there. The figures bear this out: China has been urbanising people as fast as it has urbanised its land – from around 300 million urban residents in 1990 to an estimated 540 million in 2004. In the 1980s, China's rural population accounted for some 80 per cent of the total; by 1990 the figure had fallen to 73 per cent; less than a decade and a half later, in 2004, the rural population had fallen below 60 per cent – despite the higher birth rate in the countryside. Almost 42 per cent of the country's population are now living in urban areas.[34] Some academics have begun to warn that it's a dangerous situation, which will lead to the creation of slums, continuing rural deprivation and other social problems. And there's no doubt that the authorities face a challenge in coping with the rising pressure on the resources of the nation's cities, and defusing the social tensions resulting from such rapid expansion. But it's a challenge they may have to meet, if they are to keep the country's factories supplied with workers – and satisfy the aspirations of so many rural people for a new way of life.

# 10

# The land they left behind

On the hillside, the bamboo swayed gently in the breeze, like a forest of giant green feathers. Down below in the valley, its slopes lined with the dark green bushes of the tea plantations, the sun glistened on the water of the stream as it flowed under the little bridge. A farmer was sauntering back from the fields, two big loads of duckweed suspended from the carrying pole across his shoulders. Suddenly a tiny red-cheeked boy darted out in front of him, waving. Further up the path, an old man stood and watched, leaning on his stick beside the old ancestral hall. Red paper strips pasted on the wooden doors set into its whitewashed walls promised peace and prosperity. In Wanping village in the hills of Zhejiang province, on a warm Sunday morning, the Chinese countryside seemed at its most idyllic.

There were just a few discordant notes. On the wall of a neighbouring house, the whitewash had faded to reveal rows of faint red characters, reminders of hard times not so distant. 'Revolution depends on Mao Zedong thought,' they proclaimed. Inside the old clan hall, the paint was peeling from the pillars, and the old stage which once hosted noisy opera performances was silent and empty. 'We don't use it much these days,' said the old man, pointing with his stick. He led the way through the village to his family's ancestral home, an imposing two-storey mansion next to the village's paved central square. The square was deserted. Inside the large inner courtyard of the house, its wooden pillars carved with leaves and scenes from classical stories, an old lady was cradling a small baby in her arms. 'Most of the young people have gone away now,' said the friendly old man. 'They've left to find work in Hangzhou or Shanghai, some of them for the south.'

And in the village's narrow lanes, the slogans painted on the walls of the houses were reminders of some of the pressures of rural life. 'Everyone should save electricity,' announced one. 'The Party Secretary has the ultimate responsibility for implementing family planning policies,' insisted another. Nearby, a row of posters pasted on the baked earthen wall of one old house urged villagers to 'resist evil cults'. The message was illustrated with garishly coloured cartoons, telling the story of how an honest villager was targeted by one such organisation, and ended up being cheated and eventually murdered, left dead on the ground in a pool of blood.

Elsewhere in the village there were hints at some of the other challenges facing the local residents. Beside the stream, a commemorative stone had been erected, listing the names of villagers who had contributed between three hundred and a thousand yuan each to build the concrete path leading up the valley; on the bridge, a carved memorial on one of the pillars paid tribute to a donor who had provided the six tonnes of cement needed for its construction.

The Chinese countryside is nothing if not beautiful – and nothing if not beset with problems. Wanping village is situated in one of the country's wealthier rural areas, yet even here many of the difficulties facing China's farmers were readily apparent. A lack of local government funds, which means residents often have to contribute money to build basic infrastructure; worries about crime and the lure of unorthodox beliefs; enforced family planning policies; and frequent power shortages – to say nothing of the migration of many of the young generation to the cities. For the Chinese government, which is eager to encourage more young people to remain in rural areas – not just to reduce the pressure on the urban centres, but also to ensure the country produces enough crops to feed its vast population – such problems add up to a serious challenge, one which is even tougher in remoter regions of the country, where crops are harder to grow, conditions harsher and money more difficult to earn. And in recent years, the Chinese authorities have acknowledged that improving life in the country-side is one of their most urgent tasks.

In a sense, it's rather ironic. The countryside, after all, is where China's economic reforms really got under way in the years after the Cultural Revolution, when they were enthusiastically embraced by many farming families. China's peasants were, of course, also the backbone of the communist revolution – and of the communists' armies too – and were among the earliest beneficiaries of its success, when the old landowners were overthrown and their land redistributed to the poorest farmers. Many remained enthusiastic right up to the late 1950s, when farmers around the country were grouped together in collective farms and production units known as 'People's Communes' – where for a time they even ate together in shared canteens. But the politicisation of agriculture, and a series of natural disasters, led to the great famine of 1958–61, when crops failed and millions died of starvation. Later, during the Cultural Revolution, farmers were subjected to years of enforced political study sessions, sloganeering and sometimes violence. By the late 1970s many had had enough. It was at this time, across the border from Zhejiang province in neighbouring Anhui, that villages began experimenting with a system where small areas of collective land were once again divided up and farmed by individual families. Eventually this became official policy, and many families were able to lease land to farm for themselves – or indeed to sublet to others – for the decades to come.[1] Now they could choose their own crops to grow – and even, if they were lucky, sell any surplus products on the new 'free markets' which began to appear in Chinese towns in the early 1980s – the first time for many years that individuals had been allowed to trade on their own behalf. And since, at around the same time, some people were starting to have a little more money to spend on food – after years when, for many, rice itself was a luxury – there were new opportunities for farmers who could satisfy this demand.

Mr Wang and his family had done well from the reforms. That became clear when he led me into his new tiled house in his small village in southern Anhui, and showed me up onto the second-floor balcony. As we looked out towards the hills where he had grown up, he recalled the old days. 'When I was young my family were classified as poor peasants,' he said, a slight smile playing on his sharp features. In those revolutionary times it had been an honourable label, an official confirmation that one was not a member of the exploiting classes. But it also implied serious poverty. In fact, said Mr Wang, this had been one of the poorest villages in the whole region. 'There weren't any rich peasants here at all,' he added. 'Even a few years ago, people who came here were surprised at how poor this area was.'

Certainly this part of Anhui, with its rolling green hills and fertile plains, seemed made for agriculture. It was also close to the Yangtze River, which led downstream to the big cities of Nanjing and Shanghai. But according to Mr Wang, it was not until the beginning of the 1990s that he and his fellow villagers really began to make use of these natural advantages. He pointed down below, to the small ponds behind his house, divided by little banks of earth. The water looked brown and unprepossessing, but for Mr Wang these ponds had been the passport to a better life. Beneath their muddy surface lurked the freshwater crabs – a great delicacy in this part of China – which he bred and then sold, to the seafood markets in Shanghai and other nearby cities. His business had developed rapidly, and many of his fellow villagers later followed his example, dredging out their fields, sinking concrete pits and starting to raise shrimps and crabs. Mr Wang gestured to a clump of tall houses a couple of hundred yards away in the early-evening haze. 'You can see how much has changed,' he said. 'I used to be the only one who had a big house like this, now two-thirds of the families in the village have multi-storey houses.'

He and his fellow villagers were now even being promoted by the local government as a model for others to copy, as the authorities tried to promote innovation and a more scientific approach to farming. Actually, Mr Wang admitted, business was not perfect: the price for his watery treasures had fallen by around half since he entered the trade, as large-scale commercial production elsewhere led to increased supplies and greater competition. 'Still,' he said, 'it's better than growing rice. How much do you think I could earn doing that!?' The tens of thousands of yuan he made each year enabled him to send his sixteen-year-old son to high school in the nearby county town. His two daughters, who were in their early twenties, had gone away to work in neighbouring Jiangsu province; one had a job in a clothes shop, the other worked in a beauty salon. In fact, most young women still left the area to work once they finished school, according to Mr Wang. But at least his girls weren't too far away, and could come home every couple of months. And he was proud that he had no need for them to send any money home. 'We can support ourselves,' he said, 'so anything they earn they can keep for themselves, for when they start their own families in the future.'

There are many farmers like Mr Wang, who benefited from the reforms of the 1980s and 1990s, especially in parts of the country with good natural resources, and close enough to urban centres for it to be easy to transport their produce to the market. The large tiled houses sprouting from the fields in the rural areas of northern Zhejiang province and southern Jiangsu, not far from Shanghai, are testimony to that. And the economic reforms have enabled some in the countryside to move even further away from the traditional agricultural life. During the 1980s, small factories began to spring up in villages and small rural towns all over China. These were known as 'township and village enterprises', and soon this type of light industry became one of the fastest growing sectors of the economy. Many were founded by local rural governments; but some were set up – or later bought out – by individuals or small groups of investors, becoming one of the first stepping stones towards the privatisation of China's economy. Often they simply processed the products of local farms, but others branched out into small-scale manufacturing. A few, particularly down south in Guangdong, eventually metamorphosed into major industrial corporations: stories of companies which began making electric fans and ended up making air conditioners are common; in Zhejiang province I

293

visited the headquarters of the Geely group, which started out making spare parts for fridges but now, less than two decades later, had just launched its own sports car. And in Guangdong I once drove past the premises of one of the country's largest electronics manufacturers; my Chinese guide pointed at the enormous modern factory and said, matter-of-factly: 'I've met the boss of that company, he's basically a peasant.'

Most township and village enterprises were much smaller, but they often still brought enormous changes in lifestyle to those who ran them. Mr Xu, for example, would be the first to admit that he too is 'basically a peasant' – or at least he was. A friendly, quietly spoken man in his forties, he was born in a village in northern Shaanxi province, up on the 'loess plateau', the vast swathe of bare sandstone hills which stretches for hundreds of miles across northern China from east to west. It's one of China's poorest regions, and one of the most inhospitable landscapes in the country, the result of centuries of deforestation and ever-decreasing rainfall, where crops have to be eked out of the dusty land. Mr Xu, like many local farmers, grew up in a *yaodong*, a cave house hollowed out of the hillside. 'They have their advantages,' he says with a smile. 'They're easy to keep warm in the winter, and in the summer they're cool.' But they can collapse easily too, he points out; and his family had struggled to make a living from the land. Eventually his father took up work as a carpenter, and later trained his son to follow in his footsteps. By the mid-1980s they had saved enough money to buy a hand-steered tractor, a precarious-looking contraption controlled by a pair of long handlebars, which is still one of the most popular forms of transport in the Chinese countryside. It enabled them to start a new business, digging clay from the ground up in the hills and driving it down to Xian, the nearest big city, to sell to local potteries. Mr Xu did the driving, a towel wrapped around his head to protect himself from the elements on the eight-hour journey.

These days he dresses a little more smartly, and travels in rather more style, in a chauffeur-driven Audi. His rural home is now a spacious villa – though he spends much of his time in his apartment in Xian. His children study abroad, and he himself has travelled with official delegations to Europe and the US. His transformation began in the late 1980s, when he got together with a few friends and relatives, and began using the clay they dug out of the ground in a workshop of their own, making the sculpted tiles used on Chinese temple roofs and other traditional-style buildings. Within a few years they were selling them all around north-west China, and eventually took over a small brick factory in a rural township. Soon they imported a production line from Europe and began exporting. Later they opened a rural holiday resort for tourists from the nearby city, complete with irrigated orchards where they could pick their own fruit. But Mr Xu, who, like many of China's new 'peasant industrialists', remains deeply attached to his home area, also decided he wanted to do something more. And so he began investing a significant amount of his wealth into commissioning a series of modernist buildings, built on the yellow earth hillside near his factory, to be used as an artists' village and a complex of museums of contemporary ceramics from around the world. 'I didn't have much education,' he says, 'but I want to challenge and raise the ideas of the local people, to inspire knowledge among the young generation.' He's quick to admit that it may not be easy to make something like this a success in the Shaanxi countryside, but his attitude typifies that of many of those who have rebuilt their lives in China since the 1980s. 'Some things just have to be done,' he says. 'You might make a mess of them, but you have to try. If you give it your best effort and fail that's one thing, but if you don't try that's another.'

Those who do fail – and not for lack of trying – are still many, however. Not far from Mr Xu's brick factory, I found Mr Shen, a sixty-eight-year-old farmer, with a face as brown and wizened as a walnut, squatting in an alley of apple trees. He had a newspaper clasped in one hand and a cigarette in the other, and a cheerful grin which belied his harsh existence. His home was further north, he said, up in the bare hills, where he had been a farmer all his life. But water shortages were getting worse, and it was becoming harder to earn a living from agriculture. And so he had left his children to do the farming, and travelled south to try to earn some extra money. Now he had found a job as a watchman in the orchard, working ten hours a day, seven days a week. He shared a room with three others, and was paid four hundred yuan, less than thirty pounds, a month. And he seemed happy about it – it was significantly more, he said, than most farmers in his home region could hope to earn from agriculture.

And there are still many people leading similar lives in some of China's remoter provinces. In the late 1980s the Chinese government began a series of campaigns aimed at reducing absolute poverty in the countryside. Large amounts of government money, as well as aid and loans from foreign donors, were channelled to selected counties which had been designated as being among the poorest in the nation. Much of the money went into roads and other infrastructure, in order to break the isolation of remote mountain regions. Other funds went towards tree-planting and other projects aimed at reversing environmental damage, including the loss of farmland to the spreading deserts of northern China. Smaller amounts went into loans to help individual farmers. There's no doubt that it had an impact. Official figures say that some 50 million were 'raised out of poverty' in this way during the 1990s. But there were concerns too that not all the aid money reached those who really needed it, and that some of it was diverted by local bureaucrats to pay for cars or offices or banquets, or simply for other less urgent projects.

And despite the impressive-seeming fall in the numbers of rural poor, the government eventually admitted that it had not met its previously announced – and ambitious – target of eradicating absolute poverty by the year 2000. Six years later, in fact, an estimated 23 million people were still struggling to get enough to eat and keep warm in winter, according to official figures. One of the government's top specialists on poverty alleviation, Gao Hongbin, once explained to me what this kind of poverty meant: 'For two or three months a year these people may be short of grain or rice,' he said, 'so they eat other things like wild plants instead. They live in decrepit houses, or they may not have houses at all, and just live in caves or huts up in the hills – you can't see them from the road.' Most were in remote regions of the north-west and south-west, he added, and of course they were just a tiny percentage of China's estimated 800 million rural residents. But experts have warned that many of those who have officially been 'raised out of poverty' remain at risk of falling back into it, if there's a bad harvest or a natural disaster. There have been criticisms too of the methods sometimes used in poverty alleviation work – the forcing of traditional nomadic farmers into fixed new villages, for example. And the Chinese government's official poverty line is set far lower than the international standard, used by the World Bank, of one US dollar per person per day; by that standard, China would still have an estimated 135 million people facing poverty (though this figure includes some urban residents too).[2]

And for all the development which has occurred since the 1980s, China's economic reforms have actually exacerbated the divide between richer and poorer areas, including the countryside. During much of the 1990s, and into the new century, average incomes in China's cities grew at double the rate of those in the countryside, by 8 per cent a year compared to 4 per cent. And some rural areas too did better than others. Farmers in the wealthier east moved into more industrialised, large-scale production, making life even harder for poor farmers trying to scrape a living from unproductive land in other parts of the country. The government's 'Go West' campaign, launched in 2000 to encourage investment in the less developed western regions, was designed to tackle some of these problems. But they remain deeply rooted, and have been made worse by falling prices for many agricultural products during this period. China's entry into the World Trade Organisation in 2001 also raised the prospect of more competition for Chinese agriculture from imported fruit and vegetables, as trade barriers were gradually lowered. And by the turn of the century, some of the township and village enterprises which had done so well in the past were also starting to struggle in the face of ever stiffer competition.

Other aspects of China's reforms too have made life harder for many in the countryside – and, for some, even increased the risk of falling back into poverty. For all the suffering caused during China's politicised decades, it was at least generally accepted that the reorganisation of farmers into people's communes and agricultural cooperatives brought one significant benefit – the availability of rudimentary health care to most peasants. There were simple clinics in the cooperatives, and the system also famously trained a network of so-called 'barefoot doctors', local people equipped with only the most basic of skills, but able to reach sick patients in even the remotest of villages, who were eulogised as heroes throughout the 1960s and 1970s. Such innovations contributed to a drastic rise in China's average life expectancy, from thirty-five in 1952 to sixty-eight some three decades later, according to official figures.[3] But as the commune system began to break down after the Cultural Revolution, this system started to disintegrate too. By the late 1990s, normally cautious officials at international donor institutions in Beijing were describing China's rural health care system as being in a state of collapse. (Of the network of hundreds of rural cancer prevention stations set up in the 1970s, for example, only a handful were still in operation by the early years of the new century.)[4] And on visits to the countryside, the evidence was all too visible.

In the county hospital in Lujiao, in southern Anhui province, Zhu Youfu lay on a bed in a bare whitewashed room, gazing expressionlessly at the ceiling. His father stood beside him, a pained expression on his face. It was little wonder; his fifteen-year-old son had been ill for months now – he had complained of being short of breath, and of pains in his chest, and had been diagnosed with heart and liver problems. His parents had taken him to several different hospitals, even to the provincial capital, to try to find a cure. Now they had returned to this little hospital, nearer their home village. The boy had been here for two weeks now; he was being given four types of medicine for his various ailments, and sometimes a drip-feed too, when he had no appetite. The fees for this were not exorbitant, around thirty yuan – a couple of pounds – a day, but they still added up to almost a thousand yuan a month, double the average wage of a local farmer. And the family had to pay for it all themselves.

Dr Guo, who was in charge of the boy's treatment, looked on solicitously. The family had already spent 10,000 yuan in total, he said, a significant part of their savings. In the corridor outside, the boy's mother paced up and down. She had run a little stall in the county town selling fruit and vegetables from their land, but after her son became ill she had given it up to concentrate on looking after him. His father still did some farming, but the family were starting to struggle to keep up with the costs of the medical treatment. They had put in an application to the local authorities for emergency aid, but it was a complicated process, and they had yet to receive any money.

And it was a far from unusual situation. As the then head of the World Health Organisation in China, Dr Janos Annus, put it in 2002, 'The rural health care system based on the cooperatives was abolished in around the mid-1980s, with the provision that a new system would be built to replace it.' But, he added, 'that system has not been built yet'.[5] A few wealthier rural areas, close to the big cities in the south and east, had established simple new medical insurance schemes, but most people in the countryside now lacked even the most basic cover – official figures showed that only around 7 per cent of China's 800 million peasants had any form of medical cover at all by 2002, compared to at least 90 per cent in 1979.[6] The often frustrating complexities of the new urban social welfare insurance schemes would, for most rural residents, have been an unimaginable luxury.

By the early years of the new century, the results of the collapse of the old system were becoming hard to ignore. China's Health Ministry acknowledged that around two-thirds of people in the countryside who needed hospital treatment never got it, or did not even try to seek it, because they couldn't afford the costs.[7] Which may have explained why Zhu Youfu was the only inpatient in the hospital where he was being treated. And for families like his, which did try to scrape together enough money to pay the medical fees, the consequences could be severe. As one local health official in Anhui put it, families in this position often had to borrow money at high interest rates, causing long-term problems. 'If someone gets ill in a family it can be years before they recover,' he said. 'It affects their lives, their production – and the development of the rural economy.' Dai Guangqiang, the head of the Anhui provincial health bureau, agreed. 'Our research among poorer families,' he explained, 'shows that in around 20 per cent of cases, their poverty is the result of someone in the family suffering a major illness.'

It was not that there weren't good hospitals or doctors – indeed, in Anhui I met a group of experienced doctors from the provincial capital Hefei, who had volunteered to come and work in rural hospitals, in much more primitive conditions, in order to help train the local staff in more modern methods. The problem was simply that everyone now had to pay their own way. At one rural clinic I visited, a long strip of red paper was pasted on the wall beside the entrance, with black characters painted on it in the traditional style. 'Gold will not bring eternal life,' they proclaimed. Perhaps this was intended to reassure patients as they parted with their money – but it would have been scant consolation for most.

And there was other fallout from the crumbling of the old health system. China had had a relatively good record of vaccinating its children against disease during the early decades of the communist state. But, according to official figures, by the early years of the twenty-first century the rate of inoculation against major diseases, including tuberculosis, polio and measles, had fallen to less than 75 per cent from around 85 per cent at the start of the 1990s.[8]

The problems of China's rural health system were exacerbated by another aspect of the country's reforms of the 1990s: the central government's decision to devolve most of the responsibility for providing welfare onto local and provincial governments. Some extra money was set aside to smooth the transition, but by the time this reached the lowest levels – the counties, townships and villages – there was often not much left. In many areas of the country, rural governments simply did not have the resources to pay for health care and welfare.

Eventually, in the early years of the new century, the central government began to acknowledge that action to sort out the situation was urgently required. In a village in Feixi County, in

Anhui province, in 2002, I met Dr Zhang Zhenquan, who was taking part in a pilot project aimed at rebuilding a basic medical service for the rural population. His clinic was actually the ground floor of his home, a small room crammed with medicines of all kinds. When I arrived he was just on his way out, to see a patient who lived in a nearby farmhouse. He grabbed his bag and white coat, climbed onto his motorbike and set off down the muddy road; we drove along behind him. A few minutes later, he drew up outside the home of the Wei family, a rambling old house with hens pecking at the ground in the yard outside. The family seemed to know him well; Mr Wei, a middle-aged farmer, was already waiting for him, and ushered him quickly inside. Dr Zhang took a set of glass vials out of his bag, unwrapped a disposable syringe, and headed into the darkened inner room where the family's twenty-four-year-old son was lying in bed. He had been working on buildings sites in other provinces, according to his father, and was now suffering from lead poisoning as a result of working with paint and other chemicals without wearing a mask. 'He knew he should wear a mask,' said Dr Zhang, with a shake of his head, as he emerged from the young man's room, 'but he thought it was too much trouble.' Now, he added, he needed daily treatment.

It was a sad scene, but the boy's family were just grateful that the doctor was there at all. Until recently, getting any medical treatment had been a hit and miss affair in the region. Following the collapse of the collective health care system in the 1980s, the only doctors left in many rural areas were private ones. Some were qualified, but other people who had little medical knowledge had also set themselves up as doctors. And they hadn't always gone out of their way to care for patients, as Dr Zhang himself admitted. 'In the past,' he said, 'a doctor would only go to a patient's house if they had a good personal relationship. If they didn't get on well, the doctor might not be very helpful, and wouldn't prescribe the best medicine either.' And many of these village doctors only worked part time: at certain times of the year they would shut down their clinics while they were busy with the harvest or planting crops. Anyway, according to Wang Jun, deputy head of the county health bureau, such doctors were mainly concerned with making money. 'Their starting point was their own interest,' he explained. 'They didn't care about the quality of medicine they prescribed, they just chose the cheapest ones, or put the prices up.' Hygiene was poor too, he said: few people used disposable syringes, because they were more expensive.

Now the county health bureau had introduced a new scheme designed to restore order to this chaotic situation. It had brought all the village doctors in the area back into the state system, putting them under the management of larger clinics nearby and, ultimately, of local hospitals. Some of their costs were subsidised – on condition that they maintained certain levels of hygiene, charged fixed prices, and were on call twenty-four hours a day. All the doctors had been required to take an exam, and several hundred who lacked medical knowledge had been forced to retire; medicine was purchased centrally by the county government and supplied to the clinics. As a result, according to Wang Jun, many residents had regained their confidence in the local clinics, and no longer insisted on making expensive trips to hospitals in town if someone in their family got sick. The county was also piloting a new form of medical insurance, where farmers paid a small fee of just a few yuan a year, and the local government topped this up with a little more. It wouldn't cover all their medical costs – around 20 to 30 per cent of any treatment, up to a maximum subsidy of five thousand yuan per person a year, he said – but it would certainly help. And in the circumstances, he explained, it was the best they could do. 'The rural population is very big,' he said. 'In this county alone we have 800,000 farmers, and it's impossible to provide publicly funded health care schemes like government employees get in the cities. It's unfair in a way,' he acknowledged, 'but there are just too many people. The government can't afford to pay so much money to support every farmer – we can only try to help a bit.'

This pilot project, and others like it, has now become the model for a new medical insurance scheme being promoted around the country as the government's solution to China's rural health crisis. Since 2003, collective insurance funds like the one in Feixi have been introduced in hundreds of counties across China, and are due to be in operation nationwide by 2010. Farmers pay around ten yuan a year (less than one pound), while the central and local governments add another twenty each. In theory this is supposed to cover 65 per cent of farmers' medical costs – though in practice, by 2005, the average percentage of a patient's hospital expenses paid by the scheme was just over a quarter, according to senior officials.[9] Whether such a scheme will really change lives for rural residents remains to be seen. As Janos Annus of the World Health Organisation put it in 2002, a good rural health care system is 'a prerequisite for future social stability, a cornerstone for continuing economic development of the country and continuing social development'. A couple of years earlier, a World Health Organisation ranking had placed China fourth from bottom of a list of 191 countries, in terms of the fairness of access to medical treatment. And for the moment, around 70 per cent of China's spending on health care still goes to the cities, leaving just 30 per cent for the 60 per cent or so of the country's population living in rural areas.[10]

The shortage of funding for local governments in rural areas from the 1990s on has had a serious impact on the quality of life for farmers in other ways too. When local administrations found themselves running short of revenue, their first reaction was often to impose extra taxes and levies on rural citizens. China already had a basic agricultural tax of 5 per cent on the income earned from selling crops. But soon the country's farmers, some of the poorest people in the country, found themselves expected to pay other charges of all kinds. A local government official in Wuhu, in southern Anhui, once listed for me the fees which farmers in her area had been paying. 'There was the local education surcharge,' she said, 'then there was the village road maintenance fee, next was the family planning fee, fourthly we had the pregnant women fee, and finally there was the security patrol fee.' Her administration also had the right to demand free labour – for up to twenty days a year – from the farmers, to help build dykes or irrigation projects. And this was by many standards a rather restrained list. Throughout China there were stories of local governments levying everything from 'pig production fees' to 'slaughtering levies' and 'military training surcharges'. And those were just the legal ones. There were frequent stories of local authorities adding their own extra charges, without permission. Sometimes these were for projects intended to benefit the community, insisted Wang Jianguo, a senior official at the provincial finance bureau in Anhui. 'For example,' he said, 'if a township wants to develop, but its budget is not enough, it might ask everyone to pay ten yuan, and call it a township construction fee. Perhaps they'll build a market, or a road. But the problem,' he acknowledged, 'is that not every farmer will benefit equally – and even the ones who will benefit might not have enough money to pay.'

And in many cases, taxes were imposed on farmers for projects which benefited local officials or their families more than anyone else; sometimes the money went straight into the officials' own pockets. Such demands, legal or otherwise, did little to improve the relationship between the government and the peasants. Tao Liangmin, a fruit farmer in Wuhu, described the situation. 'To be honest,' he said, as he looked out across the fields where his late crop of strawberries was ready to be harvested, 'taxes were so high that we all felt very uncomfortable whenever we saw any officials arriving in the village. We knew that when they came here, all they ever did was to ask for money.' Sometimes this type of bad feeling provoked direct confrontation. In 2000, farmers in south-eastern Fujian province clashed with police after marching to local government offices to protest against a sudden increase in the tax they had to pay on their bananas. The same year, in Jiangxi province, to the south of Anhui, two people died when police stormed a village where peasants were protesting about their tax burden. One Chinese newspaper published a study showing that in some rural areas, peasants were paying more in taxes and fees than they actually earned.[11] (It was particularly ironic considering that many urban residents, who generally earned much more, had never paid tax at all.)[12]

The problems with fees and funding have had a particular impact on China's rural education system. In the decades after the communist revolution, China did relatively well by international standards; most rural children got at least some schooling, and literacy rates in most areas of the country reached more than 90 per cent, despite the complexity of the written language. This was achieved by a system which, in theory at least, provided compulsory free education well into a child's teenage years. And children from remote rural parts of China do continue to achieve academic success, sometimes winning admission to top universities in the big cities: on a recent visit to a small rural town in Shaanxi province I was surprised to see the earnest face of a bespectacled teenage boy staring out from a huge billboard on the main street. He was, it turned out, a local student who had won a place at the prestigious Tsinghua University in Beijing; his school had put this poster up as a tribute and as a way of attracting more students.

But in practice, during the 1990s, many rural areas struggled to meet the government's new target of nine years' free compulsory education for all. Cash-strapped local authorities often cut funding for schools – in some areas of the country, only six years of education was available; in others, schools had problems paying teachers' wages. Some schools were reported to be in such dire straits that they even resorted to charging new members of their teaching staff a 'joining fee' of up to a thousand pounds. But more often the burden fell on the pupils' parents. In theory, primary and junior high schools were only allowed to charge a limited fee, of not more than a few hundred yuan a year, for textbooks and a few other specified 'miscellaneous' items. But surcharges for new buildings, heating or administration costs soon became common. For many poor parents in the countryside, it could be an unbearable burden. In one rural area of Guangdong in 2001, angry citizens burnt down part of a government building during a protest against a 3,000-yuan (£200) surcharge on pupils at the local primary school.[13]

For some families, such fees could be a barrier to sending their children to school, in an increasingly expensive society. As a senior official with UNICEF in China put it in 2002, 'Families are much more exposed to market forces now – you have to choose how to spend a limited amount of money on different things for your household.' Sometimes, he added, it came down to a question of whether 'to spend money on school fees or more food or to repair the roof on your house'.[14] And the pressure was increased by the fact that many rural families in China had two children, and some even more. The official fees for school textbooks could themselves be too much for some – even in places like Guangdong, in theory one of the country's richest areas. In the more remote parts of the province, away from the booming Pearl River Delta, several million families live below the local poverty line, as Pan Guangyi, head of the legal division at the provincial education bureau, pointed out when I met him in 2002. 'Especially in the mountain counties, where families often have two or three children, it can be hard for them to pay even a few hundred yuan each in fees,' he explained.

By the early years of this decade, there were signs that, while the percentage of children entering primary school in China remained very high – 95 per cent or more in many rural areas – a growing number of children were starting to drop out before they finished their basic education. And girls were twice as likely as boys to quit school early, according to UNICEF figures. When hard financial choices had to be made, traditional attitudes favouring the education of boys often resurfaced, it seemed. UNICEF surveys showed that in some poor regions, the school attendance rate for eleven-year-olds was only 85 per cent for girls, compared to 92 per cent for boys.[15]

Qiu Jiemei was exactly the kind of rural girl who was vulnerable to missing out on her education. She was short for a sixteen-year-old, with simply cropped hair and an open face, which lit up with a childlike smile as she showed me into the small concrete house where she lived with her younger brother. She was a little shy, but there was a maturity about her too, no doubt the result of looking after her brother for the past few years, since their father died and their mother remarried and moved away, leaving the children behind. Now they were supposed to be in the care of their uncle, who lived next door. But he wasn't always in a position to be of much help. Chengkang village, less than a hundred miles from Guangzhou, seemed quite prosperous, with its lush fields and groves of lychee trees. But as he sat at the folding table in his niece's front room, with his baby granddaughter yelling on his lap, their uncle admitted that he often struggled to make ends meet. He had a little bit of land, but some was poor quality, up on the hillside – and the fruit trees he cultivated were susceptible to bad weather and fluctuating prices.

'It depends on the heavens,' he said. 'Sometimes we have a good crop of pears, sometimes we don't have enough to eat.' Even his onions, a speciality of the region, had been hit by falling prices. As a result, he didn't always have enough money to pay for the children's school books and materials. Several times now he had had to beg the school for help. Qiu Jiemei spent some of her spare time growing vegetables to help pay her way. 'If I have enough crops I take them to the street market to sell,' she said, 'if I make a little money then I can spend it on things for school – pens and textbooks.'

She was certainly a keen student. 'I want to go to university and become an English teacher,' she told me. And she seemed to take pride in teaching her brother new English words: 'Policeman!' she shouted, as he struggled to explain his own ideal job when he left school. The children had been lucky. Their school was relatively well funded, and the headmaster, Mr Sun, said he always did his best to exempt poor families from paying the fees if they were having difficulties. Still, he said, it placed a strain on the school's resources, and he acknowledged that 'there are still quite a few children who end up quitting school early because of the expense'. But now things had improved a little. The Guangdong provincial government had recently decided to waive all the book and miscellaneous fees for primary and middle school students from poor families, in an attempt to ensure that all children in the province would get a basic education. And Qiu Jiemei's uncle had been among the first to receive assistance. 'Now the children can concentrate on their schoolwork at the weekend,' he grinned, 'they won't have to work in the fields.' His niece beamed cheerfully too. 'Now when I'm at school, I don't have to worry,' she said. Perhaps she would even have a chance of fulfilling her dream of going to university in the future.

The Guangdong government was the first in the country to exempt poor families from school fees, in 2002. It was crucial, said Pan Guangyi of the provincial education bureau, especially now that the province was trying to upgrade its industry away from simple labour-intensive production, and there was a growing demand for senior high school graduates. But in other parts of China, it was not easy for provincial governments to be so generous. In the remoter parts of Shaanxi province in the north-west, for example, a lack of funds meant that 25,000 teachers were still being paid tiny salaries of around a hundred yuan (less than seven pounds) a month in 2006, according to official media, and few schools had electric lighting. Such problems were reported to have led many rural schoolteachers to quit and look for jobs in towns and cities – with the result that rural schools around China were employing some half a million teachers who were not fully qualified.[16] Even in Guangdong, many schools in less developed parts of the province were reported to be heavily in debt in 2006; some were unable even to turn on electric fans in the sweltering summer months, others were said to have cancelled exams in order to save paper.[17]

In response to problems such as these, the Chinese government finally announced that it would provide extra funds to rural governments, with the promise that, from 2007, all rural students at primary and junior high school would be exempted from paying book fees. At the same time, the government pledged to increase the country's spending on education from some 3 per cent of GDP to around 4 per cent by 2010. These moves were part of a series of measures designed to improve the lives of China's rural residents, which were unveiled in 2005–6 under the slogan 'Creating a New Socialist Countryside'. Officially the main aim of the measures was to revive the flagging rural economy. But in practice the policy changes were also clearly designed to address some of the sources of tension in the villages. As well as more funding for education and health care, they also included plans for cuts in local government bureaucracy – and an end to the heavy tax burden on rural residents. In 2006, China's basic national agricultural tax was abolished ahead of schedule, and the

308

majority of other, local, rural taxes were also due to be scrapped.[18]

Experiments with these tax cuts began in Anhui province, with a pilot project launched in 2001. Farmers still had to pay a reduced rate of tax at this point, but other fees were axed. By the following year, provincial government officials were already hailing its impact. Friction between government officials and farmers had been reduced significantly, said Wang Jianguo of the Anhui Finance Bureau. 'There used to be a lot of disputes and clashes,' he admitted, 'but since we've reduced the burden the relationship has improved a lot.' As a result, he said, farmers were more motivated to work – and officials were wasting less time thinking of ways to extract money from the peasants. 'Now they can concentrate on what they should be doing, like planning ways to develop the local economy,' Mr Wang added.

Tao Liangmin, the fruit farmer I met in Wuhu in southern Anhui, was certainly relieved: the tax cuts had saved him three hundred yuan a year, he said, and his son's school had stopped charging extra fees too. 'We feel much more secure and confident now,' he added, as he watched the rain swirling over his fields. The Communist Party secretary of the local township was not quite so effusive, but did her best to sound upbeat. The extra money which her administration was now receiving from the central government to make up for the loss of tax income 'doesn't completely cover everything', she said, 'but at least carrying on with our work is no big problem'. In other parts of the country, though, local officials clearly found the reduction of their power to impose taxes hard to accept. In 2000, when plans for the trial tax reforms were first announced, a book giving details of the scheme quickly became popular with farmers in many areas. But government officials in one county in Jiangxi province were so alarmed at the prospect that they banned further sales of the book and attempted to confiscate copies from local villagers, provoking a riot reported to have involved thousands of people.[19]

By 2005–6, when the rural tax reforms were extended to many provinces around the country, there were some signs that they were beginning to have an influence. Factory bosses in the cities of the south and east coast, for example, cited the reforms as one reason why it was becoming harder to attract and retain workers: with less taxes to pay, they suggested, more farmers were willing to stay on the land – and some migrant workers were also thinking of returning to the countryside. Still, there were other worries for farmers – prices of fertilisers, for example, climbed sharply at around the same time. And there were continuing stories too of local governments struggling to cope as a result of the reforms. 'The farmers are happier since they cut the taxes,' said one civil servant in the countryside of central China in 2005, 'but the township governments don't have much money now – some staff haven't been paid for a year.' For all the promised subsidies, many local authorities had apparently gone into debt after borrowing money to cover their expenses.[20]

There's no doubt that the government is now paying closer attention to the problems of the countryside, after a period during the 1990s when urban areas and industrial development seemed to be its prime concerns. Amid fears that low grain prices and the loss of agricultural land to new construction were reducing the country's ability to feed itself, the Chinese authorities began, in 2004, to pay direct subsidies to the country's hundreds of millions of grain farmers for the first time, to encourage them to keep planting rice and other similar crops.[21] Huge sums have been pledged for rural reconstruction over the next few years: annual government investment in rural areas was £20 billion in 2006; by 2008 the budget had risen to some £35 billion.[22] But such spending has brought health warnings too: announcing a package of agricultural subsidies in 2005, China's Deputy Finance Minister felt it necessary to warn 'that the subsidies should not be used by local officials to buy cars, to build offices or training centres or to spend on useless projects solely aimed at showing off government achievements'.[23] The official press too has suggested that some local officials see the government's plans to build a 'new socialist countryside' as an opportunity 'to make political achievements to boost their chances of promotion', or 'an occasion to make profit for themselves'. Reports that some 30,000 officials would be sent to South Korea to study its experiences in reviving its own rural economy during the 1970s hardly helped, with warnings that some were planning to take advantage of the new policy to 'enjoy a free holiday'.[24]

Such concerns are a reminder that the quality – and honesty – of government in China's rural areas is often a major factor in the problems faced by many of the nation's farmers. Indeed, dissatisfaction with local officials has been a common cause of confrontation in the countryside. One particular source of tension has been land deals which affect the livelihoods of many rural residents. Between 1996 and 2005, China's total area of cultivated land fell by over 6 per cent, as vast areas of fields were sold off for construction and industrial development.[25] For local governments, such land deals can be big money-spinners. Land in China ultimately belongs to the state. Farmers have, in recent decades, had the collective right to use the land in their villages, and have been allowed to lease individual plots for up to thirty years. But if the land is needed for government infrastructure projects, the authorities are allowed to requisition it from the farmers who have leased it; they are supposed to receive compensation based on twenty-five times the amount of profit they have made from crops on the land in the past three years. In reality, this is often not actually a very large amount – at least relative to the commercial value of the land. State media have reported that the compensation paid to farmers is frequently as little as 5 or 10 per cent of their land's market value.[26] And in practice, many local governments sell agricultural land not for genuine infrastructure projects, but to property developers or speculators, to build factories, villas or golf courses – and keep the vast majority of the profits for themselves.

There are farmers who have done well from the process. In Guangdong, some of those in the areas around the key economic zones of Guangzhou and Shenzhen were well compensated for giving up their land in the 1980s and 1990s – and are renowned for having been able to lead a life of leisure ever since. And in the hills outside Hangzhou – which with its fertile land and tea plantations has long been one of China's richest rural areas – I visited a residential compound of three-storey town houses, each with its own small garden and garage. Cars were parked in driveways, children's bicycles stood in the gardens, neighbours chatted on the pavements. It looked for all the world like an exclusive housing estate. Yet the houses belonged to local tea farmers, who had been relocated here from up in the hills, after the city government took over their land to create a new tourist district. Most seemed to have done well from the move: some had rented their houses out, at high prices, to young couples from the city, even to foreigners. And most of the farmers still had a little land left where they could grow tea. In his split-level living room, Mr Lu, a farmer in his late fifties, rummaged around in the cupboard next to his giant television set and pulled out a basket stuffed with the latest crop of precious green tea. He divided this out into little packages; the delicate leaves were wrapped, a little incongruously perhaps, in Kentucky Fried Chicken plastic bags – but they still fetched a good price. As the late-afternoon sun faded behind the trees towards the city and its famous West Lake, it seemed a scene of rare rural calm and prosperity.

But not everyone has been so fortunate. In many parts of the country, relocations have provoked anger and conflict. Some of the most publicised cases have been down south, particularly in Guangdong, where the sheer speed of the economic juggernaut has created a voracious demand for land. Ten thousand farmers, for example, were evicted from an island in the Pearl River to make way for Guangzhou's new 'university city'. Compensation was given, but farmers who were left without jobs staged protests, and one of their leaders was later jailed.[27] In nearby Dongguan, in 2005, hundreds of police clashed with villagers who claimed that local officials had used village land to build houses and factories to enrich them-selves.[28] And in another part of the province, in the same year, three people were shot dead by police, following a riot linked to a prolonged protest over compensation for land which had been requisitioned to build a power plant.[29] And these stories have been echoed around the country. Also in 2005, a group of Catholic nuns were beaten up by thugs while trying to protect land belonging to their diocese near Xian from being seized by a property developer.[30]

Such land-grabs have also had severe environmental consequences in many areas. On the fringes of towns and cities across China, once-rural areas have turned rapidly into sprawling swathes of semi-industrialised landscapes, often shrouded in a dusty smog produced by the workshops and small factories of the township and village enterprises. Water supplies are often polluted as a result too. In 2005, in one part of rural Zhejiang province, anger over the construction of a chemical plant – which locals blamed for polluting their rivers, and for an apparent rise in sickness and the birth of deformed babies – led to a mini-insurrection, in which police cars were burnt and the township turned into a no-go zone for the authorities for several days.[31]

Not surprisingly, the number of land-related conflicts has continued to grow. In the first six months of 2004, the authorities were reported to have received more than 22,000 petitions connected to such land disputes. And in 2006 state media reported that some two-thirds of all protests in rural areas were connected to the acquisition of rural land.[32] Most alarmingly for a government which came to power with peasant support, such disputes have often turned loyal and hard-working rural citizens into rebels.

Certainly no one would ever have marked Mr Liu out as a troublemaker. In his youth he risked his life for the communist cause, first as a teenage soldier in China's civil war, and then as one of the hundreds of thousands of Chinese troops sent by Chairman Mao to support the North Koreans in their fight against the US and South Korea in the early 1950s. After returning to his home in north-eastern China he farmed the land near the Taizi River for more than forty years. Now, at the age of seventy-one, his face remained craggy and handsome, despite the lines etched into it. He still wore his old olive-green army jacket and stood with the upright bearing of a military man. But these days, his enthusiasm for those who governed him had diminished somewhat. 'They used cruel methods, cruel methods,' he repeated, shaking his head slowly, as he described how he and his fellow villagers had been evicted from their homes to make way for a new reservoir. It was a depressingly familiar story. Initially, many of the 25,000 residents who were asked to move had been willing to do so. 'We thought this relocation was a national policy and the nation would never trick the peasants,' said Mr Li, one of the old man's neighbours. 'So we just agreed to whatever the officials offered us.' But it soon became clear that those who moved away had not received all the compensation they had been promised, and so Mr Liu and his neighbours decided to stay in their homes until they were given clear information about how and where they would be relocated. The information never arrived, however – but the police did, and arrested several locals. Next came the demolition team, with orders for the villagers to leave their homes immediately.

'My wife was so upset,' Mr Liu said softly, 'that she drank poison and died.' Up to now he had been speaking clearly and methodically, all the while standing rigid as though at attention. But now deep sobs welled up from inside him. 'Didn't we fight the Nationalists?' he demanded through his tears. 'Didn't we do everything for the people?' His friend Mr Li patted him on the shoulder; some of the peasants had received a little land, he explained, but much of it was on slopes which were almost useless for agriculture, and 40 per cent of them had no new home of their own. 'Some people found work nearby,' he said. 'Some started begging, some old people had no food, some people had to steal.' Later the farmers discovered that not only had they not received all they were promised, but the local government had in fact never even offered them all the money set aside to cover their relocation by the provincial authorities, and had simply kept some of it for its own purposes.

And so, for seven years from 1992, the peasants campaigned for justice, with an almost biblical tenacity. They staged protests outside the county government offices, every day for five years. Sometimes they got inside too: 'The officials couldn't work properly – and we couldn't live properly,' said Mr Li, matter-of-factly. When senior provincial government officials came to the area, they blocked roads and tried to force them to listen to their pleas. One winter, hundreds of the farmers went to the provincial capital, and sat in protest outside the government headquarters for thirty-six hours in sub-zero temperatures. Several thousand of them even set off to march the hundreds of miles to Beijing to protest to the central authorities, only to stop when it became clear that many of the farmers were too weak to keep going. Over the years, a number of officials listened to what they had to say, said Mr Li, but did nothing. 'They had three policies,' he added, 'first hide, second placate, third lie.'

Finally he had begun reading legal textbooks. He sold the house he had built with borrowed money in order to raise funds to take the county government to court – but no local lawyer would accept the case. So he and eight others travelled to Beijing, and sought out a legal practice linked to one of the city's top universities, which they had seen on a television programme. 'These nine people told us very clearly,' recalled one of the lawyers with a sigh, 'that if they didn't find someone to take the case, they would each cut off their little finger and lay it in front of the central government offices.' The lawyers agreed to look into the case, and succeeded in taking the county government to the local court – but the verdict went against the farmers. They then persuaded officials at the provincial high court to investigate, and were eventually offered a compromise: an out-of-court payment of three million yuan for the farmers. The case was hailed in the local media as something of a legal landmark; for the farmers, though, it amounted to a payment of around 120 yuan (some eight pounds) each, as their reward for seven years of protest. They pledged to keep campaigning, but insisted they would now do so through legal channels. 'We believe in the law and the top leaders; if they care for us, then we have high hopes,' said Mr Li with a determined expression.[33]

In recent years the Chinese government has pledged to place more emphasis on protecting farmers' rights to use their land – and has talked of giving them 'long-term guarantees'. But for many it may be too late. Some official estimates put the number of farmers who no longer had any land at all at 40 million by 2006; many were reported to be struggling to find alternative ways of making a living, after using up whatever compensation they had received.[34]

And in some cases, the central government's expressions of concern for the plight of rural residents can actually make friction and clashes more likely – by increasing the determination of farmers to fight against local injustice and corruption. This has certainly sometimes been the case with one of the Chinese government's most vaunted initiatives for improving the lives of people in the country-side – the introduction of direct elections to select the members and chiefs of local village committees. Every village in China has such a committee, and experiments with elections began back in the late 1980s; by 2000, elections had been held in some 600,000 villages in every province in China. There were certainly some teething problems with the implementation of the system, and cases of abuses too, but international observers have generally accepted that in recent years most of the elections have been relatively free, with many non-Communist Party members standing and winning; and there's little doubt that these elections are probably the most genuinely democratic aspect of China's political system.[35] They seem in part to have been designed to act as a safety valve, releasing some of the tensions felt by many rural residents. And many rural citizens have indeed embraced them enthusiastically. For some, such elections have been a chance to counter the dominance of local Communist Party bosses, who had often been in power for years. Some were honest and dedicated, but others ran their areas like corrupt personal fiefdoms. The elections have allowed villagers to choose people who they believe will stand up for their rights; these officials are often younger, better educated and more entrepreneurial, and therefore better able to help farmers compete in the new economy. For Mr Tao, the fruit farmer in southern Anhui province, a village chief had to be someone 'who can do practical things for the local people, and guide us to get rich. We don't want an official who just lives in an old single-storey house, when other people are living in multi-storey buildings,' he added. 'Only those who live in good houses are qualified to help people make more money.' The current elected official had done a good job, he said: he had, for example, taken farmers to visit other villages so that they could learn how to grow grapes.

But in some areas, these new elected officials have found that they are seen as a threat by local party officials, who have often run their areas unchallenged for so many years. As a result of such powerful vested interests, some of the new village chiefs have discovered that their powers are strictly limited. In one area of eastern Shandong province, in 2001, the chiefs of more than fifty villages resigned en masse in protest at such problems, after less than two years in office. 'From the moment I was elected I was unable to do any work,' complained one of them at the time. He was a haggard-looking man in his sixties, who had once been a local Communist Party official himself. He had been persuaded to come out of retirement and run for election by his fellow villagers, who claimed that the new party secretary had sold off the village's factories and orchards, then lost most of the proceeds in various business dealings. As a result, he explained, many locals were now struggling to earn enough to get by. He had won the election comfortably, but soon found that the local party officials had simply decided to ignore him. 'They never told me when they were having a meeting,' he said. 'I didn't get my salary either – in fact they wouldn't even give me the keys to the office!' The party secretary also refused to give him the village's official seal, which meant it was impossible for him to write official letters or carry out any transactions. The old man was extremely frustrated. 'I'm still a member of the Communist Party,' he insisted, 'even if they don't acknowledge me.'

One of the other chiefs said he had tried to involve the farmers who elected him in a public discussion of issues affecting their lives. 'I wanted an open approach,' he said, 'so I organised a meeting for the villagers to discuss taxation; we were planning to take a vote and agree a standard for how people were taxed for their land.' But the local party boss had other ideas, and sent people to break up the meeting. 'They smashed my table, and kicked me to the ground,' said the village chief. The party boss was angry with the village committee, he explained, because it had tried to investigate how he was spending the local funds. 'He controlled all the money, but he wouldn't let us see the accounts,' the village chief went on, 'there was definitely something wrong.' They had reported the attack on the meeting to the local police and county government, but, he said, 'they told us they couldn't do anything'. He insisted, though, that these events had not shaken his faith in rural democracy. 'The village committee law is a very good one,' he insisted, 'I've studied it, and the provincial rules on implementing it are good too – it's just the local officials who don't support it.'

Eventually the group of village chiefs had tried to hand in a protest to the central government in Beijing, but police from their home area followed them to the capital and prevented them from doing so. In the end, some of them effectively went into hiding; one was later arrested and jailed for financial irregularities.[36] And in some cases, local officials went even further in their determination to stop elected village chiefs from interfering. In Shaanxi province in 2001, a village Communist Party secretary was charged with the murder of the elected head of the village committee. The elected official had worked hard and helped to transform the village's economy, according to the locals, but had, it seemed, discovered too much about the old leadership's past corruption.[37]

Government officials say the election process is in its infancy, and the system will improve with time. But others see such problems as a sign of the inherent difficulties of introducing a limited element of democracy into a deeply entrenched system. The village elections have clearly raised the expectations of many farmers, but in practice have, in the end, sometimes only left them more frustrated. Hopes that the elections will pave the way for a more democratic approach at higher levels, such as township and county governments, have also yet to yield any significant results. And there have been stories of other types of abuse too, with cases of village chiefs themselves accused of buying votes and falsifying elections.[38]

Such problems are a reminder that the opportunities for local officials to misuse funds and ride roughshod over the wishes of the local citizens tend to be greater in rural areas, which lack even the limited checks and balances on their actions which exist in some urban areas. It's not unusual to hear migrant workers who have left

318

the countryside to work in the cities say that rural corruption and bad government played a part in their decision to leave their homes. The slogans posted on walls and banners in many remote villages often only underline such problems, like the one I saw hanging over the entrance to one village in Shaanxi province, which warned of the need to fight against crime gangs and 'dark forces'.

And life in the countryside can be particularly hard for women. It's well documented that the suicide rate of rural women in China is among the highest in the world. Reasons vary, but oppressive traditional rural attitudes towards women are undoubtedly one factor.[39] A farmer's wife in a village in northern China once summed up her views on the status of women: 'In the villages women don't have much self-respect,' she said. 'It doesn't make much difference whether or not we've had much education – we've always felt it was our destiny to stay at home, do the washing and the cooking, and plant the land.' Now some of the women in her village had been put on a training course organised by a foreign development organisation, and had begun to try to set up their own small businesses, but many of their husbands were apparently not happy about this new assertiveness.

And women's lives are also affected by China's tightly controlled family planning system. Its implementation varies around the country, but there have been well-documented cases of abuses, as in rural Shandong province in 2005, where a blind, self-taught legal activist launched a campaign against what he said was the forced sterilisation of local women, to ensure that they did not breach the family planning quotas. The man, Chen Guangcheng, highlighted cases where relatives of women who tried to escape this coercion were detained, in order to force them to return. Lawyers from Beijing who tried to help Mr Chen were beaten up when they came to his village. Finally, in 2006, he was jailed for four years by a local court on charges of inciting villagers to cause an affray and disrupt traffic; after an international outcry a higher court later ordered a retrial, but the original verdict was eventually upheld.[40] The case was an extreme example. But the way in which family planning information is displayed in some Chinese villages does seem to

319

confirm that issues such as personal feelings and privacy relating to such matters are not always given a high priority. In one village I visited in Jiangxi province, a large blackboard hung on the outside wall of the small brick building which housed the district family planning office. It listed the names of local women and how many children they had had, and spelled out whether they had had a contraceptive coil fitted, whether they had had an abortion or whether their husbands had had a vasectomy. 'The family planning commission is my home,' proclaimed a slogan on another wall of the building.

For all the government's desire to slow the departure of Chinese peasants from the land, then, there are still many factors encouraging them to leave. Some specialists argue that easier access to bank loans and training in modern agricultural methods are the key to solving the problems farmers face in earning money. But others believe that more modern farming techniques may also leave a greater number of rural workers surplus to requirements, increasing the likelihood that they will migrate to the towns and the cities. Some experts, meanwhile, insist that farmers must be given clearer ownership rights to the land they use, in order to stimulate their enthusiasm. Others believe that individual farmers will have to form new-style agricultural collectives if they are to have any chance of competing in the marketplace.[41]

For many, the success of the government's campaign to create a 'new countryside' will be judged not just by how much money is spent, but by whether farmers are given the chance to engage in agriculture without the distortions caused by corruption and heavy-handed local government. The banning, in 2004, of a popular book which analysed the plight of farmers in badly managed rural areas raised doubts about just how far the authorities were really prepared to go in this direction.[42] There are positive examples: in one northern province I met farmers who had taken part in a 'partici-patory' project organised by a European development agency, where they had been given a greater say in the types of trees and crops planted on their village's collective land. The project had increased their interest in protecting the trees, and helped to stabilise environmental degradation, according to local officials. Many of the farmers were now growing new strains of fruit trees, which they hoped would bring them a higher income in the future. Looking out over the dry, rutted gulleys which made up much of the village's land, one local official insisted there was now fresh hope for the area. In the past, he said, many people here 'could not see a way out of poverty', and had migrated to the cities; now, he insisted, some were starting to return. Still, even here, officials admitted that implementing the project had required a significant shift in the attitudes of the local authorities towards the farmers – in order to allow them to take part in making decisions rather than simply ordering them around. And with farmers increasingly aware of their rights, and often prepared to stand up for them, such changes in official thinking may be required on a large scale in China's vast rural areas, if the problems of the countryside are to be solved.

# 11

## Consumers and citizens

In the south-eastern city of Wenzhou, Mr Song was growing tired of his old car. He'd had it for a few years, and now, as a manager in a local company, he felt it was time for something a little more stylish. After some careful research he found just the model he was looking for, a popular French car, now being manufactured in central China. He wasn't too happy about the price quoted by his local dealer, though. So he got online, and soon found a website dedicated to this particular model, which had been set up by an enthusiastic driver in Guangdong province. Through the website's discussion group, he eventually made contact with some forty people around the country, all of whom were planning to buy the same kind of car. They each agreed to go to the showroom nearest to where they lived, and see what was the best discount they could get for a mass purchase of forty vehicles; the idea was to find the cheapest place in the country to buy the car, then all meet up there to make the purchase.

In the end things didn't quite go to plan, said Mr Song, since the car manufacturer got worried about prices being forced too low, and told its dealers around the country only to sell to drivers from their local areas. Still, he and the five or six other would-be buyers from nearby parts of Zhejiang province did go to a car dealer in Wenzhou and successfully negotiate a discount of 20,000 yuan (around £1,500) each – more than a tenth off the original price. They all met at the showroom one morning, and were soon heading home in their shiny new cars. Afterwards they kept in touch through the Internet, discussing any problems they had, and whether they should get together to bring a group complaint against the manufacturer, though in the end most of them were happy enough with their purchase. They became friends too – sometimes in the summer they all drove out together into the countryside, to a famous beauty spot which was now just an hour away on the new motorway. And the next year, when Mr Song got married, he invited the other drivers too. On the day of his wedding they all met up – and drove their cars in convoy to collect the bride from her family home, as was the fashion in the city.

Indeed, buoyed by his success in getting his car cut-price, Mr Song also organised a group of half a dozen friends, who were all getting married at around the same time, to go to the local electronics store together to buy new fridges. 'It saved us a couple of thousand yuan each,' he grinned. And they weren't the only people in Wenzhou taking this approach to making a purchase. 'I've heard of people who got together to get a discount on buying imported Italian sports cars,' said one of Mr Song's friends. 'You'd be surprised what you can do if you try.'

The phenomenon of people getting together like this to negotiate a better price on a product is known in China as *tuangou*, or 'group purchasing', and has become increasingly popular in recent years, thanks particularly to the spread of the Internet. In fact, according to Mr Song, it's now so common that some car manufacturers have even set up special 'group sales' departments and are actively promoting this kind of purchase – though the discounts they offer are not as good as if you do it yourself, he says. And in market-savvy Wenzhou, even the local newspaper has organised car-buying groups among its readers, promising to help negotiate cheaper prices.

It would all have been hard to imagine a couple of decades earlier. In those days, shoppers found themselves in the position of supplicants, to the all-powerful sales assistants in the state-run stores which monopolised most of China's consumer market. In the department stores of the 1980s, many goods were shut away in glass cases, and simply attracting the attention of a member of staff to unlock them could be a challenge. These stalwarts of the planned economy sat in splendid isolation from the masses behind wide counters, where they could chat, read the paper or get on with their knitting, while studiously ignoring the crowds of disgruntled citizens queuing up to buy a pair of socks or a ballpoint pen. Customer satisfaction did not seem to be a high priority: in one department store in Xian a sales assistant once offered me a choice of new bicycles, each of which was missing either a pedal, a saddle or -- in some cases -- a wheel. Perhaps I looked a little surprised, since he gave a dismissive shrug and said, 'That's how they came from the factory.' At the local branch of the Bank of China meanwhile, a lone clerk would deal lethargically with transactions while several dozen of her colleagues, protected from customers by a glass partition, lolled at their desks drinking tea out of jars, poring over the latest novel, or simply slumped face down on the table enjoying a no doubt well-deserved rest. At the railway station, ticket staff who had to work and sleep in the same tiny booth took out their frustrations on would-be passengers, either by denying that they had any tickets at all, or simply by making sure that they offered each person one or two tickets fewer than they actually wanted.

These days, on the surface at least, much has changed: the streets of China's big towns and cities are filled with convenience stores, many open twenty-four hours a day. Walk into a trendy clothes shop on any high street and you will be greeted by loud cries of 'Welcome!' from smiling young shop assistants. In department stores it can be hard to move for overzealous sales staff trying to interest you in their wares. Sales gimmicks aimed at attracting customers are everywhere. They range from the everyday -- discounts, promotions and VIP cards -- to the downright bizarre: the real woman, wearing a flowing wedding gown, who I once saw sitting motionless in the window display of a marriage outfitters on one of Shanghai's main streets; or the restaurant in the northern city of Taiyuan where all the waiters and waitresses have shaven heads -- in order to reassure customers that they will never find a hair in their food.[1]

Growing competition in the economy has played a part in this transformation. In the past decade, new private businesses have taken on – and often defeated – China's old state-run stores. The welfare reforms of the late 1990s, meanwhile, made many people particularly careful about how they spent their money, forcing all businesses to fight harder to lure consumers. The arrival in China of foreign companies and business methods has also had an impact. The chanted greetings in many shops were first brought to the mainland by Hong Kong and Taiwanese-run fashion chains during the 1990s. And foreign supermarkets and retailers also began to open in China towards the end of that decade, shaking up their local rivals with promises of free delivery, no-questions-asked refunds and pledges to match the prices of other stores. To citizens used to decades of rude and unhelpful service, it was a welcome change. At the opening of one giant foreign superstore in Shanghai in the early years of the new century, I met a young married couple who were eagerly perusing the packed shelves. Weren't they worried, I asked, that these foreign companies might drive Chinese firms out of business? 'To be honest,' said the young woman, 'we came here specially today because we'd rather buy from foreign stores like this, we feel more confident that they won't cheat us.'

Not that it took Chinese companies long to respond. In recent years most of the country's major high street stores and main manufacturers of consumer goods have highlighted their commitment to after-sales service, and now offer long guarantees, in an attempt to win customers. Some have gone even further: the household electronics maker Haier, which grew to become one of China's biggest businesses during the 1990s, is proud of its reputation for responding to the needs of consumers. Staff from its marketing department once explained to me how, after discovering an unusually high rate of breakdowns among its washing machines in rural parts of northern China, the company realised that some farmers were actually using them to wash their potatoes. And so, they assured me, the firm began producing special machines designed for precisely that purpose.

Not that there are no traces of the old mentality left. Until recently it was almost impossible to buy a return ticket on China's railways, for example, since revenue from ticket sales traditionally belonged

325

to the railway bureau of the town where one got on the train. Service in the country's banks has improved in recent years, but it remains a source of frustration for many, not helped by a still largely unreconstructed bureaucracy, which can make transferring money from one bank to another, or from an individual account to a company account, a stressful experience. Once, when I lost my bank card, the clerk spent fifteen minutes helping me to fill in all the forms required to report this, before finally giving up in despair and suggesting that it would be much simpler for everyone if I just closed the account and opened a new one. Such frustrations may explain why many members of China's urban middle classes welcomed the country's entry into the World Trade Organisation in 2001 with open arms. While experts expressed concern about the impact of greater foreign competition on the country's farmers and domestic industries, many city dwellers hoped that the opening of the economy to increased foreign competition would bring improved service, cheaper cars and fresh opportunities, and force the old state monopolies – and indeed parts of the bureaucratic system itself – to reform. Such hopes may have been exaggerated: certainly the idea of customer service did not appear to have got through to the Beijing bus conductor who, in 2005, was alleged to have grabbed a teenage girl by the throat because she suspected she had not paid the full fare; the girl died and the conductor was later given a suspended death sentence.[2]

Still, such cases are at least guaranteed to provoke a media outcry these days. Indeed, consumer rights has been one of the more open areas of media coverage since the 1990s – one of China's first investigative television programmes, for example, focused largely on cases of businesses cheating customers – and there are now many radio phone-ins on the subject. And consumer issues are also the focus of many of the news hotlines set up by Chinese newspapers. China even has its own consumer champion, Wang Hai, an ordinary citizen who became a celebrity in the second half of the 1990s by taking up the cases of people who had bought poor-quality products or felt they had been cheated, and often winning them redress.

China now also has a national association to protect consumers' rights, with offices in every province and major city which operate their own consumer hotlines. In Shanghai I went to visit the hotline's call centre, where a couple of dozen staff received hundreds of enquiries a day. It was a warm late-spring day, and many of the calls were about problems with household appliances, particularly air conditioning, according to one of the supervisors. 'We've been getting continuous calls,' he said. 'Either people's air conditioners aren't working properly, or they're not satisfied with installation or repairs.' According to Zhao Jiaoli, director of the Shanghai Consumer Rights Protection Commission, her office took on some 60,000 cases in 2005, ranging from problems with home renovations to medical accidents. In complex cases, they call in a team of lawyers who act as volunteers, or send experts to people's homes to assess their complaints. The knowledge that consumers are more likely to take action has made companies more responsive, says Ms Zhao. It's a big contrast with the 1980s when she began working on such issues. 'Twenty years ago, when we started, I felt people didn't have much awareness of their rights,' she says. 'Now consumers' awareness of how to protect themselves is much higher – young people especially are much smarter, they know much more than older people about how to deal with lots of things in society.' Ms Zhao has been head of the commission for more than a decade now; it began in the 1980s as part of the local government, but was recently relaunched as a 'non-government organisation'. Many of its staff are in fact still seconded from the city's commerce bureau or other government departments; but the new status is designed to reassure consumers that it does not just speak for official interests. 'Being separate from the government gives people more confidence,' explains one staff member.

The passage of China's first consumer protection law in the early 1990s gave a big boost to their work, according to Ms Zhao. By 1998, when she and her colleagues held their first open day, with lawyers offering free advice, there were queues around the block. In the same year they opened the hotline, the first such citywide service in the country. It's enabled them to work much more quickly. 'Now, if we get a complaint against one of the big supermarkets, for example, we can call them immediately and ask them what they're going to do about it,' says Zhao Jiaoli. 'Often they'll give us a response on the same day.'

Not all businesses have been so cooperative, she acknowledges. 'There are some companies which take no notice,' she admits, 'and of course that's their right. But,' she adds, 'in that case we have to inform people, so we publish our findings in the media.' Sometimes this includes what she calls a 'consumer alert' – such as in the case of a local air-conditioning manufacturer which led customers to believe that they were buying the products of a much better known Japanese firm with a similar name. The company resolutely refused to respond to consumer complaints. 'So I warned consumers that this company was imitating a famous brand, and told them how many people had been cheated!' says Ms Zhao, with a glint in her eye. She herself has been threatened by angry businesses, she admits, though she says it's much rarer these days. Once she publicised complaints about work carried out by a house-decorating firm. 'They sent a lot of their migrant workers into my office,' she recalls, 'and told me, "Don't think that you're going to be able to leave your office today. If you don't let us earn enough to eat we won't even let you go to the toilet!"' The firm also brought along a TV crew to expose her as a liar – but in the end the TV reporters agreed to go and look at the homes of some of the consumers who had complained, and she was proved right, she says.

Still, there are always new types of problems appearing, notes Ms Zhao – recently there have been more complaints about hi-tech goods, and about products bought online which don't match up to the promised specification. To raise awareness, she and her association have regular slots on local radio and television, and send their monthly magazine to every neighbourhood community office. They also take part in public hearings on consumer issues, such as the price of railway tickets, bad service by airlines or how much taxi fares should be raised, to help drivers cope with higher petrol prices without harming the interests of passengers. And they have taken on Shanghai's underground railway company over the size of the deposit which passengers pay to use one of the network's swipe-card-style tickets.[3]

It all fits in with a growing awareness among Chinese citizens of how to make use of the law to protect their rights. It was only in 1999 that the concept of the rule of law was written into the country's constitution; previously this spoke only of the supremacy of the Communist Party. In recent years there has been a sharp rise in the number of lawsuits on commercial issues, as citizens have become increasingly litigious. Indeed, some of the foreign companies which moved into China's market as a result of the opening up of the country's economy following its entry into the World Trade Organisation have been surprised to find themselves on the receiving end of lawsuits from Chinese consumers. In 2002, for example, one of the first foreign banks to open up a branch in the country soon found itself facing a lawsuit from a customer who was dissatisfied with the fees it charged for its services.[4]

Yet surveys have also suggested that there are still many consumers who do not dare to speak out if their rights are infringed. Consumer rights activists too have warned that big businesses are becoming increasingly powerful in Chinese society, and are often able to exert influence over government departments to protect their own interests – and that the official consumer associations do not have sufficient power to take them on.[5] There's no doubt that attempts by consumers to use the law to defend themselves can sometimes run into sensitive territory. Zhao Jiaoli says her consumer rights organisation has been paying attention to the rising tide of disputes between urban residents and the management companies of the housing estates and compounds where they live. 'Sometimes they take people's money but the living environment is not so good,' she notes. 'Or there are disputes over people parking in public areas.' But she says they cannot intervene in cases where, for example, residents claim to have been attacked by representatives of management companies; nor does her commission have any contact with the committees of property owners which have sprung up in many residential areas as citizens seek to protect their rights.

There are now large numbers of such committees around the country – many set up in response to problems with either the construction or management of residential complexes. Some such groups of residents have taken developers or management companies to court; others have used the media, or even taken to the streets with protest banners, to demand their rights. But it can be a risky strategy. In Guangzhou, in 2006, a resident of one new housing complex who had organised a protest by several hundred of his neighbours, after their shuttle bus service was cut off, was attacked in his home by unknown assailants; the security cameras in his building malfunctioned at just that moment, according to the management, and so the attackers could not be identified.[6] And since many real-estate management companies are large and well connected, it can be hard for residents to get redress in such cases. The Shenzhen resident who called for a boycott of real-estate companies in protest at their methods in 2006, for example, was soon reported to have come under official pressure to stop talking about the issue in public.[7]

It's clear that, for the authorities, organised groups of residents actively fighting for their rights are seen as highly sensitive. This seems to be not only the result of a deep-seated suspicion of any groups of people organising outside official control, but also of specific fears that rising private property ownership could bring with it a political dimension. Indeed, some of those who wish to see greater reforms of China's system seem to agree. One prominent liberal academic once spelled this out to me in some detail. 'The people who are making money are changing Chinese society,' he said. 'This is a new force in Chinese society. By making money you have to enjoy at least the lowest extent of economic freedom,' he went on, choosing his words carefully, but speaking with obvious conviction. 'At least you have the right to occupy or enjoy what you have produced, and the money you have made. In other words, you must have some private property rights.' What's more, he added, 'if people have the chance to exercise economic freedom, and have some private property to defend, they will impose demands on the government. The market economy requires a limited government,'

330

he concluded, 'a small and effective government, but fundamentally it should be a limited government.'

It was a version of the theory, beloved of political scientists, that the emergence of a middle class, with economic interests of its own, inevitably leads to demands for greater accountability and a more open political system. And there's no doubt that official nervousness about the potential for such demands seems to have been one of the reasons for the long delay in passing China's proposed new law enshrining private property rights. After many years of discussion by legislators, the law was thought to be finally ready for approval at the annual session of China's parliament in 2006, but at the last minute it was delayed yet again, apparently due to objections from conservatives who believed it would undermine socialism.[8] Later the same year, legislators finally agreed on a new draft, which placed a greater emphasis on public ownership of state assets, but nevertheless did, for example, allow property owners to automatically renew their rights to use of the land on which their homes were built after seventy years (the previous limit under Chinese law). This was seen as an important move to reassure those who bought property that their investment would be secure in the long term.[9]

And the recent years of market economic reforms do seem to have encouraged an instinctive belief among many Chinese citizens that they should now enjoy a greater level of fairness and protection for their rights under the law. That was certainly true of one young, well-heeled businessman who I met in Shenzhen in 2002. Reclining in his chair in the coffee shop of a luxury hotel, dressed in a smart yellow jacket, he looked every inch the successful, confident member of the new middle class. But he was not happy. A few years earlier, he said, he, along with several partners, had invested in a football club in another city, which played in China's professional league. He himself had taken an active role in running the club's operations. But he and his friends quickly became disillusioned at the corruption which, he claimed, was rife in the sport. Referees routinely demanded bribes, he said, often from both the teams playing in a match.

The issue had aroused much debate in the Chinese media, and led eventually to the arrest and jailing of a well-known referee. But the investor was upset less by corrupt refereeing than by what he saw as the incompetent handling of the problem by China's football authorities. It was not what he would have expected, he pointed out. 'I'm thirty-nine,' he said, as if by way of explanation. 'I can see just how much has changed in China – we're the generation who've benefited from reform and opening up, we're "businessmen",' he went on, using the word in English, as though this gave the idea greater emphasis. 'In our "business",' he said, 'we feel that China is making more and more progress. But while so much is developing, we feel that the management of this sport is lagging far behind. We knew China had corruption,' he continued, 'but in business the government is trying to tackle it, it's getting better. We never imagined that in football it could be so serious.'

It was not too surprising to hear such comments in Shenzhen, where so many of China's experiments with modernisation have been carried out. It's a city where it's common to meet business people and members of the middle class who insist that the government ought to be serving them, and protecting their economic rights and investments. 'If you want to join the world economy you have to have a good legal system,' stressed one local businessman who I met in the run-up to China's entry into the World Trade Organisation. In Shenzhen, he said, 'a lot of ideas have come over from Hong Kong. So now if I apply to the government for a licence or to start a business, they must respond within a week – otherwise I can sue.' Such rights were, of course, limited to everyday issues relating to business and simple administrative procedures, rather than to anything more political. But they form part of an attempt by the authorities, in some parts of China at least, to respond to people's changing aspirations by offering at least the appearance of a more accountable, responsive government. Much publicity is often given, for example, to the opening of government hotlines or email inboxes where people can supposedly communicate directly with mayors or other local government officials; lower-level functionaries, meanwhile, are often sent out to answer questions from the public on local radio phone-ins.

Even the National People's Congress, China's legislature, which holds a meeting of all its three thousand or so members only once a year, and has never defeated a draft law, has been trying to present a more open and responsive image. In 2006, for example, its official website featured blogs by prominent delegates – including not only the sociologist Li Yinhe discussing her proposals for a bill on gay marriage, but also a well-known property developer expressing his concern at the increasing division between rich and poor in China. Other delegates to the session raised similarly sensitive issues, some openly criticising government ministries for making policy decisions without consulting the legislature or its leadership.[10] And such bodies have in recent years seen a growing number of well-informed academics and experts co-opted into their membership. (There are some unlikely celebrity members too: the actress Gong Li and the film director Zhang Yimou, for example, are delegates to the Chinese People's Political Consultative Conference, the advisory body to the legislature – though they have faced criticisms for not always actually turning up.)

Officials have explicitly admitted that such efforts to polish up the image of China's political structures reflect a recognition of growing aspirations for a more accountable system. In 2006, a senior official from the Communist Party's Central Party School emphasised that it was important to allow legislative bodies to provide more of a real channel for people to express their opinions, in order to head off the kind of social dissatisfaction and upheavals which led to the 'colour revolutions', the popular revolts which toppled or threatened post-communist governments in several former Soviet republics in 2004–5, causing some anxiety in Chinese official circles.[11]

At the same time, the authorities have repeatedly ruled out any ideas of moving towards a western-style multi-party democracy. Towns and cities do have local legislatures, which can relay proposals to the Provincial and National People's Congresses. And in places like Shenzhen there have been, in theory, experiments with allowing ordinary individuals to put themselves forward as candidates for these local bodies, for which, at the lowest district level, members of the public are supposed to be able to cast their vote. But in practice, the rules on becoming a candidate – and sometimes even a voter – can be highly complex, and appear designed to keep the system within carefully set limits. Would-be candidates seen as too radical by the authorities are also likely to be 'advised' to withdraw from the process.[12]

In 2005, newspapers in Guangdong reported, with some excitement, the news that a member of Shenzhen's local legislature was planning to hold regular 'surgeries', similar to those held by local councillors or members of parliament in Britain and other western countries, allowing members of the public to visit him in his office on a particular day each week to discuss their problems and grievances. It was an unusual move in a system where the members of such bodies rarely have direct official contact with the public. But later reports suggested that the authorities had swiftly made it clear to the legislator that such behaviour was not part of China's political system.[13]

And so anyone with grievances connected to the political system – cases of corruption or unjust treatment by local officials, for example – still has, in theory, to express these through an antiquated system known as *shangfang* or 'petitioning'. It's an approach which dates back to ancient times in China, and has continued in the communist era. People with complaints or injustices to report are supposed to write these down and take them to a special office run by the local government, where officials are meant to receive their petitions and pass them to other government departments for a reply. But the majority of plaintiffs receive little or no response, and these offices often become the focus for groups of disgruntled people. In recent years, for example, a kind of 'squatters' village' of petitioners grew up at the main office in Beijing, with people from the provinces camping out for days or weeks on end, in the hope of getting an answer to their complaints. The authorities eventually started trying to find ways to keep such people off the street, telling them to send letters or apply by Internet instead. But for many citizens this has not helped to solve their problems. And so in provincial capitals around China it's still not uncommon to see groups of dissatisfied citizens, often from the surrounding country-side, who have simply given up on the petition system and decided to take their complaints directly to the local government head-quarters; usually they can be found standing or sitting patiently on the pavement outside, waiting for someone to come out and listen to what they have to say – though such hopes are often in vain.

Nowadays, of course, some people prefer to take their grievances straight to the media, though political limits mean that certain cases are too sensitive for journalists to follow up or put into print. Legal reforms have also made it possible for some disgruntled citizens to bring cases to court, sometimes even against official departments – though lawyers who accept such cases may be taking a risk (not least because their licences have to be renewed once a year, and can easily be withheld if the local authorities are unhappy with them). Nevertheless, China has a growing number of lawyers providing legal aid – often via centres focusing on the rights of, for example, women or migrant workers. But many experts say such work does not receive enough financial support. One prominent legal academic who I met called on the authorities to allow more ordinary people with grievances to join together to bring group lawsuits. Such cases, known in the American legal system as 'class actions', are more worthwhile for lawyers to take on, since they may earn more money if they win. But as the legal expert put it, 'The government doesn't like to see this too much, because it involves people getting together to fight for something. Courts would prefer to split up what could be a big case into lots of small ones, and hear them separately.'

Yet despite – or perhaps because of – frustrations with China's legal and political system, a growing number of prominent academics and intellectuals have in the past few years begun to speak out publicly on social issues, and to highlight individual cases and grievances. The development of the Internet has made this easier, allowing for the publication of open letters and petitions. And

335

sometimes the official media too is willing to publish outspoken opinion pieces or commentaries. These intellectuals are, in a sense, following in the footsteps of Chinese scholars down the ages, who were traditionally expected to provide expert opinions to emperors and ministers. (Indeed, some went down in history as brave patriots for honestly expressing their views on affairs of state, even when they knew these would not be welcomed by the emperor.) It was a tradition which did not survive the early decades of communism, however – many intellectuals, for example, were rounded up and punished during the Anti-Rightist Campaign of 1957, after taking up an invitation from Chairman Mao to express their criticisms of the system a little too enthusiastically.

But some academics now again appear willing to take on the role of the 'public intellectual', as such people are known. As one professor at a top university puts it, this is a kind of duty: 'Sometimes we should reflect on civil affairs and offer some analysis,' he says. 'It may be in an area where we have some special expertise, and so we may be able to have some influence on official policy.' And, he believes, it's important that there is a public debate on the nation's social problems. 'There are lots of issues where the government should rely on the people, on this kind of debate, to get some inspiration in order to draw up reasonable policies,' he insists.

It remains a risky calling, however. Some of these 'public intellectuals' have been warned by the authorities to stop speaking out on particular subjects; some have had their websites closed down, at least temporarily; a few have been detained. 'You can only operate in a very limited space,' says the professor. 'Maybe if you go beyond this limit they will think that you've become an enemy, that you're not just a pure academic.' It means, he admits, that he and other such people think long and hard before speaking out. 'We all often impose a kind of self-censorship, and are careful in expressing our opinions,' he says. Still, these concerns have not prevented him from taking part in activities such as the issuing of an open letter by a group of intellectuals, protesting against the sacking of a news-paper editor. 'We felt this was connected with issues like freedom of expression and the survival of the newspaper,' he explains, 'so we frankly published our criticism.'

And according to this professor, such independent thinking is becoming more common in China's academic world. 'I think the concept of university independence is becoming stronger,' he says. 'In the 1970s or early 1980s, as soon as a national leader said something, everyone would start writing articles saying how important this was, how good it was. Nowadays,' he suggests, 'more and more scholars are applying their own academic standards to their work – and to analyse the work of others.'

And on a less political level, there's no doubt that increasing numbers of Chinese citizens are pursuing their own interests and concerns these days – in ways they would not have dared in the not too distant past. This can be seen, on the simplest level, in everyday life – for example in the instinctive, low-level defiance by ordinary people of rules and regulations which they don't like. In Shanghai, many citizens have, over recent years, pointedly ignored much publicised regulations banning people from hanging washing out of their windows over the street on bamboo poles, or from flying kites in public places. (The latter ban was apparently motivated by a fear that the strings were too dangerous – but it seems to have done little to deter the old men who still fly their kites in parks or on bridges across the city's creek.)[14]

More positively, people are, at many levels of society, increasingly creating their own small interest groups and informal social organisations. Visiting a family in a city in one southern Chinese town a few years ago, I was a little baffled by the continuous knocks at the door, and the stream of young women, each carrying a small child, who passed through the living room into a door at the back of the house. It was, I eventually discovered, a mother-and-baby group which gathered every weekend in the family's home. It was hardly a radical organisation – but it would still have been hard to imagine mothers organising themselves so independently a decade or two earlier. And among migrant workers, meanwhile, networks of people from the same 'native place' often spring up, offering important contacts and

337

links and some semblance of a social structure in the alien world of the big city. These networks can take unexpected forms. On a visit to Shenzhen recently I was surprised when the taxi driver, seeing a traffic jam up ahead, immediately reached under his steering wheel, pulled out a two-way radio receiver, and began shouting loudly in a strange accent. He was, it turned out, speaking the dialect of a distant northern province. He and a whole group of his friends from that province all worked as taxi drivers in Shenzhen, he explained, and had set up their own Citizens' Band radio link. 'If we have any problems on the roads, we just have to put out a call and someone will give us information or come to our assistance,' said the driver.

Other social organisations are more visible. In the traffic jams which crowd the roads out of Shanghai into the neighbouring provinces every weekend, it's not uncommon to see a line of cars with brightly coloured stickers on their doors, apparently driving in convoy. These are the members of China's car clubs, organisations which have emerged to help the nation's new motoring classes discover the joys of driving out of the big city for a weekend in the countryside. And since some drivers are still a little anxious about driving into the unknown on their own – and China also has many car-obsessives who simply like meeting other drivers and talking about their vehicles – these have become very popular. According to Yu Li, the head of Shanghai's Dark Horse Car Club, 'Many of our members are young drivers who join us to make new friends and contacts; others just like to bring along their business clients.' But the driving can be serious. Some of their trips are for seven or eight days, covering thousands of miles to Guizhou in the south-west, or Shanxi province in the north. They stay in farmers' houses or small hotels, or sometimes camp out or just sleep in their cars. 'We don't usually have a very detailed plan,' says Mr Yu, 'we just set off and see what we can find. We like to look for new places, see what real lives are like in the countryside, we can learn something about the country that way.' In remote villages they hand out school books to children; sometimes they come back later to see how the locals are getting on. And it's proved a popular approach: 'We have seven thousand members,' says Mr Yu.

Other groups reflect not just shared interests, but shared values too. At Shanghai's Fudan University, I met a young student who, after reading on the Internet about the popularity of vegetarianism in the West, had tried it out for himself. He became so enthusiastic that he set up a vegetarian society on the campus, and spent his spare time promoting a vegetarian lifestyle and the concept of animal rights. In a society where fast-food chains like McDonald's and KFC were a symbol of a modern way of life for many of the young generation, it seemed like an unfashionable message, but he had quickly attracted more than a hundred members. One nineteen-year-old student explained that she had joined despite opposition from her family. 'When I told my father that I was becoming a vegetarian he asked me, "Have you gone crazy? Are you planning to become a Buddhist nun or something?"' she said. 'He told me if I didn't eat meat I wouldn't get any nutrition and I'd get sick.' But, she insisted, she was determined to stand up for what she believed – and she and her friends were planning to set up a stall in the city centre on the next public holiday to persuade others to join them.

In recent years, China has also seen the rapid growth of charitable activity, as some of the newly wealthy begin to think about helping others – or in some cases see such benevolence as good for their image. It's something which the authorities have, up to a point, welcomed as a way of helping to tackle some of the country's social problems. Mr Du, a factory owner in Shenzhen, was far from being one of the country's richest people, but he had joined the local branch of an international organisation which brought together business people to donate money to good causes. 'You have to be a member of the middle class, and active in business, to join,' he explained earnestly. He himself had grown up in a poor village in western China, and first came to Shenzhen as a migrant worker, before eventually earning enough to set up his own business. And so he was well aware of the problems in China's remoter areas. 'We have to be concerned about rural poverty,' he said, 'and if we can help people we should.' Every few months, he and a few other members of the group went on a trip to rural areas, to look for places where they could be of most assistance. So far they had given money to rural schools in the south-west and to organisations which carried out operations to restore people's eyesight; now they were looking at problems of HIV/AIDS in rural areas. And in Shenzhen itself they were trying to help the children of families living on low incomes – including migrant workers.

But registering a charity – or indeed any other form of non-governmental organisation – in China is far from easy. A number of foreign NGOs and development agencies have been permitted to work in the country since the 1990s, in partnership with government ministries and other official bodies. But since the communist revolution, the only domestic non-governmental organisations and charitable foundations allowed to exist are those which, like the All-China Women's Federation, for example, were effectively set up under government auspices. And so the government was caught unawares when, in the first half of the 1990s, a few ordinary citizens began trying to found small groups of their own; these included several environmental organisations set up by academics and other concerned individuals in Beijing and other cities. Finally, in 1998, the authorities issued new rules governing the establishment of social organisations and non-profit-making bodies. Some citizens seized on this as an opportunity to push for a more open society: several human rights campaigners and political activists – including the veteran dissident Xu Wenli and the Hangzhou-based activist Wang Youcai – tried to make use of these rules and register a new political party, under the name of the China Democracy Party. This, it soon became clear, was not quite what the government had in mind, and in late 1998 Mr Xu and Mr Wang were arrested and sentenced, respectively, to thirteen and eleven years in jail. (Following international pressure, they were eventually released a few years later and sent out of the country to the US on 'medical parole'.)

In fact, the current rules on non-governmental organisations stress that they need approval both from China's Ministry of Civil Affairs or regional civil affairs bureaux, as well as from another government department relevant to the particular field in which the organisation works; in other words, an environmental group will need the backing of the State Environmental Protection Agency, while a migrant workers' organisation might need support from the Ministry of Labour. In practice, these rules make registering any social or charitable group a complex procedure. According to one legal academic, the rules are a reflection of continuing official anxiety about the impact of such citizens' groups. 'They think they might turn into forces which could harm the government,' he says. Even the government departments which are supposed to sponsor such groups are themselves often said to be wary of getting involved. The head of one organisation which tried to register says the official body to which his group had to apply 'made it very clear they will not endorse any independent organisation. They just don't want either the management responsibility or the political liability – they're worried that they won't be able to control what these organisations will do after they register.'

In a fast-evolving society, these rules have not actually stopped new groups from springing up – but many have had to give up on attempts to register as NGOs, charities or other 'social organisa-tions', and have simply registered as companies. This usually enables them to operate – as long as they don't do anything to upset the authorities – but it makes it harder for them to solicit donations and attract support, and they also have to pay tax on money they receive. And if they do carry out work which the authorities consider politically sensitive, their vague status leaves them doubly vulnerable to accusations of illegal activity.

In recent years a number of organisations which have tried to campaign on issues like HIV/AIDS, for example, have faced obstacles, particularly when they have tried to work on the ground in areas such as Henan province, the centre of China's biggest AIDS blood scandal, where the local authorities have been very concerned about the damage to their image caused by outside attention. It's something Li Dan knows all about. Slim, earnest and bespectacled, he first got involved in AIDS awareness activities while at university in Beijing in the late 1990s. Working as a volunteer for the Red Cross, he came into contact with people living

341

with HIV, and started to become aware of the discrimination they faced. This spurred him to go to see the situation in rural Henan for himself. What he found shocked him deeply. For much of the 1990s, poor villagers in several parts of the province had been selling their blood to earn money; often it was bought by illegal blood stations which extracted the cells they needed, and mixed the remaining liquid with that taken from other patients before injecting this back into the veins of the donors, to compensate for the blood they had lost. It was a recipe for disaster, and so it proved – in villages in some of the worst affected areas up to half the residents became infected with HIV. Li Dan was shocked to find families who had spent all their savings and could no longer afford treatment, children who had lost their parents, and others who were missing out on their education because they had to nurse sick relatives – or whose families simply had no money left to send them to school.

But when he and a group of volunteers tried to set up a school to help some of these children get an education, they found that their assistance was not welcomed by the local authorities, who closed down their first venue because it did not have a formal licence. Later they were offered a sizeable donation by an overseas Chinese group, but it would not send the money to Li Dan's organisation until it was officially registered, and local officials would not allow it to register unless it had various assets to confirm its status. 'They said we must have land first, but it isn't easy to get,' says Li Dan. 'They were just trying to give us problems.' Eventually they decided it would be simpler to sponsor children in existing local schools, after the government, following media pressure, pledged to make sure that these schools did not turn away children whose parents were HIV-positive. Li Dan and a handful of colleagues began providing support to several hundred children in villages in the areas; and they have also continued to monitor for new cases of illegal blood collection. But their work has been made harder by their lack of a clear status, and the extra stress which this places on them has led some volunteers to give up. 'They have good intentions,' says Li Dan, with a sigh, 'but when they get here they find it hard to cope; they get scared of the difficulties.'

This may be a situation which suits the government. In 2004, for example, it was reported that local authorities in various parts of China had themselves ordered a number of research institutes and other non-governmental groups working on sensitive social issues – including HIV/AIDS – to re-register as businesses. Some believed that the intention was to limit the scope of the type of work they could carry out.[15]

Yet for all the restrictions and difficulties, the number of social organisations in China has continued to grow, with some estimates putting their numbers in the hundreds of thousands.[16] They range from informal grass-roots bodies – such as self-help groups for patients with particular types of illnesses – to more formal NGOs (whether registered or not), some of which have begun to cooperate with the government to tackle various social problems. In a sense, it's a reminder of how, in recent years, the development of society in China has often outstripped the evolution of the laws which govern it. Certainly some groups have decided simply to get to work, despite grey areas surrounding their status.

In an office in central Beijing, not far from the old Workers' Stadium, you will find Lo Sze-ping – or at least you might if he's not travelling between the mainland and Hong Kong, or on one of his frequent trips to other parts of China. Mr Lo is a busy man, both a founder member of the Hong Kong branch of Greenpeace International, and now also the head of its operation in mainland China. Many are surprised to find that Greenpeace even operates in China, he says, but the organisation actually has two offices, one in the capital and one in Guangzhou. It has never been able to formally register as a mainland-based NGO, however – though not for lack of trying. 'Whenever we meet with officials we tell them we want to register, like a man thirsty for water,' explains Lo Sze-ping. 'We say "just tell us what to do and we'll do it" – but so far no one has told us.'

But this hasn't stopped Greenpeace China from playing an increasingly active role in environmental issues in the country since it began work in 2002. The fact that the group originated in Hong

343

Kong may mean that the authorities see it as less of a threat than a fully 'foreign' organisation. It has held meetings with senior environmental officials, has given advice to the government on a draft law on renewable energy, and has provided samples of what it says were illegally genetically engineered crops to China's Ministry of Agriculture. And it has conducted a number of high-profile public campaigns, which have received an increasing amount of coverage in the Chinese media: these have highlighted, for example, the logging of protected forests in southern China, the role of Chinese enterprises in the destruction of forests in Indonesia and Papua New Guinea, and the dumping of computer waste which has blighted rural areas of Guangdong.

Lo Sze-ping acknowledges that Greenpeace does not always work in exactly the same way in China as it does in other countries. 'We try to be very effective and practical in seeing changes in policies we work on,' he says. 'So if non-violent direct actions, like we do in other countries, might not be so effective, there's no reason we should be obsessed with doing them for their own sake.' In other words, the group is not going to go to Tiananmen Square and hang up a banner, since this would be 'not entirely productive'. But he believes the organisation has been able to remain 'an independent voice', criticising both official policy and big business when necessary; its work, he says, remains 'confrontational and controversial'. They once blockaded the CEO of a major international computer manufacturer in his company's Beijing office, to demand an end to the use of toxic chemicals in its products, for example. And he emphasises that the staff who take part in campaigns like that against logging in southern China are showing great courage. 'When we raise these issues, and send people to do the documentation on the ground,' he says, 'we risk being arrested with far more serious possible outcomes than from, say, hanging a banner on a building in Europe.'

Still, he insists, there's no shortage of talented and well-qualified people keen to come and work for the organisation – and often willing to take a pay cut to do so. 'They want to be environmentalists,' he explains. 'They know we do things differently from other NGOs and they want to be part of it.' The public response to their campaigns is also often greater than expected. After Greenpeace ran a campaign in universities warning students that the paper they used for photocopying might have come from protected forests, not only did some student environmental groups persuade their universities not to buy this type of paper, he says, but an association of several hundred hotels in Zhejiang province sent a memo to its members asking them to stop buying from one particular company as well. 'We didn't know them or mobilise them,' adds Mr Lo. 'They did it quite voluntarily; the level of environmental awareness is actually higher than we realised.' And he says the group is constantly contacted by people wishing to become volunteers, though since it's unable to function as a full-membership organisation, it has to disappoint many such people. 'There are more than we can handle,' he goes on. 'We tell them to stay in touch, and suggest they should start their own group, with students, colleagues, maybe dealing with local issues first.' There are now small environmental groups like this starting up all over China, he adds, though they generally lack resources and experience.

The environment is certainly an area which highlights the contradictions and inconsistencies within China's system – and society – these days. On the one hand there is an awareness – apparently genuine on the part of some officials – that only with greater public involvement can many social problems be tackled. In 2006, for example, China's State Environmental Protection Agency called specifically for 'public participation in environmental protection', and for the public to play a part in the compiling of environmental impact reports for controversial new development projects.[17] And in 2005 the agency also gave its backing to the establishment of the All-China Environmental Federation, an umbrella group of more than two thousand environmental organisations, which received a certain amount of funding from the government, and was planning to set up a centre for environmental rights to help victims of environmental damage sue those responsible.[18] Yet when such environmental work treads on the

345

territory of local officials or powerful vested interests, those involved can still be at risk. A few months later, a man who set up an environmental organisation in the eastern city of Hangzhou was arrested and put on trial accused of stealing state secrets; human rights groups said his arrest was the result of attempts to investigate serious cases of environmental pollution. In 2007 Wu Lihong, who had campaigned for years against the pollution of Lake Taihu in Jiangsu province, was jailed on financial charges – even as the authorities announced a major clean-up of the lake.[19]

It was a reminder of the continuing paranoia among many in authority about the implications of allowing more freedom for social activism. Some Chinese intellectuals see such continuing controls and restrictions as seriously damaging to society. 'I think the Chinese people are very creative,' says one academic. 'There's a lot they can do: if they had the chance, they could find ways to resolve so many of the problems in our society. But the system stops them from making the most of their abilities.' Others, though, are more positive, seeing the beginnings of a new social consciousness among China's young people, in defiance of the common perception that they are an increasingly selfish generation, uninterested in the society around them. Certainly it's increasingly common to hear young people using the vocabulary of social activism. Gay groups now talk about the homosexual 'community'; journalists write about 'marginalised members of society'; students speak of the need to do 'socially beneficial work'. At an NGO activity in Beijing not long ago, I met a student of law from a nearby university who seemed to epitomise such attitudes. 'I recently went to a forum on legal aid,' she said, 'and now I want to do some voluntary work in non-governmental organisations, to learn about real cases. I think the more you know about these things,' she added, 'the more you'll be concerned about them, and the more you'll want to work to protect the rights of weak groups in society.'

And as new ideas continue to flow into society, through the Internet, the media and the wide range of books – including many translated foreign works – which are now on sale in Chinese shops, there's little doubt that awareness of the functioning of a pluralistic society seems set to keep growing. China today is certainly not a society where all subjects can be debated – but it's one where ideas and attitudes continue to diversify, particularly among young people increasingly aware of their individuality, and of individual rights. Sometimes this openness extends to a willingness to discuss subjects which until recently remained taboo. In 2005, for example, a retired local official in Guangdong set up the country's first museum looking at the history of the Cultural Revolution – detailed discussion of which still remains highly sensitive. Yet, perhaps not surprisingly, the local authorities were reported to have quickly ordered an end to Chinese media coverage of the new museum, and told its founder not to speak to the press.[20] And in 2006 the government effectively banned the country's media from any discussion of the fortieth anniversary of the beginning of the Cultural Revolution. Just how far the authorities are prepared to go in allowing debate on such issues, and in tolerating greater social activism, may be a litmus test for judging the maturity of China's new society in the coming years.

# 12

# Culture Shock

On a January morning in Guangzhou, a watery sun rose from behind the half-finished high-rises lining the banks of the Pearl River. In the middle of the river, on Ersha Island, palm trees cast weak shadows on the forecourt of the Guangdong Museum of Art, its modern buildings, constructed in the 1990s and already looking slightly dated, glowing pale green in the morning light.

Inside, the scene was distinctly more vibrant. Groups of young people, many with the thick glasses and spiky hair so popular in southern China, were queuing for admission tickets, or poring over catalogues in the museum bookshop. Some were taking photographs of the big yellow neon sign high up on the wall, which blinked out the message, in English: 'We are good at everything, except speaking Mandarin. Pearl River Delta.' Others clambered over what looked like the sides of old wooden packing cases, which had been spread a little hazardously over the floor, and headed off down a corridor lined with giant photographs of urban life in Shenzhen. Upstairs, they stretched themselves out on comfortable sofas and settled in to watch the video artworks flickering on a bank of television screens.

The evident interest displayed by many of the gallery-goers was perhaps not surprising: it was the second Guangzhou Triennial exhibition, set up by the provincial art museum to showcase new art from China and around the world, and the theme this time was one to which anyone living within a couple of hundred miles of the museum was likely to be able to relate. 'An Extraordinary Space of Experimentation for Modernisation', as the show was subtitled, focused on the stunning growth and expansion of the cities of southern China, and the impact of this urbanisation on people's lives. The artists in the exhibition were from Europe, America and other parts of Asia as well as China – but many of the works were either about, or relevant to, life in the Pearl River Delta – the corridor of urban development which stretches from Guangzhou downriver to Hong Kong and Macao, via Foshan and Zhuhai on one side and the new mega-cities of Dongguan and Shenzhen on the other. As one of the curators put it in his introduction to the show, the region's development has been little short of 'miraculous' – but at a high cost: the wooden packing cases on the floor of the exhibition, and the metal scaffolding poles protruding from the walls, were designed to give a sense of the impermanence and inconvenience of life in the midst of what can sometimes seem like a giant construction site.[1]

The grainy reality of urban life was certainly reflected in the works on display. One featured mock-ups of buildings from inner-city areas of Guangzhou, complete with neon signs, sleazy-looking hairdressers and advertisements for the treatment of sexually transmitted diseases. Another entire room featured a photo and video installation about migrant workers in Guangzhou's poor suburb of Sanyuanli, and their sometimes desperate attempts to survive in the city. The two artists had made a film which showed rootless young men and women discussing their struggles, and their bitterness at the way they had to live. On the walls were photographs by some of the migrant workers themselves: the artists had given them cameras and asked them to take pictures of their lives over a one-year period, producing a striking and often touching array of images of building sites and factory canteens, shared dormitories and decrepit rented rooms.

The show had been put together by the Guangdong Museum of Art's own staff, the Swiss curator Hans Ulrich Obrist, and Hou Hanru, a Chinese curator who had been living in Paris for more than a decade, but had come back to his home town specially for this event. A key part of the project was the Delta Lab, a two-year series of workshops and discussions between artists and architects from Guangzhou, Hong Kong and abroad – including the celebrated

Dutch architect Rem Koolhaas, who has been a major advocate of the idea that the Pearl River Delta represents an entirely new type of urban phenomenon. Works produced for the Delta Lab included a memorable photo documentary about the people who live their lives alongside (and often underneath) the elevated sections of the highway which runs from Guangzhou to the Hong Kong border: the locals who set up their food stalls and snooker tables between its concrete pillars; the homeless people who build their shacks there; the migrant workers who meet underneath the road to play cards. Another work highlighted the phenomenon of 'inner-city villages' – areas of cramped and unsafe housing, caught between the new high-rises and office towers of cities like Shenzhen – and lamented the fact that such wealthy cities lacked the land to build social housing.

Other exhibits raised questions about the survival of the new cities: one consisted of a model of a skyline of high-rises, onto which were flashed grim messages about global energy shortages, traffic gridlock and population growth. Another work, one of the most poignant in the show, was made up of drawings by young Guangzhou schoolchildren of the environment in which they lived. The project had been organised by a South Korean community art group; the results, which filled one whole wall, were colourful childish pictures featuring an alarming array of overhead highways, car-filled ring roads, tower blocks decorated with corporate logos and, very occasionally, a tree.

There were some more personal works too, focusing on the changing lifestyles of people who, as the Shenzhen-based photographer Yang Yong put it, are 'under the continuous bombardment of globalisation'.[2] One which attracted the most attention was a video installation showing the emotional journey of a Shenzhen man before, during and after the process of sex-change surgery. People of all ages watched, apparently fascinated, as he talked of how he had always dreamed of becoming a woman, and a doctor explained how he had remodelled the faces of dozens of sex-change patients. Upstairs, a crowd of young people were gathered round TV screens showing, among others, a video of a hip-hop singer, performing what seemed to be an ironic rap based on various government slogans.

It was a vision of a pluralistic society, thought-provoking and multifaceted – and a reminder too of the drastic developments in the world of Chinese art since the start of the 1990s. Fifteen years ago, an encounter with contemporary Chinese art was likely to mean a long traipse out to a remote village on the edge of Beijing, where, in a collection of ramshackle old courtyard houses, young artists had set up studios and homes, in a kind of quiet rebellion against a society which rarely allowed them to exhibit their works officially. Now and again there would be a performance-art 'happening', but these remained strictly underground – sometimes literally, in a nondescript basement of a public housing block, or sometimes in the courtyard of one of the artists' homes. And another decade earlier, such art had barely existed at all.

For much of the 1980s and 1990s, contemporary art in China was seen by the authorities as synonymous with counter-culture, something to be treated with enormous suspicion. It was an attitude which went back to the earliest stirrings of cultural creativity in the country in the late 1970s, during the brief flurry of openness which followed the end of the Cultural Revolution and the rise to power of Deng Xiaoping. In 1978–9, ordinary people pasted their writings – poetry and fiction, as well as calls for political reform – on the so-called Democracy Wall on a busy street west of the Forbidden City in central Beijing. And in China's art schools, most of which were just beginning to admit students again after the upheavals of the previous decade, young artists also began seeking a way to express the powerful feelings of the era – the enormous pain of the Cultural Revolution, and dreams of a better future. But in a country where art had, since the 1950s, been devoted almost uniquely to propaganda purposes, the reopened academies once again concentrated on teaching the 'socialist realist' style which had been imported to China from the Soviet Union.

And so the appearance of a new group of young artists who gave themselves the name the Stars, and began experimenting with styles ranging from impressionism to minimalist painting and abstract sculpture, was considered particularly shocking. Some of the Stars, many of whom later went on to find fame, were students; others were still working in factories or government units. And since no art gallery would show their works, their first exhibition was held outside, in a small park near the National Art Museum in Beijing, where the artists hung their pictures on the railings. As the poet Yang Lian, who was present that day, recalls, 'They'd only just finished putting up the pictures when the police came and took them away. And so everyone got together and organised a demonstration to support the artists, marching through the streets to the city government.' It was, he suggests, 'probably the first protest march for artistic democracy'.

In literature, too, writings expressing the suffering of the recent past, widely known as 'the literature of the wounded', were also causing controversy. Just how shocking such creative, personal works were considered at the time can be gauged from the official reaction to the writings of China's first group of modernist poets, Yang Lian among them, whose impressionistic, abstract works appeared on the Democracy Wall. Bei Dao, one of the leading lights in this group of writers, described what happened when the police found the poems which he and his friends had written. 'They read them,' he said, 'and found they couldn't understand them, so they called in some literary experts. The experts looked at our poems and said it was impossible that we could have written such things ourselves,' he added. 'They said we must have copied them from foreigners.'[3]

In 1980 Deng Xiaoping, now safely ensconced in power, closed down the Democracy Wall movement, and some of its most outspoken participants, such as the democracy advocate Wei Jingsheng, were jailed. But gradually, during the early 1980s, some of the new generation of writers began to find magazines and publishing companies willing to publish their works. And the new generation of artists found some supporters too – in the shape of critics such as Li Xianting. 'Old Li', as he's universally known, is nowadays generally acknowledged as the 'godfather' of the Chinese contemporary art world, a distinguished-looking figure with a silvery goatee beard. But in those days he was a recently graduated student of traditional Chinese painting, who had just been assigned a job at a magazine published by the official Chinese Artists' Federation. Most of the editors of what was at the time the country's only nationwide art publication were highly critical of the young artists – and so Li Xianting, as the youngest member of staff, felt duty-bound to speak up for the new generation.

'The young artists were mainly reacting against realism,' he recalls. 'Some of them were producing abstract works, which were really a way of nullifying realism, of completely destroying its foundations. And,' he adds with a sly chuckle, 'I was quite in favour of that.' And so when, soon afterwards, he was made editor of his magazine, he decided to dedicate an entire issue to abstract art. But before it could appear, in 1983, the government launched its 'Campaign Against Spiritual Pollution', which was directly aimed at the new generation of journalists, artists and writers who had begun to challenge the Communist Party's monopoly on ideas. 'They said that we were a typical example of spiritual pollution,' says Old Li with a smile. He was suspended from his job for the next two years. But by the middle of the 1980s, controls on culture loosened a little, and he was given a job at a newly formed art newspaper. 'We made it very, very lively.'

And they were lively times. This was the period when the first wave of enthusiasm for new, foreign ideas was reaching a peak, as increasing contact with the outside world made it possible for the young generation to obtain more information. For artists like Liu Wei, these days one of China's best-known contemporary painters but then a student at the Central Academy of Fine Arts in Beijing, it's a fondly recalled period. 'The atmosphere was great at that time,' he says. 'Between 1985 and 1989 we were just starting out with modern art; everyone was beginning to think about a lot of things and follow new fashions. We were studying a lot of western philosophy then too,' he adds, 'lots of trendy western things. In fact, in those days we all wanted to study everything!' The staging of some of China's first exhibitions of modern western art in the mid-1980s also helped to inspire younger artists around the country, and by the second half of the decade many artists were moving into increasingly experimental areas – notably in the works of Huang Yong Ping and the other members of the Xiamen Dada movement, a group of radical artists inspired by the Dadaists of 1920s Europe. Installations and performance art began to catch on, often featuring artists appearing nude, either in person or in photographs. It was almost as though Chinese artists were living through their own 'hippy' era.

And indeed the interest in such ideas – in fact in almost any stimulating ideas, old or new, Chinese or foreign – during those years was summed up by the title of a popular play of the late 1980s: it was called *Jesus, Confucius and John Lennon of the Beatles*. It was one of a number of experimental works which attracted enthusiastic audiences, though some were left confused by plays such as *Bus Stop* by the future Nobel Prize-winner Gao Xingjian; loosely inspired by Samuel Beckett's *Waiting for Godot*, it featured a group of ordinary people waiting for buses which never came – or never stopped.[4]

Growing creativity was also visible in the world of Chinese cinema, where a new generation of actors and directors, many of them trained at the reopened Beijing Film Academy, also began to move away from the realism of the past decades. These film-makers, known as the 'Fifth Generation', were more interested in sweeping pre-revolutionary epics, such as Zhang Yimou's *Red Sorghum*, or mystical journeys – Tian Zhuangzhuang's *Horse Thief*, for example – or the startling rural landscapes and folk customs of Chen Kaige's *Yellow Earth*, filmed on the barren hills of northern Shaanxi province – than in socialist realism. *Red Sorghum* in particular took the nation by storm: the actor Jiang Wen became one of China's biggest stars, and the film's raucous peasant songs, written by the director, could be heard everywhere on the radio in 1988, a rare antidote to the bland Hong Kong and Taiwanese pop music which dominated the airwaves at the time. The film's story, of heroic peasants defying the invading Japanese armies in the 1940s, was guaranteed to appeal to many in China, but the patriotism was leavened with a dose of humour, something which was still rare in Chinese cinema of the era. And like many Chinese films of the late 1980s and early 1990s, it was based on a novel by a contemporary writer, in this case Mo Yan, whose sometimes fantastical stories of rural life reflected the growing influence of foreign literary trends such as 'magic realism' on China's younger writers.

Some of the films of the new generation of directors inevitably attracted official criticism, but they quickly won an international audience, bringing contemporary Chinese culture to many in the outside world for the first time. Thus the second half of the 1980s was a time of great cultural ferment: monthly literary magazines sold out, as eager readers waited for works by new young writers; cinemas were packed; a popular, relatively liberal writer, Wang Meng, was appointed Minister of Culture; the revered actor Ying Ruocheng, whose fluent English saw him cast as the jailer in Bernardo Bertolucci's 1987 film *The Last Emperor*, was made his deputy. And in the art world too the new creative movement reached its peak, with the first major exhibition at an official art gallery – though it proved to be something of a full stop too. 'China/Avant-Garde', curated by, among others, the critic Li Xianting, opened at the China National Art Museum in Beijing in early 1989. It contained works by some of the boldest painters, sculptors, photographers and installation artists of the era – but its success was fragile: when the artist Xiao Lu took her work to its logical conclusion by firing a gun at her own reflection in a mirror, the exhibition was temporarily closed down by the police.

The febrile excitement of the Beijing cultural scene in these years was captured in a film by the documentary-maker and performance artist Wu Wenguang, who followed a number of artists, theatre directors and other cultural figures in the months before – and after – the protests of 1989. *Liulang Beijing* (known in English as *Bumming in Beijing*) included a memorable scene in which one of the artists had a fit during preparations for the 'China/Avant-Garde' exhibition, and started trying to communicate with God – at which point her friends took her to a recently opened branch of Kentucky Fried Chicken, which they thought would be the best place to calm her down. Wu Wenguang later gave his film, completed the year after the Tiananmen crackdown, the subtitle *The Last Dreamers*. And the crushing of the student movement and the chill wind

355

which swept through China's cultural world afterwards certainly shattered the dreams and illusions of many an artist. (Not least the students from the sculpture department of the Central Academy of Fine Arts who built that optimistic symbol, the *Goddess of Democracy*, which they wheeled to Tiananmen Square in the last week of the demonstrations.)

The years which followed were certainly something of a low point for China's cultural scene. An ageing revolutionary poet was made Acting Minister of Culture; many of China's best-known artists chose to leave the country, moving to the US or France or Germany, where they could enjoy more creative freedom. It was at this point that many of the artists who had stayed at home retreated to the villages on the outskirts of Beijing, where, for a few years, they were able to live more or less as they wanted and indulge their taste for the avant-garde. Writers meanwhile were unable to publish works as challenging as those of the late 1980s; the witty, cynical writings of the Beijing novelist and screenwriter Wang Shuo, with their disillusioned, hapless characters, provided one of the few diversions available at the time; the film world was similarly affected.

But if the mood of this period was, for many people, one of introspection and disillusionment, it did at least seem to give rise to some creative reflections, in the works of artists who had been students during the late 1980s and were now starting their own careers. The members of one such group later established themselves as some of China's most influential contemporary artists. Their works were often deceptively simple, many consisting of enlarged images of faces, sometimes grey, sombre and almost expressionless, as in paintings by Liu Wei and Zhang Xiaogang, or pink, contorted, sometimes grotesque, as in the works of Fang Lijun and Yue Minjun. Such images seemed to point to a focus on the individual, and to feelings of depression, despair or brutality. The critic Li Xianting labelled these works 'cynical realism', since they were, in his opinion, 'moving away from idealism'. Liu Wei, the Central Academy of Fine Arts graduate who had been so enthusiastic about new ideas in the 1980s, says now that his paintings of the period – of a 'military family', with the father in army uniform – were inspired mainly by his own immediate surroundings (he grew up in an army family himself, living in a military compound) and were not designed to make any particular political point. But at the same time he acknowledges that recent events had subconsciously affected the thinking of many at that time. 'Things which seemed normal to others didn't look normal to us any more,' he recalls. 'That's why if you look at some of the pictures of faces, the features are often distorted.'

Other works which appeared around the same time played with traditional communist imagery. One of the most famous artists of this genre, Wang Guangyi, merged heroic socialist workers with the logos of the multinational companies which were starting to arrive in China; others used cartoon-like, pop-art style images of Chairman Mao. Li Xianting dubbed these works 'political pop'. Some were undoubtedly serious – and satirical – commentaries on China's past, or indeed on the curious mixture of conservative ideology and commercialism which made up the contemporary reality. But as the 1990s progressed, more artists realised that such works tended to be seen as daringly political by foreign collectors and curators, and were therefore highly marketable – with the perhaps ironic result that 'ironic' images of Mao developed into something of a cliché.

Foreign interest in Chinese art was certainly starting to grow at around this time – and becoming increasingly important to many Chinese artists. On the one hand the domestic art scene was highly restricted during the early 1990s, with limited opportunities to exhibit. And at the same time, international anger at the crushing of the 1989 protests had added to concern for and interest in the situation of Chinese cultural figures. A few film directors continued to draw attention, most notably Zhang Yimou, who enjoyed a string of international successes in the first half of the 1990s with *Ju Dou*, *Raise the Red Lantern* and *To Live*; Tian Zhuangzhuang was another, with his sensitively told Cultural Revolution story *The Blue Kite*. But it was the visual art world which really began to attract the attention of those seeking something fresh. In the early 1990s the first large-scale exhibitions of contemporary Chinese art were held abroad, in Hong Kong, Australia, Europe and the US; in 1993 a group of Chinese artists were featured for the first time in the prestigious Biennale exhibition in Venice.[5]

Such shows played a major part in establishing a place for contemporary Chinese art in the international mainstream – and in stimulating interest among international collectors for works by young, bold, iconoclastic artists. Foreigners living in Beijing also began to collect more of their works; by the mid-1990s, as the cultural climate relaxed a little, foreign-run galleries opened in Beijing and Shanghai. For the first time, paintings by some of the better known contemporary Chinese artists began to sell for significant sums of money; the growing attention they attracted also encouraged the setting up of galleries dedicated to contemporary Chinese art in several cities around the world.

As the decade went on, styles continued to diversify. Some artists stuck to painting, but others also began to experiment more and more with photography, performance and installation – sometimes on a grand scale. There were the explosive tendencies of Cai Guoqiang, who specialised in using fire and fireworks to create installations; the sometimes painful performance art of Zhang Huan, who covered himself in honey and sat naked in a village toilet, attracting swarms of flies; and the thought-provoking works of Xu Bing, who created a whole 'heavenly book' of scrolls covered with what appeared to be Chinese characters but were actually meaningless symbols of his own invention (some of which he later painted on two pigs, which he filmed as they copulated). Many of these artists had been working abroad; but back home a new generation with its own ideas was also beginning to emerge.

On a hot summer evening, a bluish light flickered through the darkness in the park in Shanghai's old French concession, casting shadows on the big granite statues of Marx and Engels under the trees. It came from a row of television sets, lined up on the ground; on each one, a man's face was shown in close-up, repeating again and again the words: 'don't move, don't move . . .' Gradually his speech speeded up, and, as it did so, the images began to vibrate, faster and faster. 'He's saying don't move – but moving in all different ways,' said an old man who was watching with interest. 'What do you think it's trying to tell us?' Not far away, a crowd were gathered around a large screen, watching a video of a young man wandering around among the skyscrapers of the new Shanghai, dressed first as a peasant in scruffy clothes, and then as a young urban worker in suit and tie. The film highlighted the different reactions of the people who watched him go by in his two different guises. Made by the young artist Yang Fudong, it was an example of the growing interest in video art among China's younger generation. And the event, organised by curators from Shanghai and Europe, was perhaps the first time this type of art had been shown in such a public place in China.[6] Not everyone was happy about it. 'I suppose this is foreign – it shouldn't be allowed,' grumbled one man out for an evening stroll in the park. But the size of the crowds pouring into a nearby tent seemed to suggest that many disagreed. Inside, they saw a video in which a young woman stood rooted to the spot on a Shanghai pavement, lost among the crowds, with a blank expression on her face. It was, according to Liang Yue, the young artist who created it, a reflection on the impersonal nature of modern city life. 'Sometimes when I stand on the street I feel as though I don't exist, no one sees me, no one cares that I'm close to them,' she said.

Her urban angst clearly struck a chord with some. And the use of video in art also seems to fit particularly well with the interests of China's young generation, who have grown up with new technology and often appear fascinated by it, both as a symbol of modernity, and as a practical tool. But in a country where the government was used to a complete monopoly over the right to make and show films, the concept of young people running around with their own cameras, acting out their visions and fantasies, clearly took some getting used to for the authorities. A previous attempt to show similarly contemporary art in a public place, in a Shanghai shopping centre in 1999, was closed down by the police, apparently because they objected to a video work by the artist Xu Zhen, showing a young man and woman dressed in their underwear, gently sniffing each other's bodies from a distance of a few inches apart.[7]

More recently, though, the government seems to have accepted that the phenomenon is here to stay. Shanghai now has a TV programme dedicated to showing digital videos made by students. The China Academy of Art, one of the country's most prestigious art colleges, situated on the banks of the West Lake in the eastern city of Hangzhou, has set up its own video art and new media department, headed by Zhang Peili, one of the pioneers of such works since the early 1990s, with assistance from the dynamic young artist Qiu Zhijie. And video art has in the past few years also begun to be featured in exhibitions in mainstream official art galleries in China's major cities. It still has its detractors. Even the critic Li Xianting, for so long a supporter of everything new in China's art world, who now says he has to spend a lot of his time watching videos, bemoans the fact that, in his opinion, video often encourages young people to focus more on technical skills than on creativity. But there's no doubt that the greater tolerance of such works is a sign that official attitudes to art are evolving – something which may have much to do with the growing commercial success of many of China's contemporary artists.

Outside the restaurant window, the steam whistles of the ships echoed across Shanghai's Huangpu River. Lights flickered on the dark water, reflections of the advertisements for Pepsi and the 2008 Olympics beamed out by the giant electronic billboard on top of one of the tall buildings on the opposite bank. It was a cold winter night, but inside, amid the muted lighting of the top-floor restaurant, the atmosphere was warm and refined, the talk at the dinner table of art – and commerce. Several of China's best-known contemporary artists were celebrating the opening of their exhibition in the Shanghai Gallery of Art, the new private gallery which had recently opened its doors downstairs. A curator from Hong Kong discussed the encouraging development of the market for Chinese art; further along the table, a businessman whose company had just listed on the stock exchange in New York was chatting to a famous painter.

360

When they finished eating, most of the diners took the lift back down to the gallery, to look again at the exhibition. The businessman took one of the artists aside and began eagerly quizzing him about the meaning of his works. In the big exhibition space, the lights from the river played across the empty white walls, on which the paintings were sparsely displayed.

By the middle of this decade, art had become big business in Shanghai. Successful Chinese companies were looking for something to hang in the office or the boardroom, and the city's increasingly fashionable reputation was attracting collectors and curators from around the world. At another exhibition in the same gallery not long afterwards, a series of works by the 'political pop' artist Wang Guangyi was on sale for a price of close to half a million pounds. And at the opening of Shanghai's official International Art Biennale exhibition in 2004, the municipal art museum in the old racecourse clubhouse in People's Square was suddenly transformed into a gathering place for some of the leading lights of the international art set, with curators from the big museums in London and New York, critics from Paris and Tokyo, and collectors who had jetted in from Europe for a night or two just to see the show.

The status of Chinese art, it seemed, had changed. International interest had grown rapidly – and had made some of the artists who emerged in the late 1980s and early 1990s very wealthy in the process. A new generation of curators was attempting to bring a fresh approach too, even to some of the country's state-run art museums. In 2000, Shanghai's art biennale included installation works and video art for the first time; over the next few years the city's art museum also began holding exhibitions by some of the artists who had left China in the 1990s and made their names overseas. In 2006 it finally put on a show of works by the late Chen Zhen, perhaps Shanghai's best-known contemporary artist, who had been banned in his native city since the mid-1990s but achieved much success in France before his untimely death from cancer in 2000. To some extent, such shows may have been a reflection of the fact that a city always keen to burnish its international image had realised it had to allow at least the appearance of a more open approach. But there was also a sense that, as society in a place like Shanghai became more modern and more wealthy, the young generation was beginning to expect – some would say demand – a more open cultural environment too (even if this tended to be less radical and more mainstream than in a city like Beijing, where life is grittier and tastes tend to be more extreme).

And there's no doubt that the authorities have also begun to realise that there can be economic benefits from encouraging the development of an art scene. In recent years, both Beijing and Shanghai have seen the growth of major areas of artists' studios and galleries in derelict old industrial buildings. In each case the authorities were initially unimpressed by the phenomenon, but later came to show more tolerance, apparently after seeing the financial advantages. In Beijing, a number of prominent artists opened studios in the '798' compound – an old East German-designed munitions factory, with striking architecture and walls still plastered with old communist slogans. The compound was initially rumoured to be due for demolition, but its popularity seemed to spare it, at least temporarily – and by the middle of this decade it had become home not only to studios, but also to an ever-expanding number of galleries – including some from South Korea, Italy and London – as well as a range of art bookshops, cafés and restaurants. Shanghai's earliest artists' area, in an old warehouse on the banks of the Suzhou Creek, was actually demolished, in 2001; and when many of the artists moved to another old factory not far away, it was generally assumed that this would ultimately share a similar fate. But this area quickly became a thriving district of studios, galleries and shops, and eventually the whole complex was cleaned up and renovated by the authorities. In fact, according to one gallery owner, the same local government official who was initially trying to get the area demolished could later be seen proudly showing visiting dignitaries round this popular art district. In the years since, district governments in other parts of Shanghai have also begun to set up their own art streets and areas of creative studios and workshops, in part as a good way of attracting foreign investment – though some artists have complained that they are

362

being priced out of such places by the growing level of commercial interest.[8]

This doesn't mean that the authorities have suddenly lost all their concerns about the content of the artworks on display. In theory, exhibitions need advance approval from the authorities – and cases of works being removed or shows being closed down do still sometimes occur. But there's no doubt that many galleries – official or otherwise – are now showing art which would not have been tolerated a few years earlier. Naked images are more widely accepted, and some politically critical or satirical content occasionally survives too. In 2005, for example, one gallery in Beijing showed a film made by a resident of a neighbourhood of the city which was about to be demolished, in which he criticised the authorities for destroying his livelihood and was shown defying the police. And there's certainly an ever-growing variety of styles of art on display. Greater freedom to experiment has even led some of the leading lights of the contemporary art movements of the 1990s to return to more traditional Chinese styles for fresh inspiration. Liu Wei, the one-time 'cynical realist' painter, is one: 'Now I feel that I like traditional Chinese painting more and more,' he says. 'When you're young you don't understand these things – but as you get older you realise they have a value.'

Not everyone is completely satisfied with the current situation. In a village outside Beijing, where several of the best-known artists are his neighbours, the critic Li Xianting now lives in a spacious newly built traditional-style house, its ceiling beams hewed from whole tree trunks, and its walls crowded with works given to him by some of the artists he has championed. His position as the elder statesman of the Chinese art scene is universally acknowledged, and he receives a constant stream of visitors – young artists from other parts of China eager to pay their respects, academics and collectors from Hong Kong, Taiwan and further afield. It's certainly a long way from the days in the decrepit old houses of the original Beijing artists' villages in the early 1990s. But these days Old Li is worried: he believes that after all these years of development, art is now facing a new threat – of becoming over-commercialised. For the more successful artists, for example, he says there's now a great pressure to stop experimenting and just keep painting in the same style, since they know that there is now a market for this. 'Nowadays you have to resist the temptation of money,' he says. 'It sounds easy, but in fact it's difficult – the temptation is very great now.'

In part this reflects his concern at the growing influence of international collectors and curators on China's art scene, particularly on younger artists trying to make a name for themselves. 'Some western curators come to China,' he says, 'and they sit down somewhere, and then all the Chinese artists queue up to come in and show them their works for ten minutes each – it's like selling socks or shoes or clothes.' Of course it's natural that these curators should have their own tastes, he says, but he fears that they often impose their own preconceptions on Chinese art – whether it's traditional culture or contemporary political satire that they're looking for. He believes this encourages many artists simply to copy the styles of those who are already successful – to become, as he puts it, the 'spring roll on the hors d'oeuvres platter of the western art world'.

To Old Li this is another example of the growing impact of globalisation, something he believes is having an excessive influence on the cities, cultures and lives of people in Asia and around the world. It's left him rather disillusioned. 'People should respect that for each place, when it begins the process of modernisation, the path it takes should be different,' he says. 'But now it's as though globalisation is turning into the Americanisation of the whole world, which I think is really terrifying.' He's quick to add that this doesn't mean there are no longer any good artworks being produced in China. 'There are still some artists working from their hearts,' he says, 'but the whole standard of values may tend towards a certain system.' And he believes that, as a result, much of contemporary Chinese art is now less relevant to the society and the environment it's created in, compared to the works of artists of the 1980s and early 1990s.

'From the late 1970s to the mid-1990s, every trend which appeared in Chinese art was linked to the movement to liberate

Chinese thought,' he explains. 'But after the mid-1990s it suddenly ended. All of a sudden,' he adds with a sigh, 'there was no longer any link between art and social thought.' It's not what he had in mind, he says, back in the early 1980s, when artists were struggling, often at some personal risk, for more openness and greater links with the outside world. 'It's a big irony,' says Old Li. 'I always believed in the idea of art emerging from a system. We all wanted to open up. And then after we opened up we discovered that we were facing another kind of system – one which is also very rigid and controlling.'

There are some, however, who believe it's a good thing that art is no longer so tightly bound up with society and with reflecting or rebelling against its reality, since this gives artists more space to delve deeper into their own imaginations. And there are those who are convinced that a globalised, more commercial market can be good for the art world too. The Shanghai Gallery of Art, the upmarket private gallery overlooking the city's river, was set up with the specific aim of putting contemporary art in the shop window. For the gallery's director, Weng Ling, it's a way of bringing contemporary Chinese artists further into the mainstream – at home as well as abroad – and of stimulating wealthy Chinese people's interest in collecting such works. Until very recently, she points out, official ambivalence about contemporary art in China meant that many of the artists who had become successful internationally were still little known in their own country, and were rarely able to take part in major shows in official art galleries. And so, says Weng Ling, 'we have a very clear, systematic plan to show these artists, to make up for some of the gaps in the way the official art museums introduce the background of Chinese contemporary art'. It seems to have been a successful strategy: the gallery has attracted visits from government officials, and Weng Ling notes with satisfaction that 'the top bosses of most of China's biggest real-estate companies have all been here'.

Nor does she feel that the development of a commercial market for Chinese art is necessarily bad for the quality of the work. 'I think it's true that a lot of artists are more and more commercial these days,' she says, 'but I believe art everywhere goes through a phase like this, and the really great artists are the ones who can still succeed after this market baptism.' Ultimately, she suggests, it's a test of their talent. 'When you're faced with money, will you choose to carry on doing new works which give you more satisfaction, or will you just paint the same kind of things every day because they sell well?' In her opinion, many of the top artists have resisted the temptation, and remained successful too.

The power of the commercial art world to bring art closer to the mainstream was demonstrated in 2006 when a wealthy private gallery in Shenzhen commissioned special works from three of China's best-known modern artists – Fang Lijun, Wang Guangyi and Zhang Xiaogang – and displayed them in three stations on the local subway network. After a few initial complaints about the bare buttocks in Fang Lijun's pictures, most commuters seemed happy to accept the art in their midst – though art experts were more concerned about how long the fragile oil paintings could survive on the wall of a subway station, and the station authorities eventually found it necessary to put up railings and post a guard in front of each painting, to protect it from the crowds.

Still, a sense that what many now remember as the idealism of the 1980s has been lost in today's more commercially driven environment is common among Chinese cultural figures of a certain generation. In some ways it's a kind of nostalgia for a time when things were far more black and white, when most people had faith that the outside world would provide new and better ideas and solutions. In the literary world, for example, it's common to hear that China has not produced as much good writing in recent years as it did during the late 1980s and early 1990s. Some put this down to the growth of the Internet, which has led to a market dominated by what many look down on as throwaway 'Internet literature'. One Chinese magazine recently summed up this sentiment with a cover story headlined 'Where have all the poets gone?' (The answer, it suggested, was that they had all become CEOs.)[9] In fact, there are many writers who rose to prominence in the 1980s who have continued to create serious works – and some of the 'Internet writers' are also highly committed to their work. It may be simply that there are now so many other types of entertainment and information that it's much harder for anything they write to have the same impact. At the same time, now that life is more complex, creating a meaning from it may also be harder. As one writer who began his career at that time puts it, 'In the 1980s we really felt we could make a difference – now that's not so easy.' But, he adds, it may also be the case that, in a world with so many other distractions, not all writers are as dedicated to their craft these days as they were in previous decades.[10] Censorship can be a problem too of course: these days it tends to take the form of retrospective bans of books which have already been published – but the issue of self-censorship still affects those writing on sensitive subjects.

And in the world of cinema too, there's a general sense that fewer truly important works have been produced in recent years. The director Zhang Yimou surprised many in 2000 with *Happy Times*, a bitter-sweet semi-comedy about lives among the ruins of China's state-owned industry in the north-east of the country. But in more recent years he has expended much of his energy on martial arts movies, winning international acclaim for *Hero* and *House of Flying Daggers*, but attracting mixed reviews at home. Chen Kaige, who made the famous *Yellow Earth*, generally seen as the first important film of the 'Fifth Generation' in the 1980s, was widely criticised some twenty years later when he released *The Promise*. It was one of the most costly Chinese films ever made, but its convoluted mythological story and eccentric casting (Japanese and South Korean actors who didn't speak Chinese, alongside the Hong Kong pop star Nicholas Tse) led many critics to describe it as an expensive failure.

Other directors, including Jia Zhangke, Wang Xiaoshuai and Zhang Yuan, have continued to make smaller-scale, more creative and stimulating films. But the development of China's film industry has undoubtedly been hampered by the fact that it's an area where the official censors have a greater direct influence over what the public gets to see than, for example, in the world of art. All film scripts and finished versions have to be approved by the powerful State Administration of Radio, Film and Television, which has tended to take a highly cautious line. As a result, directors have to choose between accepting official scrutiny, which may lead to them having to make cuts which compromise their work, and simply ignoring the censors and sending the uncut film to festivals overseas; this can often bring international awards but is a sure way of being banned at home.

(The tastes of China's cultural censors can be judged from the decision not to allow the release of the film *Brokeback Mountain* in 2006. Given the immense fame and popularity in China of its Taiwanese-born director Ang Lee, it was generally assumed that this was because the story depicted a gay love affair. There was still plenty of coverage of the film in the Chinese media, particularly after Ang Lee won an Oscar for it, but much of this managed to avoid mentioning the gay theme at all.)

Some of the directors who previously sought to bypass the censors have in recent years decided to return to making films through official channels. Others still run the risk of being banned, like the director Lou Ye, who was reported to have been told he would not be allowed to make another movie for five years, after his film *Yiheyuan* – a story of love and disillusionment set in the Beijing of the late 1980s and 1990s – was screened at the Cannes Film Festival in 2006 without getting official permission. Chinese media reports were, however, quite supportive of the director – with reporters suggesting ways in which he might be able to get round the ban![11] And having a film banned these days no longer completely prevents it being seen: DVDs can always be found in pirate video shops; I even found a copy of one banned film on sale in the official shop at Shanghai airport. Official bookstores also stocked a book compiling the scripts of several films by the director Jia Zhangke, including *Pickpocket* and *Platform*, which were never actually released in China. The growing commercial pressure on official publishing companies to produce things people want to buy can, it seems, have some advantages. (And by 2006 Jia Zhangke, now officially rehabilitated, was being featured in advertisements for China's main state-run mobile telephone com-pany, complete with clips of his appearances at international film festivals, to highlight the fact that its phone services could now be used around the world.)

And some interesting films do continue to be released. *Perpetual Motion*, generally described as China's first 'women's movie', appeared in 2006; it starred a number of well-known female actors and artists, and consisted largely of women talking about their love lives. A few years earlier, the young Beijing director Zhang Yang produced a remarkable film called *Quitting*. Its story was daring enough in itself – a true tale of how a well-known actor, Jia Hongsheng, became a drug addict, leading to tension and violence in his family. But what made it really stand out was the fact that Jia Hongsheng and his parents actually played themselves in the film. It meant reliving, and re-enacting, highly traumatic experiences: in one of the most harrowing scenes Jia Hongsheng beat up his kindly, concerned father, leaving his family little choice but to have him confined to an asylum. In a country where drug addiction remains largely taboo, and family problems are traditionally kept private, it was a bold step. As the film's American producer Peter Loehr put it at the time, 'I honestly don't think people anywhere in the world do this very often, let alone China.'[12]

The fact that Jia Hongsheng's parents were themselves pro-fessional actors made it easier; according to his father, their main motives were to dispel exaggerated rumours about what really happened, and also to inspire other young people to give up drugs through their own efforts, as their son did in the end. The film's relatively relaxed depiction of life among the inmates of one of China's mental hospitals, and its minimal scenes of drug-taking, did lead some to ask whether the film-makers had bowed to the censors. But Zhang Yang, the director, said that was missing the point. 'There are rules,' he said. 'You can't show too much drug-taking or drug-induced visions. But that wasn't my focus – the main thing was this person: his mental world, his problems.' He believed it would be of value to many of today's young people too. 'I think a lot of young people feel like Jia Hongsheng,' he said. 'Their ideals are contradicted by social reality, they can't find what they're looking for; I think a film like this can make a lot of young people think about their lives.' Such films are not guaranteed box-office success, however. And there's no doubt that the combined influences of commercial pressure and the need to pass official censorship mean that many directors have focused in recent years on making light-hearted comedies, costume dramas or martial arts films, which are less controversial – and likely to earn more money. Some hope that the arrival in Chinese cities in the past few years of new multi-screen cinemas, many with foreign investment, may allow more space for films to be shown, but this is by no means certain.

In the world of art, however, there are some who have resolutely pursued a path which has taken them far away from the commercial mainstream into much more extreme territory.

The opening of an art exhibition sounded like a pleasant way to spend a spring afternoon in Beijing – though because it was an 'underground' show, there was always the possibility that it would contain some harrowing exhibits. By this time, in 2000, some of China's more radical artists were apparently fascinated not just with the human body, but with using body parts and animals in their works too. The event was held in borrowed rooms in a suburban building, and the corridors were crowded with people, making it hard to actually see into the rooms where the exhibits were displayed. As a result the first sense of anything out of the ordinary came with the realisation that the first room I was able to push into felt extremely cold. Looking down, I discovered that the floor was made of ice, and there seemed to be something rather large and pink buried beneath it. On closer inspection, it became clear that this was, in fact, a pig's face, staring upwards. The next exhibit seemed to continue the theme: a large side of pork lay on a bed in the middle of a bare room; a small patch of skin, of a slightly different colour, had been roughly sewn onto it; there seemed little connection between this and a film showing on a television screen at the back of the room, which included scenes of surgery being carried out on

370

a patient in hospital. It was only when the artist, Zhu Yu, appeared and began lifting up his shirt and showing people a small scar on his body that it all started to become clear. He had paid a doctor to perform an operation to remove a small piece of his skin, and had then had it sewn onto the side of pork.

Along the corridor, in another room, a cluster of grey mice were scrabbling around in a glass bowl. Their movements were awkward, as though their legs had been tied together. In fact, someone explained, they too had undergone an operation: the bones of their legs had been surgically intertwined to produce this squirming mass. Beating a swift retreat, I passed a room where a naked woman stood upright, wearing only a pair of sunglasses; again the floor laid with ice provided a clue: the woman was in fact a corpse which had been propped up there, the scars on its body suggesting it had previously been used in medical biopsy classes. Finally I reached the last part of the exhibition, where a young female artist, Peng Yu, and her husband Sun Yuan were sitting next to each other on high chairs, apparently about to start a performance. As the crowd in front of them parted a little, I saw that they had drip tubes attached to their arms. Soon blood began flowing into the tubes, which were joined so that the couple's blood was mixed together. At the bottom of the tube, it then dripped out onto something which, I realised with a shock, looked remarkably like a human foetus. Turning away, I found myself looking at a display of photographs and writing on the wall. At last, it seemed, something less gruesome. In fact it was a collection of letters and pictures of an artist who, many years before, had promised that he would commit suicide on a certain date – and had recently kept that promise.

It was, all in all, one of the most unsettling events I had seen, and I can't say I was surprised to hear later the same day that the police had arrived and closed it down. The event was, I discovered afterwards, called 'obsession with hurt' (shanghai de milian). And extreme as it was, it was not particularly out of character with the works of some of the more radical performance and installation artists of the late 1990s. Two of the artists, Peng Yu and Zhu Yu, had already attracted attention, and criticism, for a previous event in a derelict Beijing basement, where the former created a 'curtain' made of live lobsters, while the latter hung a severed human arm from the ceiling, with a long rope grasped in its hand and spreading across the floor.

So what did it all prove – other than that it was apparently not too hard for artists to acquire human bodies from local hospitals? Some dismissed it as pure sensationalism – shock tactics aimed at attracting attention, from the international art world in particular, at a time when Chinese artists were already well acquainted with the controversy caused abroad when artists like Damien Hirst used animals in their works. But the critic Li Xianting, who had given the event its name, believed that it reflected some of the scars which remained in Chinese society. Most of this generation of artists had no direct experience of the excesses of the Cultural Revolution, and would still have been quite young at the time of the Tiananmen crackdown of 1989, but Li Xianting suggested that such people still felt that 'society is always harming them'. He mentioned another exhibition which had recently been closed down, not for extreme content, but because it touched on a sensitive aspect of Chinese history. 'This is a kind of hurt too,' he said, 'not to be able to sensibly discuss a state of mind.'

And, he added, even if these artists had not personally suffered during the Cultural Revolution, society as a whole was still suffering from the after-effects, which he felt had influenced the emergence of such artworks. 'I think the reason is that China does not have moral limits any more,' he said. 'The Cultural Revolution destroyed traditional morality, and then the morality established by Chairman Mao was destroyed by opening up.' The end result of what he called these 'two big cultural destructions', was, he believed, that 'an overall value system no longer exists'.

Zhu Yu, who had sewn his own skin onto the side of pork, later caused a far greater controversy when a photograph appeared showing him taking a bite out of what seemed to be a grilled human embryo. Zhu Yu, who had acquired the embryo from a local hospital where abortions were performed, claimed that he wanted to challenge the accepted limits of human society. He certainly

372

succeeded in doing this, provoking denunciations on the Internet, and the passing of new regulations by the Chinese authorities tightening controls on performance art. He has since admitted that he was violently sick immediately after the notorious 'performance', and did not dare to return to his home, where it took place, for several days. These days he has reverted to his original speciality, painting, spending long months producing precise oil paintings of the patterns left on plates by the remnants of the food he eats when he goes to restaurants for dinner. He does not talk much about the past controversy, which left him under close official scrutiny – though he is dismissive of other artists who have subsequently created extreme works, suggesting that they are simply jumping on the bandwagon and seeking only to shock. He himself seems profoundly serious about his work – with a fundamental conviction that in art there should be no limits.[13]

The critic Li Xianting says he did not like the extremity of Zhu Yu's actions – but he suggests there are cultural reasons why they had some meaning in the Chinese context; China's most celebrated twentieth-century writer, Lu Xun, for example, famously criticised society as having cannibalistic tendencies – most notably in a story in which a young man eats bread dipped in the blood of an executed convict, in the belief that it will cure his illness.[14] Still, says Li Xianting, even as they search for new art forms or seek to reflect anger towards society, artists ought to have limits. 'If there's war, murder or violence in society, can artists also kill people or start wars to criticise or reveal this society?' he asks. Nevertheless, he believes that such works reflect the fact that, for some, society still suffers from 'pain – and the lack of a moral limit'.

There are others in the Chinese art world, though, who believe that art can play a part in healing some of the pain of a society rushing so rapidly from a traumatised past to an uncertain future – and in helping to create a new system of social values. Back in Guangzhou, at the Guangdong Museum of Art, they have led the way in trying to make artistic creation relevant to people's lives. The museum was, in 2002, the first official gallery in China to hold a retrospective of contemporary Chinese art of the 1990s, and it has staged other challenging exhibitions, such as a collection of photography entitled 'Humanism', including contributions by, among others, Zhao Tielin, the photographer who spent so long documenting the lives of prostitutes in Hainan. It has also done much to emphasise the links between art and the community, running many of the type of outreach activities which are familiar in similar institutions in many other countries, but still unusual in China: lectures on contemporary art for young people, trips to artists' studios for Museum 'friends' – as well as the art activities for local youth which it holds every weekend, when hundreds of children, shepherded by their parents, cram into a big room overlooking the river to paint, take part in competitions, and create spectacular levels of noise.

The museum has gone further too: in 2003 it provided the venue for the performance of the play *The Vagina Monologues* by the staff and students of nearby Sun Yat-sen University; it has also sent its staff out to organise events and performances at a local women's detention centre, in which the inmates were given a chance to participate. 'We want to focus on marginalised people,' says curator Guo Xiaoyan. 'Few art museums in China are active in the community, but we want to go beyond the idea of being just a gallery.' Recently the museum put such ideals into concrete action, playing a leading role in the establishment of a new 'community art museum', designed partly by the Dutch architect Rem Koolhaas, which features gallery spaces, artists' workshops and studios for film and video, scattered among the various floors of a new high-rise housing block in a residential neighbourhood of Guangzhou. It's another attempt to break through the barriers between contemporary art and mainstream society.

Of course, the idea of art playing a socially active role (rather than a propaganda one) remains relatively new in China – and it's an approach which is still likely to be fraught with difficulties. More physical space for art and cultural activities is undoubtedly becoming available – not least because the government has set grand targets for promoting what it calls 'cultural construction', announcing plans to build some fifteen hundred new museums and

374

art galleries around the country during the coming decade.[15] It's not unusual these days to visit small Chinese towns and find newly built, and often very modern, museums, theatres and other cultural venues. The question will be whether the authorities are prepared to allow the ideological space and creative freedoms necessary to fill these buildings with meaningful work – and whether the artists of the new generation are able to build on the spirit of their predecessors of the 1980s, and keep taking risks and searching for their own direction, at a time when the lure of commercial success is becoming ever greater.

# 13

# Faith, hope and disillusionment

In the old black brick building, a guide was leading a little gaggle of visitors through a room filled with glass display cases. 'All of these contain precious historical objects,' she said reverentially, 'because this part of the exhibition is about the founding of the Communist party.' As the assembled employees of government work units looked on respectfully, the guide spelled out exactly why the Party had come into existence. 'It was the inevitable result of recent history,' she explained, drawing the crowd's attention to a picture of representatives of the last imperial dynasty, the Qing, signing away Chinese sovereignty over Hong Kong, and other strategic rights, to the British in the nineteenth century. 'Britain started the Opium War and used its cannons to open up our doors,' she went on, 'and the Qing dynasty government was so corrupt that it was defeated.' A cartoon of the period, on display nearby, graphically illustrated what happened next. 'This shows the western powers as animals dividing up China,' said the guide, adding helpfully, 'The tiger is Britain, the eagle is the USA, and the frog is France.'

It was the summer of 2001, and the Chinese Communist Party was celebrating the eightieth anniversary of its founding. In the small terraced house in the old French concession in Shanghai where thirteen conspirators, including the future Chairman, Mao Zedong, held their first, clandestine meeting, the occasion was being marked by a special exhibition, and state employees were being taken on trips to see it. The guide paused in front of a waxwork tableau of that meeting, featuring life-size models of those first party members in the midst of discussing how to rid China of foreign powers. 'This is very realistic,' she said, proudly, 'it's based on photographs; notice how simply they're dressed.'

Around the corner from the museum, the western owner of a recently opened restaurant was showing guests around his new establishment. He seemed to have a rather different type of party on his mind. 'All the settings are crystal and silver,' he emphasised. 'Here you have a few cases of wine – and of course champagne.' This, he added, was the key to a successful social gathering. 'Champagne is part of the party,' he said. 'Without champagne, there can be no party.' The restaurant formed part of the newly renovated complex of old buildings in the block behind the communist museum, known as Xintiandi (New Heaven and Earth), which was swiftly developing into one of Shanghai's most upmarket leisure areas. The restaurateur saw no contradiction between this kind of luxury lifestyle and the socialist shrine round the corner. 'What we're bringing to China will change the whole perception of people who come to this country,' he said. 'They'll realise how open China is today.'

It was a sentiment which would have been music to the ears of Mr Ni, head of the Communist Party committee of the party museum, as he sought to explain how the ideals of the party's founding fathers fitted together with the new development next door. The lifestyle complex was a good thing, he said, since it would attract more foreign tourists to the area to visit the museum. And, he added, it was also a symbol of the party's economic achievements in these past decades: 'The party's primary aim has always been to make the people's lives better,' he stressed, 'and now because of the policy of reform we have so many foreigners coming to invest here and contribute to our reform and opening.' After all, he said, the goal of the reforms was 'to help our economy develop faster, and to improve the people's living standards all the time'. And so, he suggested, 'I think if Comrade Mao Zedong were alive today, he'd be happy to see the people's living standards getting better and better',

Some of the visitors to the museum seemed to share his views. Mr Li, a businessman in his forties, was guiding his young daughter around a room containing a collection of Chairman Mao's personal possessions – including his heavily darned dressing gown and a pair of voluminous swimming trunks. 'I brought her to see Chairman Mao's simple way of life,' he said, 'and how he suffered to lead the Chinese people.' But he had no objection to the Communist Party museum's luxurious new neighbour. 'There's no contradiction,' he said. 'Society has to develop – and places like this show that under the leadership of the Communist Party people can live well. These foreigners are here to help us construct the nation; if they want to eat in nice restaurants, that's fine,' he continued, adding philosophically, 'there are no classes when it comes to eating. If I have money I can, if I don't have money then I have to work harder.' He himself seemed to be planning to make the most of China's growing links with the outside world – in fact he was thinking of sending his daughter to study at Oxford or Cambridge in the future. But no matter where she went, he said, she had to be proud of her country. 'That's the first thing,' he insisted. 'If I'm not patriotic people will look down on me. That's why I brought my daughter here today.'

Not everyone was quite so convinced, however. Residents in the nearby lanes, awaiting the demolition of their houses to make way for further luxury developments, were somewhat less enthusiastic. 'The Communist Party was formed to be very simple,' said a middle-aged man, 'but this area doesn't fit in with that.' His neighbour nodded in agreement: 'This is a revolutionary place,' she said. 'I don't think it's appropriate to have an entertainment complex next door – it only suits foreigners and some rich Shanghai people.' On the evening before the party's anniversary, I took a stroll around the area. On the old cobblestones of the pedestrian zone, between the restaurants and designer boutiques, stood a bright red Maserati sports car, apparently part of some promotional activity planned for the following day. It was parked just behind the rear wall of the Communist Party museum.

Living with contradictions and shifting values is something China's people have grown used to in recent years. Since the beginning of reforms, and the move away from the collective economy and traditional welfare system, many of the policies which were once the foundations of the communist state have been turned upside down. The country's leaders have on occasion tied themselves up in ideological knots in their attempts to justify the previously unthinkable. Sometimes they have tried taking a fresh look at history: when China's stock markets were reopened in the early 1990s, official media reports were quick to point out that Marx and Engels had themselves been stock-market investors in nineteenth-century Britain. At other times, they have resorted to the use of creative language: when private businesses first began to appear, for example, they were dubbed 'collective enterprises', and later 'businesses run by the people'. China's economic system is officially known these days as the 'socialist market economy', and the nation's overall policy is referred to as 'socialism with Chinese characteristics'.

And it was in fact at the time of the Communist Party's eightieth anniversary in 2001 that the reversal of many traditional values was underlined, by a decision to encourage China's new generation of private entrepreneurs to become members of the party. This was justified as a way of ensuring that the party remained relevant to the changes in society; it was also a tacit acknowledgement that the private sector was now the fastest growing area of the economy. This shift was underpinned by a new political slogan, announced around the same time, known as the 'Three Represents'. This theory, enshrined as the official 'big idea' of the outgoing Communist Party Secretary General Jiang Zemin before his retirement in 2003, suggested that the party should represent three things: advanced sectors of the economy, advanced culture and the basic interests of the people.

Some welcomed the decision to admit business people as a sign that at last the party was accepting the reality of China's changed society. Yet for others, it simply reinforced the sense that an organisation which once denounced factory bosses and landlords as the 'exploiting classes' was moving further and further away from its original ideals. Such perceptions were not helped by a string of cases of embezzlement and corruption involving senior officials during the second half of the 1990s and early years of the new century. From city officials to deputy provincial governors, from the deputy head of the Standing Committee of Parliament to the Deputy Minister of Police in charge of tackling smuggling, from the mayor of Shenyang to the party secretary of Beijing, officials around the country were arrested on corruption charges. Some were given long jail sentences, a couple were executed, several committed suicide when their crimes were uncovered. Few major cities or provinces were left unscathed.[1] In 2006, even Shanghai, which had been apparently insulated from such high-profile embarrassment, was affected, when its party secretary was sacked for involvement in the scandal relating to the use of money from the city's pension fund; the same year, down south in Shenzhen, the city's pride in having a fair and relatively transparent administrative system took a blow with the announcement that five senior judges had been detained or arrested on suspicion of taking bribes.[2]

The government hailed each arrest and each new anti-corruption campaign as a sign of its determination to root out bad officials. But the cumulative effect was, for many people, the opposite, creating the impression that as economic reforms developed, more and more officials were focused on making money and their own self-interest, and that corruption was now deeply embedded in the system. To a certain extent people came to accept this as inevitable; some no longer found it shocking. 'We just assume that all officials these days are corrupt to a greater or lesser degree,' was how one Shanghai resident put it on hearing the news of the demise of the local party boss. But the damage which this had done to the party's image in the eyes of the people was acknowledged at the highest level – the former President and Communist Party chief Jiang Zemin himself said publicly on a number of occasions that the fight against corruption was a 'life-and-death struggle' for the party.[3]

Coming, as many of these cases did, at a time when the painful reforms of China's welfare system were at their height, it was hardly surprising that many ordinary people grew disillusioned. For all the brutality and chaos of the Cultural Revolution, many of those who had grown up in the early decades of the communist era had, it seems, accepted the government's official line that the decade from the mid-1960s to the mid-1970s was just an aberration, and still retained faith in the ideals with which they had been brought up: that the party was focused on helping the poorest and most disadvantaged members of society, and that it would not take 'so much as a pin' from the people, as the saying used to go. But as they saw those old egalitarian values replaced with the dawning of a new age of individualism, many felt let down. Mr Li, a former textile worker in Shanghai who had been laid off and now got by driving a decrepit delivery van twelve hours a day, summed this up. As he watched the BMWs and Audis speeding past him on the road, he shook his head in a mixture of disbelief and resignation. 'When we worked for the state we didn't earn much,' he said, 'but there was little difference between the rich and the poor. Now there are such big divisions in society – the young can earn so much more than we do. It's very unequal,' he added, 'that's the biggest problem in China today.'

The wealth of some, and the daily struggles of many, has certainly created much bitterness. In 2005, a delegate to the annual session of China's legislature caused a storm in the media after alleging that the nation spent some 300 billion yuan (around £20 billion) a year on government cars, 250 billion on official trips abroad, and 200 billion on official banquets and other forms of government receptions – adding up to more than double the state annual investment in agriculture.[4] Anger at such perceived excess affects many people on a more personal level. On the eve of Chinese New Year 2006, I met Mr Zhang, a taxi driver, who bemoaned the conspicuous consumption of many of the new rich, and of the leaders of his state-owned company, to which he had to pay a significant amount of his earnings every month. 'We have to give so much to our bosses,' he said. 'I should be doing quite well, but they take so much – and it all gets eaten up! In China so much is just eaten up, some people spend as much on one meal as we spend on eating for a year.' He mentioned a case which had been highlighted in the local media, of a restaurant which was charging 80,000 yuan (over £5,000) a table for a New Year's feast. 'The people at the top are worse than the capitalists!' he cursed, harking back to the days when the party routinely denounced this class as the most evil of the exploiters.

And the social divide, not just between rich and poor in the cities but between permanent urban residents and the migrant labour force, which has so little access to welfare, is also something many of the older generation find shocking. 'They always taught us that we should not exploit others,' complained one middle-aged man. 'Now the system is exploiting a lot of people; even the big cities exploit other parts of the country.' Like many he was not only disillusioned by this shift in values, but also felt that life in the new society was a constant struggle to keep up. 'There's so much more pressure now,' he said. 'When I was younger we were all poor. Maybe you only had one pair of trousers, but you didn't worry about it. Now,' he went on, 'if your friend's earning more than you are, you can't sleep at night because you feel like a failure. And if you lose your job you can't sleep because you're worrying about how you're going to pay for your kid's education.'

Even among the relatively privileged, the extent of the changes can produce pain and confusion. One businessman, who came from a family of well-placed civil servants and grew up in a residential compound for elite members of the communist system, once told me that even some of his neighbours who were children of high-ranking officials had struggled to adapt to the pressures of a competitive economy. 'Some of the kids couldn't meet the challenge,' he said, 'now everything is changing so rapidly. Even though they came from a good family they still lost their job. And you look into their eyes,' he went on, 'and they're confused, angry – some of them have even gone crazy.' He himself had done well, and now ran a successful company, yet he admitted that he too sometimes found the pace of change hard to cope with. 'My head's a bit of a mess now,' he said. 'It's hard for the people who haven't made it – but for those of us who have made some money, it can be hard to accept the situation too.' He shook his head. 'Everyone was the same,' he went on. 'We all got the same wages: thirty-eight yuan a month – four dollars – there was no difference.' It was memories such as these which, he believed, made some people nostalgic for the days of Chairman Mao, like the taxi drivers who hung pendants with his image in their cars, or the old people who still kept his picture on the wall. 'They think that time was better, because everyone was equal,' he said. The businessman, however, had sought other forms of spiritual support. 'I became a Buddhist a few years ago,' he explained. 'It helped me in some ways.'

Not everyone shares his concerns, of course. Some of those who have done well are quick to emphasise their undiluted gratitude, notably to Deng Xiaoping, for the opportunities which the years of reform have brought them. But the Communist Party has been sufficiently concerned about public disillusionment that it has, since the 1990s, embarked on a series of campaigns aimed at reviving popular enthusiasm. On the one hand it still sometimes resorts to the traditional propaganda technique of promoting individuals as 'model citizens' – people whose sacrifices for the good of the nation, including sometimes of their lives, are supposed to inspire others. And since the student protests of 1989, the authorities have stepped up patriotic education in schools and colleges, in an attempt to ensure the loyalty of the young generation. This ranges from the playing of the national anthem in schools to the basic military training and half-dozen courses on politics which university students have to take, and pass, as part of their studies. Many university students also automatically become members of the Communist Party's Youth League; the brightest of them are given the chance to become full party members. It's not an opportunity extended to just anyone – the Chinese Communist Party may be, as it likes to say, the largest political party in the world, with over 73 million members in 2007 (with a similar number in the Youth League), but this is only just over 5 per cent of the population.[5] In the past, it was not uncommon to hear of people who tried and failed for their whole lives to be accepted as party members. Such dedication may have diminished in recent decades, but there are still those who see membership as a great honour.

*

Xiao Zhang is one of them. When I met him, he was finishing a degree in management at one of China's top business schools, and was hoping to get a job with a foreign or joint venture company. And he had just handed in his application to join the Communist Party. 'I've always had this feeling, since childhood, that I want to join the party,' he said with a shy smile. Perhaps it was because his parents were members, but he seemed sincere in his conviction that the party stood for noble values, as summed up by its traditional slogan of 'serving the people'. 'For me I think the Communist Party can offer a way of reaching my ideals,' he explained. 'Real happiness is to share happiness with others – if you help others or are important in their life you can get a spiritual reward.' Not all of his friends could see the point, he admitted. 'I was the first in my class to do this,' he said. 'Some of my classmates said it's useless, some said it's out of date, but I just know I want to do it.' The popular perception, he acknowledged, was that many people who joined the party nowadays were really doing it because they thought it would give them an advantage in their future career, or help them gain an official position. But Xiao Zhang said that the knowledge of the self-sacrifice of early generations of party members was all he needed to inspire him. 'It's a spiritual support,' he insisted. 'There's always a conflict between ideals and reality – and maybe sometimes when you're feeling lazy or you can't bear the pressure you're under you need something to help you.' And so, he said, 'I chose the party'.

Of course, he agreed, he knew it was not perfect. 'I think corruption is a very big problem for the party,' he acknowledged. But he believed it could be tackled, and he was convinced too that the party had succeeded in putting the shadow of the Cultural Revolution behind it. 'During those ten years of political movements, of course maybe the party hurt many people's hearts,' said Xiao Zhang, 'but now it's doing things to win back their hearts, with so much progress and development, that I still trust it.' Nor had the growing inequalities in society shaken his faith – the classes he had taken in Deng Xiaoping theory had apparently had their effect: 'If you want people to have equal wealth all the time, we'll only get equal poverty,' he stressed. 'I think equal wealth is just a goal in the long run; how to achieve it is another question. As Deng Xiaoping said, maybe we can make some people get rich first, and help others to come along afterwards.' And so, he felt, it was perfectly reasonable to be a party member and go into business at the same time. 'To get fairness you have to increase efficiency first,' he explained. Nor was he embarrassed to admit his belief that traditional ideology had to adapt to changing times. 'Marxism is just a kind of theory,' he said. 'What we understand by this theory is perhaps different to a hundred years ago – now we maybe have a different understanding of socialism and capitalism, it's maybe not as we learned in our textbooks – things they said were good may be not so good, things they said were bad may be not so bad.'

There's no doubt that many of the new Communist Party members are far from hung up on traditional ideology. 'We study Marx's ideas on economics, and I think you need to know about them,' said a student in Shanghai, who was about to join the party. 'But we study capitalist economics too – and our teachers explain to us ways you can criticise Marxist economics,' she added. 'We know that the practice is often different from the principles.'

Others are even less shy about admitting that the old ideology is not necessarily particularly relevant to their world. Jimmy Chen, from central China, was now in his final year at university, but had already become a full member of the party. On a weekend afternoon, in a café near his university which was popular with students on dates, because its mediterranean-style decor was considered romantic, he explained his political values. 'I believe in Marxism,' he began. Then he thought for a moment. 'Well, maybe I don't totally believe in it,' he went on, 'but I think there's no harm in it. It's useful – and it can guide us on how to behave.' He spoke English fluently and rapidly, with a slightly upper-class accent which he seemed to have picked up from listening to language tapes. His confident manner was leavened with a self-deprecating sense of humour.

One advantage of being a party member, he said, was being able to get good access to information about what was really going on in the country, since every couple of weeks he and a group of other student members were given a special lecture by party members from the university staff. 'They give you a lot of statistics,' said Jimmy, 'and they tell you the real facts about things that are happening.' Not that it was all interesting. 'I'd say half is useful and half is cliché,' he grinned. Still, he was proud to be a party member, like his father, an engineer, and his grandmother, who had been a worker in a textile factory, before him. 'My dad and other relatives all encouraged me to join the party,' he said. And as if to prove his dedication to the ideal of serving the people, he had volunteered to spend a year teaching in a village school in a remote rural area after graduation, for a very minimal salary. Even his own parents thought this was taking youthful idealism a bit far, he admitted. 'My mother says it's a strange place, very crude,' he said. 'She doesn't want me to stay there so long – she says if I live there I'll have to become like the local people, and I might not be able to adapt to the environment.' But he was determined to see it through. 'I want to try something different; to learn about the local culture and help people,' he said. Then he laughed, as though he realised this sounded a little pompous. 'Well, maybe that's an exaggeration, but I'm excited to try.'

This kind of positive thinking would certainly be welcomed by the party, as it seeks to inspire the young with values of patriotism and self-sacrifice. One middle-aged academic, who is worried about the direction in which society is developing, points out that university students and the young in general do tend to be more positive about life than the older generation. 'I don't think they have so much experience of society,' he says, 'so their sense of disappointment and disillusionment is not so strong. Perhaps when they enter society it will be different – but in college life is better.' It may be the case that, in the absence of real participatory politics in China, and in a society where there is little day-to-day debate on fundamental political issues, it's easier for many people to feel more distant from society's problems – since they have even less opportunity to do anything about such issues than they might in a more open political system.

Still, some of the young generation are notably less enthusiastic.

Many students seem to regard their compulsory courses on politics as a chore to be got out of the way in the first year of college. 'We don't really pay much attention to them,' says one student. A few of the lectures are vaguely interesting, she says, but most are dull. And she has seen too how hard her room-mates have had to work while applying to become party members. 'They had to write so many essays,' she recalls. 'To me this would be a big burden.' She herself sees little practical benefit in becoming a party member: she doesn't think it would be of too much help in finding a job, and her parents have never encouraged her to apply. Anyway, her heroes are of a different hue. 'I don't admire political people,' she says. 'The people I really respect are scientists – people who do things to improve the environment and the quality of life.'

Indeed, it's not uncommon to hear ordinary people talking about the Communist Party as though it's something far removed from their lives. In Shanghai, for example, I have often heard people responding to problems in society and other sources of dissatisfaction by saying, 'it's the Communist Party's fault' or 'that's typical of the communists'. Such comments frequently come from older people who have suffered in their lives; but they're a reminder too that the government's ideological campaigns and propaganda have little impact on some people – indeed, after so many decades of slogans and theories, some citizens have simply become immune to such things. A few years ago, when the party was energetically promoting the 'Three Represents' theory, I met a man in his thirties who was annoyed about the amount of coverage it was being given on television and radio. 'Why is the media always talking about these Four Represents?' he fumed, 'I'm getting really tired of it.'

There's no doubt that the ideological fervour of earlier decades can seem far away these days – particularly for the young generation. Professor Yang Xiong, youth sociologist at the Shanghai Academy of Sciences, was himself a teenager – and a Red Guard – during the Cultural Revolution years of the 1960s. When he tries to discuss that period with his own teenage son, he suggests, he meets a gulf of understanding. 'If we talk about it he immediately starts mocking me,' he says. '"How come you people were so stupid?", he asks me, "how could anyone have been so dumb as to pin a badge of Chairman Mao onto their flesh?" He just doesn't understand,' he continues. 'To him we were a generation of fools, fighting for such a hollow utopian idea.' And so, he says, 'there's not just a generation gap – it's a total gap of values'.

Still, Yang Xiong insists that this does not mean that the new generation has no ideals. 'We were just doing "empty-headed politics",' he says, 'now they're concentrating on practical economics.' If there's been a loss of idealism, he suggests, it's only 'the shattering of utopian idealism. Now it's a very practical ideal – that China should get rich, should be strong, that the people should be rich, and should be proud to be Chinese. It doesn't matter whether they're busy earning money, going to university, or studying abroad – they want the country to be successful, they want to be successful in their job, they want their family to be happy.' This pragmatic approach, he says, may make it seem that many young people are simply self-centred, but he believes that most retain a deep fundamental patriotism.

Professor Yang cites the protest marches against Japan, which took place in many Chinese cities in the spring of 2005, and in which many young people participated, as an example. The protests were in response both to the introduction in some Japanese schools of a history textbook said to downplay Japanese war crimes in China in the 1930s and 1940s, and to a bid by Japan to join the UN Security Council, which many in China opposed. There were suggestions at the time that the Chinese government had orchestrated the demonstrations, but according to Yang Xiong, the authorities themselves were taken aback at the scale of the protests, and the degree of nationalist sentiment which they revealed – not least among the young urban middle classes in cities like Shanghai and Shenzhen, which saw some of the largest marches. 'These weren't just students or the proletariat,' he says, 'they were people with jobs. In the past our surveys showed that white-collar people cared the least about politics – we thought they were only interested in a car, a house, a wife,' he adds, 'but they were the ones protesting! So people were asking themselves, how come even these kind of people are out demonstrating? Even the government didn't understand.' It's a reminder, he insists, that the feelings of this generation should not be underestimated. 'It looks like there are no ideals involved,' he says, 'but as soon as something happens to the nation, their national spirit appears.'

If patriotic sentiment is still deep, it's perhaps not surprising, given the energy the authorities have expended on promoting this in the past decade or more. The education given to young people stresses China's past oppression by foreigners, and the Communist Party's role in freeing the country both from such oppression and from the weakness which led to it. And the patriotic message is not restricted to schools and colleges: every May Day and on Chinese National Day in October, streets, buildings, even taxis are bedecked with national flags; young people are often taken on organised trips to museums and historic spots which have been designated as 'patriotic education sites' – not just places which are directly linked to the history of the Communist Party itself, but also earlier sites, like the 'Museum of Resisting British Aggression' in Guangzhou, which commemorates an uprising by local villagers against British soldiers stationed in the city after the Opium Wars. In recent years the media has also promoted the concept of 'red tourism' – holiday trips to remote parts of the country which played a part in the communists' rise to power.

And 'patriotic education' also emphasises the government's official line on the student protests of 1989, stressing that the official crackdown was necessary to prevent 'turmoil' and create the 'stability' which the authorities say laid the ground for the rapid economic growth of the 1990s. Such education also focuses on the deaths of soldiers rather than students and other innocent members of the public. It's a line which many young people seem to have accepted; even among those who believe that there's more to the story, there's often a tendency to gloss over the issue, by saying they're not interested in politics, or by suggesting that the students of that year would have been better off minding their own business

389

and focusing on their studies. 'Most of my friends think they were naive,' a trendily dressed student from one big-city university once told me.

For the party, mixing ideology and patriotism is a useful tactic, since, to most people in China, the idea of not being patriotic would be almost unthinkable; the very word for patriotism in Chinese, *ai guo*, literally means to 'love the country', and few people, even those who might have differences of opinion with the government, could imagine feeling otherwise. For many people this instinctive reaction extends to the strategic issues which the Chinese government considers most fundamental, such as sovereignty over Tibet and Taiwan (though these days business people will also often express the hope that there will be no confrontation with Taiwan as it would be bad for the economy) – and a deep sensitivity towards any signs of the continuing influence in Japan of the type of right-wing attitudes which gave rise to Japanese militarism and its expansion across Asia in the 1930s. The official teaching about the stains of colonial history – China's partial subjugation by foreign powers after the Opium Wars, for example – also seems to have left a residue of suspicion towards any foreign government or organisation believed to be treating China in an arrogant way. This can be seen in the feelings of hurt national pride which sometimes surface in response to, for example, cases of foreign companies found to have misled or short-changed Chinese consumers.[6]

Despite the government's best efforts, though, there are, it seems, still some who can draw a line between patriotic feelings and support for the party. 'I'm a patriot,' said one young graduate I met, 'but I don't have too much faith in the Communist Party.' This seemed to be something of an understatement. 'In fact, I don't think I've ever met anyone who really believed a lot in the party,' he continued. 'Who believes in the party nowadays? The party doesn't even believe in itself now – it's like the story of the emperor's new clothes: everyone knows, it's just that nobody dares to say it!' His views no doubt owed something to the experience of his father, who had been a factory worker and a loyal party member, in the days when the big state enterprises were still the core of the economy. 'With the development of the market economy, he's seen how so many state assets have been taken over by the managers, and how hard things have been for the ordinary people,' said his son. 'So I don't think he has any faith any more. Sometimes he asks, "What kind of communism is this?"'

And even patriotic sentiment can itself be hard to control. Such concerns have meant that, over the past decade, several Chinese citizens' groups involved in anti-Japanese activism have found that their activities have often been restricted by the authorities. And while there's no doubt that a government-backed petition on the Internet opposing Japanese membership of the UN Security Council contributed to the spread of the anti-Japanese protests of spring 2005, in some cities, where those protests became violent, there was a sense that they might still spiral into chaos.[7] Such upsurges of nationalistic feelings can certainly be useful for the authorities, but they do pose potential risks: they may slip out of control, and they can sometimes also become a focus for other grievances; and if the authorities then try to intervene to restrain the protestors, they can find themselves accused of not being sufficiently patriotic, or of being weak and failing to stand up for the nation's interests – something which can be deeply damaging to the credibility of the leadership.

In May 1999, for example, there were demonstrations outside the embassies of NATO countries in Beijing, and at their consulates in other Chinese cities, after NATO missiles destroyed the Chinese embassy in Belgrade, killing three people. It was widely assumed abroad that the protests were entirely organised by the authorities. But many of those who took to the streets hurling rocks at embassies and consulates, and indeed burnt down part of the US consulate in Chengdu, had undoubtedly joined in of their own accord – and it was not uncommon to hear anger at the bombing spilling over into criticism of China's own government for being too weak in its response. In fact some people were convinced that NATO had carried out the bombing intentionally, and insisted this had only happened because China's leadership was not strong enough. Many harked back to the old days. 'If Chairman Mao were still alive this would never have been allowed to happen,' insisted one man in the crowd outside the US embassy in Beijing that first night. Around him, some of the rock-throwing protesters spontaneously began to chant old slogans from the Maoist era.[8]

Nor do feelings of patriotism necessarily prevent people from showing an interest in other ideas which the authorities may find less welcome. I was struck by this one winter morning in Beijing in the late 1990s. As we drove out into the suburbs the snow on the roads was just starting to turn to slush, but it was still bitterly cold. My destination was the spot where, in 1937, a clash between locals and Japanese troops – who had already been in north-eastern China for some years – sparked the full-scale Japanese invasion of the east and south of the country as well. A museum on the site now marks the incident, depicting, in often graphic detail, the violence and suffering visited on China in the years that followed. And since this particular day was the anniversary of an important incident during those years of conflict, a group of students from one of Beijing's top high schools had also been brought to visit the museum. They had not driven here, however – they had walked all the way from the city centre, through the sludge and ice, since their teachers thought this would concentrate their minds on the suffering of previous generations. Inside the museum, the students filled in question-naires as they made their way around the exhibits, which included bloody three-dimensional models of scenes of death and destruction. One fifteen-year-old girl emerged from the exhibition, shaking her head. 'It's important to see this,' she said. 'We have to make sure we never allow something like this to happen again.' Her friend who was with her nodded in agreement. Then they glanced at each other, and the first girl said she wanted to ask me a question. 'Do you know whether it's true what people are saying?' she said. When it became clear that I had no idea what she was talking about, she explained a little more. 'You know,' she said, 'that the world's going to end next year? That's what we've heard – we're quite worried about it.'

And the two girls were not the only people in China that year who seemed fascinated by the doomsday theory, derived from the writings of Nostradamus, which predicted that the world would end in 1999. It was just one example of the increasingly diverse range of beliefs and ideas which, despite all the official propaganda, have surfaced in China over the past decade and a half. In the early 1990s, for example, there was a striking upsurge in the popularity of practices such as *qi gong* – the ancient Chinese breathing exercises with deep roots in traditional philosophy and cosmology. Every morning and evening, parks in towns around China were thronged with people practising *qi gong*, and other traditional exercises, in little clusters under the trees. Such exercises had always been popular with old people, but during the 1990s growing numbers of younger people began to take them up too. The fact that they were good for the health was one reason for their popularity, at a time when medical costs were rising. But it was also widely believed that their success was inspired partly by a kind of escapism, as people sought solace and spiritual reassurance amid the disillusionment which followed the crushing of the 1989 protests. With their links to traditional ideas such as Taoism – the ancient Chinese philosophy which over the centuries evolved into a spiritual belief system – these practices offered an alternative to the sometimes grim reality of everyday life.

And sometimes, such beliefs took on a quasi-mystical character: I once visited a dusty, decrepit lane in an obscure Beijing suburb, where, in the small courtyard of a ramshackle old house, a group of miserable, impoverished-looking people were standing, waiting to be ushered inside. The handwritten signs posted on the walls explained why they were there: they promised cures for all types of diseases, and lifelong good health. In one of the rooms off the courtyard, the source of these claims was holding court. An energetic-looking middle-aged man with closely cropped hair and a confident manner, he greeted me courteously and, with some enthusiasm, began to describe the secret of his success. 'If you channel your body's internal energy,' he said, 'the results can be very powerful. For example,' he went on, 'I only need to sleep for forty seconds at a time – that's enough to make me feel completely refreshed for hours.' He gave me a quick demonstration, closing his eyes, a beatific smile on his face. When he reopened them, he presented me with a name-card, which was filled with a string of impressive titles, as chairman or board member of a whole list of *qi gong* associations, medical research institutes and meditation organisations of all kinds. It was easy to understand why he inspired so much confidence in people seeking to improve their health – and their lives.

Around China, a number of *qi gong* masters and exponents of other similar practices gained rapidly in popularity throughout the 1990s. One of the fastest developing forms of practice in China during the mid-late 1990s was Falun Dafa – popularly known as Falun Gong. It combined *qi gong*-style breathing exercises with elements of traditional Chinese philosophy and religion, Buddhism and Taoism in particular, and above all it promised good health for those who practised it, and the possibility of curing many ailments without the need to resort to any form of medicine. It was a popular message, and the practice spread quickly around the country, transmitted from one group of practitioners to another, with the help of books and videos. These featured the teachings of Falun Gong's founder, a former civil servant from north-east China by the name of Li Hongzhi. Master Li, as he was known, had a charismatic quality which helped Falun Gong to attract not only elderly people but young, well-educated people as well. By the late 1990s there were significant groups of Falun Gong practitioners in some of China's top universities. Officials at China's State Sports Administration, which in theory oversaw *qi gong* and other similar disciplines, estimated that it could have tens of millions of practitioners. Falun Gong supporters claimed the number was even higher.[9]

But as the movement grew, it also attracted criticism, notably from a famous Chinese scientist who published papers accusing the movement of promoting 'superstition'. It was a loaded term, in a country where the communists had always vowed their determination to wipe out 'feudal superstitions' of all kinds. And it provoked an angry response from Falun Gong practitioners. In April

1999, a group of them staged a protest in the city of Tianjin, not far from Beijing, at a university publishing house which had printed the professor's articles. After around a week, this protest was broken up by the police – who were accused by the demonstrators of using violence against them. The message spread quickly among Falun Gong followers – and another protest was organised, this time in the Chinese capital itself.

And so on a balmy spring Sunday morning, guards at the compound housing the offices and homes of most of China's top leaders, in a leafy side street to the west of the Forbidden City, were surprised to see crowds of people, many of them middle-aged or elderly, congregating on the pavement opposite. Dressed in simple clothes, they stood calmly and quietly, and could easily have been mistaken for a group of out-of-town tourists, waiting for their buses after a visit to the nearby Beihai Park. But a few representatives of the crowd made their way to the entrance to the leadership compound and asked to speak to senior officials. They were Falun Gong practitioners, they said, and wanted redress against those who had criticised and mistreated them. They were received relatively politely, and told that their demands would be noted. Yet the crowd – which most estimates put at around ten thousand people – initially refused to disperse; the Falun Gong practitioners simply stayed where they were, silent and well disciplined, for most of the day. Finally, after dark, police shepherded them away from the scene, putting many of them onto buses and driving them out of the city centre.

No immediate action was taken against the participants – but for China's leaders these events came as a serious shock. Beijing was supposed to be under especially tight security at the time, since the tenth anniversary of the crushing of the 1989 Tiananmen protests was fast approaching, and later in the year the Communist Party was planning a lavish celebration of its fiftieth anniversary in power. And despite the peaceful nature of the protest, the idea that a movement which many in the government had barely heard of could suddenly organise such a massive demonstration right on their own doorstep – apparently without the security services having the slightest advance knowledge – was particularly galling. For some in the leadership, this represented a direct challenge to their authority.

And so, after several months of frantic investigations, the authorities announced that they were banning Falun Gong, labelling it a 'cult' (literally a *xiejiao* or 'evil teaching'). They accused it of stealing the clothes of Buddhism and Taoism – and claimed that, by encouraging people to avoid using conventional medicine where possible, Falun Gong had caused hundreds of deaths. Falun Gong practitioners responded angrily, and there were more protests in many cities around the country. The government began rounding up hundreds of people accused of being 'ringleaders', many of whom were sent to prison or re-education camps. And tens of thousands of Falun Gong practitioners, perhaps more, were forced to write signed 'confessions', renouncing their support for the movement.[10] The crackdown, supported by a massive propaganda campaign in the media, was generally agreed to be the toughest ideological 'rectification' campaign since the crushing of the 1989 protests. In the months that followed, supporters of Falun Gong accused the government of torture and brutal methods against those detained, in some cases of murder – and indeed practitioners outside China have continued to make such allegations ever since. The authorities denied them, and counter-accused the movement of brainwashing followers into committing suicide. Falun Gong followers said the government had concocted the evidence. And for more than a year after the clampdown, Falun Gong practitioners, many of them middle-aged women from the provinces, continued to defy the authorities by making their way, alone or in groups, to Beijing's Tiananmen Square on an almost daily basis. Some attempted to unfurl protest banners, others simply sat down on the square in the midst of the crowds of tourists, and began practising their exercise routines. And almost without fail, they were quickly pounced on by plain-clothes police and dragged away into waiting vans.[11]

Eventually such scenes became less common, and the government announced that its nationwide campaigns had succeeded in crushing Falun Gong; a number of other *qi gong*-based movements were closed down too. Yet Falun Gong supporters continue to protest in other countries – and there are still occasional reports of TV transmitters in various parts of China being briefly hijacked by the movement's supporters, in order to broadcast their message. In 2005–6, banners in lanes and side streets in Shanghai and Beijing, for example, urged vigilance against the movement, calling on citizens to 'protect the integrity of the cable television network and defend against evil cults'. Others warned them not to 'listen to, believe or spread' the message of such organisations.

The Falun Gong phenomenon, and the dedication of many of its supporters, seemed to be further evidence of the search of many in China for new beliefs. There has been a growing sense in recent years of a crisis of values in Chinese society, as political ideology has become less powerful, and less influential on most people's lives. Some have expressed the opinion that many people no longer believe in anything other than making money: even a trainee priest I once met in Beijing seemed to lament the passing of the old days of ideological purity. 'A lot of young people growing up now don't know what faith is, or why they're living,' he said. 'Young people are all searching for money and advantage, they're interested in stars and big business people. When I was at school,' he added, 'there was a lot of teaching about belief – even though at the time it was promoting atheism, it was still a kind of belief.' And such ideology had exerted an influence over how people behaved in their daily life, he insisted. 'They would do good things, and try to control their bad sides,' he explained, 'but young people today are much less like that.' And he believed the increasing pressure of earning a living had fuelled the growing materialism. 'Since the reforms began and the economy developed, a lot of parents spend most of their time working and earning money,' he said, 'so it makes the children spend all their time thinking about earning money too.'

Some, of course, would say that many people had little choice in a society still struggling to rebuild its social safety net, where many do have to work so hard to survive that they have little time for anything else. As one academic told me, 'Like Confucius said, it's only when you have food and clothes that you can think about manners and morality.' And there are those who believe that the loss of a strong overriding sense of values has actually contributed to China's rapid development over the past decade and a half. According to Victor Yuan, the Beijing-based opinion pollster, a survey of Chinese people's values which his company carried out in 2005 revealed an extreme flexibility in many people's thinking. 'Basically they don't really strictly adhere to anything,' he says, 'they are just open to change. If you compare it with Europe, Chinese people are more dynamic; they are looking forward to innovation and change – and the period it takes for things to change is much shorter compared to the US or Japan, for example.' But while this may be good for the economy, Mr Yuan suggests it can also bring with it a moral vacuum. 'Of course some people care about right and wrong,' he says, 'but some are overly liberal in terms of morals. That's good to some degree because they support aggressive change. But,' he adds, 'the problem is you need to have some fundamental things – and for them it can seem like nothing is absolute. You might think that they have no principles.'[12]

His concerns are shared by a man who has experienced many of China's ideological upheavals of the past half-century at first hand. At the age of almost ninety, Bishop Aloysius Jin looks frail, though rather serene, as he sits in an armchair in his official residence in Shanghai, a plate with a picture of Pope Benedict XVI on the table next to him. Through the window behind him, the twin spires of St Ignatius, the old French Jesuit cathedral, are silhouetted against the grey sky. Bishop Jin's fragile appearance is hardly surprising, given that he has had several years of serious illness, to say nothing of a life which has included more than its share of ups and downs. But his views are still forcefully expressed. 'I have great fear that moral values are disappearing,' he says. 'Many young people are only after money – the mentality is changing.' And while the government talks about pursuing 'socialism with Chinese characteristics', the bishop fears that the nation is now overly influenced by what is, he feels, 'basically an American characteristic – Americanism, consumerism'. The half a dozen huge shopping centres clustered around a single intersection just a couple of minutes' walk from his residence may perhaps have influenced his thinking. 'American culture has a bad side,' he continues. 'It's worrying to me.' But the bishop also believes that some people are reacting against this type of spiritual void. 'Yes,' he says, 'there are more and more people coming to church. Some young people are still very sincere and search for the truth, and when they can't find it elsewhere they come to us.'

The revival and growth of religion over the past two decades has been a striking counterpoint to the growing materialism of much of Chinese society – and this in spite of the virtual obliteration of religion during the Cultural Revolution. In those years all religious sites were closed down, some of them physically destroyed, and many monks, nuns and priests were sent for re-education. Yet from the early 1980s, religion began tentatively to emerge from the shadows. Buddhism, which had been intricately bound up with Chinese culture for over a thousand years, experienced perhaps the most visible revival, and the ochre walls of reopened temples could soon be seen in many cities. But Christianity, which had been first introduced by missionaries as early as the sixteenth century, and had spread rapidly in some parts of China during the nineteenth century, also began to revive, slowly at first in the 1980s, but faster in the 1990s. The activities of all China's five officially sanctioned religions – Buddhism, Taoism, Islam, Protestantism and Catholicism – remained under official control, under the supervision of China's State Administration for Religious Affairs; each had its own 'patriotic' organisation in charge of the day-to-day running of its affairs. But there was an upsurge too in 'unofficial' religions – including traditional folk beliefs, unofficial Muslim groups in China's north-west, and the 'underground' Christian church. Some of these Protestant and Evangelical Christian groups had links to foreign missionaries, who began returning to China in the 1980s, sometimes in the guise of English teachers, sometimes on trips from Hong Kong during which they distributed Bibles among the populace. Many of these groups espoused beliefs which did not fit well with the control of religion by the government. 'We pay allegiance to God, why do we need the government to tell us what to do?' as one underground Protestant pastor put it.[13]

The emergence of an underground Catholic church, meanwhile, had more complicated historical roots. After the communist revolution the Chinese government eventually began ordaining new Catholic bishops, without consulting the Vatican. This led to the Pope denouncing the communist regime, and ties between the two sides were broken off in 1958; from that time on, the Vatican maintained formal links only with the Catholic church in Nationalist-controlled Taiwan. China's official Catholic organisation, meanwhile, paid allegiance only to Beijing, not to Rome. But the Vatican also continued, effectively in secret, to appoint its own new bishops to the church in the mainland – leading to the creation of a parallel underground church, which met mainly in 'house churches' in private homes. Its members have over the years been faced with frequent harassment by the authorities. 'It was like guerrilla warfare,' as one member of the underground church once put it, describing how she and her fellow believers had moved their meetings from place to place to avoid detection. And the split in the Catholic movement also left a legacy of tension between believers on both sides.

It's something Bishop Jin in Shanghai knows all about. He grew up on the rural outskirts of Shanghai, in a family which, he says, had been Catholic for 'ten generations'. He was sent to a school run by French Jesuits, and entered the clergy in the 1940s. Even some seventy years later, the legacy of his education is evident in his fluent French and delicately French-accented English. After the turmoil of the Japanese occupation, Bishop Jin was sent to Rome, where he studied religious doctrine for two years in the late 1940s, returning to China just as the revolution erupted. For a few years the Catholic church tried to continue to operate normally; but eventually foreign priests were forced to leave the country, and the religion was placed under the control of the official Catholic Patriotic Association. Later, during the Cultural Revolution, churches and other religious buildings were closed down, and turned into warehouses or factories. Many Christians were subjected to re-education, their leaders to imprisonment or persecution. Aloysius Jin was no exception, spending some two and a half decades in jail. But despite all he had suffered, on his release in the early 1980s he agreed to work with the official government-backed Catholic movement, which was just starting to reopen churches around the country. It was not an easy decision, he says, and he acknowledges that it caused anger among many of his former colleagues who refused to follow the official line, and were given even longer punishments as a result – like Joseph Fan, the bishop of the 'underground' Catholic church in Shanghai, who has remained under effective house arrest since his release from jail in the 1980s.[14]

'Many accused me of being a traitor, of compromising,' says Bishop Jin. But he insists that he, and others like him, did what they did in order to improve the chances of the church's survival in China. 'There are just half a dozen old priests like me left in Shanghai now,' he says. 'Ten years ago people were still saying you shouldn't open seminaries or publish books, they said the government wouldn't last long – they told me "wait, wait, for the fall of communism". But I said it will exist for a long time. If I'd listened to their advice there would only be six old priests left in Shanghai now – and the Shanghai diocese would be finished.' And so he pursued what he depicts as a pragmatic approach. 'What we want is not politics, it's evangelisation,' he says. 'If they give us the freedom, even a limited freedom, to evangelise, then we should be on good terms with the government.'

One of the most concrete symbols to which Bishop Jin can point as a justification of his strategy can be found on a hill outside Shanghai – the site of the old Jesuit church and observatory at Sheshan. Here, on a warm day in early summer, ageing believers genuflect in front of the shrine to Joseph in the woods at the foot of the hill; a little further on, an old woman crosses herself, praying in a whisper, as she kneels on the steps before a statue of the Sacred Heart. On the winding path leading up through the trees, families picnic in front of the Stations of the Cross, before continuing their climb to the top, where the tall red-brick basilica looms high above the surrounding countryside. Some are just here for a day out, but others are fervent believers – and their numbers swell each May when pilgrims from across China come to pray at the shrine to the Virgin Mary for which Sheshan is famed. But it's a busy place all year round: Sheshan is also home to the Shanghai Catholic Diocese's seminary, its religious training college, which was reopened by Bishop Jin in the 1980s. One of the four major Catholic centres in China, it had, by the middle of this decade, trained some 350 priests, who are now working all over the country. In Shanghai alone, says Bishop Jin, there are now more than sixty priests – most of them trained here too – and some 120 Catholic churches, many situated in the rural areas around the city where the early missionaries were busiest. It's still a far cry from the old days, before the communist revolution, when the city and its surroundings had some three hundred churches – but it marks a significant revival nonetheless. And compared to the 1980s, when most of those attending services in China's churches were elderly believers who had kept the faith since pre-revolutionary times, these days many of the faithful are much younger.

And for all the bitterness of the original split between the official and unofficial Catholic churches in China, the lines between them have in recent years become increasingly blurred. Official priests say that they still pray for the Pope, books about whom can be found in their church shops; some priests from the official church have themselves travelled to the Vatican and taken part in services presided over by the Pope. And while harassment of the underground church continues sporadically, some clergy from the two sides have remained in contact, despite past differences of opinion. In the last few years there have even been a few occasions where, in defiance of the authorities, priests from both sides of the church have jointly presided over services, particularly funeral ceremonies for old colleagues. Rome too has shown signs of seeking to heal the rift, giving its seal of approval to many of the new priests and bishops of the official church who have been ordained in recent years to replace those of Bishop Jin's generation. Some 'patriotic' bishops have even sought approval from Rome for new appointments of priests and bishops, before submitting them to Beijing.[15] According to one official priest, this is popular with believers who now 'prefer to have a bishop nominated by the Pope'. This, he suggests, is a reflection of the fact that ordinary Catholics these days 'tend to be better informed', and less willing to accept clergy ordained only by Beijing. By the middle of this decade, the Chinese government did appear to be turning a blind eye to the practice, perhaps hoping that this would at least help to reduce the appeal of the underground church, and might encourage the Vatican finally to break diplomatic relations with Taiwan. But major obstacles remained too, not least Rome's insistence on complete religious freedom for the church to operate, without interference from the bureaucrats of the official patriotic association. And Beijing has continued to irritate the Vatican by further occasional appointments of new clergy who have not received approval from the Pope. But Bishop Jin, who is in favour of members of the official church seeking the Pope's blessing, believes that despite the difficulties, there will one day be 'no split, only unity' between China's Catholics.

For the ordinary people who have joined China's churches in recent years, which side of the official/unofficial divide they stand on often seems to make little difference to how seriously they take their faith. Jennifer Chen turned to Christianity in her mid-twenties. A university graduate with a good job in a foreign company, she seemed, on the surface, like a typical successful member of the new urban middle class, spending her spare time meeting friends in cafés or going to karaoke bars. But she felt a sense of confusion about what she wanted from life. 'I often told myself, I want money, I want a really good life,' she recalls. It was, she points out, an understandable reaction to the practical problems of life in an increasingly expensive society. 'For example, I live far out of town, so I have to spend a lot of time every day travelling to work; if I had more money I could live downtown and my life would be a lot easier,' she says. 'And I'm an only child, and my parents' pension isn't high, so I feel like they'll have to rely on me in the future too.' But she also knew that many around her were less well-off, and she began to feel concerned about how little attention many people seemed to pay to this or other social problems. 'I felt everyone was very selfish, with no sense of social responsibility,' she says now, adding, 'most rich people wouldn't think of giving money to the poor.' And so she began to question her own values. 'Sometimes I couldn't help thinking, is a lot of money what I really want? I felt like I was in the middle of nowhere; sometimes I felt very confused, very lost. The pressure seemed very great, and I couldn't see a way out. So I felt I needed a spiritual support, a guide.'

After a chance meeting with a Christian, she stumbled on what she was looking for. First she joined a Bible study group run by the official church, and quickly forged a bond with the other members. 'I felt I needed to have a sense of community, people to exchange feelings with,' she says. Within a year she was baptised. Of course it hasn't changed everything in her life, she acknowledges. 'It hasn't made all the practical problems go away,' she says with a smile, 'but at least now I have a way to reduce the pressure. If I feel really depressed I can go and pray or read the Bible.' There are also church meetings where members of the congregation talk about their emotions and experiences and sing together. Many of the others she meets there are also young people, mostly students, who have recently joined the church. 'Most of them say they felt their life was very confused, with no sense of direction,' she explains, 'and so they wanted to find a goal in life.'

Now, Jennifer says, one of the goals is to help others, including in the charitable activities organised by the church of which she is now a member. 'If you love God you have to start from the people around you,' she says, 'that's what the priest told us.' And she believes that these are values which Chinese society as a whole would do well to learn from. 'Most people have no particular faith, no fear of hell or anything like that,' she says, 'so they'll do anything for their own advantage – I think they need something to restrain them.' It's a problem which she feels has been exacerbated by the damage done to China's traditional beliefs – such as Buddhism, with its emphasis on good deeds and storing up virtue – during the decades of political movements. 'All this was cut off by the Cultural Revolution,' says Jennifer. 'There was a big gap. If we had kept these

404

aspects of traditional culture maybe things would be more harmonious today. But we cut them off for decades,' she adds, 'and then we opened the door to western things all at once, so it was easy for people to be led astray.'

There's no doubt that many share her desire to seek a new set of values. Protestantism has perhaps grown fastest of all religions in recent years – with 18 million believers, according to official figures, though the number is thought to be significantly higher if members of the underground church are included.[16] One of the main churches in Beijing, for example, relays services by loud-speaker into the courtyard outside to cope with the size of its congregation. And for some young people, particularly students, Christianity seems to have become quite fashionable in recent years, partly because of its status as a foreign import. In many cases, such interest is very superficial: Christmas, for example, has caught on with the young generation, but mainly as an opportunity to send cards or go out for dinner with friends; a smaller number of young people attend midnight Mass on Christmas Eve out of curiosity. For China's retail industry, meanwhile, it offers a new commercial opportunity: Christmas songs, greetings, trees and decorations have in recent years become almost as common in the department stores and shopping centres of major Chinese cities as they are in Hong Kong or most western countries. Knowledge of exactly what it's all about, however, often remains a little vague. In one Beijing hotel a few years ago I met the young manager in charge of organising the Christmas decorations – including women in Santa Claus costumes and an Alpine chalet with fake snow. I asked what Christmas meant to him. Well, he replied enthusiastically, as far as he knew Christmas was 'a festival to commemorate the death of Jesus, who died maybe a couple of hundred years ago'.

But however superficial and commercial, the sight of families carrying Christmas trees home through the streets, or giant inflatable Santas lolling on the roofs of Shenzhen department stores, still seems a long way from the tense atmosphere of the early 1990s, when students in some Chinese universities were officially warned not to celebrate Christmas in any way. The official media still does its best

405

to avoid any mention of the religious aspects of Christmas – nevertheless, in recent years its popularity as a festival has become such that some commentators have expressed concern that so many people are worshipping western customs at a time when traditional Chinese festivals are felt to be on the wane. And there's undoubtedly a more serious side to interest in Christianity too, with a growing popularity in intellectual circles. In an officially atheist society, it seems, faith for some may also be a kind of rebellion against the status quo. The spread of religion has certainly brought it into some unexpected places – I once met a young graduate who asked me with a worried look whether I thought there was any contradiction in his being a member of the Communist Party – and a Christian too.

Christianity, of course, still remains a minority belief among China's vast population, with 'only' tens of millions of faithful. Buddhism, on the other hand, is closer to the mainstream: it has at least a hundred million believers, and continues to grow. Temples have reopened and expanded, and new ones have been built, often with donations from overseas. The influx of money can sometimes make the atmosphere seem rather commercial, but on weekends and festival days the temples are often crowded with people – many of them young and praying fervently. Young women, for example, may make offerings to Guanyin, the Goddess of Mercy, who is linked to fertility; other believers attend religious lectures by revered masters. At one temple in Shanghai, on a quiet weekday afternoon, I met a young mother who was enquiring about religious lessons for her small son at the temple's education department. Outside in the courtyard, two middle-aged women laid down their shopping bags, lit up several sticks of incense each and began bowing energetically in front of a small shrine. In one of the temple's main halls, a young woman was walking slowly round the room, chanting prayers and reverentially rubbing the case of each of the various Buddhist statues with her hand as she went.

For the Chinese government, dealing with the rebirth of religion is a balancing act. Up to a point, there's a sense that the officially atheist Communist Party sees a certain benefit – or at least no great disadvantage – in organisations which promote good citizenship and moral standards, especially at a time of growing social fragmentation. As the head of China's State Administration for Religious Affairs, Ye Xiaowen, put it in 2006, 'Religious force is one of the important social forces from which China draws strength.'[17] (One of his deputies once proudly explained to me that China even had a number of Christian 'model workers' nowadays, including a Mr Wang, who he described as a famous designer of light bulbs.) And there's no doubt that religious organisations are once again quietly beginning to play something of a charitable role. The Catholic diocese in Shanghai, for example, runs several charitable homes for the elderly, as well as a computer training centre aimed at helping disabled people to improve their skills and find work. Buddhist organisations also play a social role. At one temple I visited in southern Fujian province, a display in the entrance featured photographs of elderly people who were so poor that they had had to work to support themselves when they were well into their eighties – but were now being looked after with donations from the temple and its congregation. Buddhists in Shanghai, meanwhile, have sponsored poor rural students at some of the city's universities, and provide aid to poor elderly and disabled people who live alone. Such developments are still on a relatively small scale, but they are a sign that whatever the official ideological reservations about allowing religion a wider role in society, the pressing nature of many social problems means that this is starting to happen anyway. In poor rural areas, too, a lack of funding and the urgent desire for development have encouraged some local governments to accept donations from Christian organisations.

Still, the official attitude to religion remains, to say the least, cautious. Representatives of China's official religions are among the delegates to the annual session of the National People's Congress and its advisory body, often appearing dressed in full religious regalia. But at the grass-roots level, many churches are only permitted to open their doors to the public at the specific times when they have a service or Mass, and do not seem to be encouraged to play the same round-the-clock community role which they fulfil in many other countries. Sermons in the official churches, meanwhile, include compulsory appeals for patriotism and prayers for the nation and its leaders. And there are tight controls on any kind of missionary work or public activities outside designated religious venues. A religious affairs official in Shanghai once explained the rationale to me: 'China has freedom of religious belief,' he said, 'so in churches or in your home you can promote whatever you like, and in religious places no one is allowed to promote atheism.' But at the same time, he added, China's 'guiding thought' remained atheism, which meant that 'in public we can only promote atheism, not religion'. This was necessary, he suggested, to prevent social tension. 'The majority of our population are still atheists, or tend towards atheism,' he said, 'so if you promote religion to a big audience in public this could create some ideological clashes and cause instability in society.'[18]

At the same time Chinese officials go to great lengths to dismiss the idea that there is any contradiction in the idea of an atheist state controlling religion. When I met Wang Zuo'an, then Deputy Director General of the State Administration for Religious Affairs, in 1999, he suggested that being an atheist made him a neutral 'honest broker' when it came to dealing with religious matters. 'If there's a dispute between Muslims and Christians, and I'm a believer in one of these religions, how can I resolve the dispute?' he asked. 'I could be biased. But we have no emotional attachment,' he stressed. 'We just follow the law.' This lack of emotional attachment, and perhaps the influence of traditional communist attitudes too, also seemed to inform his comments on the future of religion. 'We think the development and disappearance of religion is an objective process,' Mr Wang said. 'No one can change it . . . Religion will exist for a long time, we don't know until when, so the only way is to respect this.' It was hard to avoid the sense that he retained certain doubts as to whether society would always need religion. 'From the party's point of view,' Mr Wang added, when pressed further, 'if you want to defeat religion, you can't use power or administrative means, you have to rely on the level of social development, on raising people's social awareness, so this is a long-term process.'

Such comments are a reminder of the continuing ambivalence which religion inspires among some in officialdom. In some ways this applies to Christianity above all, since it has traditionally been seen by many in China as representing a foreign value system – indeed, in the past, as Wang Zuo'an noted, it was once widely referred to as a *yang jiao* – a 'foreign religion' – though he insisted these days were now over. But there's no doubt that Christianity is still sometimes seen as a vehicle for the political interests of foreign governments. Buddhism, on the other hand, generally seems to be seen as less political, and therefore less of a threat – indeed, the religious affairs official I once met in Shanghai told me that though he was an atheist, he had grown up listening to his grandmother's Buddhist stories. 'These gave me lots of ideas about aspirations and values,' he said. 'So there's no contradiction – our family's fine, we're all working together for its development. And the nation's the same,' he went on. 'You have your faith and I have mine, as long as these don't clash with the aims of the nation then we're all members of the same family.' The major exception to this happy family, of course, has been Buddhism in Tibet, where the exiled Dalai Lama is, according to Tibetan tradition, regarded as a god-king, which means the separation of religion and politics is far harder for the Chinese authorities to impose. Monks and nuns who have openly supported the Dalai Lama have been repeatedly jailed. And the young boy selected by the Dalai Lama as the reincarnation of the Panchen Lama – Tibetan Buddhism's second most important figure – was rejected by Beijing in 1995 and has been held at an undisclosed location ever since.[19] And in China's far north-western region of Xinjiang, which borders on central Asia and has a mainly Muslim population, Islam similarly became an object of heightened official suspicion in the 1990s, when a relatively small number of its followers took up armed resistance against the Chinese authorities, often with support from across the border in former Soviet Central Asia.[20]

The government therefore continues to tread a fine line, on the one hand not wishing to antagonise members of the official religions, but at the same time remaining anxious about the potential of religion – and indeed of any unauthorised spiritual movements – to rally challenges to its authority. In the years after the crackdown on Falun Gong in 1999, it launched a series of campaigns aimed at promoting 'scientific thinking' – which some saw as a code word for atheism – and at stamping out practices which it saw as reflecting 'superstitious beliefs'. The authorities even sought to limit celebrations of Qing Ming, China's traditional 'grave-sweeping festival', which takes place every April, when families go to pay their respects and make offerings at their ancestors' graves. Traditionally, relatives burned incense and sometimes 'temple money' (mock banknotes, believed to help the dead live more comfortably in the afterlife). But over the past decade such offerings have also been upgraded to reflect society's growing aspirations, and there have been reports of people burning paper models of gold bars and complete luxury villas, two metres high, equipped with paper stereos, televisions and, in some cases, domestic servants too.[21]

Stamping out such customs has not been easy, however – and the shops outside many temples continue to sell such paper products, even though they have technically been banned. And beliefs of all kinds have continued to surface over recent years – many of them linked to traditional Chinese folk rituals, and the diverse blend of Buddhist, Taoist and Confucian ideas in which many Chinese people have believed over the centuries. A few years ago, for example, members of the local Communist Party branch at a court in a small town in Hunan province were disciplined after they hired a Taoist priest to perform rituals in the court compound. Their aim had been to drive evil spirits out of the courthouse, after a member of staff died in an accident.[22] And in 2005, the authorities announced a ban on advertisements for fortune tellers, warning that they were peddling superstitious and pseudo-scientific ideas and could harm young people's minds. (Fortune tellers have grown in popularity in the past few years – indeed some are now available for consultation via the Internet.)[23]

But however many official edicts are announced, there's no doubt that some traditional Chinese ideas die hard. A superstitious belief in the power of numbers, for example, is deeply rooted in Chinese society. The number four is particularly inauspicious,

410

since it sounds like the word for death; fourteen is even worse, as it has echoes of the phrase 'going to die'. Eight and six, on the other hand, are considered lucky – because they sound similar to the words for 'getting rich' and 'happiness'. In recent years such superstitions seem to have become, to an extent, officially enshrined: China's state-run mobile phone company, for example, charges customers extra if they want a phone number containing lots of eights or sixes; numbers which include the sequences 14 or 44, on the other hand, are far cheaper. And foreigners checking into Chinese hotels are often given rooms with a number ending in 14, since such rooms are unpopular with Chinese guests. Similarly, some buildings simply do not have a fourteenth floor. Since the number thirteen is also considered unlucky by some in China these days, partly as a result of influence from Hong Kong, this can lead to some confusion: friends who moved from the twelfth to the fifteenth floor of the same apartment building in Shanghai were surprised to discover that they had only actually gone up one storey – since the thirteenth and fourteenth floors did not exist.

The government's attempts to stamp out superstition are not helped either by the fact that several historical movements founded on some rather unscientific beliefs have long been officially praised as patriotic and heroic. The museum at the site of the Communist Party's first meeting in Shanghai, for example, includes a display commemorating the Taiping rebels, a movement which fought against the Qing dynasty, and against foreign armies around Shanghai, in the second half of the nineteenth century. For the Communist Party, it's the Taiping's nationalistic opposition to the Manchu Qing emperor which is of greatest significance. What the official exhibits do not mention is that the rebellion was led by a Cantonese peasant who had been influenced by the teaching of Christian missionaries, and impressed his followers with his claim that he was actually the younger brother of Jesus Christ. The society which the Taipings set up in the city of Nanjing, which they controlled for more than a decade, was known as the 'Heavenly Kingdom'.[24] Members of the anti-foreign Boxer movement, meanwhile, which rose up against foreign occupation in 1900, claimed

411

mystical powers, such as the ability to stop the bullets of foreign soldiers' guns with their bare hands.

And for the Chinese authorities, maintaining a grip on religion has been made more challenging by the growing diversification of society. While the 'house churches' run by underground Christian organisations remain illegal, and still face sporadic crackdowns, in some parts of the country at least the attitude of the authorities seem to be that they will tolerate them provided they do not do anything too overtly provocative – and indeed in practice there are now so many such groups that it would probably be hard for the authorities to stamp them all out even if they wanted to. And public confidence in defying official control has also grown. In 2000, for example, the local government in the city of Wenzhou in Zhejiang province launched a crackdown on religious organisations it said were either unregistered or spreading superstition, and demolished a number of religious buildings which it described as illegal structures. But some locals did not seem scared by this show of strength. One business-man from the area began calling foreign media organisations, expressing his fury at the government's actions. 'How dare they do this?' he demanded to know. 'We've invested so much money in our temple, how can they just come along and demolish it?!'[25] His attitude seemed to reflect the local mentality: the countryside of that part of southern Zhejiang is dotted with massive churches towering over small villages, the huge red crosses atop their spires visible from many miles away across the fields. Some have been built with donations from wealthy locals, some are affiliated to official Christian organisations, others apparently not. And even in poorer rural regions of China, local people – such as ethnic minority groups in south-western Yunnan province, for example – sometimes also simply go ahead and build their own churches without any reference to the government.

The Communist Party has in recent years shown a growing aware-ness that it needs to respond to the increasing diversification of society, and of belief – and to the damage done to its credibility by corruption and greater social inequality. And so it has taken a series of measures aimed both at recapturing the moral high ground and improving its standing in the eyes of the public, and at strengthening its ability to maintain a grip on a fast-changing society.

Attempts to improve the 'health' of the Communist Party itself have ranged from renewed promises to take a tougher line on corruption – which claimed some prominent victims in 2006 – to improving the party's capacity in terms of management and organisation.[26] In 2005, for example, the party required all members to take part in study sessions aimed at making it a more 'advanced' organisation; and it also set up three new training schools for senior officials and party members. Their locations were highly symbolic: two of the schools were designed to provide reminders of the party's revolutionary past – they were located at either end of the route of the famous 'Long March', the journey of several thousand miles made by the communist army in the mid-1930s, which enabled it to escape Nationalist annihilation and regroup for its eventual push for power – a story which has long been mythologised as proof of the party's courage and self-sacrifice. The third college, on the other hand, was apparently intended to emphasise the party's links with the modern world – it was given the impressive-sounding name of the China Executive Leadership Academy and was located in Shanghai's Pudong New Area, the laboratory for many of China's experiments with economic reform in recent years. Its campus seemed to have been designed as a symbol of everything that was modern about China: golf buggies ferried visiting journalists through the carefully manicured grounds, tastefully decorated with bamboo groves, to a complex of brightly coloured modernist buildings. The spacious libraries and lecture rooms seemed to have been modelled on those of top business schools at universities in western countries. And the staff of the academy were keen to stress that they were promoting new ideas among the party bureaucrats and local government leaders who were sent here for training. 'All our lecturers are under thirty-five,' said one staff member proudly. And he emphasised that the courses taught included not just the workings of the global economy, but also training in crisis management – local leaders, he explained, had to take part

413

in role-playing exercises, where they were forced to deal with, for example, challenging questions from the media in the event of accidents or disasters.

It was part of an official strategy to make the leadership appear more responsive to public concerns. And the Communist Party has also taken some steps to get its message across to a young generation with very different interests and attitudes: these include not just measures such as employing people to respond to criticisms of the government in Internet forums and chat rooms, but also attempts to capture young people's imagination by developing fashionable-looking 'manga'-style cartoon books and animated films based on revolutionary stories – including the Long March itself. Even Lei Feng, the young soldier of the 1960s who was for decades used in propaganda campaigns to promote a self-sacrificing spirit (he died in an accident after a life apparently dedicated to helping others and praising Chairman Mao), has recently been reinvented as a trendy, Che Guevara-style fashion icon – his image appearing on T-shirts and in a recent book which included pop-art-style paintings and compared his status as an icon to that of Marilyn Monroe, who died in the same year. To the young generation, the book acknowledged, Lei Feng might seem 'mysterious and remote', but it suggested that in fact, 'everyone is looking for their own Lei Feng' – and 'the nation is looking for its own Lei Feng too'.[27]

In 2006, there were also reports that the party was planning to pour millions of pounds into a renewed campaign to promote the study of Marxism, in order to update it for a changed society.[28] And in practical terms, many of the policies announced by the authorities in recent years have been aimed at rebuilding public faith in the system, not least by addressing some of the roots of popular dissatisfaction. The campaign to create a 'harmonious society', launched in 2005, seemed specifically designed to reassure the public that social inequality was being tackled. The announcements of pledges to bring fully free education to rural children, to reintroduce rural health insurance, to establish basic welfare insurance schemes for migrant workers in the cities, and solve the problem of education for their children, reinforced the message. The leadership now frequently refers to the aim of creating a *xiaokang* society, one which is 'reasonably well-off' and in which all can share. It's a phrase initially popularised back in the 1980s, and its use seems designed to give hope to those who feel they have missed out on the benefits of reform.

The Communist Party has also set about trying to fill what many see as the moral void left by the shattering of so many of the old certainties. In 2006, it launched a campaign to promote what was described as 'the socialist concept of honour and shame'. The campaign included what appeared to be a new moral code – a kind of socialist Ten Commandments known as the 'eight honours and the eight shames' (*ba rong ba chi*). It's been prominently displayed on billboards and neighbourhood noticeboards around the country, on trains, at stations and in other public places. Its advice includes 'honour to those who love the motherland and shame on those who do harm to her; honour to those who are hard-working, and shame on the indolent; honour to those who are united and help each other, and shame on those who gain at the expense of others; honour to those who are honest, and shame on those who forget righteousness for the sake of their own advantage; honour to those who practise frugality and perseverance, and shame on those who wallow in extravagance and pleasure'. These prescripts have been described by official media as 'a perfect amalgamation of traditional values and modern virtues'.[29]

Some have seen the promotion of this new 'moral code', along with the call for a harmonious society, as a sign that China's leadership is dabbling with the idea of reviving some of the ideas of Confucianism – once the dominant traditional teaching in China, which stresses righteousness, humility, manners and rituals – in its attempts to find a new unifying ideology. It is certainly an idea which appeals to some; a number of private schools offering an education in the Confucian classics (some even featuring traditional Confucian scholars' costumes) have opened in several Chinese cities (though some have subsequently been closed for operating without a licence). And a mere three decades after the end of the Cultural Revolution, when China was swept up in a nationwide campaign to denounce Confucianism, senior officials can now be found inaugurating Confucius Institutes – officially backed centres for the study of Chinese culture – in major cities around the world.[30]

But many people wonder whether, in such a changed society, it's still possible for the Communist Party to revive either the idealism of its early years, or the rigid, upright values of Confucianism. Some feel the party will simply have to get used to tolerating a growing range of different beliefs. For all the new emphasis on morality, the official list of 'eight shames' is, for some, simply a reminder of problems which have become widespread in contemporary China, problems which many associate in particular with those in positions of power. (The depth of official worries about corruption was highlighted in 2005 by reports that primary schools in one Chinese city had introduced an anti-corruption textbook, which was intended to teach pupils how to prevent their parents from becoming corrupt.)[31]

And some people believe that such propaganda campaigns can have only a limited impact in a more pluralistic society. 'The problem is that whatever the government says, most people just get on with their jobs and don't pay attention,' says one intellectual, who adds, 'even I myself don't even really know what all these eight things are . . . So it's not a question of coming up with a slogan which everyone will forget in three months – these kinds of things have to be really implemented, they have to become a part of daily life; only then will people feel that these are values we can hang on to and follow.' Some have suggested too that the authorities will need to go further to unravel some of the policies which have created an increasingly divided society, if they are to make such moral codes a reality. As one academic puts it, 'You need basic social justice to have a foundation for morality – if you don't have this you can't expect the people to have such a morality.'

It seems the battle for people's hearts and minds may involve striking a balance between maintaining the rapid economic growth which has brought hope to many in China over the past two decades, and, at the same time, mediating some of the more drastic side effects of that development, which have brought struggle and disillusionment to others.

# Epilogue

If you want to see something of the state of modern China, the Huaihai Road is not a bad place to start. The main street of Shanghai's former French concession – and still, to many, the heart of the city – it stretches from the poorer neighbourhoods on the edge of the old Chinese town, through the new downtown business district and one of Shanghai's most fashionable shopping areas, before heading off towards the quieter pavements of some of the city's most exclusive residential quarters. All of modern China is here: I walked it on a winter's day, just as they were hanging up the red lanterns and gold New Year's greetings outside the latest Hong Kong-owned shopping centre. Further along, a brass band, half a dozen men in red jackets and white trousers, were sat out on little chairs on the pavement, playing jaunty tunes to celebrate the launch of a sale in a luxury brands mall. In the window of a nearby sushi restaurant, businessmen in pin-striped suits were chatting over lunch. At the Cybermart, where you can buy the most up-to-date computers, digital cameras and other electronic paraphernalia, hip sales guys with spiky hair and baggy jeans played nonchalantly on their PSPs and X-boxes as they waited for customers.

But taking a walk along the Huaihai Road was for me not only about catching a glimpse of the latest trends; it was also, in a sense, going back to the past, since this is the part of Shanghai where I lived, and spent a lot of time, when I first moved to the city in 2000. Not that that's very long ago, of course . . . Or is it? Strolling down the busy street on this crisp, sunny afternoon, I had the growing feeling that we had already moved into another era. It wasn't just the renovated frontages of many of the old shops, or the new office

417

towers which had appeared in several places, nor indeed the half-dozen city blocks and street corners which had vanished in the past few years; these included one very modern shopping plaza, and a row of shops which was now in the process of being demolished for the second time since I moved to Shanghai. The shops themselves had changed in nature too. The rows of local chains and government owned stores were now giving way to the big foreign brands: Adidas, Swatch, Sephora, Swarovski Crystal. The old state-run food shop where the sales assistants, most of them laid-off former factory workers, would give me a cheery greeting when I bought my bread and milk, and invariably ask my opinion on pressing international questions such as why so many British cows were going mad, was now long gone. I had watched the staff's white overalls grow progressively greyer and their mood ever glummer, until finally it closed down, to be replaced by a luxury furniture store.

Along the road, the old Cathay Cinema, an art deco relic of the 1930s, where five years ago you could still sit in the original grand auditorium – though it was a bit chilly and the seats were rickety – had been divided up into a modern multiplex, and part of the lobby had been taken over by a fashionable hair salon. The cash machine outside now belonged to a foreign bank. On the news-stand on the nearby street corner the local publications now had to vie for space with ranks of glossy Japanese and Taiwanese magazines, imported legally or otherwise, their headlines sprinkled with English phrases: 'Bling', 'Sex Bible.' A couple of trendy girls and a young man with orange hair gave them a cursory glance as they walked past.

The pace of change in urban China certainly remains spectacular. I know that from the two twenty-storey high-rises which have appeared on the skyline outside my window over the past half year. Not everyone is happy about the ongoing transformation – one academic I met, a specialist in architecture and urban planning, said he finds the experience of living in a Chinese city so exhausting that he has to go abroad for at least a month every year to recover, usually to Europe, where, as he put it, the pace of life is so much slower. But the degree to which this state of continuous change has permeated many people's mentality is brought home to me whenever I tell someone that the first time I came to China was in the 1980s. Often, they react with a surprised look and say something like, 'Really, so *early*?' Or as one man in Guangzhou put it: '1986? That's when China was just starting out'. In one of the world's most ancient civilisations, such comments can seem faintly absurd – but they're a reminder of just how far many people see their lives, and the society in which they live, as defined by the time-scale of China's reform era since the late 1970s, and a reminder too of just how much has changed in the interim.

One of the more revealing sets of books published in China in recent years is a series of four small volumes, combining whimsical drawings and short texts, focusing on aspects of life which, as the title of the set puts it, 'are in the process of disappearing'. The subjects covered include 'objects', 'phrases', 'professions' and 'crafts', and make it clear just how much of the detail of the fabric of everyday life in China has been utterly transformed – and in some cases totally erased – since the 1980s. The vanished phrases range from old slogans of the Cultural Revolution years – 'down with', 'imperialist running dog', 'barefoot doctor' – to those of the optimistic days of the early reform era: *wan yuan hu*, a 'ten-thousand-yuan family', a description which implied great financial success for farmers in the early 1980s, but which, as the book puts it, now sounds 'very poor'. From a little later in the reform period there's *xia hai*, 'jumping into the sea', a phrase heard constantly at the turn of the 1990s, which described the process of leaving one's state job and going into business – in the days when this was still seen as a bold plunge into the unknown. The disappearing objects, meanwhile, include the abacus (still common in the late 1980s), aluminium lunch boxes (ditto) and steam trains (in use in some parts of China until the 1990s). But it was the inclusion of the fax machine as one of these doomed objects which really struck me: with the onset of the 'e-era', the authors suggest, 'its days will surely soon be numbered.'[1] This is a gadget which would have seemed like an extraordinary modern convenience in China just fifteen years ago

419

– now it has already been deemed obsolete. It's an indication of how fast the nation is moving to embrace new technology, and also of a mindset that expects things to be constantly replaced and upgraded. It's visible everywhere: when I first came to China in the 1980s, most ordinary people were only just starting to buy their own fridges, and many were still dreaming of owning a colour TV set. Even in 1997, when I moved to Beijing, barely more than a million people in the country were said to own a computer. Now, in the lane where I live in Shanghai, I often wake up to the cries of the junk collectors wandering through the neighbourhood, calling out for 'unwanted fridges, colour TVs, old computers'.

For many Chinese people, these years of change have meant a rapid improvement in their material living conditions. Average living space for urban residents has increased, life expectancy has improved and for many, of course, income has grown significantly too. Back on the Huaihai Road, I watched a young woman nosing her new red Mini Cooper into a gap in the traffic, among the Land Rovers and Buicks. On the pavement, outside a big department store, young well-dressed couples giggled as they tried new perfumes at a Calvin Klein promotional stall. Inside, a crowd of smart young women listened earnestly to a lecture about the advantages of a popular Japanese brand of cosmetics. Next door, in the 24-hour McDonald's, a pair of well-fed businessmen in their late thirties seemed to be trying to impress a couple of heavily made-up young women with talk of a trip to Thailand; on the table opposite, a teenage girl with a pierced lip and plucked eyebrows, wearing a tartan jacket and tie, was texting furiously on her mobile phone.

Such people now have far more opportunities, and often a greater confidence in their own individuality. More generally, this also often translates into a sense of a greater confidence in their nation and its place in the world. I was reminded of this when I looked into another fast food restaurant further down the Huaihai Road. KFC was the earliest of the foreign chains to move into China. When its first outlet opened in Beijing in 1988, it provoked near hysteria, with people queuing around the block, desperate for a taste of the western dream. Its expansion since then has been spectacular: now the company has more than a thousand restaurants in China, and counting. So I was a little surprised to be handed a leaflet explaining that its Chinese outlets were planning to abandon what was described as 'the traditional foreign fast-food model', and were instead going to be 'changing for China'. Years of research, the leaflet announced, had revealed that western fast food was 'limited in choice', 'focused on deep-fried products', 'didn't include many vegetables' and 'encouraged people to eat a lot', while its products often 'didn't change for years'. In the light of these startling discoveries, the company was therefore planning to introduce a 'new type of fast food', which it said would be more suited to Chinese tastes. This was all, of course, perhaps just a good example of a localised marketing strategy. But there was still something slightly bizarre about one of the giants of the US fast-food industry seemingly criticising its own past, in an apparent attempt to retain the loyalties of Chinese consumers – and it was a reminder too that those consumers were now increasingly selective and well-informed, and even the biggest foreign brands could no longer take them for granted.

But the process has not been without pain. Further along the Huaihai Road a middle-aged man from Beijing was sitting on the pavement in front of a modern office tower, with a young boy in his arms and a hand-written plea in front of him, explaining how his restaurant had failed and he needed money to pay for his son to be treated for pneumonia. At the traffic lights not far away a woman dressed in rural clothes led a little girl among the cars shaking an empty plastic cup at their windows when they stopped. On the pavement a raggedly dressed old man dodged through the crowds, a few old plastic bags of belongings slung over his shoulder on a bamboo carrying pole. A sweet-potato seller from the rural suburbs stood on the corner of the street, offering his hot earthy wares for a yuan a piece. A young woman who looked like she had recently arrived from the countryside pulled a map out of a plastic bag and checked the way to her destination; at the entrance to a nearby lane, an old man, wrapped up in padded clothes against the cold, leant on a pair of home-made crutches and watched the world go by.

China's divisions are obvious, even on the most upmarket street of the country's wealthiest city. Again, it's a significant transformation from the 1980s. Back then, the sharpest divide was between Chinese people – most of whom, in the cities at least, were on roughly the same income level – and the rich visitors from abroad who were just starting to arrive in significant numbers. Such was official nervousness about the opening up to foreign tourism in those days that ordinary Chinese citizens were forbidden from entering most of the country's newly-built tourist hotels. This led to surreal scenes where crowds of (often well-educated) Chinese people would congregate outside the fences of such establishments, peering through the railings in an attempt to catch a glimpse of the luxuries from which they were excluded, while even the most slovenly foreign tourist could stroll in without anyone complaining. These days things are different: Chinese citizens are now only too welcome to visit the luxury shopping and leisure complexes lining Shanghai's waterfront, the Bund, for example – but only if they look prosperous enough; the smartly liveried doormen discreetly keep out any scruffy looking out-of-town tourists and less well-heeled locals who might try to wander inside.

In a sense, these divisions are the side-effects of Deng Xiaoping's pronouncement that some of the people should be allowed to get rich first. What he actually said – in one of the officially quoted versions of the saying at least – was that 'some regions and some people may get rich first, in order to bring along and help other places and other people, and to gradually achieve a common prosperity.'[2] But as many commentators have pointed out, it's become increasingly clear that, for many years, there has been rather more focus on the first part of the phrase, and somewhat less emphasis on its conclusion[3] – and indeed, that China as a whole can be seen as having put the overall goal of getting richer as a nation first, without spending too much time worrying about some of the problems resulting from such development. This is visible in the damage to the environment caused by rapid urbanisation and industrialisation, in the jettisoning of so much of the country's architectural heritage, and the break-up of traditional communities.

And many individuals feel that they too have paid a price – in the loss of the old socialist guarantees and the increased responsibility for their own welfare which has resulted. It's become a source of growing popular concern, and not only for the urban poor, or the rural masses who, until recently at least, were largely neglected: it was apparently with the new urban middle classes in mind that the headline of one article in an official newspaper recently asked: 'as we get wealthier do we get happier?' The answer, according to one survey, was 'no', at least for close to a third of those questioned. Such people's concerns, the article noted, 'include but are not limited to: rising housing prices, a tight and unstable job market, [and] back-breaking schooling expenses and medical bills.'[4] By early 2007, one official study by the Chinese Academy of Social Sciences in Beijing was warning of growing 'social panic' among ordinary people at the stratospheric rises in the price of property in the capital.[5]

The authorities have more recently begun taking steps to tackle some of these issues, with a series of measures aimed at cooling the housing market, and equally significantly, a range of policies aimed at alleviating the burdens of the country's farmers. But there's a long way to go. And overall, in the past couple of years, there have been signs of a growing debate within China's leadership about the direction of the country's development – in effect, about whether it's time to retreat from the rush to 'get rich first' and focus on the creation of that 'common prosperity' which Deng Xiaoping originally spoke of. This has been reflected in attempts to rein in economic growth, apparently in order to concentrate on addressing pressing social problems. Even Shanghai, symbol of breakneck expansion, set a reduced growth target in 2007 of around 9 per cent, after fifteen consecutive years when its annual GDP growth was in double figures.[6] It's a difficult balance to strike – to some extent the wealth needed to tackle China's problems is the result of the same forces which have created many of those problems. Still, these moves reflect growing official awareness of public anger at some of the more extreme results of the development of the last decade and a half – not least the phenomenon of official corruption, which

423

many see as a by-product of the 'getting rich first' mentality. Indeed some see this as just the tip of the iceberg, a reflection of the way in which the changes in society have eroded the country's moral fabric. 'Relationships between people in cities are all about money these days,' said one disillusioned intellectual, one of the generation in their mid-forties to mid-fifties who tend to be among the most cynical about what's going on. 'It's all about profit and advantage, using each other.'

Not everyone feels so strongly, but awareness of popular disillusionment at some of the ways in which society has changed in recent years is undoubtedly spurring the authorities to seek ways of shoring up public confidence and ideological values. As I walked along the Huaihai Road, a woman called out to me from the entrance to an old lane. 'Free ticket to visit the Museum of the Former Site of the Socialist Youth League, sir?' she cried. It was an offer I couldn't refuse. And so I found myself gazing at black-and-white pictures of the long-lost revolutionaries who had helped organise left-wing activism from this old house in the French concession during the 1920s. But the museum was bigger than it looked from outside: several old houses had been knocked together, to create a separate large exhibition space upstairs, which was devoted to the role of youth in contemporary society. At its entrance hung a row of pictures of several generations of Communist Party leaders photographed with groups of smiling young people. An elderly couple were looking at the display with their small grandson, who couldn't have been more than three years old. 'This is Mao Zedong,' said the grandmother, 'remember we showed you his picture before?' 'And this is Deng Xiaoping,' added the old man, gesturing at another photo, 'and that one is Jiang Zemin.' The little boy seemed unimpressed: 'I don't want to look at these, I want to go and play,' he said.

I wandered into the next room, which was called the 'youth models section'. It was designed, according to the sign by the door, to inspire young visitors to become a 'useful person in building China into an all-round well-off society.' Just inside was a display of pictures of young people who had died in the service of the nation, all of them in the 1950s or early 1960s, before the Cultural Revolution. There were model factory workers and military heroes, including the famous martyred soldier, Lei Feng. The black-and-white images sent a clear message, an attempt to inspire today's youth by appealing to more innocent, idealistic times. Round the corner some of those youth were gathered, a group of fifteen-year-old high-school students in baggy school tracksuits, watching a video about more recent Chinese heroes. This featured some impressive technology – several young people had been super-imposed, three-dimensionally, on a small stage in front of the main screen, apparently asking questions of Yang Liwei, the astronaut who took part in China's first manned space flight in 2003. 'Wow,' they swooned, as pictures of the earth viewed from space appeared on the big screen. 'These are pictures which we Chinese people took ourselves!' Next up was Yao Ming, the seven foot six inch Chinese basketball player who has been such a success since moving to the US to play in the NBA in 2002. After the film finished, one of the museum's guides got up and addressed the teenage audience: Yao Ming was someone China could be proud of she said, an ideal role model, because, although he had gone to America, 'he has never worshipped foreign things'. She repeated this phrase several times, increasingly enthusiastically: he hadn't tried to become an American citizen, she added, and always made sure that he came back to China to do things for the nation.

I left the museum – an officially approved Red Tourism site, according to a sign on the wall outside – and walked back out onto the Huaihai Road. Just round the corner, a jeweller's shop was selling gold figurines of the God of Wealth; across the road was a Rolex store where many of the watches in the window retailed for some four to eight thousand pounds each. A little further down the street, on an electronic billboard, Yao Ming appeared again, this time in more commercial mode, advertising a mobile phone network. This was followed by an advertisement for a financial services company, which boasted that it had already helped a million people to 'get rich'. Nearby, in the courtyard of an old mansion set back from the road, a crowd of make-up artists and stylists were swarming round a bare-chested male model, in what seemed to be a fashion shoot for Levi's jeans. There were some reminders of the Communist Party's appeals for people to show more public spiritedness too: a billboard encouraged people to be 'loveable citizens' and abide by the traffic regulations; another called on them to do voluntary work; outside one department store the local branch of the Red Cross had parked its mobile blood donation van, and was asking people to give blood 'without reward'. They weren't so busy today, said the man sitting at a little table outside, but they still had a steady number of donors.

In such an increasingly diverse society, maintaining ideological values is undoubtedly a growing challenge for the authorities. There's no doubt that, for all the collapse of many of the old social structures over the past two decades, some elements of social cohesion – particularly in terms of the family system – remain generally stronger in China than in many western societies. The nation does now also seem to be witnessing the emergence of what are, potentially at least, some of the trappings of a new civil society – whether in the efforts of its media to write about real issues, or in the willingness of more ordinary citizens to organise their own groups and associations. Nevertheless, the limits which the authorities continue to impose on these sectors still prevent their full development. And some people remain convinced that, for all the urgency of dealing with many of the problems of the present day, China will not be a society truly at ease with itself until it has faced up more fully to some of the excesses of its recent history: I have been struck, in talking to people for this book, by just how many have referred to the continuing damage done to the nation and its society by the Cultural Revolution and its after-effects. To many such people, it seems, the events of Tiananmen Square in 1989 are of secondary importance – though others believe these will one day have to be reappraised too.

There is little doubt that some of China's leaders have a sense that they will have to take some new steps in the years to come – though the focus of these, as usual, seems likely to remain economic rather than political. In late 2006, many Chinese people were glued to their television screens watching a TV series called 'The Rise of the Great Nations'. Apparently commissioned by President Hu Jintao himself, it looked at how nine countries around the world had become economic powers over the centuries, and was widely praised for analysing their success without resorting to traditional ideological rhetoric.[7] In the episode on the UK, for example, British academics were filmed talking dispassionately about the factors which gave rise to the expansion of the British Empire in the nineteenth century, without any particular criticism of such imperialist tendencies.

China's leaders are clearly still looking for models which can enable them to maintain development – and their grip on power too. Some believe that they are trying to achieve the impossible – both in their attempts to combine one party rule with an ever freer economy, and in embracing the information technology revolution while seeking to maintain controls on the flow of information. So far the leadership has been helped by the fact that economic development has been fast enough to keep many people believing in the dream of 'getting rich first' – the sense that many in China, however poor they may be themselves, remain motivated by aspiration and the hope of emulating those who have done well, rather than reacting with jealousy or bitterness. Maintaining this belief will be a challenge: the nation is rich in dynamism – as I was reminded by the two-year-old girl from a small town I met recently, who could respond in rapid-fire English to every Chinese word her mother asked her to translate – but, as has been described in some of the preceding chapters, it's rich in problems too. How these problems are dealt with may colour how we look back at China's development since the 1980s, particularly since the speeding up of economic and social reforms in the early 1990s: whether the era of 'getting rich first', and all the side-effects and difficulties it has brought with it, comes to be seen as an often painful but ultimately necessary stepping stone on the road to creating a more prosperous and less divided society – or whether the price paid will be deemed to have been too high.

427

# Notes

Abbreviations:

CD      *China Daily* (Official English-language paper),
www.chinadaily.com.cn

CRI     China Radio International, (Beiing's official international
broadcaster), english.cri.com

PD      *People's Daily* (Official Chinese-language paper, with
Chinese and English websites), www.people.com.cn,
english.peopledaily.com.cn

SD      *Shanghai Daily* (Official English language local paper),
www.shanghaidaily.com

SCMP   *South China Morning Post* (Hong Kong's main English-
language newspaper), www.scmp.com

Xinhua   Xinhua (New China) News Agency (China's official news
agency, with bilingual website), www.xinhuanet.com

## 1: Cities in motion

1. Lin Yutang, *My Country and My People*, The John Day Company,
New York, 1935, p. 315.
2. Wang Bin, 'Brick Pagoda Hutong: the root of Beijing's hutongs', in
*Beijing City Planning and Construction Review*, 2005, no. 4.
3. Mao Qizhi, 'Review and suggestions on the hutongs and courtyards
of Old Beijing', ibid.; Nancy Pellegrini, 'Past imperfect', *Time Out
Beijing*, October 2005.
4. Gu Xiaoyang, 'Hutong: The Lane' (tr. Duncan Hewitt), in Henry
Zhao and John Caley (eds.), *Under Sky Under Ground: Chinese
Writing Today*, Wellsweep, London, 1994, p. 150.
5. See e.g. Ewen MacAskill, 'Amnesty accuses China of breaking
Olympic promises', *Guardian*, 21 September 2006.
6. Ma Zhefei, 'Will the world's tallest building be built in Beijing?',

*Southern Weekend* (*Nanfang Zhoumo*), Guangzhou, 24 May 2001.

7. The website is www.oldbeijing.net; see also 'Resident builds virtual museum about old city', *CD*, 15 December 2006; You Nuo, 'Don't turn blind eye to hutong', *CD*, 27 November 2006.

8. Julia Colman (ed.), *Critical Mass*, China Contemporary, London, 2004; Melinda Liu, 'A Great Leap Backward', *Newsweek*, 17 January 2000.

9. Gero von Boehm, *Conversations with I.M. Pei: Light is the Key*, Prestel, Munich, London, New York, 2000, p. 19.

10. Louisa Lim, 'China tourist town's culture clash', BBC News, 28 June 2004.

11: See Jonathan Spence, *The Gate of Heavenly Peace*, Penguin, London, 1982, pp. 271–4.

12. Yang Lian, 'Foreword' (tr. Duncan Hewitt) in Mark Leong, *China Obscura*, Chronicle Books, San Francisco, 2004 (author's revised translation).

**2: Shanghai between old and new**

1. See Barbara Baker (ed.), *Shanghai: Electric and Lurid City*, Oxford University Press, Hong Kong, pp 83–5.

2. J.G. Ballard, 'Look back at Empire', *Guardian*, 4 March 2006.

3. Pan Guang, *The Jews in Shanghai*, Shanghai Pictorial Publishing House, 1995, p. 59.

4. Gero von Boehm, *Conversations with I.M. Pei*, op. cit., p. 22.

5. Liu Xiaokang, 'Dwellings slated for demolition', *SD*, 18 December 2000; some twenty million square metres of old buildings were demolished in the 1990s, according to the Shanghai Construction Commission, author interview, 2001.

6. See e.g. Xing Bao, 'The long goodbye', *Shanghai Star*, 23–29 January 2003.

7. Ibid; see also 'Construction builds up', *Shanghai Star*, 23–29 January 2003.

8. 'Relocation company starts fire and burns elderly couple to death – all suspects punished', Xinhua, 9 October 2005.

9. '"Shanghai's richest man": the life of Zhou Zhengyi', *Shanghai Morning Post* (*Xinwen Chenbao*), 26 October 2006.

10. For details of lawyer Zheng Enchong's jailing, see 'Shanghai lawyer's 3-year jail term upheld', *PD Online*, 19 December 2003;

after release he was kept under effective house arrest, see Human Rights in China, press release, New York, 5 July 2006.

11. The Hong Kong developer is Vincent Lo of the Shui On group; see e.g. Dan Levy, 'Harnessing the tiger in China – Hong Kong developer [...] seeks more territory to conquer', *San Francisco Chronicle*, 1 January 2006.

12. Press conference for the Shanghai World Expo 2010, June 2006.

13. 'Shanghai's resident population is 16.14 million', Xinhua, 12 July 2002; 'Shanghai: resident population is 17.78 million', National Population and Family Planning Commission of China (NPFPC), www.chinapop.gov.cn, 20 March 2006; the growth appears set to continue, see 'Shanghai: resident population to reach around 19 million in 2010', NPFPC, 21 July 2006.

14. Er Dongqiang, 'Foreword' (Chinese version) in *A Last Look Revisited: Western Architecture in Old Shanghai*, Tess Johnston and Deke Erh, Old China Hand Press, Hong Kong, 2004.

15. Ibid.

### 3: Aspiration nation

1. See e.g. Lynn Pan, *The New Chinese Revolution*, Sphere Books, London, 1987, p. 146.

2. Xia Jun and Yin Shan, *Housing has Changed China (Juzhu gaibian Zhongguo)*, Tsinghua University Press, Beijing, 2006, p. 1.

3. Nie Meisheng, 'Policies and measures on housing of Chinese low-income households', CRI, 30 May 2006.

4. Duncan Hewitt, 'China ends low rent public housing', BBC News, 6 April 1998.

5. Jiao Yang, 'Press conference of Shanghai Municipal Government', english.eastday.com, 19 November 2003.

6. Xue Wen, 'Rising prices see owners become a "housing slave"', *SD*, 16 May 2006.

7. Ibid.

8. Duncan Hewitt, 'Sanya authorities to blow up half-finished buildings', BBC News, 1 February 2001.

9. 'B&Q to sell more electrical appliances', *CD*, 19 September 2006.

10. Huang Haibo, *Petty Bourgeois Woman (Xiaozi nuren)*, Huawen Publishing, Beijing, 2002.

11. Wang Shouzhi, *Hello! Middle Class (Haluo! Zhongchan)*,

Heilongjiang Fine Arts Publishing, Harbin, 2005.

12. Sun Wei, Executive Director for International Relations, Shanghai Media Group, author interview, May 2005.

13. The trend has spread into the commercial sector too, see He Shuqing, 'Nearly 100 European themed commercial streets in 38 Chinese Cities', *New Weekly (Xin Zhoukan)*, Guangzhou, 1 Jan 2006.

14. Jane Cai, 'Plea to stop "the mindless pursuit of urbanisation"', *SCMP*, 14 July 2006.

15. See e.g. Liu Wei, 'Shortage of electric power an ordeal for China's economy', *PD*, 28 July 2003.

16. Advertising for Buick Royaum, www.gmchina.com, 2006.

17. He Shuqing, 'Sick cars', *New Weekly*, 1 June 2006.

18. 'China to remain "kingdom of bicycles"', Xinhua, 15 June 2006; Shi Jiangtao, 'Wheel of fortune turns for cyclists', *SCMP*, 16 June 2006.

19. Song Mo and Wen Chihua, 'Turning full cycle', *CD*, 28 September 2006; Mark O'Neill, 'Dream stalls for China's car industry', *SCMP*, 6 June 2005.

20. 'Ranking of top 100 real estate firms announced', *CD*, 31 March 2006.

21. Hu Jiujiu, '90 square metre dividing line [...]', *New Weekly*, 15 June 2006.

22. 'Clinton earn $150,000', Briefs, *Shanghai Star*, 30 May 2002; Wang Shouzhi, *Hello! Middle Class*, op. cit., p. 119; Zhou Zhuyi, 'Eriksson's property pitch in Shanghai', *SD*, 8 April 2006.

23. Wang Gang, 'Homeowners detained', *China Newsweek (Zhongguo Xinwen Zhoukan)*, Beijing, 14 November 2005.

24. Mark O'Neill, 'Taking easy way out in property crisis', *SCMP*, 22 May 2006.

25. 'China moves again to curb soaring house prices', Xinhua, 29 May 2006.

26. Hu Jiujiu, '90 square metre dividing line [...]', op. cit.

27. Bill Savadove, 'Five sentenced for looting Shanghai pension fund', *SCMP*, 28 September 2007.

28. 'Stop illegal land use now', Opinion, *CD*, 8 June 2006.

29. Xie Chuanjiao, 'Economists warn of real estate bubble', *CD*, 13 January 2007.

**4: Farewell to Welfare?**

1. In 1992 there were 108 million state employees, including 35 million in factories, 8 million in mining and quarrying and 6 million in construction. *China Statistical Yearbook 2005*, China Statistics Press, Beijing.
2. Lawrence Brahm, Naga Group Consulting, author interview, 28 September 1999.
3. See e.g. Duncan Hewitt, 'Shenyang sells enterprises for one yuan', BBC News, 22 March 1998.
4. Professor Song Xiaowu, senior advisor to the State Council, author interview, 1999.
5. One notable case was in the north-eastern cities of Daqing and Liaoyang in 2002, see Duncan Hewitt, 'China's unemployment challenge', BBC News, 16 March 2002.
6. *China Statistical Yearbook 2005,* op. cit.
7. Baroness Thatcher, 'Speech in Bermuda', 7 August 2001, www.margaretthatcher.org.
8. More than half a million textile workers were laid off in the first seven months of 1998 alone. See 'Creating a new world for the placement of a million laid-off workers from the textile industry', *PD*, 23 July 1998.
9. You Lantian, quoted in Duncan Hewitt, 'Beijing re-employment', East Asia Today, BBC World Service, 24 March 1998.
10. Author interview, March 2002.
11. *Shanghai Statistical Yearbook 2006*, Shanghai Statistical Bureau.
12. Shao Ning and Yao Liping, '"Five welfare" safety net benefits 1.2 million people', *Xinmin Evening News (Xinmin Wanbao)*, Shanghai, 15 October 2006; and *Shanghai Statistical Yearbook*, op. cit.
13. Lin Yongsan, quoted in Duncan Hewitt, 'China calls for more servants', BBC News, 24 November 2000.
14. *Yangcheng Evening News (Yangcheng Wanbao)*, Guangzhou, 28 February 2002; according to Sheng Huaren, head of the State Economic and Planning Commission, only 13 million of 21 million workers laid off between 1997 and 2000 were re-employed as of 2001 – see Duncan Hewitt, 'China state enterprise reforms', BBC News, 9 January 2001.
16. Li Xing, 'Elderly must contribute in ageing society', *CD*, 2 March 2006; also 'Adjust retirement policy', Opinion, *CD*, 11 July 2006.

17. Lehman Brown, 'Reform of pension insurance enters a "minefield"', quoted in *BizShanghai*, May 2006.
18. Janos Annus, WHO, Beijing, author interview, May 2002.
19. Hu Yan and Jiang Qiongji, 'Alzheimer's often goes undiagnosed, untreated', *CD*, 11 April 2006.
20. 'Appeals hotline', in *Fraternity (Bo'ai)*, Shanghai Charity Foundation, 4/2006.
21. China Central Television, Channel 10, 20 October 2006.
22. Chow Chung-yan, 'Health system needs foreign cash', *SCMP*, 14 March 2006.
23. He Huifeng, '4 months, 9,000 treatments: widow fights 1.2m yuan bill', *SCMP*, 17 December 2005.
24. Jane Cai, 'Record 5.5m yuan treatment probed', *SCMP*, 1 December 2005; and Wang Hongliang, '5.5m "sky high medical fee"', *Lifeweek (Sanlian Shenhuo Zhoukan)*, Beijing, 12 December 2005.
25. Chow Chung-yan, 'Health system needs foreign cash', op. cit.
26. 'Health sector criticised', Xinhua, in *SD*, 5 August 2005.
27. Ibid.
28. Liu Shinan, '"Fair-price" hospitals won't solve the disorder', *CD*, 8 February 2006; Ma Lie, 'Shaanxi cuts health care bills for poor', *CD*, 30 November 2005; Mickey Ng, 'Commission shames 8 hospitals for overcharging their patients', *SCMP*, 26 August 2006.
29. For the Hospitals Association appeal, see 'The health ministry will set up a commercial bribery blacklist', Xinhua, in *Daily Sunshine (Jing Bao)*, Shenzhen, 13 June 2006.
30. Duncan Hewitt, 'China passes medical accidents law', BBC News, 25 April 2002. Staff at one Shenzhen hospital were even briefly ordered to wear helmets to protect them from angry relatives: 'Hospital staff shed helmets after two days', *CD*, 27 December 2006.
31. See Lu Youqing, *Diary of Death (Siwang Riji)*, Shanghai, Huayi Publishing, 2000.
32. See Liu Shinan, '"Fair-price" hospitals [...]', op. cit.; and Chow Chung-yan, 'Health system needs foreign cash', op. cit.; also Xu Qin, 'Warding against wasteful wards', *SD*, 14 August 2006.
33. Zhang Feng, 'Team to tackle healthcare woes', *CD*, 19 September 2006.
34. 'As we get wealthier do we get happier?', Opinion, *CD*, 10 February 2006.

## 5: A half-open media

1. See e.g. Liu Binyan (tr. Perry Link), *'People or Monsters', and Other Stories and Reportage from China after Mao*, Indiana University Press, Bloomington, 1983.
2. Duncan Hewitt, 'Guangzhou's commercial media', BBC World Service, 28 March 2002.
3. *Southern Weekend*, cited in Duncan Hewitt, 'Shijiazhuang bomb trial warning', BBC News, 30 March 2001.
4. *Southern Weekend*, cited in Duncan Hewitt, 'China's new tabloid press', *East Asia Today*, BBC World Service, 28 December 1997.
5. 'BBC pays attention to our paper', *Southern Metropolis News*, 2 March 2002.
6. These magazines included notably *China Newsweek* and *Caijing* magazine, as well as *New Weekly* and *LifeWeek*.
7. A series of unconnected bombings and explosions around China in 2001–2 were one example: see e.g. Duncan Hewitt, 'Guangzhou bus explosion', BBC News, 31 January 2002.
8. Wang Yong, Shu Wen and Wang Zijiang, 'Embarrassment for China's "warm-up team"', *Shenzhen Evening News (Shenzhen Wanbao)*, 8 June 2006.
9. 'Farcical games ruin spirit of competition', *CD*, 24 October 2005.
10. Duncan Hewitt, 'Guangxi mine accident arrest', BBC News, 4 August 2001.
11. Duncan Hewitt, 'Doubts over journalist's jailing', BBC News, 12 January 2001.
12. Wang Yong, 'Model scholar judge stashes US$3.4m', *SD*, 10 November 2006.
13. Jane Macartney, 'Editor dies after police beating', *The Times*, 7 February 2006.
14. Verna Yu, 'Law review sought after custody death', *SCMP*, 17 May 2003; '84 Days and Nights in Guangzhou', *Wuhan Evening News (Wuhan Wanbao)*, china.org.cn, 8 July 2003.
15. Joseph Kahn, 'Police raid newspaper that reported new SARS case', *New York Times*, 8 January 2004; Irene Wang, 'Ex-tabloid boss' sentence a sad day for mainland justice system', *SCMP*, 22 March 2004; Philip Pan, 'In China, an editor tries and fails', *Washington Post*, 1 August 2004; 'Chinese journalist awarded

UNESCO World Press Freedom Prize', UNESCO press release, Paris, 7 April 2005.

16. Jonathan Ansfield, 'Pressure on the press', *Newsweek*, 27 June 2005; 'Top Chinese press editor sacked', BBC News, 29 December 2005.

17. Ching Cheong was eventually released early, on 'medical parole,' in February 2008. Zhao Yan is thought to have previously angered the authorities by helping farmers to campaign for their rights: see Josephine Ma, 'Fraud count was used "to justify arrest of journalist"', *SCMP*, 26 August 2006; Wang Xiangwei, 'Jailing of journalists raises the question of different treatment', *SCMP*, 4 September 2006.

18. Robert Saiget, 'Beijing students protest over rape-murder', Kyodo News, 24 May 2000; 'Students mourn death of classmate', *PD Online*, 26 May 2000.

19. 'Special force tackles negative chat on Net', Reuters, in *SCMP*, 20 May 2005; Shi Ting, 'Search on for 4,000 web police for Beijing', *SCMP*, 17 June 2005.

20. Alex Pham, 'Yahoo to pay Chinese families', *Los Angeles Times*, 14 November 2007.

21. Duncan Clark, BDA China Consultancy, quoted in Duncan Hewitt, 'China's net generation', BBC News Online, 25 July 2001.

22. Matt Forney, 'China's web watchers', op. cit.; Geoffrey A. Fowler and Mei Fong, 'China tightens grip on internet with new content, media rules', *Wall Street Journal*, 27 September 2005.

23. '"The Promise" director calls parody immoral', *PD Online*, 14 February 2006; 'Chen not amused by steamed bun spoof', *CD*, 22 February 2006; 'China to identify internet bloggers', Agence France Presse, in *SCMP*, 23 October 2006.

24. George Wehrfritz and Duncan Hewitt, 'One billion couch potatoes', *Newsweek*, 6 June 2005.

25. See e.g. *5 Weekly (Xingqiwu)* magazine, Shjiazhuang, 2/2006; Liu Shinan, 'Paparazzi set poor example', *CD*, 17 May 2006.

26. The series *Waves wash away the sand (Lang tao sha)*, also known as *Deep Throat (Shen hou)* starred Xia Yu, who found fame as a teenager in Jiang Wen's film *In the Heat of the Sun*, 1994.

## 6: The 'me' generation

1. Notably in Huang Jianxin's *The Black Cannon Incident (Hei pao shijian)*, 1986.

2. 'Shanghai rocks with US band', *CD*, 8 December 1986.

3. 'Beijing warns on demonstrations', *Sunday Morning Post*, Hong Kong, 21 December 1986; see also Jeffrey N. Wasserstrom, 'Backbeat in China', *The Nation*, 1 July 2002.

4. Sheldon Hsiao-Peng Lu, 'Postmodernity, popular culture, and the intellectual: A report on post-Tiananmen China', *boundary 2*, Summer 1996.

5. MC Hot Dog (*Ha gou bang*), *Street Music* (*Jietou Yinyue*), Magic Stone Records, Taiwan, 2001.

6. *Guangzhou Daily*, cited in Duncan Hewitt, 'Student haircut row', BBC News, 2 March 2002.

7. 'After the "Meteor" has passed', *Southern Weekend*, 4 April 2002.

8. 'Off-screen love and hate for TV idol drama' and 'Defending against and curing the poison of idol dramas', *Guangzhou Daily*, 14 March 2002; Hei Ma, 'Is F4 a virus?', *Global Times (Huanqiu Shibao)*, Beijing, 4 April 2002.

9. Zhou Qian, 'Live report: travelling ten thousand miles and spending money to see F4', www.eastday.com, 19 May 2002.

10. 'Defending against and curing the poison of idol dramas', op. cit.

11. Yang Yongming, Shanghai Education Commission, author interview, July 2001.

12. Duncan Hewitt, 'Private detectives investigate children', BBC News, 20 April 2002.

13. Duncan Hewitt, 'Summer camps for pampered kids', BBC News, 10 August 2001.

14. Talk at the Foreign Correspondents' Club, Shanghai, 29 June 2005.

15. Kevin Huang, 'You say "lei ho", we say you're fired', *SCMP*, 15 September 2005.

16. Wang Xiaofeng, 'Birth of a Super Idol', *LifeWeek*, 19 September 2005; Benjamin Joffe-Walt, 'Mad about the girl: a pop idol for China', *Guardian*, 7 October 2005; '*Supergirls* champion to appear on stamps', Xinhua, 17 January 2006; 'China moves to clean up TV screens', Xinhua, 12 January 2007.

17. Qiu Minye, 'Eighteen-year-olds generate electricity', *City Pictorial (Chengshi Huabao)*, Guangzhou, 27 May 2005.

18. Chen Jiu, 'Me generation', *New Weekly*, 1 June 2006.

19. Wang Shanshan, 'Foreign cartoons banned from prime time', *CD*, 14 August 2006.

### 7: Unsentimental education

1. Liam Fitzpatrick, 'Asia's overscheduled kids', *Time*, 27 March 2006.
2. Liu Weifeng, 'Students complain of teachers' language', *CD*, 2 March 2006.
3. 'Cell phones on campus prompt debate', *CD*, 24 March 2004.
4. 'Overburdened students refuse weekend classes', english.eastday. com, 1 November 2004.
5. Yan Zhen, 'Primary schools reduce Chinese character list', *SD*, 10 February 2006; see also 'China reduces schooling burden of students', Xinhua, 15 April 2005.
6. Zhang Minxuan, Shanghai Education Commission, author interview, September 2005
7. 'Tuition becomes parents' burden', *CD*, 25 August 2006
8. Yu Zhong, 'High tuition fees drive mother to suicide', *CD*, 22 September 2005; Vivien Cui, 'Son's elation turns to devastation', *SCMP*, 3 July 2006.
9. Wang Ying, 'Banks urged to dig deep to help students', *CD*, 22 September 2004.
10. Deputy Minister of Education Zhang Baoqing, quoted in '20 per cent of Chinese university students face financial difficulties', Xinhua, 1 September 2004.
11. Ibid; and 'Minister slamming unreasonable school fees to retire', Associated Press, 1 November 2005.
12. 'Enthusiasm for overseas study rationalised', Xinhua, 30 May 2005.
13. *Guangzhou Daily*, quoted in Duncan Hewitt, 'Chinese students go west', BBC World Service, 1 October 2001.
14. 'Internet helps, but addiction kills', *CD*, 8 February 2006.
15. Duncan Hewitt, 'China's tiny tycoons', BBC News, 2 December 2000.
16. Yang Xiong, Shanghai Academy of Social Sciences, author interview, June 2006; see also Mark O'Neill, 'Labour produces a mismatch', *SCMP*, 8 May 2006.
17. The number of people aged over 65 in 2005 was estimated at just 100 million: see 'Day for senior citizens', *CD*, 31 October 2006; for US comparison see Stephanie Hemelryk Donald and Robert Benewick, *The State of China Atlas*, University of New South Wales Press, 2005, p. 75.
18. Duan Jianhua, Guangzhou Population and Family Planning

Committee, quoted in Qiu Quanlin, 'Only-children parents urged to have two kids', *CD*, 10 November 2006.

## 8: The great proletarian sexual revolution

1. 'China's college students get okay to tie knot', *CD*, 30 March 2005; 'Fudan relaxes sex rules for students', SD, 19 July 2005; Jiao Xiaoyang, 'New rules still curb students' pre-marital sex', *CD*, 18 July 2005; 'Guangzhou university to regulate student sex', Reuters, quoted in *CD Online*, 27 October 2005.
2. David Bonavia, *The Chinese: A portrait*, Penguin, Harmondsworth, 1982, p. 87.
3. Li Yinhe and Wang Xiaobo, *Their World (Tamen de shijie)*, Shanxi People's Publishing House, 1992.
4. Prominent writers in this category included Wang Anyi, Zhang Xianliang and, in the early 1990s, Jia Pingwa (see Jianying Zha, *China Pop*, The New Press, New York, 1995, for a discussion of the controversy provoked by the latter).
5. Esther Zhao, 'A sexual revolution silently going on in China', *CD*, 3 June 2005.
6. See e.g. Zhi Chuan, *Separate when the day breaks (Tian liang yihou fenshou)*, China Film Publishing, Beijing 2003.
7. Li Yinhe, speaking at a debate on the new marriage law organised by the All-China Journalists' Federation, Beijing, 22 January 1999.
8. Wang Jiaquan, 'Divorce rises with changing marriage and love', *CD*, 30 November 2004.
9. 'China passes sweeping changes to marriage law', Xinhua, 28 April 2001.
10. 'Poll finds early sex a norm in big cities', Xinhua, in *CD*, 6 July 2005.
11. Survey by Li Yinhe: see Esther Zhao, 'A sexual revolution silently going on in China', op. cit.
12. Talk at the Foreign Correspondents' Club, Shanghai, 24 January 2006.
13. Ibid.
14. 'Health services grow to meet increase in teen pregnancies', *PD Online*, 7 August 2003.
15. *Southern Weekend*, quoted in Duncan Hewitt, 'Yunnan teenage prostitution case', BBC News, 22 January 2002.

16. Ai Xiaoming, quoted in Zhou Liming, 'Sex, lies and surveys', *CD*, 15 December 2005; see also Huang Junjie, 'The new generation lacking in sexual IQ', *New Weekly*, 1 January 2006.

17. Zou Hanru, 'Shed more light on campus sex', *CD*, 23 June 2006.

18. Xie Chuanjiao, 'Website takes the embarrassment out of sex talk', *CD*, 21 November 2006.

19. Lei Huiling and Li Ying, 'Accidental teen pregnancies up nearly thirty per cent since start of winter holidays', *Oriental Morning Post (Dongfang Zaobao)*, Shanghai, 31 January 2006.

20. 'Single mother sparks moral debate', Xinhua, in *CD*, 15 October 2006; 'Single mother issue in spotlight thanks to blog', *CD*, 17 October 2006.

21. 'Teen mom escapes charge of killing baby', *CD Online*, 26 December 2003; 'Teen mom kills baby to please her lover', *SD*, 24 January 2006; Cao Li, 'Teenage mother sentenced over death of unborn baby', *CD*, 21 November 2006.

22. Zhang Yu, 'Number of divorces rockets in Shanghai', *CD*, 27 October 2006; 'Marriage no longer top priority for young', Xinhua, in *SD*, 4 April 2006.

23. Duncan Hewitt, 'China's first condom ad', BBC News, 30 November 1999, and 'Condom ad banned', 2 December 1999.

24. *Beijing Youth Daily (Beijing Qingnianbao)*, quoted in Duncan Hewitt, 'China's first condom ad', op. cit.

25. 'Shanghai's first hotel provides free condoms', *Shanghai Evening News (Xinwen wanbao)*, 1 December 2005.

26. China had 183,000 registered cases of HIV by December 2006; in 2002 the number was just over 30,000, though official estimates of the real figure were far higher: see e.g. 'Number of HIV carriers hit 850,000', *PD Online*, 12 April 2002.

27. 'Handshake highlights fight against AIDS', *PD Online*, 2 December 2003; 'Leaders' handshakes epitomize nation's resolve against AIDS', Xinhua, 30 November 2004.

28. Chung To of the Chi Heng Foundation, Hong Kong, author interview, September 2006.

29. Wu Jiao, 'Condom use to be promoted among gays', *CD*, 1 December 2006; Zhang Liuhao, 'Safe-sex chat draws controversy', *SD*, 16 October 2006.

30. Howard French, 'The Stones rock, by China's rules', *New York*

*Times*, 9 April 2006; the US TV series *Friends* has likewise never been shown on Chinese television, apparently because of official concern about the lifestyles and morality of its characters.

31. Liu Ji, 'Divorce between TV marriage and reality under fire', *CD*, 3 October 2006.

32. '47% of spam SMS are pornographic', PacificEpoch.com, 21 November 2006.

33. Echo Shan, 'College girls go nude before camera for eternal beauty', *CD Online*, 18 November 2004; 'Nude photo exhibition shatters Chinese taboo', Reuters, 28 January 2001.

34. 'Star says sorry for controversial advert', *Beijing News*, quoted in *CD*, 15 June 2006.

35. Xiao Xin, 'Can you resist attraction?', and 'Tips', both in *Better Life* (*Meihua Shenghuo*), Shanghai, December 2005.

36. Nü Ren Yi, 'My dream of working in a sex shop', *City Pictorial*, 28 July 2006.

37. See e.g. Li Shaohong's film *Blush*, 1995, which tells the moving story of the fate of two Shanghai prostitutes 'rehabilitated' after the revolution.

38. *Fatal Decision (Shengsi Jueze)*, Shanghai Film Studio, 2000.

39. 'Masterminds of Japanese orgy get life', *CD*, 17 December 2003.

40. '"Prostitute parade" in Shenzhen stirs debate in China', CRI, 8 December 2006.

41. Hu Jie, *The Vagina Monologues: Stories from China*, Gender Education Forum, Sun Yat-sen University, Guangzhou, 2004.

42. John Gittings, 'China drops homosexuality from list of psychiatric disorders', *Guardian*, 7 March 2001; Zheng Guihong, 'Chinese society more tolerant of homosexuality', china.org.cn, 31 October 2001.

43. 'Mainland's first gay organization approved', *New Express Daily* (*Xin Kuaibao*), Guangzhou, in 'China Scene', *CD*, 3 November 2006.

44. Wu Jiao, 'Condom use to be promoted among gays', op. cit.

45. Chung To, Chi Heng Foundation, lecture at Fudan University, Shanghai, 7 September 2006.

## 9: Floating people

1. Laurence Rouleau-Berger and Shi Lu, 'Migrant Workers in Shanghai', *China Perspectives*, Paris, Hong Kong, March–April 2005.

2. Ibid; and Jasper Becker, *The Chinese*, John Murray, London, 2000, pp. 102–3.

3. 'Educational opportunities open up for migrant population in Shanghai', *PD Online*, 9 January 2004.

4. 'Foundation to fund education of migrant workers' children', *PD Online*, 14 January 2004.

5. '37 migrant schools shut in Beijing', Xinhua, in *SD*, 25 August 2006.

6. Ibid; and Hu Yan, Xu Jitao and Mark South, 'Education still dilemma for children of migrants', *CD*, 10 March 2006.

7. 'Don't leave kids behind', Opinion, in *CD*, 30 May 2006; Kristine Kwok, 'Migrant workers leave millions of children behind', *SCMP*, 20 October 2006.

8. 'Children left behind face tough road', *PD Online*, 2 June 2004.

9. 'Don't leave kids behind', op. cit.

10. Yang Xiong, Shanghai Academy of Social Sciences, author interview, June 2006.

11. Wu Jiao, 'Sexual suppression frustrates migrants', *CD*, 16 August 2006.

12. Ibid; Echo Shan, 'The sex oppression of migrant workers voiced', *CD*, 1 July 2005.

13. Echo Shan, 'Migrant workers barred from tourist resort', *CD Online*, 18 October 2005.

14. For Wenzhou's migrant population, see 'One in three is a "new Wenzhou citizen"', *Wenzhou Evening News (Wenzhou Wanbao)*, 3 March 2006; for prejudice, see Duncan Hewitt, 'China's vulnerable migrants', *From Our Own Correspondent*, BBC World Service, 4 May 2001.

15. Raymond Zhou, 'Henan stigma highlights regional bias', *CD*, 16 June 2005; Chen Hong, 'Police apologise for discriminatory banners', *CD*, 10 February 2006; 'Bid to kick out Henan people causes fury', *CD*, 15 June 2006; Liu Kaiming, China Labour Research and Support Network, author interview, June 2006.

16. Duncan Hewitt, 'Bridge disaster compensation row', BBC News, 8 February 2001.

17. *Shanghai Statistical Yearbook 2005*.

18. Lu Jianwu, author interview, December 2004.

19. 'Medical insurance regulation benefits migrant workers', *CD*, 16 May 2006; 'Migrant workers' rights better protected', *PD Online*, 11

January 2005; Michelle Chen, 'Shanghai insurance scheme adds insult to injury', *Asia Times*, 10 June 2004.

20. Melinda Liu, 'Migrants' rights: opening up the system', *Newsweek*, 31 January 2005.
21. 'Migrant wave drives Shanghai's population growth', Xinhua, 6 April 2006.
22. Tang Min, 'Downtown beggars can be choosers', *CD*, 18 March 2003; 'Shanghai publishes guide to spot beggars', Associated Press, in *CD Online*, 25 September 2005.
23. 'Respecting rights of migrant workers', *CD*, 20 September 2005, citing *PD*. In late 2006 an official survey suggested the average gross income of migrants was 12,000 yuan a year, but some experts believe this is overstated.
24. GTZ and Yunnan Provincial Poverty Alleviation Office, *General report on urban poverty research in Yunnan province*, Beijing, Kunming, 2004.
25. Jane Cai, 'Back pay claims pile up', *SCMP*, 8 March 2006.
26. Wang Pu, 'A year's labour re-education for latest "suicide show"', *Yangcheng Evening News*, 4 June 2005.
27. Wang Zhenghua, 'Convicted migrant worker killer waits for final verdict', *CD*, 21 September 2005.
28. 'Wage system protects migrant worker rights', Opinion, in *CD*, 29 March 2006; 'No more wage defaulting', Opinion, in *CD*, 27 October 2006.
29. Zong He, 'Let's protect migrant workers', *CD*, 4 April 2005.
30. 'Migrants learn about legal rights', *SD*, 19 April 2005.
31. 'China now has 150 million migrant workers', Xinhua, in *CD Online*, 29 October 2006.
32. Dongguan Statistical Bureau, dgs.gov.cn.
33. David Barboza, 'China, new land of shoppers, builds malls on gigantic scale', *New York Times*, 25 May 2005.
34. National Bureau of Statistics of China, 2005. Some experts suggest urbanisation could reach 58% by 2020: 'China's urban population to reach 800–900 million by 2020', *PD Online*, 16 September 2004.

**10: The land they left behind**

1. Famine: see Jasper Becker, *Hungry Ghosts: China's Secret Famine*, John Murray, London, 1996. Reforms: see Richard Baum, *Burying*

*Mao*, Princeton University Press, 1994, pp. 68–69; John Gittings, *The Changing Face of China*, Oxford University Press, 2005, pp. 120–130.

2. Gao Hongbin, author interview, November 1998; '10% of Chinese live in poverty', CRI, 1 November 2006; '23 million cannot afford food, clothes', *SD*, 29 March 2006.

3. Wen Chihua, 'County hospitals offer hope for cancer victims', *CD*, 4 March 2006.

4. Ibid; also, Yukon Huang, World Bank country director, briefing in Beijing, 10 April 1998.

5. Janos Annus, author interview, May 2002.

6. Cited in ibid.

7. Duncan Hewitt, 'China's rural health crisis', BBC World Service, 24 June 2002; 'Curing China's ailing health care system', World Bank, 2003; Josephine Ma, 'Poor farmers left to die in their homes', *SCMP*, 6 November 2004.

8. Zhang Feng, 'Officials told to step up inoculation drive', *CD*, 2 March 2006.

9. 'Nation launches new rural medical plan for farmers', Xinhua, in *SD*, 31 March 2006.

10. See 'Volunteers heal rural poor with free service', *PD Online*, 30 March 2001.

11. *Southern Weekend*, in Duncan Hewitt, 'Unrest in rural Jiangxi', BBC News, 16 October 2000; Duncan Hewitt, 'Anhui tax reforms', BBC World Service, 19 June 2002.

12. The income tax threshold for urban citizens was raised from 800 yuan to 1600 yuan in 2006, and to 2000 yuan in 2008. Farmers paid tax while earning just a few hundred yuan a month.

13. Duncan Hewitt, 'Guangdong school protest', BBC News, 16 February 2001.

14. David Parker, Deputy Representative, UNICEF, Beijing, author interview March 2002.

15. Ibid.

16. Ma Lie, 'Rural school teachers to enjoy better conditions', *CD*, 15 February 2006; Zhu Zhe, 'City teachers will work in rural schools', *CD*, 8 March 2006.

17. Liang Qiwen, 'Report: schools in Guangdong in colossal debt', *CD*, 29 March 2006.

18. Elaine Wu, 'Central government scraps tax on farmers', *SCMP*, 20

December 2005; 'Hu pledges to improve farmers' lot', *CD*, 15 February 2006; Cary Huang, 'Rural spending plan a huge policy shift, says Wen', *SCMP*, 6 March 2006.

19. Duncan Hewitt, 'Unrest in rural Jiangxi', op. cit.
20. World Bank, quoted in Fu Jing, 'Local authorities warned about rising debts', *CD*, 10 February 2006.
21. 'China offers farmers 11.6 billion yuan direct grain subsidies', Xinhua, 15 October 2004.
22. Cary Huang, 'Rural spending plan a huge policy shift'; op. cit.
23. 'China to subsidise farmers with 5.5 billion yuan', Xinhua, in *CD*, 3 March 2005.
24. 'Listen to rural voices', Opinion, in *CD*, 3 November 2006; 'Stop wasting public funds on overseas trips', *CD*, 15 June 2006.
25. 'China endeavours to increase its arable land', Xinhua, 30 August 2006.
26. 'Land deals unreasonable', Opinion, in *CD*, 23 June 2006.
27. Edward Cody, 'China's land grab raise specter of popular unrest', *Washington Post*, 5 October 2005.
28. Elaine Wu, 'Violent end to dispute over land', *SCMP*, 20 October 2005.
29. Minnie Chan, 'Villagers reportedly shot dead during power dispute', *SCMP*, 8 December 2005; 'China reveals report on violence in south', Xinhua, 11 December 2005.
30. Chan Siu-sin, 'Family of beaten Xi'an nun holds no grudge', *SCMP*, 3 December 2005.
31. Didi Kirsten Tatlow, 'In riot village, the government is on the run', *SCMP*, 13 April 2005.
32. Zhao Huanxin, 'Landless farmers must be helped', *CD*, 8 March 2006; in 2005 China's police reported 87,000 'mass incidents', or protests, around the country.
33. For background to the case, see Li Xuemin, 'Final word in suit against government which drew national attention', *Liaoning Workers' News (Liaoning Zhigong Bao)*, 14 March 2000; Mark O'Neill, 'Farming the fields of injustice', *SCMP*, 14 May 2000.
34. Zhao Huanxin, 'Landless farmers must be helped', op. cit.
35. The Carter Centre, set up by former US President Jimmy Carter, is a long-term supporter of the process, and runs a related website, www.chinaelections.net.

36. One of the village chiefs was later reported to have committed suicide in despair at their plight: see Hannah Beech, 'China's fantasy of freedom', *Time*, 25 January 2007.

37. Wei Yahua, 'Democratically elected village chief killed', *China Newsweek*, 9 July 2001.

38. Minnie Chan, 'Victory for villagers in battle over "rigged poll" for chief', *SCMP*, 2 May 2006.

39. Wu Chong, 'Doctor in life and death struggle', *CD*, 31 October 2004.

40. Josephine Ma, 'Court upholds jail term for blind birth-control activist', *SCMP*, 2 December 2006; see also Hannah Beech, 'Chen Guangcheng: A blind man with legal vision', *Time*, 30 April 2006.

41. Melinda Liu and Jonathan Ansfield, 'Down on the farm', *Newsweek*, 15 May 2006; Liu Shinan, 'Price hikes should bring benefit to our farmers', *CD*, 13 December 2006; 'Canadian support enables Gung Ho to keep cooperative spirit alive', *China Development Brief*, 5 July 2006.

42. The authors were later sued by one of the rural officials they criticised; see Joseph Kahn, 'Expose of peasants' plight is suppressed by China', *New York Times*, 9 July 2004.

**11: Consumers and citizens**

1. Duncan Hewitt, 'China's bald-headed restaurant', BBC News, 22 December 2001.

2. Wang Zhenghua, 'Teenage girl dies after bus "strangling" ', *CD*, 19 October 2005; 'Bus conductor sentenced to death for strangling', Xinhua, 13 May 2006.

3. Dong Zhen, 'City transport card in dispute', SD, 1 December 2006.

4. 'Citibank Shanghai branch sued by a Shanghai citizen', *PD Online*, 18 April 2002.

5. Vivian Wu, 'Consumers continue to struggle for rights', *SCMP*, 16 March 2006.

6. He Huifang, 'Owners come home to misery and violence', *SCMP*, 20 March 2006; 'Attack arrests', *SCMP*, 22 March 2006.

7. Andrew Browne, 'Blogger hits home by urging boycott of Chinese property', *Wall Street Journal*, 12 June 2006.

8. Joseph Kahn, 'A sharp debate erupts in China over ideologies', *New York Times*, 12 March 2006.

9. Irene Wang, 'Property law wins legislators' support', *SCMP*, 31

October 2006; 'Draft property law tabled to legislature for seventh reading', *PD*, 16 December 2006.

10. 'NPC bids for public attention with delegate blogs', Associated Press, 5 March 2006; Jane Cai, 'Consult us first on the big issues, say deputies', *SCMP*, 11 March 2006.

11. Li Junru, quoted in 'Political advisory system can help China avoid "colour revolution" – advisor', *PD Online*, 10 March 2006.

12. Chow Chung-yan, 'Tough test for activists seeking office', *SCMP*, 9 September 2006.

13. 'People's Congress delegate fixes day for receiving visitors', commentary, *Southern Metropolis News*, 27 July 2005.

14. Duncan Hewitt, 'Shanghai laundry ban', BBC News, 23 November 2001; 'Kites to be grounded', *Shanghai Star*, 31 October 2002.

15. Benjamin Kang Lim, 'China activist quits amid crackdown on NGOs', Reuters, 7 February 2006.

16. Julia Greenwood Bentley, 'The role of international support for civil society organisations', *Harvard Asia Quarterly*, Winter 2003.

17. Shi Jiangtao, 'Emphasis on public role in environmental projects welcomed', *SCMP*, 23 February 2006

18. Qin Chuan, 'Government turns up NGO volume', *CD*, 26 April 2005.

19. Christopher Bodeen, 'Trial begins of environmentalist charged with theft of state secrets', Associated Press, 15 May 2006; Joseph Kahn, 'In China, a lake's champion imperils himself', *New York Times*, 13 October 2007.

20. Leu Siew Ying, 'Museum's dark lessons rile authorities', *SCMP*, 22 May 2005.


**12: Culture shock**

1. Hou Hanru, in *Beyond: An Extraordinary Space of Experimentation for Modernisation*, Triennial Catalogue, Lingnan Art Publishing, Guangzhou, 2005, p. 34.

2. Yang Yong, in ibid., p. 222.

3. Bei Dao, talk at the Chinese Cultural Society, Edinburgh University, November 1987; as a result of such incomprehension, these writers were known in China as the 'misty poets'.

4. *Jesus, Confucius and John Lennon of the Beatles* by Sha Yexin, 1987, partial translation in *Renditions*, Chinese University of Hong Kong, No. 43, 1995. 'On seeing the play *Bus Stop*: He Wen's

447

critique in the *Literary Gazette*', *Renditions*, No. 19/20, 1983.

5. Lynn MacRitchie, 'Precarious paths on the mainland: art in China'; *Art in America*, March 1994.
6. 'Don't Move', by Yang Zhenzhong, in *Homeport*, curated by BizArt, Shanghai and Homeport, Rotterdam, Fuxing Park, Shanghai, August 2001.
7. Alexander Brandt, Xu Zhen, Yang Zhenzhong, *Art for Sale*, Shanghai, April 1999.
8. Yan Zhen, 'Art zones create high rent, not talent, says designer', *SD*, 25 January 2007.
9. 'China, I've lost my poetry', *New Weekly*, 8 November 2006.
10. Qiu Xiaolong, author of *When Red is Black*, talk at the Foreign Correspondents' Club, Shanghai, 28 August 2006.
11. 'Lou Ye surprised by five year ban', *Shanghai Morning Post*, 5 September 2006.
12. Duncan Hewitt, ' "Quitting" surprises China', BBC World Service, 7 December 2001.
13. Meiling Cheng, 'Violent Capital, Zhu Yu on file', *The Drama Review*, MIT, Winter 2005.
14. Lu Xun, 'A Madman's Diary', in *A Call to Arms*, Foreign Languages Press, Beijing, 2000.
15. Hu Fei and Chen Mo, 'Springtime or Greap Leap Forward for Art Museums', *New Weekly*, 15 March 2006.

**13: Faith, hope and disillusionment**

1. The officials in question are, respectively, Li Jizhou, Cheng Kejie, Mu Suixin, Chen Xitong.
2. 'Shenzhen judiciary gripped by graft probe', *CD*, 8 November 2006.
3. Chen Qun, Miao Changfa and Sun Yeli, 'What party is to be built? And how?', *PD Online*, 2 December 2001.
4. Ren Yuling, quoted in 'Government urged to trim the fat', *Shanghai Star*, 10 March 2005.
5. 'CPC holds grand rally to celebrate 85th anniversary', Xinhua, 30 June 2006.
6. The Japanese cosmetics brand SK-II, owned by P&G, was a case in point, attracting media criticism in 2006 after official tests found banned chemicals in its products; see e.g. 'Watchdog urges tighter checks on Japan imports', *CD*, 15 September 2006.

7. See e.g. 'Massive anti-Japan protests spread to Guangzhou, Shenzhen', Kyodo News, 11 April 2005.

8. Duncan Hewitt, 'Protests grow at US embassy in Beijing', BBC News, 8 May 1999.

9. For popularity of *qi gong* in the 1990s see Jasper Becker, *The Chinese*, op. cit., p. 233; for official figures see Duncan Hewitt, 'Beijing slams meditation rally', BBC News, 28 April 1999.

10. See e.g. John Gittings, *The Changing Face of China*, op. cit, pp. 319–20.

11. See e.g. Duncan Hewitt, '100 Falung Gong protesters held', *Guardian*, 26 April 2000.

12. Victor Yuan, author interview, December 2005.

13. See Duncan Hewitt, 'Religion in China', BBC World Service, 15 September 1999.

14. See M.A. Thiessen, 'A Tale of Two Bishops', *Crisis* magazine, 1 February 2002.

15. On funerals, see 'Bishop Zhang Bairen: Obituary', *The Times*, 12 October 2005; 'Chinese Bishop Liu Dies at 90', ZENIT news agency, Rome, 16 December 2001. On links with Rome, see Melinda Liu and Duncan Hewitt, 'A "single" church', *Newsweek*, 13 February 2006.

16. Hemelryk Donald and Benewick, *The State of China Atlas*, op. cit. p. 84.

17. Huan Xin, 'Buddhism "contributes to a harmonious society"', *CD*, 11 April 2006.

18. Ma Dinghua, deputy director general, Shanghai Religious Affairs Bureau, author interview, February 2000.

19. See e.g. Isabel Hilton, *The Search for the Panchen Lama*, Penguin, London, 2000.

20. After many years of downplaying the scale of such resistance, the Chinese authorities, in the aftermath of 9/11, began warning of links between Xinjiang rebels and al-Qaeda.

21. Duncan Hewitt, 'Qing Ming superstition ban', BBC News, 5 April 2002.

22. Duncan Hewitt, 'Court hires Taoist priest', BBC News, 25 October 2000.

23. David Fang, 'Ads touting fortune-telling banned from the airwaves', *SCMP*, 1 February 2006.

24. See Jonathan Spence, *God's Chinese Son*, Flamingo, London, 1997

25. Henry Chu, 'Illegal houses of worship targeted in China crackdown', *LA Times*, 15 December 2000.
26. Jiao Xiaoyang and Wang Zhuoqiong, 'Party affairs to be more transparent', *CD*, 2 March 2006; 'Party thunders against "sex, gluttony and drink"', Agence France Presse, in *SCMP*, 29 January 2007.
27. Shuai Yonggang, and Liu Jiongxiong, *Lei Feng 1940–1962*, Joint Publishing, Beijing, 2006.
28. Cary Huang, 'Millions pledged to revive Marxism', *SCMP*, 20 January 2006.
29. Xinhua, quoted in Wang Xiangwei, 'Hu's bland preaching will fail to revive time-honoured social traits', *SCMP*, 20 March 2006.
30. Benjamin Robertson and Melinda Liu, 'Can the sage save China?', *Newsweek*, 20 March 2006; 'Confucius Business Institute inaugurated in London', *PD Online*, 10 April 2006.
31. 'Anti-graft education enters primary school', Xinhua, 27 September 2005.

**Epilogue**

1. Lu Zhi, Jiang Lan and Gu Yan, *Objects/ Phrases/ Professions/Crafts Which are in the Process of Disappearing (Zheng zai xiaoshi de wupin/ ciyu/ zhiye/ yishu)*, Shanghai Far East Publishing, 2002.
2. 'Deng Xiaoping: Let some of the people get rich first' (comments to Time Inc. delegation, 23 October 1985), Xinhua, 16 January 2005.
3. 'China's development at a critical point: common prosperity or half in poverty', *PD Online*, 12 August 2004; 'New five year plan called revolutionary', *Asia Times*, 13 October 2005; Wang Yong, 'Education in integrity can fight corruption', *SD*, 25 October 2006; 'China Q & A', china.org.cn.
4. 'As we get wealthier, do we get happier?', op. cit.
5. Zhao Huanxin, 'House prices "harm building of harmony"', *CD*, 30 January 2007.
6. Han Zheng, Mayor of Shanghai, 'Report on the work of the government', Shanghai Municipal People's Congress, 28 January 2007; in practice, however, Shanghai's GDP growth actually speeded up, totalling 13.3% in 2007.
7. Irene Wang, 'Propaganda takes back seat in fêted CCTV series', *SCMP*, 27th November 2006.

# Further reading

Among the best standard histories of China are *The Rise of Modern China* by Immanuel C.Y. Hsu (Oxford University Press, 2000), *China: A New History*, by J.K. Fairbank and Merle Goldman (Belknap, 2005), and *Mao's China and After* by Maurice Meisner (Free Press, 1999). The leading historian Jonathan Spence's *The Search for Modern China* (Norton, 2000) and *The Gate of Heavenly Peace* (Penguin, 1982) are particularly readable accounts of China's struggles to come to terms with the modern world – the latter focusing on the stories of writers, political idealists and intellectuals in the early to mid twentieth century. The same author's *Mao* (Phoenix, 2000) is a straightforward introduction to the man who shaped so much of China's recent destiny. John Gittings's *The Changing Face of China: From Mao to Market* (Oxford University Press, 2005) brings the story up to date with a careful, detailed analysis of the communist era, while Richard Baum's *Burying Mao: Chinese Politics in the Age of Deng Xiaoping* (Princeton University Press, 1994) is a highly readable academic account of the twists and turns of policy, from the beginning of the reform era to the aftermath of Deng Xiaoping's southern tour of 1992.

A sense of how China changed during the 1980s can be found in David Bonavia's *The Chinese* (Penguin, 1982), Fox Butterfield's *Alive in the Bitter Sea* (Bantam, 1983), and Lynn Pan's *The New Chinese Revolution* (Sphere, 1988). Jan Wong's *Red China Blues* (Anchor, 1997) adds a personal twist: the author, a Canadian journalist who worked in Beijing through the Tiananmen era, first came to China as an idealistic left-wing student during the later years of the Cultural Revolution.

The excitement of China's first experiments with new thinking in literature, cinema, philosophy and politics in the 1980s is brilliantly conveyed in Geremie Barmé and John Minford's *Seeds of Fire: Chinese Voices of Conscience* (Hill and Wang, 1988); *New Ghosts, Old Dreams: Chinese Rebel Voices*, by Geremie Barmé and Linda Jaivin (Times Books, 1992) updates this to cover the Tiananmen generation. George Black and Robin Munro's *Black Hands of Beijing* (John Wiley, 1993) focuses specifically on those who participated in the protests of 1989, while Perry Link's *Evening Chats in Beijing* (Norton, 1993) is a thoughtful assessment of the concerns of China's intellectuals from the late 1980s to the early 1990s. Jianying Zha's *China Pop: How Soap Operas, Tabloids and Bestsellers are Transforming a Culture* (The New Press, 1995) provides a lively insight into how China's cultural and media world developed in the post-Tiananmen years.

James Miles's *The Legacy of Tiananmen: China in Disarray* (University of Michigan, 1996) focuses on the many social problems which came to a head during the early 1990s, while John Gittings's *Real China: From Cannibalism to Karaoke* (Simon and Schuster, 1996) is an in-depth look at social change and environmental issues in the middle of that decade; Nicholas Kristof and Sheryl WuDunn's *China Wakes: The Struggle for the Soul of a Rising Power* (Vintage, 1995) is a lively account of the same period. Jasper Becker's *The Chinese* (John Murray, 2000), meanwhile, covers the broad sweep of China's political, social and economic development from the 1980s to the turn of the new century.

Two interesting oral histories are Zhang Xinxin and Sang Ye's *Chinese Lives: An Oral History of Contemporary China*, edited by W.J.F. Jenner and Delia Davin (Macmillan, 1987) – a fascinating reminder of the concerns of ordinary people in the 1980s – and Calum Macleod and Zhang Lijia's *China Remembers* (Oxford University Press, 1999), which focuses on successful and historically significant individuals. Sang Ye's later *China Candid* (University of California Press, 2006) brings the picture brilliantly up to date. Further insights into ordinary lives come in John Pomfret's *Chinese Lessons: Five Classmates and the Story of the New China* (Henry

Holt, 2006), and *Wild Grass: Three Stories of Change in Modern China* (Pantheon, 2004) by Ian Johnson; *River Town* and *Oracles Bones* by Peter Hessler (John Murray, 2002 and 2006) and Rob Gifford's *China Road* (Bloomsbury, 2007). Ian Buruma's *Bad Elements: Chinese Rebels from Los Angeles to Beijing* (Phoenix, 2003) covers the motivation of dissidents and campaigners for greater social and political freedoms in mainland China, Hong Kong and further afield. Kai Strittmatter's *China A to Z* (Haus, 2006) fills in some of the cultural background to life in contemporary China.

On the economy, Joe Studwell's *The China Dream* (Profile, 2002) casts a caustic eye over the ebb and flow of official policy in the 1990s, and over the rush to invest in China, and the successes and many failures, which resulted; James Kynge's *China Shakes the World: The Rise of a Hungry Nation* (Weidenfeld and Nicholson, 2006) looks at China's growing economic impact on the outside world, and the motivations of the individuals involved in this 'economic miracle.'

For more on old Beijing, see *The Search for a Vanishing Beijing* by M.A. Aldrich (Hong Kong University Press, 2006) and Jasper Becker's *A Farewell to Old Peking: The Destruction of an Ancient City and the Creation of the New Beijing* (Oxford University Press, 2007). The atmosphere of the old city is perhaps best captured in the novel *Camel Xiangzi* (also known as *Rickshaw Boy*) by Lao She (Foreign Languages Press, 1981), never fully or perfectly translated, but still a classic story of 1930s life by one of the wittiest and most humane Chinese writers of the twentieth century.

*Shanghai* by Harriet Sergeant (John Murray, 2000) provides a vivid portrait of life in that city in the decades before the revolution, though it focuses mostly on the foreign community. Pan Ling (Lynn Pan)'s *In Search of Old Shanghai* (Joint Publishing, 1982) and *Old Shanghai: Gangsters in Paradise* (Cultured Lotus, 1999) provide a colourful, more local perspective, while *Shanghai: Electric and Lurid City*, edited by Barbara Baker (Oxford University Press, 1998) is an interesting anthology of writing from the 1920s and 1930s. The books of Tess Johnston and Deke Erh, notably *A Last Look* (1998, revised 2004), *Frenchtown Shanghai* (2001), and *Shanghai Art Deco*

(2006) – all published by all Old China Hand Press – provide a vivid photographic and anecdotal record of the city's unique architecture and history. Qiu Xiaolong's Shanghai-based detective novels – notably *When Red is Black* (Sceptre, 2006) – brilliantly portray the atmosphere of Shanghai life and offer perceptive insights into the changes in contemporary Chinese society.

On the media, see Liu Binyan, *People or Monsters* (Indiana University Press, 1983) and the same author's autobiography, *A Higher Kind of Loyalty* (Pantheon, 1990); the China Media Project at Hong Kong University offers valuable insights into current developments: http://cmp.hku.hk.

For the sexual revolution, see James Farrer's *Opening up:Youth Sex Culture and Market Reform in Shanghai* (University of Chicago Press, 2002) and Harriet Evans's *Women and Sexuality in China* (Polity Press, 1997).

*The State of China Atlas*, by Stephanie Hemelryk Donald and Robert Benewick (University of New South Wales Press, 2005) provides useful figures and an introduction to social trends, while China Development Brief (www.chinadevelopmentbrief.com) provides in-depth analysis of social, and particularly rural, issues. Rural problems are the focus of Chen Guidi and Wu Chuntao's *Will the Boat Sink the Water? The Life of China's Peasants* (Public Affairs, 2006), a translation of the banned *China Peasant Survey*, while *The Diary of Ma Yan: The Struggles and Hopes of a Chinese Schoolgirl*, edited by Pierre Haski (Harper Collins, 2005) highlights the challenges for rural education. For civil society, see *From Comrade to Citizen: the Struggle for Political Rights in China* by Merle Goldman (Harvard University Press, 2005). On contemporary art, see *Performance Art in China*, by Thomas J. Berghuis (Timezone 8, 2006) and *China! New Art and Artists* by Dian Tong (Schiffer, 2005). For contemporary literature, try *Red Sorghum* by Mo Yan (Penguin, 1994); *To Live* by Yu Hua (Anchor, 2003); Wang Anyi's *Love in a Small Town* (Renditions, 1988) and *Baotown* (Viking, 1989); *The Noodle Maker* by Ma Jian (Chatto and Windus, 2004); Wang Shuo's *Playing for Thrills* (Penguin, 1998); and *Candy* by Mian Mian (Little, Brown, 2003).